Apostle of the Lost Cause

1872

Apostle
of the
Lost Cause

J. WILLIAM JONES, BAPTISTS, AND THE DEVELOPMENT OF CONFEDERATE MEMORY

Christopher C. Moore

America's Baptists / Keith Harper, Series Editor
Knoxville / The University of Tennessee Press

The America's Baptists series will bring broader understanding of the places Baptists have occupied in American life. Many of these works will be historical monographs, but the series will embrace different types of primary and secondary works, including but not limited to annotated collections of diaries, letters, and personal reflections as well as biographies and essay collections.

Copyright © 2019 by The University of Tennessee Press / Knoxville.
First Edition.

Frontispiece: J. William Jones as chaplain of the 13th Virginia Regiment.
From *J. William Jones, Christ in the Camp, or Religion in the Confederate Army* (Atlanta: The Martin and Hoyt Company, 1904), 61.

Library of Congress Cataloging-in-Publication Data
Names: Moore, Christopher C., author.
Title: Apostle of the Lost Cause: J. William Jones, Baptists, and the
   development of Confederate memory / Christopher C. Moore.
Other titles: America's Baptists.
Description: First edition. | Knoxville: The University of Tennessee Press, [2019] |
   Series: America's Baptists | Includes bibliographical references and index.
Identifiers: LCCN 2019008132 | ISBN 9781621905394 (hardcover)
Subjects: LCSH: Jones, J. William (John William), 1836–1909. |
   Baptists—Southern States—Clergy—Biography. | Baptists—Southern States—
   History. | Confederate States of America—History. | Southern States—History.
Classification: LCC BX6495.J57 M66 2019 | DDC 973.7/13092 [B] –dc23
LC record available at https://lccn.loc.gov/2019008132

Designed and typeset
by Nathan Moehlmann,
Goosepen Studio & Press

Contents

Illustrations

Following page 99

Acknowledgments

I am overwhelmed with gratitude for all the people who have contributed to the completion of this book. Thank you to Scot Danforth, Dr. Keith Harper, and the University of Tennessee Press for allowing me the opportunity to grapple with Confederate memory in print. I am also grateful to my friend and mentor Dr. Doug Weaver, whose unwavering support has proved invaluable for many years now. Thank you also to Dr. Bill Pitts, whose encyclopedic knowledge and kind spirit has been such an inspiration to me during my academic journey. Thanks, too, to Dr. Michael Parrish for the ways in which he has cultivated and deepened my interest in American Civil War history. I have also treasured Dr. Bill Leonard's advice throughout the writing process, and I am thankful to Drs. Mikeal Parsons and Joel Burnett, both of whom read earlier versions of this manuscript.

I would like to express my deep appreciation for the financial support of Baylor University's Religion Department, especially the awarding of the Donald A. Driskell Endowed Fund for the Glenn O. and Martell B. Hilburn Endowed Graduate Research Scholarship Fund—a scholarship that enabled me to make essential research trips. I am also thankful for the archivists who assisted me along the way, particularly Dr. John Coski at the Museum of the Confederacy in Richmond, Virginia, and Adam Winters at Southern Baptist Theological Seminary in Louisville, Kentucky.

There are many others to whom I am indebted, both professionally and personally. Two of my former professors at Campbell University deserve special mention. Thank you to Dr. Steve Harmon for your friendship, your theological guidance, and for encouraging me to pursue a career in academia. Thank you also to Dr. Glenn Jonas, who ignited my now insatiable interest in the history of Christianity. You have been a tireless mentor and friend for over a decade and a half, and I am grateful. I am also appreciative of my close friend Jason Lee for helping me procure images for this work.

Finally, I would like to thank my family. Thank you most of all to my wonderful wife, Amie, who has made sacrifices for me that others can only imagine. I do not pretend to think that without her love, encouragement, and dedication, this book would have been remotely possible. Thank you to my darling little girls, Clara and Olivia, who light up my life, and who will be almost as happy as I am that this project is completed. Thank you to my in-laws, Dr. Wilbur and Mrs. Brenda Smith. Your love and generosity are a constant inspiration. Thank you to my grandparents, Audie and Albert Edwards, and to my late grandmother, Pauline, for the unconditional love and the warm memories you have given me. Thank you to my siblings—Jennifer, Elizabeth, and Michael—who have never let me take myself too seriously. Lastly, thank you to my parents, Rose and Carlton. I am grateful to my mom, who never let me lose sight of the importance of education. I am also grateful to my dad, who molded me into the Civil War buff I am today. I love you both dearly.

Foreword

On the eve of the American Civil War, Georgia Senator Robert Augustus Toombs allegedly quipped that the South could "whip those Yankees with cornstalks." Once hostilities ended and the South lay in ruins, someone reminded Toombs of his failed prophesy. Undaunted, Toombs simply noted, "They wouldn't fight us with cornstalks." In his mind, the South really could have won if only Northern forces had fought on the South's terms. But that war never materialized.

Prior to 1861 most Southerners and many Northerners agreed with Toombs. Southern leaders boasted about the region's great wealth. Why not? Cotton was King, and who could stand against such might? The South's upper-class culture featured gracious hospitality and unparalleled refinement. Who could stand against such finery? And great military leaders like P. G. T. Beauregard, Albert Sidney Johnston, and Robert E. Lee virtually guaranteed victory in any armed conflict. But when neither wealth, cultural pretensions, nor military leadership could wring victory from Union forces, dispirited Southerners after the war looked for consolation in what came to be known as the "Lost Cause."

Christopher C. Moore's *Apostle of the Lost Cause: J. William Jones, Baptists, and the Development of Confederate Memory* is a welcome addition to the America's Baptists Series. In it, Moore details the labors of one of the Lost Cause's greatest apologists. As a chaplain in Lee's Army of Northern Virginia, Jones revered his commanding officer's memory and dedicated himself to preserving it. Beyond his admiration for Lee, Jones wanted to let the world know that the South was a good place with good people, and it always had been. In fact, no one worked more tirelessly than J. William Jones in preaching the gospel of the "good South." In defeat, the South's cause was noble. In defeat, the South's war aims were just. In defeat, there remained a measured defiance. While Baptists were not the only Southerners to buy into Lost Cause ideology, they played a significant role in shaping the post-war narrative that emerged, and Jones wove that narrative more effectively than anyone else. It is a story that Moore tells well. Moreover, Moore uses Jones's story to convey a far more nuanced understanding of the complexities of Lost Cause thinking—many of which historians have overlooked since Jones's important contributions to Lost Cause ideology have become obscured over time.

J. William Jones died on March 17, 1909, but thanks in large part to his labors, the Lost Cause had already assumed a life of its own. Succeeding generations of Southerners took up their cornstalks to refight the Civil War, this time on *their* terms. Long after the Civil War ended, many pushed for segregation and engaged in "massive resistance" as they harkened back to a romanticized, mythical South that never existed. Christopher Moore's work is a timely reminder both that actions have consequences and that words have a life beyond the printed page.

KEITH HARPER
Southeastern Baptist Theological Seminary

Introduction

> In the relation between myth and history myth proves to be
> the primary, history the secondary and derived, factor. It is not
> by its history that the mythology of a nation is determined but,
> conversely, its history is determined by its mythology.
>
> — ERNST CASSIRER

I n 1892, Mary Anna Jackson, widow of the famed Confederate general, Thomas J. "Stonewall" Jackson, completed a biography of her husband. Reflecting on the last picture ever taken of the general, she wrote the following: "It was during these last happy days that he sat for the last picture that was taken of him — the three-quarters view of his face and head — the favorite picture with his old soldiers, as it is the most soldierly-looking; but to my mind, not so pleasing as the full-face view which was taken in the spring of 1862 . . . which has more of the beaming sunlight of his *home-look*."[1] With this observation, Mary Jackson encapsulated one of the major themes of her book. Throughout her account she had tried to paint her husband less as a fierce warrior and more as a tender husband. But despite her best efforts, Confederate soldiers had already chosen the picture of Stonewall Jackson that they wanted to remember.

The study of the so-called "Lost Cause" is, at root, an examination of the picture that postwar white Southerners wanted to remember. Among other elements, Lost Cause mythology entailed a sacralization of Southern history, a veneration of Confederate heroes, and an apology for the Confederate cause, largely in an attempt by white Southerners to preserve a distinctive identity vis-à-vis Northerners. White Southerners envisioned themselves a virtuous people — defeated by Yankees but chosen by God — and weaponized their sacred history in order to win a war they had already lost.[2]

Among the most ardent of Lost Cause apologists and hagiographers was former Confederate chaplain, John William Jones. Having been commissioned by Robert E. Lee to preserve an accurate account of the

Confederacy, Jones extended his mission by canonizing Southern leaders, most notably Lee, Stonewall Jackson, and Jefferson Davis. Because of his many books, and through his position as secretary of the *Southern Historical Society Papers* (*SHSP*), Jones became one of the most celebrated proponents of the Lost Cause tradition.[3]

Jones was also a Baptist, and to approach his oeuvre without this point distinctly in mind is, to borrow the expression of one Confederate general, to enter the fray with "one boot off." Throughout his adult life, Jones pastored Baptist churches. Before the outbreak of the Civil War, he had intended to be a Baptist missionary. He was an active participant in the Southern Baptist Convention, serving as assistant corresponding secretary for the Home Mission Board. He was a Baptist fundraiser. He lamented the lack of Baptist ministers, and he wrote into Baptist newspapers in order to defend Baptist doctrines. His enormously popular *Christ in the Camp* was first published as a serial in the Baptist *Religious Herald*. Four of Jones's sons became Baptist ministers. Of course, as with any historical figure, the factors motivating Jones — internal, external, conscious, or subconscious — were variegated. Still, any study of Jones's life and career that neglects his unapologetic "Baptistness" is incomplete.

Scholars have traditionally interpreted the Lost Cause as an ecumenical movement, highlighting the willingness of former Confederates like Jones to de-emphasize sectarian differences in order to maintain Southern unity.[4] Unfortunately, terms such as "ecumenism" can have so many meanings that they end up meaning little at all. Historians' usages vary dramatically, with some scholars using ecumenism to indicate the participation of various denominations (or religions) in a common effort, regardless of whether or not these various groups consciously cooperated with one another. At the other end of the spectrum, some writers employ ecumenism to mean the intentional blurring or dismissal of doctrinal particularities, even to the extent of organic union among denominational bodies.

With such a broad continuum in play, classifying Jones as an ecumenist is problematic. For one thing, labeling him as such obscures the importance of denominational loyalty in the shaping of Lost Cause literature, and by extension, white Southern memory. What many scholars have deemed "ecumenical"— at least in Jones's case — is better understood as "cooperation," or even "denominational networking." For his part, Jones was willing to collaborate with non-Baptists in pursuit of a common goal (disseminating the Lost Cause narrative), but he ultimately remained a product of his time, deeply influenced by the historical and sometimes intense denominational rivalries of nineteenth-century America.

When Jones partnered with non-Baptists, he did so in service to the central animating mission of his postwar life: to serve as the Confederacy's "apostle." Jones's self-perception as apostle — one commissioned to spread the Confederate "gospel" and to venerate Southern "saints" — is the interpretive lens for this study. Instead of stifling his sectarian tendencies, Jones's mission allowed breathing room for such commitments. Far from being a thoroughgoing ecumenist, Jones locked arms with those of differing denominations only to the extent that such cooperation facilitated his dual charge of preserving a distinct Confederate narrative and revering those he considered to be incarnations of Southern virtue.[5]

For decades, historians have explored memory and mythologizing in the postbellum South. Of particular interest is the way in which religion influenced the Lost Cause mythology. With this in mind, some writers have emphasized the role of ex-Confederate clergy in the forging of white Southern memory, even going as far as to place Jones at the center of the amalgamation of the Lost Cause and Protestant Christianity.[6] But despite his acknowledged importance, Jones remains a largely unstudied figure. Such a lacuna has remained, despite a late 1990s revival of work on religion and the American Civil War. Likewise, books on Reconstruction and memory have given Jones but scant treatment, and works that have concentrated specifically on postwar Southern Baptists have afforded Jones only passing reference.

In short, the historical portrait of Jones remains incomplete, and writers who have chronicled his career have often painted contrasting pictures. Some historians have focused on Jones as a veritable "evangelist" of the Lost Cause, or even as a model for Christian evangelism in general. Others have taken a decidedly less charitable approach, characterizing Jones as a petty sycophant who ran roughshod over rival writers, and who was almost as obsessed with his own reputation as he was with the legacy of his Confederate heroes.[7] What scholars have yet to do, and what this book hopes to accomplish, is to provide an extended study of Jones's life, situate him in a nineteenth-century Baptist context, and address how his deep-seated denominational identity fashioned Confederate memory in a predominantly Protestant and perpetually factionalized postbellum South.[8]

This monograph contributes to Lost Cause scholarship in two ways. First, this study provides the only in-depth survey of Jones's life and work, emphasizing both his Baptist identity and his function as Lost Cause advocate. Second, this book nuances recent interpretations concerning the role of denominationalism in the development of the Lost Cause. More broadly, Jones's story challenges the way many writers have approached Southern religion and the Civil War. Prevailing treatments have focused on how churches compromised Christian principles ("sacrificed their witness") in order to buttress the South's peculiar institution. In particular, Baptists acrobatically defended church-state separation and at the same time baptized the Confederacy's "Christian nation." To be sure, churches were in some sense "culturally captive,"[9] as white congregations of the South mounted defenses of chattel slavery that were as resilient as they were repulsive. And while most white churches in the South exchanged a potentially prophetic message for the pottage of white hegemony and economic exploitation — in effect valuing profits over prophets — many white Southerners refused to surrender their sectarian loyalties. Denominational fidelity thus profoundly influenced the burgeoning Lost Cause tradition, and it is here that Jones's life and career sheds much-needed light.

Guided by his self-identification as an apostle of the Confederacy, Jones utilized denominationally neutral language for the purposes of hagiography. An overarching theme of his writing was the veneration of Confederate leaders, and throughout his postwar career Jones's central objective was to testify to the virtues of three Confederate stalwarts (Lee, Jackson, and Davis), none of whom were Baptist. By de-emphasizing the sectarian particularities of his three Confederate heroes, Jones directed readers toward figures whose virtues transcended denominational scruples. In so doing, Jones — a committed Baptist and commissioned apostle — led disciples from various denominations to the shrine of Lee, Jackson, and Davis.

As an apostle of the Confederacy — commissioned by Lee himself — Jones saw as his two-part mission to apotheosize Confederate icons and to preserve a faithful Confederate narrative.[10] His intimate knowledge of Confederate leaders provided readers with embodiments of Southern morality who transcended denominational boundaries and who enabled white Southerners to locate their champions (and themselves) in a biblical narrative that both explained defeat and ensured ultimate vindication. While Jones sacrificed much in this endeavor, he did not forfeit his denominational identity. Instead, his commitments to the Lost Cause tradition and to the Baptist denomination were inextricably linked: Jones the apostle was also Jones the Baptist. As such, he is an ideal model for investigating the crucial way in which denominationalism influenced the growth and spread of Lost Cause mythology.[11]

CHAPTER ONE

From the Mission Field to the Battlefield: Jones's Early Life and Prewar Years

Jones, you may have seen; he has great zeal, an unusual turn for practical working, and I am sure he will make a very useful man.

— JOHN ALBERT BROADUS

Robert E. Lee died on the morning of October 12, 1870. Former Confederate general William Nelson Pendleton, who had served as Lee's chief of artillery, was distraught at the loss of one he would thereafter describe as a "model Christian, patriot, and soldier." According to Pendleton, Lee's greatness "could not but ripen into a tender yet venerating love on my part for one so pure, so true, so great and good." As did so many others, Pendleton resolved to preserve Lee's memory at any cost. Within a month of Lee's death, Pendleton had organized the Lee Memorial Association, setting out to raise funds for a statue and mausoleum dedicated to the general. For the next five years Pendleton worked tirelessly; he gave speaking tours, distributed pamphlets, and deployed agents to raise funds, all in an effort to honor a cherished leader who, in Pendleton's mind, remained the paragon of military acumen and Christian piety.[1]

Pendleton was also determined to publish a definitive account of Lee's life, and along with the Lee family and Lee's colleagues from Washington College, he began work on a biography. They enlisted Lee's former soldiers and friends to contribute to the volume, but when former aide Charles Marshall disclosed that he was no longer able to complete his assignment — a section surveying Lee's military career — the project essentially collapsed.[2] With the aborted attempt to memorialize the South's most treasured hero, Lee's family and friends were deeply concerned. Lee's memory would now be at the mercy of sundry memorial associations, each jockeying to be the authoritative interpreter of Lee's legacy.

One Lee devotee, who was already composing his own biography of the beloved general, was keen to be that authoritative interpreter. Offering to rescue the faltering endeavor, former Confederate chaplain John William Jones asked for access to the Lee family papers and for a copy of the incomplete manuscript. Not only would he complete the biography, Jones insisted, but he would divide the proceeds with the association. Publishing his work in 1874, Jones's account set the bar for future Lee biographers. Leaders at Washington and Lee University — where Lee had served as president for five years — were so taken with Jones's *Personal Reminiscences, Anecdotes, and Letters of Gen. Robert E. Lee* that they awarded Jones an honorary doctorate of divinity. The biography's success ensured that Jones would be the authority on Lee's life for years to come. Moreover, for the next three decades Jones would position himself in the hottest part of the battle for Southern memory. As a result, he became the lens through which countless white Southerners would refract memories of the American Civil War.[3]

A complex individual with a storied career and a penchant for the dramatic, Jones was a man driven by a vision. Balancing on the fulcrum of Southern history, he felt commissioned — divinely chosen, perhaps — to preserve a South that was but a hair's breadth from being swallowed in defeat. Contemporaries called him the "fighting parson"; writers since have labeled him the "historian of the Confederacy" and the "evangelist of the Lost Cause."[4] Yet if there was a guiding principle in his post-war career — one that galvanized Jones from his pulpit to his publications — that force was his role as apostle of the Confederacy. There is no more fitting description of one whose life was so utterly dedicated to the spread of the Confederate gospel.

Jones mirrored the biblical apostles, who possessed intimate knowledge of Christ, as well as personal commissions to preserve the narrative of his life, death, and resurrection. Jones, however, prized what he believed to be a directive from Lee to chronicle a faithful account of the Confederacy. Furthermore, as biblical apostles directed their hearers to Christ — God incarnate — so too did Jones point his readers to those he believed were incarnations of Southern virtue. His means of executing this commission were single-minded but also pragmatic. A deeply religious man, he interpreted Confederate history in light of a divine drama, offering white Southerners penetrating clarity into the mysteries of Providence. At the same time, he was resolutely Baptist, and he navigated a denomination-ally competitive landscape by joining with non-Baptists for the sake of gospel evangelism on the one hand and cultural indoctrination on the other. Examining his early life and prewar years, one finds a Jones who nursed a missionary's heart, but who also strained to discern the divine will. Ironically, it would be in the din of cataclysmic military defeat that Jones came to hear God's voice most clearly.

✣ ✣ ✣ ✣ ✣

John William Jones was born on September 25, 1836 in Louisa County, Virginia. The Baptist tradition ran deep in Louisa County, dating back to the work of Shubal Stearns, Daniel Marshall, and Martha Stearns Marshall in the mid-eighteenth century. Baptists made the most of their preponderance in the area, where the number of Baptist churches was relatively high (fourteen in 1850) compared to other counties of the Old Dominion. Jones came from Welsh stock; his father was Francis William Jones, and his mother was Ann Pendleton (Ashby) Jones. John William had an older sister, Helen Mary, who was two years his senior. His broth-ers, Francis Pendleton ("Pen") and Philip Edloe ("Ed"), were four years and six years younger, respectively. Jones was nine years older than his sister, Lucy, and eleven years older than his youngest sibling at the time, Robert.[5]

Jones's father was active in his community, serving as both militia col-onel and magistrate of the county. According to the 1850 census, Francis worked as a "merchant," a common designation in census records. One can only infer as to how successful he was in business. Josephus W. Anderson, forty years old and listed as a merchant's clerk, lived with the Jones family in 1850 and may have been in Francis's employ.[6] If so, Francis was well-off enough both to pay a clerk and to support a large family. Another clue as to his means was the fact that the Jones family owned slaves.

Census records list fifteen-year-old Alphonso Gray as a resident of the Jones household in 1850. Gray's placement in the census has led some to believe that he was a family slave, yet this was unlikely. First, the census did not record Gray's race — "white, black, or mulatto" — in the allotted space. Second, and more significantly, Gray's age and gender do not match the "slave schedules" of Louisa County. The US Census first used these so-named schedules in 1850, listing general information about slaves (gender, age, color, but not name) on separate documentation from that of the slaveholding family. Schedule records indicate that the Jones family owned six slaves in total: men, women, and children, ranging in age from two to sixty.[7]

Little is known of Jones's childhood years, aside from general details about his early education at academies in Louisa and Orange counties. There are also precious few specifics concerning his religious conversion, or his initial involvement with the Baptist denomination. That Jones would one day dedicate much of his career detailing the spiritual journeys of fellow Confederates makes it all the more striking that he so rarely commented on his own. The first salient facts regarding Jones's religious life come from August 1855, when he experienced conversion and underwent baptism during a protracted meeting led by George Boardman Taylor at Mechanicsville Baptist Church in Louisa County. Even while Jones said little of this pivotal moment, the event deeply shaped him, and he would later opine that if an individual did not come to Christ at a young age, the person likely never would. The young Jones also saw that revivals were a well-suited environment for bringing lost sheep into the fold.[8]

In the autumn of 1855, Jones enrolled at the University of Virginia (UVA). His father, Francis, wrote that after "prayerful consideration," he had no objections to the path his son was taking. Francis hinted, however, that the financial burden could be considerable. "You can fully appreciate the feelings I have when I think of the many loved ones I have to provide for, with no means of doing so as I desire, but it is all right. God will take care of those who trust in him as they out [sic] to." In order to defray the costs of attending the university, Jones took out loans from friends and taught classes at UVA. Edward S. Joynes, a former UVA professor, remembered Jones entering the university as an "uncouth country boy" who was "never distinguished for intellectual attainment." Regimental records would one day describe Jones as blue-eyed, brown-haired, and fair-skinned. At five feet tall, however, he was not the picture of self-assertion. Jones was so unprepared for college life that Joynes felt compelled to take "John William" — as he was known to his friends — under wing.[9]

In October 1858, Jones participated in the formation of a Young Men's Christian Association (YMCA) at UVA, which boasted being the first college YMCA in the United States. Jones served as treasurer. The group organized prayer meetings and Bible studies in boarding houses (where students lived) and throughout campus. The association also deployed its members to Sunday schools and worship services in impoverished areas within a ten-mile radius of UVA. Jones cared little for the walking, but each Sunday he trekked five miles into the mountains in order to lead classes. He was also active in the YMCA's initiative to coordinate a Sunday school for African Americans.[10]

While at college, Jones made his temporary home at the "Daniel House." The accommodations befitted him, as John Lipscomb Johnson — a UVA student and future Confederate chaplain — described the Daniel House as a "sort of Baptist Headquarters at the University." Jones shared a room with John C. Hiden, and since the apartment was in close proximity to the dining area, the spot was a natural place for friends to gather after the evening meal. But the meetings were not simply for leisure; in fact, Jones treated the conversations with great seriousness, utilizing opportunities to probe the spiritual conditions of his colleagues. Of the eight students at the dormitory, four were professing Christians and four were not. According to Jones, he and his three Christian roommates prayed for the wayward four, a revival occurred, and the students converted. From that incident Jones learned a lesson that would serve him well for the remainder of his ministry. He later recounted that "the work of that session at the University thoroughly convinced me that young men are easy to reach when properly approached."[11]

Although stationed in the "Baptist Headquarters" of UVA, Jones retained friendly relations with non-Baptists. In one letter from the late 1850s or early 1860s, his cousin Julia thanked him for visiting a Methodist church with her. Notwithstanding, one of Jones's sisters included an addendum to the message, in which she expressed her fond memories of the "many happy hours I've spent in *the Baptist Church*." In another letter,

Jones's sister Helen Mary related that she had attended both Episcopalian and Methodist churches, but concluded that "our *denomination* can certainly *boast* of decidedly the *best* ministers." While letters of this nature were not extraordinary, the correspondence was indicative of a family that fostered cordial relations with non-Baptists, but remained firmly planted in the Baptist denomination.[12]

Jones left university a changed man. His former mentor took notice, remarking that he was "surprised to see into what a self-possessed, forceful man the awkward boy of 1855 had grown." Jones's flair for evangelism was evident, and the budding minister established what would become lifelong relationships with prominent Baptist leaders. He attended Charlottesville Baptist Church, where leading Baptist pastor and denominationalist, Alfred Elijah (A. E.) Dickinson (1830–1906), ministered. Another Baptist stalwart, John Albert Broadus (1827–1895), served as UVA chaplain for Jones's first two years in Charlottesville and then as his pastor for Jones's last two years in college. Long after Jones's time at UVA, he continued to look up to Broadus, and Jones regularly consulted with Broadus on theological matters.[13]

Because the impressionable Jones held Broadus in such high esteem, there is good reason to believe that Broadus's work at UVA influenced Jones's attitude toward non-Baptists. Though a devoted Baptist, Broadus thrived in the nonsectarian setting of a public university. While chaplain, he ministered to a diverse student body, many coming from non-Baptist backgrounds. Well aware of denominational sensitivities among faculty and students, Broadus cast a wide net, and his ostensible neutrality won the respect of fellow evangelicals. One student, who would go on to become an Episcopalian rector, credited his religious influence to Broadus. In an even clearer affirmation of Broadus's interdenominationalism, one Presbyterian professor lobbied for Broadus to remain at UVA even though a Presbyterian chaplain traditionally came next on the appointment rotation.[14]

After graduating from UVA in 1859, Jones enrolled at Southern Baptist Theological Seminary (SBTS) in Greenville, South Carolina, which opened the same year. He was one of the first names to matriculate at SBTS, along with Crawford H. Toy (1836–1919), who graduated from UVA in 1856 and who would become Jones's close friend. Jones studied a variety of subjects at seminary, including New Testament, homiletics, systematic theology, and church government. The incoming student body was active in the town of Greenville and beyond, and their endeavors to organize Sunday schools and promote revivals won the admiration of observers. As he had at UVA, Jones adopted and encouraged the school's missionary spirit.[15]

The seminary's "Abstract of Principles" may very well provide insight into Jones's theological beliefs at the time. While the Abstract exhibited the influence of Reformed theology, it remained intentionally broad. Concerning the Bible, the Abstract attested that the scriptures were "given by inspiration of God" and were "the only sufficient, certain and authoritative rule of saving knowledge, faith and obedience." The Abstract denied that the Lord's Supper was a "sacrifice," yet offered no opinion on issues of "open" versus "closed" communion. Neither did the Abstract endorse a particular eschatological position (premillennial, postmillennial, or amillennial), aside from the general belief that Christ would judge the world. The goal of the Abstract was to remain common but not commonplace, and to circumvent the most potentially divisive issues among Baptists. Of course, even generalities could provoke controversy, as Landmark Baptists would have demanded a more detailed treatment of the Lord's Supper (in particular, an affirmation of closed communion).[16]

While Jones attended SBTS, the seminary invited Broadus to join the faculty. Both Jones and Toy objected to the move, reasoning that Broadus was irreplaceable in his Charlottesville pastorate. Broadus accepted the call nonetheless and served the school as professor of New Testament interpretation and homiletics. Jones thereafter enjoyed regular contact with his mentor; he and Toy even boarded with the Broadus family. During that time, Broadus learned much about Jones and Toy. For example, the pair shared a passion for missions, but displayed markedly dissimilar aptitudes toward religious studies. "Toy is among the foremost scholars I have ever known of his years, and an uncommonly conscientious and devoted man," Broadus wrote. He continued, "Jones, you may have seen; he has great zeal, an unusual turn for practical working, and I am sure he will make a very useful man."[17] Broadus's assessments of Toy and Jones would prove prescient.

The Civil War would derail both Jones's and Toy's dreams of becoming missionaries, and both would instead serve as Confederate chaplains. For Toy's part, the war did not squelch his appetite for study, and fellow soldiers were well aware of his proficiency with languages. In March 1863, Jones wrote to Broadus that Toy had left his Syriac books in Virginia and was thus "compelled to fall back on German for amusement."[18] After the war Toy taught in various schools, and in May 1869, he returned to SBTS as professor of Old Testament interpretation and oriental languages, a position he held for ten years. During his time with the school, the seminary moved to Louisville, Kentucky (1877).

At SBTS, Toy became increasingly interested in the works of Charles Darwin and Julius Wellhausen. As these interests became more pronounced in Toy's work, the objections of faculty at SBTS compelled him to resign in 1879, though his colleagues continued to hold him in high regard. Toy then became professor of Hebrew and Oriental languages at Harvard University, teaching in that capacity for eight years. Eventually, Toy began attending a Unitarian church.[19] Toy's successes certainly confirmed Broadus's assessment of the seminarian's scholarly acumen, even while Toy's ultimate trajectory likely dismayed his former mentor.

Broadus's evaluations of Toy and Jones were noticeably different, but Broadus's insight into Jones's character was no less accurate. Broadus had noted Jones's "great zeal" and his "unusual turn for practical working." Jones's postwar work would show that he was nothing if not zealous and practical, yet even in his seminary days, he displayed an unwavering enthusiasm for ministry. In a letter to Abram Maer Poindexter (1809–1872), co-secretary of the Southern Baptist Convention's Foreign Mission Board, Jones admitted that his post-seminary ambitions had been to "settle down in some quiet little pastorate." After hearing Poindexter speak on the need for missionaries, however, Jones had a dramatic change of heart. In August 1859 he wrote to Poindexter, "In response to the call made for men by the board, the missionaries, and the cries of perishing millions in heathen lands, I've only to say as did the prophet of old, '*Here am I — send me.*'" Less than a year later — in June 1860 — Jones and his close friend Toy were ordained as Baptist ministers. Both anticipated missionary work in East Asia.[20]

Unfortunately for Jones, much of 1860 entailed one frustration after another. He had preferred an appointment to Japan, since Toy would be serving as a missionary there. Instead, Poindexter encouraged Jones to consider China. After mulling over the matter Jones accepted the placement, and by July 1860, he was chomping at the bit to depart. He wanted to sail for China by early October, but his desire to travel with Toy delayed matters since Toy would not be ready to leave until late autumn. Jones resolved to wait on his co-laborer, not just for the sake of companionship, but with the anticipation that Toy would help him brush up on Greek.[21]

With his departure postponed, Jones grew anxious about what he was to do in the interim. Toy counseled patience. Estimating that he could sail with Jones no earlier than December, Toy urged Jones to wait. Toy suggested that Jones could take a pastorate, but preferred that Jones "do the work of an Evangelist." By this Toy may have meant for Jones to embark on a speaking tour, during which he could focus not only on the need for missions, but address "every department of Christian effort." Concerned that his friend not lose heart, Toy recommended that Jones continue his personal study of missions in general, and China in particular.[22]

Another issue that hung in the balance concerned whether or not Jones would enter the mission field as a married man. He debated between working in Shanghai and Canton, believing the latter to be "peculiarly unhealthy for females." Even if he journeyed alone, he preferred Shanghai on account of the climate. Warm weather, he confessed, did not befit his "constitution." Nevertheless, he left the final decision with the board. By late September 1860, a disappointed Jones seemed convinced that he would remain unmarried before leaving for China. He continued to suggest to Poindexter the possibility of accompanying Toy to Japan, in part because it was doubtful that Toy's intended companion would be able to make the voyage.[23]

Knowing now that he would be unmarried while abroad, Jones was more receptive (weather notwithstanding) to Canton. He sent word to James Barnett Taylor, another secretary of the Foreign Mission Board, accepting the appointment. "You ask if I will be ready to go as early as December," Jones wrote, "Yes! Or even earlier should it be deemed best." He continued, "I am very anxious to reach my field and go to work at the language in which I hope to preach all my life." Zealous as he was, Jones was still willing to wait until December so that he could leave with Toy, for whom Jones continued to show great fondness. Making the most of his waning weeks in the US, Jones began visiting churches and requesting their prayers.[24]

By late November 1860, Jones received the message he had been dreading: political affairs had prompted the indefinite postponement of his departure. Jones was at a loss. Not only had he begun to envision Canton as home, but he was now in a situation he aptly described as "awkward." Since he was likely to leave for the mission field whenever circumstances permitted, he doubted that a church would hire him in the meantime. With a hint of panic, he asked, "So if the Board should decide not to send me now it will become a very serious question with me — *what am I to do* while awaiting the issue of events?"[25] As matters would have it, he would not have to wait long before political circumstances commanded his attention and his future. Within a month of Jones mailing this letter, South Carolina would secede from the Union.

When December came, Jones knew his position was precarious. On December 17, 1860, he wrote to Broadus, "The secession feeling is growing in Virginia very fast." For Jones, however, all was not despair. On December 20 — the same day as South Carolina's secession — he married Judith Page Helm (1836–1924). Even though Jones had not identified Judith by name in his correspondence, her presence in his life goes far in explaining Jones's palpable angst over his marital status as an aspiring missionary. Judith's family boasted deep roots in Virginia, tracing their lineage through Carter Braxton, a Virginian signer of the Declaration of Independence. Jones's writings suggest that Judith was strong-willed and undaunted by her husband's robust personality. In an 1861 letter to Broadus, Jones described Judith as "an invaluable auxiliary in my efforts to correct my faults." He went on to observe that "a *good wife* is certainly the best critic that a young preacher can have." Over the course of a nearly five-decade marriage, the couple would have ten children, five of whom survived to adulthood. Of those five, four became Baptist ministers.[26]

Even as a married man, Jones had not given up hope of becoming a missionary. By January 1861, however, he was growing desperate. He wrote to Taylor requesting permission to visit churches and raise funds, believing that this would enable the board to send him abroad. He pled, "I do not want to remain here *a single day* longer than I am forced to remain, and am anxious to make every effort in my power to hasten my departure." Jones shared that Judith was equally eager to reach Canton, and he even posed the idea of sailing to China and supporting himself until the board could take over the responsibilities. He may have gotten this idea from Toy: less than a month earlier, Jones had conveyed to Broadus that Toy was considering "taking the chances" and going to Japan without board support.[27]

Although Jones was reticent to take a temporary pastorate, in January 1861 he accepted a once-a-month appointment at Little River Baptist Church in Louisa County. He would serve at the church until May of that year. Little River was an interesting choice for Jones. The church dated back to 1791, and records suggest that at one point the church had a prickly relationship with non-Baptists. In 1855, the pastor of Little River so harshly criticized the actions of "Pedo-baptists" that a local Methodist pastor took offense.[28] Whether or not Jones knew of the kerfuffle is unknown. What is known is that Jones himself usually avoided public conflict with fellow evangelicals when at all possible.

Jones never made it to Canton, China. Yet by the spring of 1861, he would find himself plunged into a new and terrible mission field. Perhaps his zeal for missions had blinded him to the full extent of political turmoil in the early 1860s. Even so, as with the Apostle Paul, a crisis would prompt Jones to redirect his consuming passion. When war came, Jones would concentrate all his efforts toward the conversion of Confederate soldiers, and he would cooperate with ministers of other denominations in order to invite and sustain revivals. The wartime interdenominationalism he would espouse, however, never led to a fundamental doctrinal shift in his thinking. No matter how much he maintained cordial relations with non-Baptists, Jones was and remained a dyed-in-the-wool Baptist from Louisa County, Virginia — a frustrated missionary looking for a great revival.

✢ ✢ ✢ ✢ ✢

By Jones's account, on the brink of the Civil War, he had been waiting, trunks packed, ready to sail for China. He had considered himself a "strong Union man" until — in his words — "Abraham Lincoln issued his proclamation to subdue the sovereign States of the South, who had exercised their constitutional right of seceding from the Union, and claimed their inalienable right of free government." On April 17, 1861, the Virginia Convention passed an ordinance of secession. The "Louisa Blues" — a volunteer company Jones would join — was drilling at the Louisa Court House when news reached them that the ordinance had passed. The company received a telegram around noon that instructed them to be on trains before sundown. A large crowd gathered at the depot to see off the soldiers. A minister led the group in prayer, asking God to protect the men from wounds on the battlefield and vices in the camp. By nightfall the company was en route to capture an arsenal at Harpers Ferry.[29]

Jones's tone in a May 1861 letter revealed that his attention was shifting from the mission field to the battlefield with a whiplash-like intensity. To James P. Boyce, the visionary behind the founding of SBTS, Jones expressed his concern that the North's "invading army" would try to prevent Virginia's vote of secession. This statewide vote in May 1861 would determine the ratification status of the convention's April 17 decision to secede. There was trepidation among Virginians that the presence of Federal troops would interfere with the vote. Knowing this, Jones guaranteed Boyce that Virginians would vote, even if they had to "pull the triger [sic] with one hand and deposit their ballots with the other." Jones went on, "[I]f an Abolition army does invade our soil every man capable of bearing arms will at once take the field." Worth noting is Jones's reference to an "Abolition army." In his postwar writings, Jones dismissed slavery as a peripheral issue in the onset of the war. In this 1861 letter, however, he specifically associated the Union Army with an abolition force.[30]

With war looming, Jones cast his lot with the Louisa Blues. The Louisa Blues would become Company D of the 13th Virginia, a regiment organized by Ambrose Powell (A. P.) Hill in the spring of 1861. The 13th would eventually form a portion of Stonewall Jackson's Army of the

Valley, and after the Battle of Fredericksburg in the winter of 1862, the regiment became part of Jubal Early's Brigade, Richard Ewell's Division, and Jackson's Corps. When and where Jones enlisted, however, are unclear. Some authors state that Jones had joined the Louisa Blues by April 17, yet regimental records indicate that he enlisted as a private with the Louisa Blues on June 8 at Harpers Ferry. If these records are correct, then Jones's brother Francis ("Pen") enlisted on June 15, 1861 (in Winchester), while brother Philip ("Ed") enlisted on April 17, 1861. Other sources specify that the three brothers all enlisted at the same time, on April 17. Even Jones himself gave conflicting accounts, at times recalling that he joined the Louisa Blues on April 17, and at other times implying that he arrived at a later date. A letter from Jones's brother, Ed, adds credence to the regimental records. Ed wrote his mother on June 9, 1861, describing Jones as a new recruit who had just come to the outfit. Ed also mentioned that he looked forward to seeing their brother, Pen, the next week. While Jones may have been present with the Louisa Blues on April 17, Ed's correspondence supports records showing that Jones and his brother Pen formally enlisted with the 13th in June 1861.[31]

Although regimental reports establish that Ed enlisted only two months before Jones, by June 1861, Ed wrote home as if already a grizzled veteran. "I am getting very tired of hearing 'Dixie,'" he told his mother. "I hear it played about a dozen times a day more or less." He also noted to his brother Pen that measles, mumps, and stomach ailments had already become perpetual issues among the soldiers. As far as camp religion was concerned, Ed acknowledged that "a camp is certainly the most *corrupt* & demoralizing place in the world." Perhaps motivated by the immorality of camp life, Ed expressed willingness to reach across denominational lines. He recorded attending Methodist, Episcopal, Lutheran, and Roman Catholic services.[32]

Ed also wrote that he had become accustomed to drilling on Sundays, though he believed the practice had come as a shock to Jones. Indeed, Ed predicted that it would take time for Jones to adjust to the rigors of camp life. When Jones first arrived with the 13th, Ed playfully spied on his older brother taking a camp meal for the first time, but expressed disappointment that Jones ate his ration of beef and bread "without even frowning." Meals were not the only adjustment for Jones; Ed lamented the bunking conditions, informing his father that the men had to sleep "like *hogs, piled up together on the ground* about *four deep*." Jones also had trouble keeping step while marching, a shortcoming that led one observer to tell him that he "pitied the *man's heels* that he [Jones] *walked behind*."[33]

As Ed anticipated, Jones's first month with the 13th was a time of difficult transitions. He and Judith had been married less than six months when he joined the army. Jones did his best to comfort his new bride, pleading with her to "bear the separation better." He reminded her that the two of them had once resolved to go "far hence to the heathen." Just as his sense of duty had called him to the mission field, he wrote, so too did duty draw him to the battlefield. Perhaps in an expression of his Calvinism — or at least in a manifestation of the fatalism that was so common among soldiers — Jones told Judith: "Remember that if God so wills it (and He hears prayer) I am as safe in the camp or on the battlefield as within the quiet shades [of Virginia]." Jones also advised Judith not to imagine him as a "poor soldier man" living on bread and water, but instead as a "fat, sleek individual . . . eating fried chicken, bread & butter, and molasses, drinking butter milk." Jones continued to paint a rosy picture for his worried wife, adding that his friends in the area had offered him multiple dinner invitations, and that as a result he was often able to avoid camp food.[34]

Ed likely spoke for all the Jones brothers when he reassured his uneasy mother by affirming, "You know it is our duty as Virginians to be here to defend our rights." He continued, "We're engaged in a noble and just cause and God will aid us on to the victory which we will gain as sure as we fight." Envisioning the possible battles ahead, Ed expressed a sentiment that his brothers may have echoed: "I do not believe myself that we are going to have a fight here directly, but if we do I will try to do my duty & to kill one of the rascals at *least* if no more."[35] Tragically, the Jones brothers would have that opportunity soon enough.

The 13th saw action in numerous battles. Two of the most significant engagements for the regiment included Second Manassas (Second Bull Run) on August 28–30, 1862, and Spotsylvania Court House in May 1864. The 13th also participated at Sharpsburg (Antietam) on September 17, 1862;

Fredericksburg, December 11–15, 1862; Chancellorsville, April 30–May 6, 1863; and Petersburg, June 1864–March 1865. The regiment suffered the most losses at Gaines's Mill, June 27, 1862, losing more than forty percent of the regiment (twenty killed, eighty-five wounded). Also noteworthy is that the regiment lost more men through capture than from battle and disease combined. Likewise, the desertion numbers were nearly as high as the figures for death and disease.[36]

For Jones, the costliest times of the war occurred between the summers of 1862 and 1863. At Gaines's Mill in June 1862, Ed received a wound in the lungs and returned home to convalesce. While caring for Ed, however, Jones's mother died. Lamenting the loss, Pen described the matriarch as a "tender, virtuous, Christian mother." There was still hope that Ed would recover from his injuries, but by early 1863, he took a turn for the worse. With this in mind, Jones corresponded with Judith concerning the state of Ed's soul. "I rejoice to believe that he [Ed] is fully prepared (if it be God's will to take him from us) to enter a better house," Jones wrote. "He says that he is not afraid to die — that he trusts in Christ — that His blood is sufficient — God grant that he may be spared to us, or if not that his hope may be brightened and his faith strengthened."[37] On February 19, 1863, Ed died at home. He was nineteen years old.

In an anecdote near the beginning of *Christ in the Camp* — which Jones wrote in 1887 — Jones ruminates on his brother's death, albeit indirectly. In the illustration, a young soldier of the 13th Virginia is wounded at Gaines's Mill and later dies at home. As Jones narrates, the soldier had not succumbed to vices in camp and, lying on his deathbed, assured those gathered around him that he trusted Jesus and was unafraid to die. Jones's musings on the soldier's demise reflected the high premium that nineteenth-century Americans placed on having a "good death." Such a death entailed being surrounded by loved ones and affirming one's faith in Christ.[38]

Jones did not mention Ed by name, but the particulars of the *Christ in the Camp* account match Ed's story. Ed too enlisted with the 13th, was wounded at Gaines's Mill, displayed courage while dying, and was preceded in death by his mother. That Jones did not identify Ed might be surprising, but it was not uncharacteristic. In Jones's discussion of Gaines's

Mill in the *Southern Historical Society Papers*, he chose not to comment on Ed's death, even while offering a poignant incident of casualties amongst a set of brothers in the Louisa Blues.[39] Such an omission is intriguing considering that Jones was quick to speak of his personal associations with prominent Confederate leaders; when it came to his brothers, however, Jones was either silent or content to praise his brothers from afar.

Even with the loss of his mother and brother weighing heavy on Jones, his heartbreaking year was not yet over. Pen was wounded in the mouth at Gettysburg and died at home two months later, at age twenty-two. In the wake of yet another tragedy, Jones wrote to Broadus:

> It is indeed a sad trial to see another noble brother thus cut off in the open-
> ing of his manhood, but we have abundant cause of comfort in the fact that
> he fell while gallantly doing his duty — that he reached home to have all the
> attention that the hand of affection c[oul]d bestow — and above all that he
> sank calmly and peacefully to rest — leaning on the bosom of the Saviour in
> whom he trusted. Oh! that I had two more such brothers to take the places
> in the army of our country made vacant by their fall. Perhaps it may become
> my duty to fill the place of one of them — if so I trust I shall be ready.[40]

In private correspondence, Jones naturally grieved the deaths of his brothers. His public writings, though, were a different matter. As he had done with Ed, Jones was strangely taciturn regarding his relation to Pen. When recounting Pen's death in *Christ in the Camp*, Jones never revealed that Pen was his brother.

The passing of Pen stands out since he was wounded at Gettysburg, a battle in which the 13th was not engaged. Pen had been promoted to lieu-tenant and served on the staff of his uncle, General John M. Jones (who himself was killed in the Battle of the Wilderness, May 1864). Because of his transfer, Pen fought at Gettysburg while the 13th remained on garrison duty at Winchester, Virginia. The 13th had begun their garrison duty in mid-June 1863, and it was an assignment to their liking. The men reported having plenty of clothes and food, and also being impressed with "lots of pretty girls." The 13th did not rejoin Lee's army until July 23, during the retreat from Gettysburg. For all their fond memories of Winchester, the soldiers of the 13th deeply regretted not being on the field at Gettysburg.[41]

The summer of 1863 was a trying time for Jones. For one thing, at Winchester Jones likely contended with soldiers who had found new opportunities for mischief. Another issue concerned Jones's separation from Pen; while the 13th indulged at Winchester, Pen was mortally wounded leading a charge at Gettysburg. The deaths of his brothers greatly burdened Jones, and the day would come when he made it his mission to determine exactly why the Gettysburg campaign had failed. In an attempt to defend Lee from criticism, Jones would come to place blame on General James Longstreet. Pen's valiant charge could have also driven Jones to find a scapegoat for the Gettysburg defeat. He was likely motivated — in part — by the same feelings he expressed to the *Christian Index* in early 1865. Discussing Confederate soldiers who were hunkered down in the trenches of Petersburg, Jones tried to fortify his readers: "They are not yet prepared to swear, on the Evangelists of Almighty God, that they have been traitors to the 'best government the world ever saw,' and that the comrades who have so nobly fallen at their sides on many a bloody field, perished in an unholy and wicked attempt at treason."[42] As Jones would maintain later in life, Confederates faltered at Gettysburg because Longstreet had not followed Lee's orders. Lee was not to blame; God had not sided with the Union, and those who perished on the sanguinary fields of Pennsylvania — men like Francis "Pen" Jones — had fallen in a righteous cause.

✠ ✠ ✠ ✠ ✠

From early in the war, Jones aspired to be a regimental chaplain. Even before arriving at camp, he requested from Boyce a recommendation to that effect. Jones did not want to enter the matter lightly, though. He wrote Boyce: "The life of a chaplain will be a toilsome, and dangerous one, but I have accustomed myself to be unmoved by hardships when they beset the path of duty, and I shall enter upon my duties (if I secure the appointment) with a firm reliance upon God's promised help and a firm determination not to be carried away by the excitement incident to the camp, but to preach the Gospel — so far as I am able." Jones did not hide his intentions. His brother Ed wrote home on June 9, 1861 (one day after Jones enlisted with the 13th) that Jones hoped to be chaplain of the regiment, or at least Company D. But by September 1861, Jones grew frustrated that he had not yet received his commission. The next month, however, he finally got his wish. In October 1861, Jones was discharged and appointed as a chaplain. Although he remembered serving in the ranks for a year before transferring to chaplain, regimental records indicate that Jones became a chaplain on October 9, 1861, less than six months after enlisting with the Louisa Blues.[43]

As a Baptist, Jones joined what was an evangelical dominance among Confederate chaplaincies, with Baptists, Methodists, and Presbyterians holding most of the positions. Methodists enjoyed the greatest number of chaplains, with estimates ranging anywhere from 300 to 500. Presbyterians and Baptists jostled for second place, with Presbyterians ranging from 125 to 200 chaplains, and Baptists ranging from 100 to 300. Despite these figures, Jones felt that that quantity of chaplains — particularly Baptist ones — was woefully inadequate. Furthermore, it irritated him that Baptists were not keeping pace with fellow evangelicals.[44]

Jones often expressed concern that the number of Baptist chaplains did not reflect the proportion of Baptists in the South. Yet an individual in his position had to address denominational concerns delicately. Many Baptists viewed state-supported chaplaincy as a violation of church-state separation. Some Baptists also balked at the idea of using government money to support chaplains whose theologies (or denominations) Baptists considered suspect. In fact, it was those groups who feared a breach of church-state separation that spearheaded efforts to create new roles, such as that of "army missionary."[45] While the government funded chaplains, denominations took responsibility for army missionaries. By war's end, Jones would transition from the former to the latter.

Jones's labors to recruit more Baptist chaplains may have been hurt by — of all people — Baptists, but the Confederate government hindered matters as well. Although wartime and postwar white Southerners lionized the Confederacy as chosen by God, the Confederate government initially treated chaplaincy with little regard, when addressing it at all. Chaplains had to be content with a private's wage and rank — a concession the Confederate Congress only reluctantly allowed. Furthermore, the regulations for chaplains were as paltry as the remuneration. No guidelines existed concerning chaplains' ages, denominational endorsements, arms, uniform, or responsibilities. By contrast, the Union Army uniformed their chaplains while ranking and paying them as officers. Many white Southerners took notice, questioning how the Confederacy could fulfill its divine potential while treating its own clergy as second-rate soldiers.[46]

The Confederate Congress also waffled on the compensation for army chaplains. In May 1861, Congress provided chaplains an eighty-five-dollars-per-month salary but reduced pay to fifty dollars per month less than two weeks later. That same month there was a failed effort to cut pay to forty dollars per month. Congress members reached a compromise at fifty dollars even while some continued to lobby for higher pay. In April 1862, Congress finally set wages at eighty dollars per month, the earning of a second lieutenant. Some scholars have assessed the Confederacy's indifference toward chaplaincy as an honoring of church-state separation, but these interpretations can be overly charitable. After all, some officials justified ministers' meager compensation by arguing that chaplains only preached once a week.[47]

With the Confederate government's laissez-faire approach toward army chaplaincy, Jones was perhaps fortunate that his role in that capacity was temporary. In September 1863, Dickinson asked Jones to become an army evangelist. Jones attempted to convince Broadus to take the position, but when Broadus refused, Jones accepted. There are a number of possible reasons for Jones's move. He could have been following the guidance of Dickinson, his former pastor and good friend. Jones might have felt pressure from denominational leaders who were less than enthusiastic about state-supported chaplaincies. Jones himself could have seen the chaplaincy as compromising church-state separation, but this seems unlikely since he served a lengthy tenure as chaplain and initially hesitated to give up the position. Also in play may have been a financial motivation, since denominationally supported army missionaries often received better pay than chaplains. More curious than Jones's motives for accepting the new role are Jones's reasons for offering the position to Broadus instead. Factors likely included Jones's friendship with Broadus, as well as his continuing hope that Broadus would come and preach to the soldiers. As one scholar has suggested, Jones may have also worried that if he vacated a chaplaincy position, a non-Baptist might fill the spot.[48]

When surveying Jones's work after the autumn of 1863, the title "army evangelist" can be misleading. Historian Frank Hieronymus provides a helpful delineation of the nomenclature and roles of ministers in the army. First, there were "chaplains," clergy funded by the Confederate government. Next, there were "army missionaries." Individual denominations deployed these parsons, and supported them in the way of pay and (when possible) rations. Army missionaries remained in a semi-permanent role with the army, though they frequently traveled from one regiment to the other. Army missionaries were also more beholden to denominational leaders than were chaplains. Last, there were "evangelists," who received support from a local congregation, not a denominational mission board. Oftentimes, evangelists served with the army on a temporary basis.[49]

While Hieronymus's categories are useful, none of them accurately describe Jones's service after his appointment to "army evangelist." Jones became an evangelist at the request of Dickinson, then superintendent of the Virginia Baptist Colportage and Sunday-School Board. On October 1, 1864, Jones sent a report to Dickinson that summarized Jones's work over the past year. He recalled that it had been one year since he "entered the service of your [Dickinson's] board."[50] Unlike other evangelists, Jones answered to a Baptist board, not to a local congregation. Also, Jones did not treat the status of evangelist as a temporary one; he was actually one of the few ministers who served from the beginning of the war until its conclusion. With his link to a Baptist board and his permanent connection with the army, Jones's role seemed akin to that of an army missionary.

To complicate matters more, Jones simultaneously referred to himself as both a "missionary" and an "evangelist." In January 1865, he stated in a letter to the Goshen Baptist Association that he had been appointed their "missionary" at the last board meeting. Nevertheless, he signed the letter as an "evangelist" of the Third Corps (commanded by A. P. Hill). In the same correspondence, Jones referenced "permanent missionaries," a designation that only muddies already turbid waters. Furthermore, some historians have described Jones as a missionary or "missionary chaplain" to Hill's corps, while others have classified Jones as an evangelist. Rather than assume that scholars are playing fast and loose with the terminology, it is just as plausible to suppose that Jones was. For example, there is good reason to believe that he made no nominal distinction between missionaries and evangelists. When he headed up a veterans' reunion in 1901, he invited only Confederate chaplains and missionaries. He would not have ignored a separate category of evangelists, especially since he had identified himself as such during the war. More likely, he subsumed "evangelists" under the general heading, "missionary."[51]

Pinpointing Jones's precise status is difficult, but understanding his ministerial function is not nearly so. Historian William Earl Brown states it well in observing that the shift to evangelist "simply sanctioned the ministry Jones was already performing."[52] For his part, Jones seemed content to define his title by his work, not vice versa. In any event, a move toward either missionary or evangelist meant that Jones's ministry became more explicitly connected with the Baptist denomination. No longer was Jones a chaplain who happened to be Baptist; now he was a Baptist minister who happened to serve in the army.

Some chaplains looked down on army missionaries and evangelists since these ministers were not only paid more but often did not endure the same privations as the common soldier. For this reason, Jones guaranteed readers that he had suffered the same trials as anyone else. Indeed, he served as a private for months before becoming a chaplain and then as a chaplain for two years before becoming an army evangelist. For Jones, as with all Confederate soldiers, military life was arduous and provisions were meager. Soldiers often ate once a day (or less) and sustained themselves on hardtack. If they were fortunate, there would be bacon or rye coffee. One sergeant of the 13th remembered that soldiers prepared for long marches by gathering five days' rations, a knapsack, a blanket, five pounds of ammunition, and their regular twelve-pound musket. Unfortunately, soldiers often ate their rations in the first two or three days and then "starved the rest of the time." Jones wrote that on these grueling marches he relieved his blistered feet by walking barefoot.[53]

During a three-month stint ministering with Jones in the Confederate camps, Broadus provided a snapshot of everyday life with the 13th. Sleeping arrangements were unenviable, and Broadus noted his futile attempt to soften his bed — which consisted of a "little wooden frame" — with an oilcloth and blanket; for a pillow, he used his overcoat. In August of the same year, Broadus described his exhaustion in a letter to his wife. According to Broadus, he had fallen asleep, fully clothed, on the floor of Jones's tent. As did soldiers, camp ministers often endured punishing hours. In an article for the *Religious Herald* in August 1863, Jones relayed to Dickinson that Broadus had temporarily stopped preaching due to hoarseness. Sore throats plagued not only Broadus, but many other camp preachers. The ailment's prevalence even led one observer to name the condition "clergyman's sore throat."[54]

Enduring long hours, however, was often a chaplain's least worry. Specifically, chaplains were confused as to what their role was to be in battle. Were they to fight? Even though Jones earned the moniker of "fighting parson," he never claimed the name for himself, and the epithet need not suggest that he fought while serving as chaplain. The nickname could instead reference Jones's pre-chaplain role in the ranks. The Chaplains' Association, of which Jones was a charter member, declared that there was no official policy about clergy fighting, and that chaplains "shall be wherever duty calls him, irrespective of danger." That said, the association continued, "[O]rdinarily it is thought wrong for him to take a musket."[55]

Chaplains had to walk a fine line. By not fighting, they could lose the respect of the soldiers, which would in turn hamstring efforts at evangelism. Either way — whether arming themselves or not — chaplains suffered a perilous existence. While seven Confederate chaplains died in battle, thirty-two died of disease in camp. Also, chaplains often had "litter duty" and were responsible for helping transport the wounded to field hospitals. In the execution of this task, chaplains ran the risk of being captured. The emotional toll on chaplains was also great: they had the heart-rending job of writing to the next of kin when a soldier was wounded or killed.[56]

As chaplain, and then as army evangelist, Jones worked at a feverish pace. He often preached two or three times a day. In his characteristic "evangelical" tone, he spoke to soldiers about personal conversion, on one occasion exhorting a colonel to "seek after a personal interest in the Savior's blood." Jones's ministry reflected his continued adherence to the theological positions marked out by SBTS's "Abstract of Principles." For example, the Abstract emphasized the liberty of conscience. Jones too valued such liberty, believing that soldiers could follow their consciences to any denomination of their choosing. His work also reflected a belief in regeneration and repentance as defined in the Abstract. Regeneration was a "change of heart, wrought by the Holy Spirit, who quickeneth the dead in trespasses and sins enlightening their minds spiritually and savingly to understand the Word of God." Repentance was an "evangelical grace, wherein a person being by the Holy Spirit, made sensible of the manifold evil of his sin, humbleth himself for it, with godly sorrow, detestation of it, and self-abhorrence."[57] Jones's ministry focused on personal conversion, rooted in genuine repentance from sin.

In one year, Jones reportedly preached 161 sermons and baptized 222 converts. Some historians have highlighted that Baptists — influenced by the ecumenical spirit of camp religion — relaxed their emphasis on baptism. To the contrary, Jones demonstrated that he had not strayed from his understanding of baptism since his time at SBTS. The seminary's Abstract described baptism as "an ordinance of the Lord Jesus, obligatory upon every believer, wherein he is immersed in the water in the name of the Father, and the Son, and of the Holy Spirit." In fact, Jones went to great and even dangerous lengths to ensure that soldiers received baptism. He baptized in full view of Federal troops, and even gave the "men in blue" credit for not firing on the services. In order to baptize soldiers by immersion, he famously cut a hole in a frozen lake. He would also baptize in rivers made fast and swollen by recent rains. Jones recorded that, by war's end, he had baptized 410 soldiers.[58]

Peril was not limited to the baptismal waters. Once, Jones refused to dismiss his congregation until he had finished a prayer, even though an artillery battle began during the service. Other anecdotes portray Jones as less intractable. For example, on one occasion he tried to cancel a service due to rain. When soldiers protested, the service continued until artillery fire compelled the congregation to relocate. Jones also distributed tracts in the trenches of Petersburg, where shells could fall indiscriminately at any moment.[59]

A significant aspect of Jones's chaplaincy was his participation as a founding member in the Chaplains' Association of the Second and Third Corps, Army of Northern Virginia. The association began in March 1863, and its duties included anything from combatting camp immorality to recruiting chaplains. With founders coming from denominationally diverse backgrounds — Jones (Baptist), B. T. Lacy (Presbyterian), and W. C. Powers (Methodist) — the group was a testament to the willingness of evangelicals to band together for sake of soldiers' spiritual welfare. The association also provided a means of regulating the chaplaincy, something the Confederate government had left largely undone. The organization addressed a variety of issues ranging from whether chaplains should fight to whether chaplains should have a distinguishing badge. Important for Jones's postwar work, it was through the association that Jones first met Robert E. Lee in February 1864. Jones and Lacy requested an audience with the general in order to appeal for a reduction of work on the Sabbath. According to Jones, Lee readily honored the petition.[60]

Even outside of association work, Jones leagued with ministers from non-Baptist denominations. In October 1863, he reported to the *Religious Herald* the numbers of the recently baptized from each denomination. His figures had Methodists at sixty-two, Presbyterians at twenty-two, Disciples at two, and the Episcopalians, Lutherans, and United Brethren all at one. He also noted that he had baptized ninety-three into the Baptist fold. Writing to a Baptist newspaper, Jones understood the need to add that "others of our Baptist chaplains have baptized still larger numbers." For Jones there existed a perpetual tension regarding how to ally with fellow evangelicals while at the same time promoting specifically Baptist interests. In an 1863 letter, Jones wrote to Broadus with measured optimism, "I am beginning to do *something* at filling up the Regts with good Baptist Chaplains but have been greatly retarded by the want of *the right sort of men*." Even while joining in the interdenominational push for more chaplains, Jones wanted Baptists to fill the vacancies.[61]

In early 1865, and from the trenches of Petersburg, Jones entreated Georgia Baptists. He asked for religious material — whatever "Sherman has not taken" — and, in a common refrain, pled for more Baptist chaplains. With a less than subtle jab at Georgia Baptists, Jones disclosed that Georgia soldiers had been speaking ill of their state's clergy for not visiting the army. He added: "I have tried to defend my brethren, but have found it very hard to get over the fact that Sorrell's [sic], Wofford's, Benning's, and Colquitt's Brigades are all without a Baptist Chaplain or Missionary — that the artillery and cavalry from Georgia are equally destitute — that there are at present only five chaplains, and not a single missionary to represent the great Baptist denomination of Georgia in this army."[62] Two weeks later, the *Christian Index* printed another supplication. This time Jones discussed a meeting of the Chaplains' Association, during which members unexpectedly concluded that the numbers of chaplains had increased over the past year. *Index* readers, however, were not off the hook. "I regret to have to say," Jones reprimanded, "that there has been a decrease of Baptist Chaplains, (and I might add, Missionaries too) within the past twelve months."[63]

Of course, Jones was not the only minister concerned about Baptist numbers in the camps. Asking for more chaplains, Dickinson observed that "there is a very extensive Baptist sentiment in the army." In October 1863, a soldier writing to the *Biblical Recorder* noted that Jones and army missionary G. W. Bagley had visited camp. The soldier stated that "our hearts have been made glad, for they are Baptists, zealous for good works, and we have not been blessed with Baptist preachers for about twelve months." The writer continued by referencing Jones's recent transition to "General Evangelist": "I do hope that God will bless his labors and enable him to stir up the Baptist ministers to at least an ordinary sense of their duty."[64]

Just as influential on Jones as the carnage of the battlefield was the religion of the camps. The rains of revival watered the seeds of the Lost Cause, and for the remainder of his life, Jones would employ his recollection of camp religion in order to mold white Southern memory.[65] In the Confederate revivals Jones also came to appreciate in a new way the effectiveness of interdenominationalism. Nonetheless, because soldiers and chaplains held so firmly to their denominational identities, even in the extraordinary circumstances of war, the fraternal relations of camp religion were just as symbiotic as they were ecumenical. All along, Jones was a thoroughgoing Baptist with a missionary drive to convert the masses, even if this meant networking with non-Baptists. Eventually, he would exercise the same cooperative spirit in order to promulgate the Lost Cause.

Jones's wartime correspondence may have betrayed his uncertainty over the prevalence of Baptists in the army, but his writings also bore witness to what he believed to be the guiding hand of Providence. In Jones's mind, neither the vagaries of politics nor the butchery of warfare could prevent him from fulfilling his mission, whatever that might be. That purpose had once seemed quite clear to him, especially as a freshly minted minister eager to carry the gospel abroad. Now, in the throes of national upheaval, he would channel the same ardor into the evangelism of soldiers who daily subsisted in the shadow of death. Instead of clouding his calling, secession had brought it into sharper focus. Finally, he would embrace his "Damascus Road" moment, not in the midst of a Louisa County revival, but in the fiery baptism of war.

"We Mingled Together in Freest Intercourse": Jones the Baptist and Wartime Confederate Religion

"Religion in the army" was a peculiar type or phase of piety. I mean not that it differed from religion in other armies, but that it differed from religion at home and in peace; identical in essence, but modified in manifestation by the extraordinary circumstances amid which it sprang up and developed. It was a variety in the fruit of the manifold grace of God; it had its own form, color, flavor.

— J. C. GRANBERRY, *Christ in the Camp*

For many nineteenth-century Lost Cause advocates — especially those of a religious bent — the wartime revivals within the Confederate camps represented irrefutable evidence that God favored the Southern cause. These times of heightened religious fervor and mass conversions not only confirmed God's presence in the Confederate ranks, but also bolstered claims that white Southerners remained God's chosen people. Because of the centrality of these revivals in the way many white Southerners viewed themselves after the war, understanding the origins and ramifications of these religious phenomena is crucial. In fact, there was no wartime event that affected Jones's postwar thinking as much as the Confederate revivals.

The fire of revival began sweeping through the Confederate armies in the winter of 1862–1863. For Jones, this move of God represented a pivotal period in the life of the Confederacy. Jones recalled that just one year earlier the "moral picture of the army" had been "dark indeed." In the winter of 1861, he wrote to Richmond's *Daily Dispatch* asking readers to donate books to the army. Jones added that the texts could be religious or otherwise, since his goal was to occupy soldiers with reading lest they occupy themselves with vices (a particular problem in winter quarters, when soldiers had less to do). The "irreligion" of 1861–1862 was at least partly due to the indifference of the Confederate government toward the chaplaincy system. Jones, however, believed the problems stemmed from the Confederate Army's battlefield successes early in the war. According to Jones, after the Confederate Army's victory at First Manassas (First Bull Run), Southerners began relying more on themselves and less on God. Only when Southerners realized that Lee's army was not invincible, the reasoning went, could a revival descend.[1]

Especially in light of Jones's suggestion that the revivals followed Confederate setbacks, the timing of these spiritual awakenings is significant. Scholars generally agree that the revivals began in late 1862 in Virginia and then expanded rapidly in 1863 to the Western theater. Historians diverge, however, on the sequence of events in late 1862. Some hold that the revivals began while Confederate troops were in winter quarters along the Rappahannock, soon after the Battle of Fredericksburg — a resounding victory for the Confederates — in December 1862. Other writers posit that the services followed on the heels of Confederate defeat at the Battle of Sharpsburg (Antietam). Jones himself wrote that the revivals began after Sharpsburg, in September 1862, as Lee's army returned from the first Maryland campaign.[2]

What may appear as tedious, academic hairsplitting is actually important for assessing the psychology of pre-revival Confederate soldiers, who were either flush with victory or dispirited from defeat. The latter of these options — that revival services ignited after Sharpsburg — goes far in illuminating a common theological mindset of white Southerners. For the first two years of the war, optimism ran high in the Confederacy. With setbacks in late 1862, this optimism waned and set the stage for renewed religious vigor. Southerners began to question the invincibility of Confederate armies, and they attributed military reverses to God's chastisement. Southerners thus felt that a return to God would result in Confederate victories.[3]

White Southerners' theological response to defeat was characteristic of what is sometimes referred to as "retribution theology." The fundamental premise of this theology was that God blessed those who were good and cursed those who were bad. An adherent to this way of thinking not only had a degree of control over the future (if one acts rightly, one will receive good), but also had a lens through which to interpret the past (if bad things happened, then one must have acted wrongly). Jones appealed to this sense of God's retributive justice when recounting camp revivals. As Jones saw the matter, once an overconfident South tasted the bitterness of defeat, Southerners remembered their need for God. When Southerners submitted themselves before God, Jones thought, hearts were then prepared for a great outpouring of God's spirit.[4] For many nineteenth-century evangelicals, revivals were times of acute and renewed religious awareness that often followed periods of perceived spiritual torpor. That revivals would follow in the wake of military setbacks is thus unsurprising. If defeat was a means of chastisement, a return to God would invite spiritual renewal, and perhaps lead to success on the battlefield.

By 1863, revivals were burning through the Confederate camps. During the revivals' peak, there were sometimes six meetings a day. One of Jones's goals in his 1887 *Christ in the Camp* was to take readers inside one of these meetings, and as a result, he painted a vivid picture. He wrote that in early 1863 soldiers were so eager to attend religious meetings that the commotion to find a seat made some think a circus had come to town. He remembered scores of soldiers squeezing into a packed church, and he insisted that while the men waited there was no "idle gossip"; instead, congregants began a hymn that seemed "almost ready to take the roof off of the house." Admitting that he might be an "old fogy," Jones inserted that the hymns were glorious despite not being accompanied by a "grand organ" or "quartette choir." After singing, one man prayed. This prayer, according to Jones, did not mention the causes of the war. Likewise, the presiding minister alluded neither to the war nor to slavery, but was content to preach "the Gospel." Jones avowed that in this ethereal atmosphere, men who were unaccustomed to the "melting mood" were brought to tears. By the end of the Fredericksburg revival, Jones had counted more than five hundred conversions.[5]

Jones wrote that the Battle of Chancellorsville briefly interrupted meetings in the spring of 1863 but that revivals culminated in August of that year, spread to other armies thereafter, and continued in some form until Appomattox. With these services came a flurry of opportunities for Jones. For example, he recounted a particularly grueling day that occurred in September 1863. At 6:00 a.m., he preached to his brigade; at 11:00 a.m., he attended a baptismal service; at dusk, he preached by the light of fire stands to about five thousand men, where he was glad to report around two hundred conversions. Such an arduous day was not uncommon for Jones. In fact, he remembered attending four protracted meetings a day for a period. While he usually preached at least once a day, he might also deliver four sermons in the same time frame. On occasion he would perform four baptismal services without ever changing his clothes. When Broadus visited Jones in the summer of 1863, Broadus too preached up to four times a day, after which, Jones declared, there was "scarcely a dry eye in the vast throng."[6]

Jones recalled one instance when he witnessed a chaplain preaching outside in the snow. Surveying the congregants, Jones observed at least fourteen soldiers without shoes. On another occasion, he delivered a message in a steady rain for forty minutes—this in large measure because soldiers demurred at the idea of canceling the service due to weather. Jones provided such anecdotes not only to praise the spiritual resiliency of Confederate soldiers, but also to instill the same vigor in his readers. He jibed Southerners missing church services due to inclement weather, and he encouraged readers to follow the example of Confederate soldiers whose spiritual resolve enabled them to brave the elements. Jones also hoped that readers would take a cue from the unpretentiousness of Confederate worship services. He assured readers that he preached the "old, old story, Of Jesus and His love," and he judged that a "grand organ" was superfluous in congregational singing. Drawing inspiration from these humble services, he prompted Southerners to appreciate the simplicity of the gospel message and Christian worship.[7]

The nature of revivals in the Army of Northern Virginia changed with the Petersburg campaign, when Lee's and Grant's armies engaged in trench warfare from the summer of 1864 to the spring of 1865. Jones wrote that while religious services continued during this time, it was often dangerous to conduct meetings outside of bomb shelters. In postwar accounts, Jones maintained that revivals had continued through the end of the war, yet his Petersburg correspondence evidenced that months of brutal fighting had dampened both military and spiritual morale, and that while he anticipated revival in the Army of Northern Virginia, one was not presently underway. Even if soldiers' enthusiasm had waned, Jones recorded a flurry of activity, estimating that troops had built up to sixty chapels along the lines from 1864 to 1865, a significant number considering wood shortages in Petersburg. Praising the assiduity of chapel-building in the beleaguered city, Jones compared Confederate troops to those rebuilding Jerusalem's walls in the time of Nehemiah.[8]

Returning to his emphasis on the modesty of Confederate worship, Jones underscored that the lowly Petersburg chapels boasted no frescoes, gas lighting, steeples, bells, organs, or refined congregants. The improvised sanctuaries often consisted of pine logs or slabs, with planks serving as seats. Chapels had one or more chimneys, and most importantly, a pulpit, toward which all seats were directed. Jones claimed that these cabins doubled as schools for soldiers, where troops could learn not only how to read and write, but also mathematics, Latin, Greek, French, and German. Just as he lauded makeshift chapels as outshining fanciful church buildings, Jones praised these chapel-schools as excelling many of the "so-called 'universities' of the land today." As was common with Jones, his panegyrics knew no bounds. Not only was Confederate worship loftier than that of civilian congregations; Confederate education also rivaled that of civilian colleges.[9]

While at Petersburg, Jones was not content merely to report on religious services. He also felt it his duty to encourage Southerners who were disheartened after four years of war and who were particularly concerned about attrition in the Petersburg ranks. Jones testified that Confederates were "not prepared to give up their homes to pillage, their wives, mothers, and sisters to insults, and themselves to be slaves of a hireling soldiery." Moving from encouragement to reprove, Jones thundered, "Shame on the faint-hearted coward who would seek to escape the ills of war by flying to the far greater evils of subjugation." Despite what looked like a dire situation for the South, Jones was convinced that Confederates were but one campaign away from ultimate victory.[10]

Jones estimated that by the war's end, the Army of Northern Virginia had seen fifteen thousand conversions. He was quick to add that perhaps this figure should be as high as fifty thousand but that he did not want to be accused of exaggeration. He concurred with Methodist chaplain William W. Bennett that conversions throughout the Confederate armies were upwards of 150,000. While scholars have provided various revisions of Bennett's number, some approximations still range as high as one hundred thousand conversions.[11] For Jones, such figures only advanced his argument that Christ's presence had permeated the Confederate camps. Jones's firm belief in the piety of Confederate leaders and troops—exemplified in the camp revivals—proved foundational for his postwar writings, especially as they related to the developing mythology of the Lost Cause.

✣ ✣ ✣ ✣ ✣

More than any other event in his life, Jones's experience in wartime camp revivals shaped the way he viewed the postwar South. The revivals also influenced the way he understood his own denominational identity. Even though the numbers of religiously active Confederates were relatively low before the revivals of late 1862—the most charitable estimates offer a figure as high as one-third[12]—the average church-going soldier would have found camp life to be a denominational hodgepodge. For a staunch Baptist like Jones, preserving a distinct denominational identity in a sea of non-Baptists was a perilous endeavor. While such a quandary may seem quite foreign to modern readers, for Jones the stakes were high. In essence, the trick was to bend without breaking—to unite with non-Baptists for the sake of wartime evangelism without simultaneously abandoning doctrinal beliefs that were uniquely Baptist. Jones's ability to walk this theological tightrope would serve him well in the postwar period as he leveraged the narrative of wartime denominational fraternity in order to disseminate the Lost Cause message.

That Jones would successfully navigate the sectarian waters of camp life was certainly not a given. Along with the exigencies of war, the denominational mélange could have tempted some chaplains to de-emphasize doctrinal particularities in order to cast the evangelical net as wide as possible. Yet there is no need to exaggerate these tendencies. Scholars who have surveyed the interdenominationalism of camp revivals tend to overstate the case, characterizing as "ecumenical" what is better understood as "cooperative."[13] Indeed, networking was common among evangelicals, but by and large, denominational partnerships fared better in camps than they did in the soldiers' home churches, especially when those soldiers were Baptist.

Among Baptists, the first and most substantial challenge to evangelical cooperation was intense denominational fidelity. Interdenominational collaboration was not entirely foreign to Baptists, though. In the early nineteenth century, Baptists banded with other denominations in the camp meetings of the Second Great Awakening. Baptists did so, however, while still honoring their Baptist particularities. Of course, even in the wake of these revivals, denominations were not above "stealing sheep" from one another, and with the formation of the Southern Baptist Convention (SBC) in 1845, Southern Baptist identity and regional loyalty fused indivisibly.[14]

The ultimate expression of denominational loyalty among nineteenth-century Baptists was the movement known as Landmarkism. James R. Graves (1820–1893), editor of the *Tennessee Baptist*, coined the term "Landmarkism" when Graves's colleague, James Madison Pendleton (1811–1891), published the 1854 pamphlet, "An Old Landmark Reset: Ought Baptists to Invite Pedobaptists to Preach in Their Pulpits?" Years earlier, in 1848, Graves had criticized immersion performed by non-Baptists ("alien immersion"). Graves's argument was twofold. First, he held that the local Baptist church was the only true, New Testament, church. Only Baptists, he contended, could trace their origins to Jesus and John the Baptist. Graves supported his belief in successionism by identifying various groups throughout Christian history as Baptist. Second, Graves believed that only Baptists properly practiced the ordinances of baptism and communion. For him, this meant baptism by immersion and communion only for the baptized ("closed communion").[15]

In the 1890s Landmarkers railed against the research of William H. Whitsitt, who dated Baptist origins to the seventeenth century and traced baptism by immersion to 1641. Whitsitt, a church history professor, had served as president of Southern Baptist Theological Seminary (SBTS) since 1895. When influential Texas Baptist pastor B. H. Carroll threatened to make a motion for the SBC to end its relationship with SBTS, Whitsitt resigned from his post in 1898. Interestingly, Whitsitt expressed a deep appreciation for Jones's life and writings. After Jones's death, Whitsitt—who would make his own contribution to Lost Cause mythology—delivered a rousing encomium at the 1909 meeting of the SBC. The fact that Jones had supported Whitsitt during the SBTS turmoil and that Jones had shown no inclination toward Landmarkism were reasons enough for Whitsitt to praise the minister's work.[16]

Another hurdle for denominational networking came from non-Landmark Baptists. Many Baptists were cagy about the alleged interdenominationalism of Confederate camps. One writer to the *Biblical Recorder* asked, "In the terrible crisis through which we are now passing, are we not in danger of underrating the great truths which constitute our denomination a peculiar people?" The writer continued with a passionate plea:

> Nor can we agree to the assertion, so often made, that the errors of those who differ from us are slight; while they hold much that is good and true in common with us, and we need not therefore be so earnest in the maintenance of our peculiar principles. With the teachings of history before us, we can agree to no such thing. When we remember the sad results of these seemingly slight errors, the truth as it is in Jesus totally obscured, the most monstrous superstitions and idolatries substituted in its place, and a nominal Christianity in alliance with the civil government, hunting down and putting to death all who venture to dissent from its dogmas, we arrive at the conclusion that in religious matters there can be no slight errors.[17]

Another writer to the *Biblical Recorder* announced, "[w]e have never agreed with those Baptists who hold that the present is no time for proclaiming the peculiar views of our denomination." The writer continued: "If they are worth contending for in times of peace, when the currents of society flow smoothly along in their accustomed channels, much more should we keep them before us and earnestly advocate them in these seasons of upheaval when no one can tell whither we are drifting."[18] For this contributor, even warfare was no excuse for diluting denominational commitments.

Particular sticking points for Baptists concerned the ordinance of baptism and the formation of "army churches" in the Confederate camps. For example, a small crisis regarding the protocol for camp baptisms surfaced in the summer of 1863. Many Baptists expressed agitation when a Baptist chaplain from South Carolina, T. W. Gwin, sent a letter to the *Confederate Baptist* that discussed his work with non-Baptist denominations. Gwin wrote, "Bro. Walters and myself (Baptist), immerse for the other chaplains, and they sprinkle for us when candidates desire it." Baptists swiftly denounced what they believed to be Gwin's openness to non-immersion baptism. Gwin issued an explanation the following month insisting that he only baptized by immersion but that there existed an informal baptismal-exchange system in the army. When non-Baptist chaplains received converts who wished to join the Baptist church, the chaplains referred the individuals to Gwin and his coworker. Likewise, when Gwin received someone who wanted to join a non-Baptist church, he sent the candidate to a chaplain of that denomination.[19]

Having clarified his response, Gwin did not let the matter rest. He asked the *Confederate Baptist* what should be done for non-Baptists who had already been baptized as infants but wished now to be immersed (though not become Baptist). Gwin wrote: "It may not be baptistic to recommend (after immersion) these candidates to the Presbyterian and Methodist Church for membership, yet, under all the circumstances, should we not immerse and recommend them to the churches of their choice, or should we simply give them certificates of baptism and a recommendation to the Christian regard of all the brethren in Christ?"[20] Many Baptists suffered neither of Gwin's options. The *Confederate Baptist* rejected Gwin's proposal, and the *Christian Index* and *Biblical Recorder* picked up on the story. Since baptism was the "appointed and indispensable antecedent to church membership," the *Confederate Baptist* concluded that Gwin should not baptize anyone who wished to join a "Pedo-baptist" church.[21]

Another issue that rankled Baptists involved the idea of "army churches." Many Baptists were hesitant to organize formal churches in the camps lest Baptist soldiers have to transfer their memberships from home churches. Other denominations shared Baptists' concerns, and as a result, what developed in camps were less formal army churches. These army churches were nonsectarian and often adopted articles of faith that appealed to multiple denominations. While a few denominational congregations formed in the army, a key feature of army churches was their interdenominational character. As a result, some Baptists were uneasy about the idea of army churches, fearing that in such gatherings chaplains and soldiers would ignore denominational particularities.[22]

There was no consensus among Baptists as to the practicality of organizing formal Baptist churches in camp. In the summer of 1863, the *Christian Index* disagreed with the *Religious Herald* as to the feasibility of establishing Baptist congregations in the army. When the *Religious Herald* showed openness to the idea, the *Index* countered: "There is too much ... that militates against the successful accomplishment of the ends for which churches are formed, to render it expedient to constitute them. They would most surely die a violent death, and then where is the disorder to end which will be created by want of proper letters of dismission, or vouchers of baptism?"[23]

The *Index* expressed concern that formal churches in the army would include only "new converts" since Baptists who joined the army would not have brought with them membership letters from home churches. Instead, the *Index* proposed that soldiers wishing to join the Baptist denomination be baptized and then given a baptismal certificate in order to "secure admission to any home church which is satisfied of the candidate's conversion." Certificates from Baptist ministers would vouch that the candidate had been "properly baptized in the army upon a profession of faith in Christ." This was Jones's standard practice, as he explained: "It may be of interest to mention how we received and baptized men without a church to authorize it. Well, we baptized them just as Philip did the eunuch, upon a profession of repentance toward God and faith in the Lord Jesus Christ, and gave them a certificate to that effect." Such baptismal certificates were important, as one of the primary ways nineteenth-century Baptist churches accepted new members was through a letter of transfer from another Baptist congregation.[24]

Despite Baptist uneasiness toward interdenominational services in Confederate camps, Jones reached across sectarian boundaries for the sake of evangelism, believing he could do so without compromising his Baptist identity. In fact, a hallmark of his activity during the Confederate revivals was his collaboration with non-Baptists. He lobbied for interdenominational cooperation, later identifying this fraternal spirit as one of the most "potent factors" in the success of chaplains and army missionaries. He quoted Presbyterian minister William J. Hoge, who had visited a Confederate revival in Fredericksburg in the spring of 1863. Hoge remembered, "[W]e had a Presbyterian sermon, introduced by Baptist services, under the direction of a Methodist chaplain, in an Episcopal church. Was not that a beautiful solution of the vexed problem of Christian union?"[25]

In one of Jones's clearest affirmations of denominational collaboration, he reminisced:

> [I]nstead of spending our time in fierce polemics over disputed points, we found common ground upon which we could stand shoulder to shoulder and labor for the cause of our common Master. Bound together by the sacred ties of a common faith in Jesus, a common hope of an inheritance beyond the skies, and a common desire to bring our brave men to Christ and to do all within our power to promote their spiritual interests, we mingled together in freest intercourse, took sweet counsel together, preached and prayed and labored together, and formed ties of friendship — nay, of brotherhood — which time can never sever, and which, we firmly believe, eternity will only purify and strengthen.[26]

One of the most striking examples of this shared labor was the practice of camp baptisms. Prior to the baptism, chaplains inquired as to the candidate's denominational preference. If there was no minister of that particular church present, the attending minister sent for one. Jones remarked that he was involved in these exchanges, receiving soldiers sent to him from ministers of other denominations, and in return, sending soldiers who wished to join non-Baptist churches. He was confident that other army ministers practiced a similar baptismal-exchange system.[27]

Jones and others also organized "associations"—coalitions with the specific goal of promoting partnerships among denominations. The role of an association was broader than that of an army church and included distributing tracts, leading prayer groups, and encouraging pious living among the soldiers. Jones himself was one of the founders of the Chaplains' Association of the Second and Third Corps, Army of Northern Virginia. Goals of the Chaplains' Association, which began meeting in March 1863, were to combat vice, recruit chaplains, provide religious instruction to soldiers, and increase the efficiency of army chaplaincy. Notably, the first participants in the association came from a variety of denominational backgrounds: Baptist, Presbyterian, Methodist, and Episcopalian. Presbyterian minister and co-founder of the Chaplains' Association, B. T. Lacy, observed that through the work of chaplains "ministers of the different denominations are brought into closer and more harmonious co-operation, thus promoting the unity and charity of the whole church."[28]

The Chaplains' Association was not the only officially interdenominational body in the Confederate armies. Jones recorded a letter from H. B. Richards, who helped organize the Soldiers' Christian Association of the Ninth Virginia Calvary. Richards's motivation was that "all the Christians in the regiment should be *united*, and contend side by side and shoulder to shoulder in the cause of Christ." Richards continued that the association would be composed of "all the professors of the religion of Christ . . . without regard to denomination or sect."[29] Another association's goal was "uniting the members of the various Churches . . . in the work of saving souls, of gathering the results of the night meetings, and of hearing the recitals of religious experience."[30] One writer described the work of a chaplains' association in "breaking down barriers and removing denominational prejudices." The Evangelical Tract Society, organized in Petersburg, Virginia in July 1861, represented an interdenominational effort to distribute religious literature to soldiers. In order to maximize the success of colportage, tracts needed to remain nonsectarian.[31]

Important to note here is that neither army churches nor associations dismissed denominational distinctions as unimportant, and neither group understood itself as interfering with the denominational loyalties of participants. Soldiers who wished to join the Baptist denomination often had to present a public testimony, after which the Baptists of the unit would vote. If accepted, the neophyte was then accountable to the other Baptists of the group. Hence there existed denominational subdivisions within the interdenominational association.[32]

Jones emphasized the cooperative nature of camp revivals as well, averring that the typical revival minister shunned "fierce polemics against Christians of other denominations." Jones and other preachers received warm welcomes from soldiers of various denominations, and one Presbyterian artillery private noted the "marked absence of sectarian feeling" in the sermons of visiting ministers. Jones also held his non-Baptist colleagues in high esteem. For example, he described Methodist chaplain J. C. Granberry as "one of the ablest preachers and most efficient workers I know." Jones continued to admire Granberry after the war, even asking him to write the introduction to *Christ in the Camp*. Beyond Granberry and Methodists, Jones included copious citations from Presbyterians, Baptists, and Episcopalians in his six-hundred-page tribute to Confederate religion. Because of the substantial space the book dedicated to non-Baptists, Jones's *Christ in the Camp* was itself a clear expression of denominational comradery.[33]

Jones's account of the Confederate revivals illuminated more than the practice of interdenominationalism; it also highlighted the extreme circumstances that compelled hitherto rivals to join together in the first place. In short, the brotherhood of Confederate revivals was circumstantial by nature—born not of theological dialogue, but of rank necessity. While the exigencies of war did not abrogate denominational loyalties, practical matters demanded collaboration. For example, one circumstance necessitating the cooperation of ministers was the scarcity of chaplains. Jones relished the opportunity to preach to troops, but he fretted that there were so few clergy to accomplish the pressing work. Others shared his concern. Jones recorded that in one instance, a desperate Episcopalian soldier requested a chaplain—any chaplain—regardless of the minister's denominational affiliation. The shortage of chaplains perplexed Jones and his fellow ministers not only because soldiers desired preaching, but also because civilian churchgoers viewed army camps as hotbeds of immorality. Even Jones, who was determined to show that Christ was in the Confederates' midst, had to admit that sundry vices had infected army camps. Most common among these transgressions were card-playing, profanity, Sabbath-breaking, and perhaps most treacherous, drunkenness.[34]

Jones told the story of an inebriated officer falling off his horse while trying to inspect troops (Jones had to stand guard at the tent while the officer recovered). Jones believed that drunkenness increased when soldiers were idle, and he confessed that one-time teetotalers indulged in the bottle while in camp. He was also ashamed to admit that soldiers and officers engaged in drunken brawls. Furthermore, he remembered that, alarmingly, army surgeons had some of the worst reputations for drunkenness. Writing on behalf of the Chaplains' Association, Lacy asserted that the "carelessness and open apostasy of professors of religion are here—as well as everywhere else—a great hindrance to the success of the gospel." Jones concurred that many soldiers had made "shipwrecks" of their faith and that "wickedness of every description held high carnival in our camps." With iniquities running rampant, many felt an acute need for more chaplains. In the absence of enough chaplains, however, armies organized interdenominational associations "for the promotion of morality and piety."[35]

The lack of chaplains also led to mixed worship services. As he did so often, Jones agreed with Stonewall Jackson, who showed little patience for sectarian sermons in mixed assemblies. Jackson opined: "Denominational distinctions should be kept out of view, and not touched upon. And, as a general rule, I do not think that a chaplain who would preach denominational sermons should be in the army. His congregation is his regiment, and it is composed of various denominations. I would like to see no question asked in the army of what denomination a chaplain belongs to; but let the question be, Does he preach the Gospel?"[36] In the context of mixed congregations, interdenominationalism served the dual function of preventing chaplains from preaching sectarian sermons while simultaneously protecting the denominational loyalties of the soldiers who were listening. In one sense, ministers muted denominationally specific messages; in another sense, these neutral sermons honored the denominational leanings of soldiers. Chaplains cooperated not in order to blur doctrinal distinctions but to respect the denominational fidelity of those in their charge. Their congregations demanded as much, as many soldiers bristled at sermons redolent of sectarianism.[37] With the paucity of chaplains, religious soldiers had limited options, and they expected regimental chaplains and visiting ministers to respect the denominational commitments of their captive audiences.

The scarcity of chaplains could also bring denominational anxieties to the surface. Jones, for example, worried that there were too few Baptist chaplains in the army. He wrote, "[T]here is one thought which strikes me painfully in looking over these statistics—the proportion of Baptist chaplains to those of our Methodist and Presbyterian brethren is so *small*, when we consider the relative membership of each Church." He continued, "I rejoice that the ministry of these denominations have awakened to some appreciation of what they owe the army. I mourn that our Baptist ministry seem *behind them* in this respect." Jones repeated his appeal for Baptist chaplains, so much so that he feared Georgia Baptists would accuse him of "harp[ing] on one string." By Jones's estimation, one Georgia regiment was "largely Baptistic in sentiment," and he maintained that "a large mass of its converts . . . desire to connect themselves with Baptist Churches." The problem, he pressed, was that the regiment lacked access to a Baptist chaplain. The issue galling Jones was not simply that Baptist soldiers had no ministers of their own, but that those inclined to be Baptist were unable to join the denomination. Networking among evangelicals did not mean that chaplains set adrift their denominational distinctions. Nonsectarian sermons were well and good, but Jones still wanted Baptist chaplains for would-be Baptist soldiers.[38]

Soldiers were particularly sensitive to what they perceived to be sectarian messages. On one occasion, a disgruntled soldier accused Jones himself of exhibiting denominational bias. Presbyterian chaplain T. D. Witherspoon relayed to Jones that an offended congregant asked that Jones not be invited back to perform camp baptisms. When Witherspoon inquired as to why, the soldier responded that "it is generally understood that, inasmuch as we have all of the evangelical denominations repre-sented in our brigade, no man ought to present his *own particular doc-trines.*" Witherspoon protested, denying that Jones had preached sectarian sermons. The soldier agreed that Jones had not *preached* such sermons, but insisted that Jones had "read to the crowd *all of them Baptist Scriptures.*"[39] Not willing to concede the point, Witherspoon disagreed that the scrip-tures in question were in fact "Baptist" passages. While Witherspoon shared this account in jest—and while Jones shared the story in order to defend himself against the allegations—the incident demonstrated that the impetus for denominational cooperation was as much a bottom-up as a top-down phenomenon.

Besides chaplain shortages, another circumstance compelling min-isters to band together was the unique opportunity for wartime evange-lism. Many chaplains shared the exuberance of A. E. Dickinson when he exclaimed, "What a field of usefulness this war has opened!" Chaplain A. D. Cohen wrote that he had more opportunity to do good during the war than at any other time during his ministry, and when reflecting on the eagerness with which regiments gathered for worship services, one chaplain asked, "What Richmond pastor has such an advantage?" "The field of labor opened here for the accomplishment of good is beyond measure," a colporteur commented. "An angel might covet it."[40] Jones also rejoiced in the enthusiasm of soldiers to hear the gospel, and he claimed that chaplains who were willing to suffer the privations of the soldiers had a "golden opportunity of pointing the sick and wounded to the great Physician; the hungry to the 'bread of life;' the thirsty to 'the water of life;' the weary to the 'rest that remaineth for the people of God,' and the dying to 'the resurrection and the life.'" The war offered ministers access to a breadth and diversity of congregants unlike any they had seen before and any they would likely see again. Here chaplains found that soldiers who were ill, wounded, or on the brink of battle were especially receptive to the gospel message. For these chaplains, interdenominationalism was a provisional means of reaping fields white with harvest.

In particular, hospitals provided chaplains a bountiful mission field. Jones wrote that the "world's history has never presented a wider field of usefulness to the humble colporter who tried to do his duty than the camps and hospitals of the Confederate armies, and rarely have Christian workers more fully improved their golden opportunities." In fact, Jones dedicated an entire chapter of *Christ in the Camp* to the work of chaplains and colporteurs in the Confederate hospitals. Dickinson called the hospitals a "most inviting field for religious effort," and minister J. B. Hardwick described one hospital as a "Bethel," perhaps intimating that he felt God's presence more acutely in hospitals than anywhere else. Referring to hospitalized soldiers who were far from home and deathly ill, James B. Taylor reported, "What an opportunity for the child of God!"[41] Hospitals provided a unique occasion for chaplains to minister to sick and wounded soldiers. In a context where soldiers felt but a hair's breadth from death, the denominational affiliation of chaplains was of little importance. Likewise, chaplains were reticent to discuss sectarian concerns while attending an ailing soldier's bedside.

Jones recorded the observations of one correspondent, who noted that the "thoughts of the sick are naturally turned to religion, under any circumstance, but a soldier in a hospital, away from home, surrounded by many sick, and seeing men die daily around him, is peculiarly susceptible of good impressions." In the same letter, the correspondent affirmed that soldiers "did not stop to ask me to what denomination I belonged, but they hailed me as one who loved the same Saviour as themselves, and therefore, a friend and brother."[42] Chaplains and soldiers alike recognized that hospitals were an ill-suited setting for denominational squabbles. Here, chaplains were satisfied to put aside sectarian concerns and seize the precious opportunity to minister to soldiers who, at any moment, would stand before God's judgment.

Another reason that chaplains combined their efforts was the critical need to convert soldiers before they were killed in battle. Expressing the precariousness of the situation, Jones shared a story of receiving nine candidates for baptism. Before he could administer the ordinance, however, three of the candidates were killed, two were wounded, and one was captured. Although Jones believed that any soldier intrepid enough to face battle could not be scared into conversion, camp chaplains repeatedly reminded listeners that a soldier's life could be cut short at any moment. Soon before the Battles of Second Fredericksburg and Chancellorsville in the spring of 1863, Jones exhorted his congregants to "accept Christ as their personal Saviour *then and there*." "How know you but that ere to-morrow's sun shall rise the long roll may beat, and this brigade be called to meet the enemy," Jones cautioned. "It may be that some of these brave men *are hearing now their last message of salvation*." Jones recalled that he and other chaplains had preached no better sermons than those "under the inspiration of the circumstances which surrounded us and the consciousness that we were preparing to deliver the last message of salvation which many of those brave fellows would ever hear." With battles looming, many soldiers would be "summoned from that season of worship into the presence of their Judge."[43]

As were other clergy, Jones was well aware of his listeners' anxieties. He remembered one occasion when a shell fell among his congregation. The round did not explode, and the congregants swiftly relocated the service. En route to safer ground, however, another shell fell, killing or wounding five men in the artillery. When the service resumed, Jones's sermon was morbidly appropriate: "Except ye repent ye shall all likewise perish." Jones knew that fear of death made soldiers more receptive to religious instruction. He stated, "As men stood amid the leaden and iron hail of battle, saw comrades fall thick and fast around them, and were made to feel, 'There is but a step between me and death,' they were brought to serious reflection and solemn resolve." According to Jones, when battles neared, soldiers would cease their gambling and profanity, quickly adopting "a most tender frame of mind to hear the Gospel." He also expressed the weighty responsibility of recognizing "that in every congregation we probably address those who will fall in the impending battle." Under these circumstances, chaplains had little time for denominational rivalry. They had to reach the soldiers' souls before bullets reached the soldiers' bodies.[44]

Jones was not the only chaplain who recognized that battle stresses produced singular opportunities for evangelism. One army correspondent believed that every soldier asked himself, "Whose turn will come next?" The correspondent concluded, "[i]n this aspect, the recent battles have done more to make converts than all the homilies and exhortations ever uttered from the pulpit. A man who has stood upon the threshold of eternity while in the din and carnage of the fight, has listened to eloquence

more fiery and impressive than ever came from mortal lips."[45] One minister observed that many men converted immediately after battle; Baptist
pastor Andrew Broaddus noted that the aftermath of battle "is a most
favorable time for presenting the claims of the Gospel"; and Dickinson
declared that "the shock of battle has been sanctified to the saving of
souls."[46] As did ministers of the Second Great Awakening, who pushed
their transient congregations to make immediate decisions, Confederate
chaplains combined their efforts for the sake of immediacy.

One reverend avowed that the army was a "vast field, ready and ripe
to the harvest, and all the reapers have to do is to go in and reap from
end to end." Calling for more chaplains, he claimed that soldiers did not
have time to wait for "slow men, mere reasoners and expositors, however learned or eloquent," since the soldier knew "he may die tomor-
row." Jones connected the imminence of death with interdenominational
work, asserting that a respectable chaplain "indulges in no fierce polemics
against Christians of other denominations. He is looking in the eyes of
heroes of many a battle, and knows that the 'long roll' may beat ere he
closes — that these brave fellows may be summoned at once to new fields
of carnage — and that he may be delivering them the last message of salvation that some of them may ever hear."[47] Lacy also linked nonsectarian-
ism and the menacing specter of death: "The intercourse and communion
of Christian brethren in the army is as intimate and precious as anywhere
upon earth. It is an interesting fact, that by this work ministers of the
different denominations are brought into closer and more harmonious
co-operation, thus promoting the unity and charity of the whole Church,
and greatly encouraging each other. Many of the greatest temptations to
vice are excluded from the army. There is much time for profitable reflection. The near approach of death excites to serious thought."[48] Ministering
in the shadow of death reminded chaplains that there was little time to
quarrel publicly over denominational particularities.

One last factor inspired chaplains to bridge the sectarian gap: the
opportunity for Confederate victory. The correlation between camp religion and battlefield successes rested on significant theological presuppositions, one being that white Southerners were God's chosen people.
Closely related to this notion of chosenness was Southerners' belief in

God's retributive justice. Underpinning this theology was the assumption that if Southerners were good, God would bless them; conversely, if Southerners were bad, God would curse them. When evil (or defeats) befell the South, white Southerners quickly shored up the edges of their theology by pointing to God's chastening hand. Just as Israel suffered God's discipline, so too did the South have to endure divine reprimand in order to be a faithful people. On the other side of the coin, military victories surely revealed God's favor. Retribution theology not only enabled white Southerners to interpret past events, but allowed them a degree of control over future events. If Southerners blessed God, the reasoning went, God would bless Southerners. An 1863 prayer in the *Christian Index* exemplified this line of thinking: "Your country needs your prayers; for she is in danger, and God, the God of nations, can rescue her from danger. But God will prosper the righteous only, therefore confess and forsake your sins . . . and this chastening . . . shall afterward yield the peaceable fruit of righteousness unto us. Then God will bless us, and then will our invaders be hurled back, and then will the bright beams of Peace and Prosperity light up our darkened land."[49]

Jones readily appealed to notions of Southern chosenness and divine retribution, and his jeremiads explicitly linked Southern holiness with Confederate victory. At the first session of the Chaplains' Association in March 1863, attendees encouraged "humility and penitence on the part of the Church at home under the chastening rod of God." Clergy did not leave piety exclusively in the hands of civilians, though; ministers also trusted that God would bless a holy army with victory. One writer exclaimed, "O, for a humble, Christian army! We can never obtain liberty and peace until we humble ourselves in the dust before God." Jones too encouraged Southerners to pray, assuring them that "the sure road to peace" was the "conversion of the army."[50]

Jones printed few jeremiads as explicit as that of Lacy. Writing for the Chaplains' Association in 1863, Lacy unapologetically identified the Confederates as God's chosen people: "He who has led our armies to victory, conducting them like the hosts of Israel with pillars of cloud and of fire by night and by day, has also encamped round about us, and the tabernacle of the Lord has been in the midst of our tents." Lacy echoed retribution theology by encouraging the church to "humble herself before her Lord" and by imploring readers to repent from sin. If Southerners responded thusly, Lacy believed that "God . . . will deliver us from our enemies." "Zion should lift up her voice without ceasing unto her Saviour and her God," he wrote; "[t]his war must be regarded by all Christian men as a chastisement from the hand of God on account of our sins."⁵¹

Just as sin had invited God's chastisement, Lacy supposed that piety would invite God's blessing. Lacy continued by expressing that the "object of all chastisement is purification," and that Southerners could "indulge the hope that the results which God designed are following from the war. And when they are accomplished the war will cease." In presenting his solution to the South's woes, Lacy anchored his exhortations in Southern civil religion. "Let love of country be joined to love of God," he urged, "let the temporal interests be connected with the eternal." Put more blatantly, Lacy declared that "the cause of the country is the cause of the Church."⁵²

Jones cited numerous writers who associated Confederate righteousness with military success. Lacy held that a pious army would be a victorious army: "[W]e believe that the final success of our arms is intimately connected with the fidelity of the Church in fulfilling its duty to the army, and closely related to the religious character of the army itself." Some observers even noted the practical benefits of camp religion. One writer explained that a good chaplain raised the morale of the army, and that even irreligious officers recognized as much. Another witness pronounced, "I was never so well satisfied as I am now, that the religion of Christ is essential to the existence—not to say the efficiency—of a *volunteer* army." For these correspondents and others, Christian soldiers carried with them an air of fearlessness. One onlooker characterized a "true Christian soldier" by saying that "[h]e did not know what fear was." Describing a Christian officer, another writer proclaimed that "[d]eath had no fears to him." C. H. Dobbs, a Presbyterian chaplain, wrote that "[i]t is a little remarkable that very few of our church members survived the war. Perhaps the explanation is that they were more fearless, but it is true."⁵³

For some, it was axiomatic that Christians made exceptional soldiers. One admirer lauded a Confederate officer by stating that his "example taught that the best soldier of the Captain of Salvation made the best soldier of the Confederate camps." Baptist chaplain R. W. Cridlin stated that "[i]t was fully and satisfactorily proved in our regiment that true 'soldiers of the Cross' made the best soldiers for their country." Well-known Baptist chaplain J. J. D. Renfroe agreed: "I believe it was generally conclusive that religious men made the best soldiers."[54]

Not only was a Christian soldier a better soldier, many reasoned, but a Christian army was an invulnerable army. Lacy cited one general as decreeing, "Were all the soldiers sincere Christians and praying men, in a cause like ours, they would be invincible." Another chaplain noted the following: "It was the religious fanaticism of Cromwell's puritanic army which made it invincible. It is the genuine religious tone of Jackson's which, under a pious commander, has thus far rendered it unconquerable, and we trust that the powerful religious element in this command will inspire sentiments of the highest order of patriotism when the occasion comes from every man to stamp himself a hero!"[55] Jones quoted a writer from the *Petersburg Express* who contended, "If we can make good Christians of our fighting men, our armies will be invincible against all the hosts that can be brought against them." Jones cited a contributor to the *Atlanta Register* who put the matter just as starkly: "Our army seems to be impressed with a high sense of overruling Providence. They have become Christian patriots, and have a sacred object to accomplish—an object dearer to them than life. They have also perfect confidence in their commanders. Such an army may be temporarily overpowered by vastly superior numbers, but they can never be conquered.—Our armies, God being with us, are invincible."[56] A writer to the *Christian Index* encouraged readers with these words: "Courage, ye men of the South! *Ye cannot be conquered.* Gather beneath the folds of your war banner; and with your trust in Him who hitherto has helped you, shout the shout of defiance."[57] Such sentiments fueled white Southerners' belief that God would not only protect a righteous people from disaster, but would bestow on them final victory.

Jones's citations reveal that many felt there were both practical and theological benefits when Christian soldiers filled the ranks. As the thinking went, not only would religious soldiers have higher morale, but

confident in the states of their souls and assured of their eternal desti-
nations, they would be fearless on the battlefield. There also existed the
confidence that God would bless a holy army with victory even in the face
of overwhelming odds and hopeless prospects. With these factors in mind,
it behooved chaplains to work together, not only for the sake of the gospel,
but for the sake of the Confederacy. Time was too precious to engage in
sectarian bickering, especially since, as chaplains saw it, the fate of the
Confederate nation hung in the balance. If chaplains pooled their time
and resources, more soldiers would accept the Christian message. If more
soldiers adopted the faith, then God would bless the Confederate troops,
not only with revivals in the camp, but with victories on the battlefield.

Even while interdenominational networking was a prominent feature
of camp religion, it remained an emergency measure, stimulated by the
harsh and peculiar circumstances of war. During the conflict, denominational identity remained central for chaplains and soldiers alike, even
while sectarian rivalries went temporarily dormant. When the war ended,
however, the familial attitudes amongst evangelicals changed as well. The
postwar South saw denominationalists re-entrench, and it was in this
context that ex-Confederates cultivated the Lost Cause mythology.

Lost Cause authors took inspiration from the interdenominationalism of the Confederate revivals.[58] Although the cannons had fallen silent,
a rhetorical war against the Yankees continued, and Lost Causers understood the necessity of broad support—including denominational cooperation—in order to win the battles ahead. Indeed, Jones would parlay
his wartime connections with non-Baptist chaplains in order to further
the Lost Cause message. But denominational fraternity in the postbellum
South could not reach the levels of collaboration experienced during the
war. No longer did evangelicals renounce sectarian sermons or encourage
the kind of baptismal-exchange programs common in the Confederate
camps. When the fog of war lifted, old rivalries crystallized once more.

✢ ✢ ✢ ✢ ✢

Jones had willingly allied with non-Baptists during the war, but he harbored residual and inherent prejudices that even the stresses of battle did

not overcome. Ironically, *Christ in the Camp*—in which Jones touted non-sectarianism—exhibited some of the pervasive biases common among nineteenth-century evangelicals. The key term here was *evangelical*, and Jones seldom let his readers forget it. He peppered his writings with the descriptor, especially when addressing chaplain efforts and army revivals. For Jones, "evangelical" was both a versatile and coded term. On one hand, the name suggested that Confederate chaplains were concerned by-and-large with conversion; on the other hand, the label delimited the scope of denominational cooperation. Jones embraced the wartime activity of his Methodist and Presbyterian brethren, but largely ignored the participation of Roman Catholics in the Confederate revivals. By doing so, Jones employed "evangelical" language for the purposes of both inclusion and exclusion.[59]

Jones observed that all "evangelical denominations" were well represented in the Confederate Army; he specified when soldiers were aligned with "some evangelical church"; he was concerned that soldiers were and continued to be connected with "some evangelical denomination"; he lauded the friendship among "evangelical preachers"; and he maintained postwar correspondence with those of "all creeds of evangelical Christianity."[60] Even in sections of *Christ in the Camp* where Jones used the boldest interdenominational language—for instance, when he insisted that camp sermons were founded on "common ground" and not on sectarian polemics—he continued to insert evangelical qualifiers. He avowed that "[u]nquestionably one of the most potent factors in the grand success of our work was the union of hearts and hands on the part of chaplains and missionaries, and indeed of all Christian workers of the evangelical denominations." Still on the topic of interdenominational collegiality, Jones continued: "This cordial co-operation of the chaplains and missionaries of the different evangelical denominations had the very happiest effect on our work."[61]

Keeping Roman Catholics at arm's length was a telling move for Jones, since Roman Catholics not only partook in the Confederate revivals, but also played a key role in the spread of Lost Cause mythology. In fact, their participation has led a number of scholars to characterize the Lost Cause as a broadly ecumenical movement.[62] But Jones's *Christ in the*

Camp paints a different picture of Confederate religion, and by extension, the Lost Cause. Since Jones could but awkwardly situate Roman Catholics in his account of the revivals, his work not only betrayed his ambivalence toward Roman Catholic involvement in the Lost Cause, but also illuminated key aspects in his theological interpretation of Confederate history.

Roman Catholics were noticeably absent from *Christ in the Camp*, but when Jones deigned to mentioned them, the portrayals were hardly glowing. In one story, the peaceful death of a Christian soldier (who was "dying very happily") caught the attention of two soldiers nearby. One was a Roman Catholic who, overcome with emotion, offered a cryptic admission: "I never want to die happier than that man did." The other was an unbeliever who, because of witnessing the triumphant death of a Christian soldier, determined to seek religion himself. Jones was unclear as to whether readers should associate the Roman Catholic patient with the irreligious patient; still, Jones described the Roman Catholic as moved by the experience and example of this "Christian soldier."[63]

In another instance, Jones cited a letter from minister James B. Taylor in which Taylor reported on a recent visit to a Confederate camp. There, only two soldiers had refused Taylor's tracts; one was a Roman Catholic, and the other was unable to read. A letter from the Chaplains' Association noted one brigade's lack of a "Protestant chaplain"; later, Jones wrote of this same brigade's reputation for being "irreligious." He provided a revealing explanation: "They had no chaplains except two Romish priests, who, no doubt did their duty as they understood it, but were, of course, entirely out of sympathy with evangelical religion as we understand it, and up to this period there had been few, if any, efforts made for the conversion of these brave fellows to the simple faith of the Lord Jesus Christ."[64] Jones's backhanded compliment notwithstanding, he took for granted that Roman Catholics were out of step with the revivalist disposition. Furthermore, he suggested that priests had neglected to convey the "simple faith of the Lord Jesus Christ." Simplicity of faith and worship was common stock for Jones, and he recoiled at practices he felt compromised the plain truth of the gospel.[65]

While his references to Roman Catholics were often perfunctory, Jones acknowledged the Roman Catholic presence in Confederate ranks.

In one account, a chaplain related his friendly interaction with a soldier wishing to join a church. As to which church, the soldier responded, "The Roman Catholic, sir; I know no better." Whether this statement signified pride in the church or merely a retreat into familiarity is uncertain. The attending chaplain apparently leaned toward the latter, as he added, "I scarce need to add that he was a son of Erin's Isle." Yet while some correspondents found that "Israelites, Catholics and Protestants exhibited profound interest on the subject of religion," others blithely overlooked Roman Catholic participation in Confederate religion. One minister happily conveyed that the chaplains' work "pervades all classes of the army . . . and elicits the co-operation of all denominations. We know no distinction here. Baptists, Cumberlands, Old Presbyterians, Episcopalians, and Methodists, work together, and rejoice together at the success of our cause." Here again, descriptions like "all denominations" and "no distinction" did not include Roman Catholics.[66]

Among his evangelical contemporaries, Jones's cautious attitude toward Roman Catholics was not unique. Still, it is curious that he did not accent Roman Catholic participation in Confederate religion in order to further his contention that God had been intimately present among Southern troops. There are a number of possible reasons for why he did not, the simplest being that he had very little interaction with Roman Catholic chaplains. This explanation is plausible considering the low numbers of Roman Catholic chaplains in the Confederate Army. Furthermore, Jones's 1887 edition of *Christ in the Camp* focused on Lee's Army of Northern Virginia. How familiar Jones could have been with Roman Catholic chaplains is debatable, since most Roman Catholic chaplains were concentrated in areas like Tennessee and Louisiana.

Jones would likely have had some knowledge of the work of Roman Catholic chaplain S. B. Barber of the 47th Virginia Regiment. J. M. Meredith, an Episcopalian chaplain, was also from the 47th Virginia, and Meredith participated with Jones in the Chaplains' Association. Even so, Meredith was first involved with the Chaplains' Association in April 1863; Barber did not join the 47th until April 1864. If Jones knew of Barber's work, Jones neglected to mention it.[67] Jones was also silent concerning the ministry of Father James Sheeran, chaplain of the 14th Louisiana.

Sheeran's regiment came to be associated with "Lee's Tigers" and saw action in many of the same battles as Jones's 13th Virginia. By his 1904 edition of *Christ in the Camp*, Jones only indexed Sheeran, locating him in the 1st Louisiana and misspelling his name.[68]

Jones intentionally limited the scope of his work, as the 1887 edition of *Christ in the Camp* centered primarily on the Army of Northern Virginia. In 1888, he published another edition, this time broadening the book so as to encompass not only Lee's Army of Northern Virginia but the entire Confederacy. Here he added an additional appendix, entitled "The Work of Grace in Other Armies of the Confederacy." Still, Roman Catholics received scant reference. One reason for this may be because Jones relied so heavily on the account of William W. Bennett, Methodist chaplain and author of *A Narrative of the Great Revival Which Prevailed in the Southern Armies*. Bennett's massive treatment also largely excluded Roman Catholics.[69]

Even while Jones himself may have had infrequent contact with Roman Catholic chaplains, it is difficult to imagine that he was unaware of their activity. In fact, some priests enjoyed enormous postwar popularity, not only for their service on the battlefield but for their contributions in shaping white Southern memory. For example, Father Abram J. Ryan was sympathetic to revivalism during the war and an adamant Lost Cause advocate after it. Because of Ryan's poetry, by the 1870s white Southerners had ordained him the "poet-priest" of the Lost Cause. In the spirit of many other prominent Lost Cause writers, Ryan's poems glorified both the Confederate Army and Confederate leaders. White Southerners were more than familiar with Father Ryan; they made him one of the Confederacy's most celebrated veterans.[70]

Jones knew of Ryan's service, too. In the early 1880s—well before the first edition of *Christ in the Camp*, and while serving as editor of the *Southern Historical Society Papers* (*SHSP*)—Jones printed correspondence and poems from Ryan.[71] Yet Ryan's most prominent (and oddest) inclusion in Jones's work came in the early twentieth century, when Jones featured the poet-priest in a full-page photograph for the 1904 edition of *Christ in the Camp*. What Jones did not provide, however, was any corresponding text for the photo. That is, unless the content of the opposite page was meant to serve as context, which would only complicate the photo's presence in the first place. The page opposite Ryan's picture included one of the few references to Roman Catholics in Jones's book. Jones recorded a letter from Baptist chaplain J. J. D. Renfroe, of the 10th Alabama Regiment, in which Renfroe rejoiced in the decrease of camp vices. Renfroe stated, "Card-playing and the like ceased to be public in this brigade, except among the Irish Catholics, of whom there were three companies, who seemed 'neither to fear God nor regard man;' only they were very good soldiers."[72] Surely, Father Ryan's image was not intended to correspond to such a disparaging account of Roman Catholic soldiers. Instead, Jones (or his publishers) retrofitted Ryan's picture—unmoored from context—for a work that had essentially ignored him.

✢ ✢ ✢ ✢ ✢

As Jones would have had at least a general knowledge of Roman Catholic chaplains when he published *Christ in the Camp*, his decision to disregard Confederate priests reflected the *milieu* of anti-Catholicism in the United States. Nineteenth-century America had witnessed a tremendous influx of immigrants—many Roman Catholic—and as these numbers swelled, so too did Protestant uneasiness. In the 1840s alone, the rate of Roman Catholic growth outpaced Protestants threefold. The spike in Roman Catholic population galvanized nativist organizations, and throughout the 1830s and 1840s, frictions escalated into anti-Catholic and anti-ethnic riots. Anti-Catholicism during this time stemmed not only from fear of papal control, but more practically, from anxiety that Roman Catholics would take jobs away from Protestants. This is why, when panic from the 1837 fiscal crisis finally subsided, tensions between Protestants and Roman Catholics relaxed as well.[73]

When immigration rose again in the 1850s, nativism experienced a revival. Nativists founded a variety of anti-Catholic fraternities, the most famous of which was the "Know-Nothing" Party. Two of the primary objectives of the Know-Nothings were to reduce the influence of foreign voters and concurrently to ensure that only native-born Protestants were elected to office. To achieve this latter goal, the Know-Nothings either endorsed Protestant candidates or elected their own candidates to run for office. By the outset of the Civil War, the Know-Nothings had faded from the political scene; the anti-Catholicism they embodied, however, had not.[74]

Not every Protestant shared the Know-Nothings' suspicions. In fact, the Civil War softened the prejudices of many Protestants.[75] While personal accounts testify to the dynamic nature of Protestant attitudes toward Roman Catholics during the war, Protestant-Catholic relations did not thaw overnight. The rhetoric of Northern and Southern periodicals made that fact clear. In both sections, newspapers served as a means either to foster or to temper anti-Catholicism. In the North, one writer for *Harper's Weekly* addressed what he believed to be the "all-powerful influence" of priests over parishioners, including the clerical demand for "blind submission." Another writer, couching statements in the form of a "political catechism for children," even compared the Roman Catholic Church to slavery. In January 1865, a writer for *Harper's Weekly* railed against an encyclical letter by Pope Pius IX. The letter in question was Pius's 1864 *Syllabus of Errors*, which criticized, among many other things, American democracy. Asserting that the letter was "a bull against Protestantism," the author attacked the pope for wanting to destroy religious and political liberty and for believing that "liberty of conscience and of worship is a 'delirium.'"[76]

Similar to their Northern counterparts, Southern papers were highly critical of Roman Catholicism. In North Carolina's *Biblical Recorder*, one writer listed Roman Catholics among the world's "unconverted." Even while admitting that some Roman Catholics had found Christ despite the "mummeries" of the church, the contributor alleged that "the great masses are ignorant of Him." In another *Biblical Recorder* article—one with the bitingly self-explanatory title, "Intellectual Superiority of Protestantism"—the correspondent praised the scholarly accomplishments of German Protestants while dismissing German Catholic accomplishments as negligible.[77]

Writers to Virginia's *Religious Herald* could be just as scathing with their remarks. One author denounced the dogma of papal infallibility, calling it the "climax of human arrogance" and declaring that "[n]o higher

pretension can be put forth by moral man." Another contributor celebrated the pope's loss of power vis-à-vis the Italian states. In one instance,
the writer's criticism was so vituperative that it prompted a response from
Herald editors. The critic condemned any Baptist openness to the "false,
idolatrous, *wicked* religion" of Roman Catholicism. The *Herald* editors
responded that Roman Catholics should be treated with respect. As to
Roman Catholic "errors," the editors continued, "These we should condemn, oppose, loathe and avoid, just in proportion as they tend to deceive,
enslave, degrade and ruin the souls of men."[78] As religious periodicals
demonstrated, Southern Baptist animus toward Roman Catholicism mirrored the attitudes of most nineteenth-century American Protestants.

While Jones's work did not express the deep hostility toward Rome
vocalized by so many of his contemporaries, neither did his writings escape the ether of anti-Catholicism, and it was these presumptions and
prejudices that deeply influenced his interpretation of Confederate religion. Since he estimated Roman Catholics as being "entirely out of
sympathy with evangelical religion as we understand it,"[79] Jones sensed a
fundamental incompatibility between Roman Catholicism and the tenor
of revivalism. Yet it was the camp revivals that stood as an ultimate testament to God's presence with the Confederate armies and vindication of
the Confederate cause. In Jones's mind, Confederate religion was at its
core—in the description of historian Gardiner Shattuck—"a place where
faith was democratic, nonhierarchical, and nonclerical."[80] For a staunch
nineteenth-century Baptist, treasuring the democratic and eschewing the
hierarchical was part and parcel of evangelicalism in general and camp
revivals in particular. Jones thus exerted little effort in situating Roman
Catholics within the broader narrative of Confederate religion.

Exactly how Roman Catholics viewed camp revivals is a matter of
debate. Some scholars have contended that revivalism was a foreign concept for Roman Catholics, while others argue that Roman Catholics
engaged in comparable worship activities before, during, and after the
Civil War.[81] Even if Roman Catholic soldiers were familiar with the revivalist impulse, this did not equate to a wholesale acceptance of revivals
as they were practiced in the Confederate camps. In fact, historians have
suggested that Protestant hegemony in nineteenth-century America

motivated Roman Catholics to embrace a form of revivalism themselves. Perhaps by doing so, they could compete in the religious market and ensure that Roman Catholics did not convert to Protestantism.[82] While some Roman Catholics did participate in Confederate revivals, the apprehension of other Roman Catholics may have had less to do with an inherent aversion to revivalism and more to do with a fear of predominantly *Protestant* revivalism.

For Roman Catholics, the decision of whether or not to participate in Confederate revivals was a two-way street. The matter consisted of more than Protestants excluding Roman Catholics; many Roman Catholics willingly avoided the revivals. Such avoidance caused no small amount of tension in the camps. Especially in a context where evangelical denominations were largely in concert, Roman Catholics who did not participate in the revivals stood out in sharp relief. Many Protestant soldiers remained suspicious of Roman Catholic teachings, and many resented the efforts of Roman Catholics to spread their faith. For Jones and others, Roman Catholics alloyed what evangelicals understood as the greatest achievement of the revivals—what historian Drew Gilpin Faust describes as a "homogeneity of religious outlook."[83]

Jones's repeated stress on the evangelical nature of camp revivals exposed key aspects of his understanding of Confederate religion. His emphasis also complicates modern-day interpretations, as scholars continue to debate what the term "evangelical" means and meant.[84] As historian Samuel Hill hypothesizes, nineteenth-century Christians often relied on the term evangelical in order "to register 'alternativity,' a position at some variance with conventional religious culture."[85] For Jones, however, "evangelical" represented more than an alternative to the prevailing religious ethos; the term also served as a convenient and coded means of identifying the "non-Catholic."

Indeed, Jones embodied the evangelical focus on scripture, personal trust in Christ, and conversion. He also lobbied for a religion of the people—a religion that rejected any accoutrement that might detract from the simple truth of the gospel. Yet as did many nineteenth-century Christians, Jones deployed "evangelical" as both a positive and negative descriptor. As historian John Wolffe discusses, anti-Catholicism, whether in the United States or Europe, was "very much the essence of evangelicalism," and "antagonism to 'popery' served, in a positive as well as negative sense, to help define evangelical identity." Anti-Catholicism was much more than a "mere negative prejudice"; it was a core identifying feature of nineteenth-century evangelicalism.[86]

The evangelical instinct to unite against Roman Catholicism was on full display in the creation of the Evangelical Alliance, which formed in London in 1846. Initially, the alliance seemed to find support from Britain, the United States, and other European nations. At the 1846 London meeting, however, the United States broke away from the group and did not form its own branch of the alliance until 1867. The reason for the United States' departure centered on whether or not to exclude slaveholders from participation. The United States did not appear to have any qualms with the alliance's stated purpose of defending against the "encroachments of Popery and Puseyism." Interesting here is the inclusion of Puseyism, commonly associated with E. B. Pusey (1800–1882) and the Tractarian Movement. The alliance stood not only against Roman Catholics, but also against High Church Anglicans who were open to Roman Catholic liturgy and theology.[87]

What is fascinating about the alliance is that the organization never achieved great unity. Ironically, a major reason for this failure was the alliance's raison d'être itself. The individualistic impulses of evangelicals kept unifying efforts in check and even countermanded them. The more closely evangelicals bound together, the more they resembled—in their minds, at least—the Roman Catholic Church.[88] Exclusion bred exclusion, and the alliance struggled to join against a common foe without becoming the very thing they had united to oppose. The inherent paradox of nineteenth-century ecumenism was that evangelicals were seemingly united in their opposition to union. With this mind, a discussion of "evangelical ecumenism" in the Confederate revivals is, in one sense, oxymoronic. While it is true that many nineteenth-century evangelicals were willing to cooperate, evangelical networking was by its very nature limited. Anti-Catholicism not only served as an impetus for evangelical union; anti-Catholicism also made union amongst evangelicals tenuous and contradictory.

The timing of Jones's 1887 *Christ in the Camp* was significant, as Jones's portrayal of evangelical Confederate religion impacted the interdenominational character of the still-developing Lost Cause mythology. In fact, some Southern denominations went as far as to advocate for organic union among evangelicals as a means of preserving regional and religious identity in the postwar South. Other Southern evangelicals feared that such a union would dilute the faith and would occasion an inevitable slide toward Roman Catholicism. In the end, white Southerners prized sectarian purity over religious solidarity, and denominationalism won the day.[89]

How Lost Causers like Jones related to postwar merger efforts is not altogether clear. Highlighting the unifying effects of the Lost Cause—in particular the coalition among evangelicals, Roman Catholics, and Jews—historians have suggested that Lost Cause literature fed efforts to unite denominations formally. In particular, Jones's accounts of wartime denominational fraternity inspired some postwar Southerners to embrace the same ecumenical spirit in order to salvage white Southern identity.[90]

The association of Lost Cause partisans with postwar ecumenism, however, is problematic for at least three reasons. First, while Southerners pushing for formal mergers may have taken their cues from Lost Cause writings, there is no evidence that Jones was sympathetic to such a movement. Second, by Jones's own account, wartime interdenominationalism emerged from practical necessity rather than doctrinal harmony. Third, Jones's ambivalence toward Roman Catholicism calls into question that either wartime revivals or the Lost Cause was broadly ecumenical in nature. Indeed, Lost Causers of various religious backgrounds allied for the sake of sacralizing white Southern memory. But such an alliance emerged primary from pragmatic collaboration.

As far as Jones was concerned, wartime denominational cooperation had not extended into the realm of doctrine. Still, he felt that interdenominational networking could benefit the post-Reconstruction South. In *Christ in the Camp*, he shared the story of Confederate soldiers mistakenly firing on their own men. He then compared the debacle to postwar denominational rivalries: "And so I never see bitter controversies between evangelical Christians that I do not feel like crying with all my feeble powers: 'Cease firing into the ranks of your brethren, and trail your guns on the mighty hosts of the enemies of our common Lord." Even while he grieved factionalism, Jones sensed that camp religion had in some ways spilled over into local congregations: "I am glad to believe that the fraternal spirit which has so largely prevailed for some years among evangelical Christians at the South is in no small degree due to the habit of cooperation which so generally prevailed during the war."[91] Once again, Jones directed his comments toward evangelicals, beseeching them to unite for a common cause. Beyond joining forces in order to defeat the unspecified "enemies of the Lord," Jones trusted that interdenominationalism could rally white Southerners to fashion a Confederate apologia. Cooperation was essential in order to vanquish the Lord's enemies, be they spiritual, temporal, or on the other side of the Mason-Dixon.

✞ ✞ ✞ ✞ ✞

Jones knew the benefits and necessity of denominational networking in light of the extraordinary circumstances of war. He also understood the limits of interdenominational relationships. His example thus calls into question the assessments of historians who have downplayed wartime Protestant-Catholic tensions or insisted that Baptist chaplains relaxed their emphasis on doctrines such as baptism.[92] To the contrary, Jones held fast to his evangelical identity and to Baptist distinctions in particular. Specifically, he remained unmoved on the necessity and mode of baptism, and he was willing to risk his life and that of baptismal candidates in order to carry out the ordinance.[93] Furthermore, he maintained that non-Baptist chaplains were aware and respectful of his denominational fidelity: "And it gives me pleasure to testify to the courtesy and kindness with which I have been treated by the chaplains of the different denominations, all of whom know that I am a decided Baptist. Indeed, there seems to be in the army a truce to denominational bickerings—there are no sectarian sermons preached and no sectarian tracts circulated, but all seem to work together to make men Christians, and then leave it to their consciences and their Bible with what denomination they will connect themselves."[94] While war compelled Jones to network with various denominations, he never ceased to view himself as a "decided Baptist." In fact, he believed army religion was particularly suited for Baptists, as chaplains honored the conscience of the individual, trusted congregants to interpret the scriptures for themselves, and accepted the denominational leanings of churchgoers and converts.

The denominational "truce" occasioned by the war did not survive unscathed in peacetime. Even while many Southerners drew inspiration from camp revivals, sectarian competiveness stymied initiatives to merge evangelical denominations formally.[95] Still, certain aspects of wartime interdenominationalism—cooperation with members of other denominations who themselves were firmly rooted in their own traditions—did extend into the Lost Cause era. At the same time, other features of evangelical fraternity—such as "mixed" worship, softened denominational rivalries, and nonsectarian sermons—were circumstantial, brought about by the stresses and constraints of war. In any event, Jones would have been alarmed to discover that denominational unionists were using his writings to advocate for the obliteration of sectarian distinctions.

Jones's writings also challenge the scholarly contention that Protestants and Roman Catholics set aside theological differences for the sake of wartime revivals, or for the purpose of disseminating the Lost Cause.[96] As chaplain, Jones remained wary of Roman Catholic belief and practice. As author, he dismissed Roman Catholics—or incorporated them cumbersomely—in his accounts of Confederate religion. In the context of nineteenth-century American Protestantism, Jones's attitude toward Roman Catholics was unremarkable, mirroring the stance of most Southern evangelicals. What makes his neglect of Roman Catholics important, however, is that it tempers assumptions of the Lost Cause as an ecumenical movement that welcomed Roman Catholics as full participants. Even more significantly, Jones's exclusion of Roman Catholics reveals that crucial tenets of Lost Cause religion may have indeed been oriented *against* Roman Catholicism. For Jones, the Confederate revivals were rooted in individual experience and personal faith in an unmediated gospel. His praise of Confederate soldiers was thus inextricably tied to his view of them as specifically evangelical Christians, each one endowed with the freedom of conscience.

By viewing the piety of Confederate soldiers through an evangelical lens, Jones augmented a key platform of Lost Cause mythology—that Confederate soldiers were better (evangelical) Christians than Northern soldiers. Regarding Roman Catholics, Jones felt that they were fundamentally out of step with the Confederate revivals and with evangelical religion in general. This being the case, Roman Catholics were thus out of step with the very foundation of Lost Cause religion as Jones understood it. As historian Zachary Dresser notes, "[w]artime cooperation and revivalism convinced many southerners that their region possessed a unique religious element, a spiritual quality that defined the very essence of what distinguished Dixie."[97] Since Jones imagined that wartime interdenominationalism and revivalism were so closely related to Southern identity, his dismissal of Roman Catholics from revival narratives insinuated that between Roman Catholicism and Southern identity there existed a tension at best and a contradiction at worst.

Although Jones demonstrated no support for efforts to unite Southern denominations formally, he still believed that trans-denominational networking was foundational for the preservation of white Southern memory. Within five years of the war's end, he would emerge as one of the chief figures of the Lost Cause. Thereafter, his interdenominationalism would no longer be in service to circumstantial, wartime evangelism. Instead, it would become a primary means of sustaining Southern identity and codifying a distinctively pro-Confederate religious history. Embodying his role as apostle of the South—personally commissioned by Lee to preserve a faithful narrative of the Confederacy—he immersed himself in the lives and legends of Lee, Jackson, and Davis. He would also take the helm of the *SHSP* and as editor forge a Confederate narrative that endured long after his death. All along the way, he remained an unwavering Baptist who understood the necessity of denominational cooperation when fighting a war—even a war in print.

CHAPTER THREE

"Our Cause" and the Lost Cause: Jones's Rise to Prominence

The American people have never known the chastening
experience of being on the losing side of a war.

—C. Vann Woodward, *The Burden of Southern History*

Fifteen years after the end of the Civil War, a writer for the *Religious Herald* reported that J. William Jones's ship had sunk, literally. The article recounted that Jones and his son had been rowing down the Pamunkey River in eastern Virginia when a sudden storm pummeled their boat, causing the craft to sink. Fortunately, Jones and his son were able to seize low-hanging tree branches and escape to safety. With his clothes drenched, Jones borrowed an old Confederate uniform from one of Robert E. Lee's sons.[1] Although the *Herald* offered this story in humor, the anecdote was a fitting description of Jones's postwar career. Even though the ship of Confederate independence had foundered, Jones continued to find solace in the Confederate gray.

Jones's rise as the veritable high priest of Lost Cause religion did not happen overnight. Furthermore, his eventual prominence in the Lost Cause movement was inextricably tied to his Baptist ministry. As his influence grew among Baptists, Jones positioned himself as the postwar authority of religion in the Confederate Army. He spoke and wrote to Baptists with sometimes reckless confidence, quoting Confederate leaders as if reciting scripture and mounting formidable apologies for the Confederate cause. Within a year after the war's end, Jones had also positioned himself as a personal friend of Lee, relishing intimate contact with him during the general's tenure as president at Washington College and thereafter claiming a special knowledge of Lee's religious character. By the mid-1870s Jones's influence had extended beyond Baptists, and white Southerners began to see Jones as he had long seen himself: an eyewitness to God's manifest presence with the Confederate Army, and an apostle commissioned to proclaim good news to a defeated people.

Jones's postwar career saw his ascent in both the Baptist denomination and the Lost Cause movement. As his reputation grew, he negotiated what some saw as an implicit tension between the Lost Cause and the Baptist cause. For Jones, however, there was no conflict between these two causes, which is one reason there existed a permeable wall between his work as a Baptist minister and his work as a Confederate historian. Just as his Confederate loyalties colored his thoughts on Baptist life and practice, his Baptist loyalties led him to craft a specifically evangelical interpretation of Lost Cause religion. This denominational fidelity significantly impacted how Jones cooperated with non-Baptists for the sake of establishing and defending white Southern memory. In the two decades following the war, he transitioned from an obscure chaplain who offered the occasional missive for religious newspapers to a denominational leader who moonlighted as one of the chief guardians of Lost Cause orthodoxy.

✣ ✣ ✣ ✣ ✣

After Lee surrendered the Army of Northern Virginia on April 9, 1865, Jones received parole and returned home. He had hoped to dedicate much of his time to study, but instead found it necessary to farm. He held open the possibility of becoming a foreign missionary, but the war had left the Foreign Mission Board (FMB) unable to support him financially in an overseas venture. He still worked as a voluntary agent for the FMB in 1865, traveling more than seven hundred miles and preaching sixty-eight sermons between August and October. By the fall of 1865, he was back in the pastorate. He accepted positions at two Baptist churches in Rockbridge County, Virginia: Goshen Bridge and Lexington. Commitments to these churches initially prevented Jones from becoming a paid agent of the FMB (in Kentucky) or taking a position with the Southern Baptist Sunday School Board. In a letter to James Barnett Taylor, secretary of the FMB, Jones also suggested that Kentuckians would not receive him, writing that "my perhaps too ultra, southern feelings would probably get me into trouble."[2]

Jones boasted of revivals at Goshen Bridge and Lexington, in which both whites and African Americans received baptism. He wrote to the *Religious Herald* that he tried to "preach especially for the colored people of my charge every Sunday afternoon," with the hopes that doing so would stave off "meddlers from abroad." Jones's emphasis here reflected the fear of many white Southerners that Northerners would "poison" the minds of former slaves and turn them against whites. In the summer of 1866, Jones turned down an offer to be an agent for Southern Baptist Theological Seminary (SBTS), admitting that his two congregations had shown some frustration with his frequent absences.[3]

Even though Goshen Bridge was a larger church than Lexington (and provided him with a parsonage), Jones left Goshen Bridge after one year and became a full-time pastor at Lexington. A factor doubtless influencing Jones's decision was Lee's installment as president of Washington College (in Lexington) in September 1866. Jones began his full-time tenure at the Lexington church in November 1866. He made financial sacrifices by accepting a position at Lexington, a congregation William H. Whitsitt once called the humblest church in town. These financial troubles prompted the Jones family to take in boarders. Nevertheless, Jones's determination to be near Lee would pay dividends in other ways. Jones was one of the only Lexington pastors available to help lead religious services for the students at Washington College, and he jumped at the opportunity to serve with his old commander once again.[4]

Jones became increasingly involved at the college. He signed on as one of the rotating chaplains at the school, and Lee asked him to begin a YMCA there as well. Jones also joined the Friends of Temperance, a nonsectarian organization at the college. The superintendent at the nearby Virginia Military Institute (VMI) also solicited Jones's help. Jones led revivals at both locations, reporting around 150 conversions. In addition to his ministerial duties at the institute, he taught New Testament Greek at VMI. A man prone to keeping multiple irons in the fire, he led morning prayers at Washington College and evening services at VMI, all while continuing to serve as pastor of his Lexington church.[5]

In the fall of 1867, the African American members of the Lexington congregation petitioned to leave and begin their own church. In Jones's mind, there existed no animosity between whites and African Americans either before or after the split. In fact, he noted his position as a "presbyter" in the new church. Still, Jones once again betrayed his fear that outsiders would stir up racial discord. At the dedication of the new church, Virginia minister J. P. Corron charged the congregation to guard against politics in the pulpit. Furthermore, congregants were to remain wary of anyone who claimed to be the freedpeople's friend. Not only could these "friends" swindle the members, but such imposters could lead the congregation astray. For this reason, Corron exhorted congregants to accept advice only from those they knew. Jones's beliefs appeared in line with Corron's. Jones wrote that while he was strongly in favor of religious instruction for African Americans, he was also "one of those who believe that the religious instructions of the colored people among us can be best accomplished by *Southern bred men*."[6]

Much of what occupied Jones's mind from 1868–1870 was the construction of a new church building for the Lexington congregation. With a hint of denominational rivalry in his tone, Jones complained that a new building was necessary because the current location was distractingly close to a Presbyterian church. According to Jones, the Presbyterian organ was drowning out the Baptist pastor's voice. He stressed that the Lexington congregation wanted nothing elaborate, only a "neat, comfortable house of worship, in good taste, conveniently arranged." Perhaps influenced by his ministry in humble wartime chapels, Jones prized simplicity in worship. But even a simple building did not come cheaply, and for two years Jones petitioned the readers of the *Religious Herald* for contributions.[7]

While he pled for help with his church's building fund, Jones continued to experience personal financial difficulties. On more than one occasion he was unable to pay installments on his Seminary bond. He griped that a new boarding house at the college was "seducing" his boarders and that "city prices" were too high. With a growing family, he was tempted to take a position as an agent for the Domestic Mission Board in Kentucky and Tennessee (he declined the offer). Eventually, Jones suggested to

Broadus that he publish some of Jones's articles and apply the profits toward the Seminary bond.[8]

In late 1870 and early 1871, Jones faced weighty decisions, and a number of considerations prompted him to make a career change. First, financial hardship had hobbled him. Second, Lee died in October 1870. With his chieftain gone, Jones lost one of his primary connections to Lexington. Furthermore, he wanted to dedicate significant time to organizing Lee's memorial volume, a work that commenced within a month of the general's death. Third, doctors recommended that Jones move his family to a different climate for the sake of his wife's health. Even with these factors in play, Jones was apprehensive about leaving his Lexington congregation. In early 1871 he wrote James P. Boyce, "You know I have greatly set my heart on our cause in this grand old Valley and had about made up my mind that it was to be my home (so far as I could see) for all my life and labor on earth." Jones's dedication to Virginia Baptists not only prevented him from taking an agency with the Domestic Mission Board, but also kept him from accepting an agency with Washington College. He worried that the travel required for such positions would take him away from promoting the "cause" in the Shenandoah. After deliberating, however, Jones made the decision in early 1871 to leave Lexington Baptist Church and accept an agency with the Southern Baptist Theological Seminary (SBTS).[9]

For a year Jones canvassed the South raising money for his dear seminary. He faced a number of challenges during his tour. In November 1871, he wrote from Georgia that he had traveled through two counties thought to be the "headquarters of 'Klukluxism' (so called) in Georgia." Dismissively, he asserted that he had seen "none of those monsters, and did not meet anyone else who had seen them." Jones's fundraising slowed in early 1872 when his son, Ashby, was injured in a fall. Fearing that Ashby might lose one if not both of his eyes, Jones took his son to a doctor in Atlanta. March 1872 brought glimmers of hope, with the health of both Jones's son and wife improving.[10]

Since the end of the war, Jones had honored the two great causes in his life: the Baptist cause and the Confederate cause. While serving as the pastor of Lexington Baptist Church, he cultivated his relationship with

Lee at Washington College and threw himself into work on a memorial volume after Lee's death. Now as an agent for SBTS, Jones took time on his tours to give lectures on religion in the Confederate Army. While he saw no ideological contradiction between the Baptist and the Confederate causes, he did sense a financial tension. He expressed this sentiment in an 1872 letter to Boyce, writing that he believed it would be difficult to solicit funds from Virginians since they would be "absorbed in the raising of the [Lee] 'Memorial' fund."[11]

Jones resigned from his SBTS agency late in the summer of 1872. He expressed concern that he was becoming a financial burden to the seminary; furthermore, he had been offered a position as the general superintendent of the Sunday School and Bible Board of the General Association of Virginia. He accepted the post and began a new tour of the South, requesting funds and promoting Baptist Sunday schools. He remained in the superintendent position until June 1874, after which he was unemployed and seeking another pastorate. One matter hindering Jones's search was his desire to find a location conducive to his wife's health.[12]

The year 1874 marked a turning point in Jones's career. A major Lee memorial volume conceived by former Confederate general William N. Pendleton, along with the faculty of the then Washington and Lee University, collapsed when one of the primary contributors dropped out of the project. The aborted biography dismayed the university faculty and Lee's family. But as he had done ever since the end of the war, Jones inserted himself into the fray over Southern memory. He offered to complete a Lee biography himself if given a copy of the incomplete manuscript and access to the Lee family papers. In 1874, Jones published *Personal Reminiscences, Anecdotes, and Letters of Gen. Robert E. Lee.* The book was a success, selling more than twenty thousand copies.[13] As was his custom, Jones included so many letters and direct quotations that the work served as a virtual sourcebook for future biographers.

Even as Jones's star was rising in the Lost Cause movement, he held firmly to his Baptist roots. These roots, however, could not hold Jones in one place. In 1875, he became pastor at Ashland Baptist Church in Hanover County, Virginia. Over the next twelve years, he served as pastor at a number of Virginia churches: West Point, King William County,

1881–1883; Cool Spring, Hanover County, 1881–1886; Berea, Louisa County, 1884–1886; and Lyles, Fluvanna County, 1886–1887.[14]

Jones's Baptistness was inextricably tied to his Southernness, and for this reason he rejected efforts to reunite Northern and Southern Baptists. A prolific contributor to the *Religious Herald*, Jones criticized the paper for dedicating what he thought was too much attention to the American Baptist Publication Society (ABPS). He commented that the paper had lost its "Virginia character" and had become too "national" for his liking. "I thought the time had come," he wrote, "when we should publicly let the editors know that we want a distinctive *Southern, Virginia*, Baptist paper." While he ostensibly denounced bitter feelings toward the North, and while he encouraged Southern Baptists to exchange "fraternal courtesies" with their Northern brethren, his conciliatory attitude went only so far. Just as postwar Southerners desperately clung to their distinctive identity, so too did Southern Baptists.[15]

The years 1875–1877 were pivotal for Jones both personally and professionally. In addition to his nagging financial problems, Jones mourned the loss of two children. In the spring of 1877, he returned from a trip to find that his house had burned. Although he lost his library, he was thankful that his manuscripts had survived. Still, he lamented the "bitter trial" that now left his family homeless. During these years Jones also made perhaps the most significant move in his career as a Lost Cause advocate: in 1875, he moved from temporary to permanent secretary of the Southern Historical Society (SHS). Between 1875 and 1887 he would edit fourteen volumes of the *Southern Historical Society Papers* (SHSP), a publication dedicated to preserving a faithful, pro-Confederate account of the Civil War.[16]

In addition to his position at the SHS, Jones continued writing. In 1880, he published the *Army of Northern Virginia Memorial Volume*[17] at the request of the Virginia Division of the Army of Northern Virginia Association. The book consisted mostly of addresses from well-known ex-Confederates such as Jefferson Davis, Jubal A. Early, John B. Gordon, Charles Marshall, C. S. Venable, and others. Jones also printed the addresses from various reunions of the association as well as several eulogies of Lee. The work was mostly the words of others, but it contained numerous Lost Cause tropes: the greatness of Lee, the exoneration of Lee's Gettysburg's campaign, the overwhelming numbers of the enemy, the unpreparedness of slaves for emancipation, and the anticipation of historical vindication.

Census records reveal that by 1880, Jones was living in Richmond. What exactly his financial situation was at this point is unclear. On one hand, he was only three years removed from a devastating house fire. Also, in addition to his five sons, Jones's sister-in-law, Sallie Helm, now lived with the family. The inevitable financial strain may explain why the Joneses boarded E. B. Garrett, a twenty-five-year-old school teacher. Yet on the other hand, Jones possessed enough means to employ two African American servants: fifty-eight-year-old Edith Jones, who also served as a cook, and fifteen-year-old Ida Jones.[18] Frustratingly, one can only guess as to the circumstances that brought Edith and Ida into the Jones household. That they share the family's surname could suggest that Edith was a former slave to Jones's father and that Ida was her daughter. As tempting as such speculation is, it remains only that, as the 1850 census indicates that Jones's father owned slaves, but lists no names.

Around the same time that Jones published his memorial volume, he was denied an agency for the Peabody Educational Fund, an organization established in 1867 to aid with education in the postwar South. Even with the rejection, he worked feverously. He continued in his pastorates and as secretary of the SHS, and from 1885 to 1886, he served on staff at the *Religious Herald*. He finally resigned his position at the SHS in 1887 and began work as the assistant corresponding secretary of the Home Mission Board (HMB) of the Southern Baptist Convention in Atlanta—a post he would hold until 1893.[19] As he left the SHS, Jones wrote: "[W]hilst another might have surpassed me in efficiency I think I may, without impropriety, claim that no one could have brought to the office greater love for our work, more zeal in the discharge of its duties, or more devotion to the cause of vindicating at the bar of history the name and fame of our Confederate leaders and people."[20] In 1887 Jones published one of his most well-known works, *Christ in the Camp*. By the time of the book's publication, Jones was already viewed as an authority on Southern memory. He claimed that Lee had personally requested an authoritative account of the Confederate revivals, and *Christ in the Camp* provided just that.

By the late 1880s, Jones had become not only a prominent Baptist, but also a well-known Lost Cause writer. Along the way he solidified his reputation as an apostle of the Confederacy, one commissioned both to preserve a faithful narrative of the Confederacy and to direct readers toward incarnations of Southern virtue. Important to remember, however, is the interconnectedness between Jones's commission as Confederate apostle and his calling as Baptist minister. This link—and even tension—elucidates some of the crucial ways that denominational identity shaped the developing mythology of the Lost Cause.

✠ ✠ ✠ ✠ ✠

As Jones moved on with his life and ministry after the war, he still maintained a relative openness to non-Baptist evangelicals. He wrote the *Religious Herald* in the fall of 1866 that he had baptized nearly forty congregants at Goshen Bridge Baptist Church, but that "[f]ive or six of our converts will probably unite with other denominations." While his report suggested that certain elements of wartime interdenominationalism—namely, the referring of converts to other denominations—had carried over into the postwar period, Jones still couched his comments in the context of revival. "Truly, the Lord seems to be pouring out his Spirit in this region," he continued. "I hear of revivals also among our brethren of other denominations."[21]

As he had demonstrated during his time as army chaplain and evangelist, Jones was willing to cooperate with other denominations in the context of revival. Furthermore, in the same *Herald* correspondence Jones made the following plea to readers: "Our Baptist cause is in pressing need of more preachers in this section. I believe that if we can get enough of *the right sort of men*, all these feeble churches could be built up and new churches established through the Valley." Even though denominational fraternity was well and good—especially in the exceptional circumstances of wartime and postwar revivals—Jones made clear that his primary concern continued to be the health and welfare of the Baptist denomination.[22]

Although his 1887 *Christ in the Camp* would recount the evangelical comradery of Confederate revivals, Jones's public and personal correspondence immediately after the war seldom harkened back to the halcyon days of wartime interdenominationalism. Instead, he contributed to the sectarian re-entrenchment of many white evangelicals in the postwar South. Over the next twenty years, Jones consistently painted other evangelicals less as Baptists' co-laborers and more as Baptists' competitors.

In the fall of 1865, Jones was optimistic about Baptist prospects in Virginia's Shenandoah Valley. He cosigned a letter to the *Religious Herald* stating, "In our judgment, the Valley presents a wide and inviting field to the Baptists of Virginia. While our views are comparatively little known in large sections, there is still a disposition to receive them." The article went on to say that there were many towns without a Baptist church, but that establishing such churches would be simple if Baptists in eastern Virginia would contribute "the men and means." The writers also testified that they had visited communities that had never witnessed a baptism by immersion. The letter continued by offering what was meant to be an inspiring anecdote. The story told of a woman who was married to a Presbyterian, but who ventured twenty miles on horseback in order to attend the first Baptist sermon she had heard in twenty years. Upon arriving, the woman "made a profession of religion and united with the Goshen Bridge Church."[23] While Jones was not one to count Presbyterians among the world's unconverted, he did attest to the superiority of Baptist faith and practice.

Jones authored a similar letter in March 1866. Writing the *Religious Herald*, he refuted the truism that eastern Virginia was unable to produce two things: sweet potatoes and Baptists. He went on to bemoan the hegemony of non-Baptist evangelicals: "The whole land has been occupied by our Pedobaptist brethren; our principles are unknown, and the prejudice against us is hard to be overcome." Not only were Baptists combating prejudice, he maintained; they were also battling ignorance. He noted that there were so few Baptist churches between Lexington and Winchester, a traveler "would find the grossest ignorance of our views." He continued, "We have scarcely a name in this magnificent region, not because of a want of adaption of our principles to the people; not because of an unwillingness to receive our views, but simply because the Baptists have not put forth proper efforts to 'possess the land.'" With more means, "there is no doubt that Baptist churches would spring up rapidly all through the Valley."[24] If Jones's correspondence is any indication, then the evangelical collegiality of camp religion was quickly fading into memory. While wartime and postwar revivals remained a unique time of denominational cooperation, Jones continued encouraging and envisioning Baptist preponderance in the Shenandoah Valley. For him, the postwar religious landscape was as much about survival as it was about revival.

Jones revealed his private attitudes toward non-Baptist evangelicals in a series of letters to his former mentor and friend, John Albert Broadus. In early 1866, Jones wrote Broadus of a vacant professorship at Washington College. Jones knew Broadus would be reluctant to leave SBTS but believed that Broadus's actions on behalf of "our principles" would challenge the prevailing denominational sentiments of the college, an institution Jones referred to as "that 'Gibraltar of Presbyterianism.'" Less than a month later, he wrote again, informing Broadus that there would be opposition from the "ultra Presbyterian element" to his appointment as professor. Jones was undeterred. "General Lee is doing his best to break down the strong sectarian (Presbyterian) bias that the institution has heretofore had," Jones wrote, "If you could get your consent to come there is no telling the influence you might exert for the general cause and for the Baptist cause." When Broadus declined the offer, Jones requested that Broadus recommend another Baptist for the position. Jones indicated that well-known Virginia Baptist George B. Taylor was "deeply impressed with the importance to our cause of having a Bapt[ist] professor at W. C." and was willing to be considered for the post if it would secure a Baptist influence at the institution.[25]

Not one to be easily discouraged, Jones was still pleading with Broadus in the summer of 1866. Jones relayed that he had heard from others a desire "to break down the Presbyterian regime" at Washington College. In December 1866, Jones invited Broadus to visit the school in order to "do great good for the cause of Christ and the Baptist cause." In May 1867, Jones indicated to Broadus that Washington College had twelve to fifteen Baptist students and that Broadus was needed to "help the Baptist cause." In another letter from May, Jones was more blatant. Referring to a recent revival, he wrote to Broadus, "The young converts are taking hold like men and I shall be sadly disappointed if it is not the dawn of a new era for our cause here. The Pedoes are growling, but I'll let them growl all to themselves and in the meantime I hope to baptize some more of their flock."[26] Jones's sentiment here is jolting, as it reflects a departure from the evangelical cooperation that Jones described as central in wartime revivals. Soon after the war's end, Jones was unequivocal in his view that Presbyterians were competitors. Even more remarkable, he was not above "sheep-stealing" from those with whom he had worked so closely just two years prior.

Jones's attitude stood in stark contrast to the fraternal spirit that he would one day identify as pervasive in wartime revivals. His letters reveal that, far from disappearing in the postwar period, evangelical competition quickly resurfaced when the cannons fell silent. Indeed, denominationalism squelched the efforts of some Southern evangelicals to collapse denominational distinctions. Instead of attempting to recreate the harmony of wartime interdenominationalism, evidence suggests that prominent Lost Cause figures like Jones were willing participants in the renewal of sectarian rivalries in the postwar South.

Baptist interests drove Jones for the decades following the war. In June 1866, he declined an offer to serve as an agent of SBTS, explaining that there existed a high demand for protracted meetings in eastern Virginia and that areas would be "left destitute unless I supply them." He grumbled, "I am the only Baptist preacher within *30* miles of here in two directions, within *60* miles in another and within *100* miles in another direction. And there is a constantly growing demand for Baptist preaching and an increasing readiness to accept Baptist views." In the winter of 1867, he wrote the *Religious Herald*, "From every direction I hear calls for Baptist preachers." He measured the relative strength of the local Presbyterians, Methodists, and Episcopalians, but assured readers he was not complaining. In public comments, as would be expected, he was more reserved in his criticism of other evangelicals. Even so, he stressed that there was "'a future' for the Baptists in Virginia."[27]

Jones was also a firm supporter of a distinctively Baptist education. In November 1871, he printed an advertisement pleading for Georgia Baptists to support SBTS, for which he was currently serving as agent. He declared that only through the support of Baptists would SBTS be able to "show to the world the sure foundation of the distinctive views of Baptists." In the same month, Jones cosigned a letter that defended SBTS against accusations that the faculty espoused questionable theology. In response, Jones attested that "*all* the Professors of the Seminary are gentlemen, scholars, Christians and '*sound* Baptists.'"[28]

In March 1870, Jones enthusiastically endorsed the Hollins Institute, a women's college in Roanoke, Virginia. Before becoming a women's college, the school had been founded as a seminary by Baptist minister Joshua Bradley in 1842.[29] Jones encouraged *Religious Herald* readers to send their daughters to the college, informing parents that students would be held to a high academic standard and would flourish in a Baptist context. He wrote that "with such schools Baptists have not the shadow of an excuse for sending their daughters to the institutions of other denominations." On another occasion, he avowed that a Baptist parent who passed up such an institution and "sends his daughter to a Pedo-baptist school . . . commits a most serious blunder, and inflicts a grievous wrong upon his child."[30] Even in the realm of education, Jones kept a wary eye on evangelical competitors.

Although there were postwar efforts among evangelicals to unite denominations formally, Baptists were particularly reluctant to the idea, many recoiling at what they considered to be a dismissal of denominational particularities.[31] Some of the issues Baptists debated in the postwar period had arisen during wartime. For example, one writer to the *Religious Herald* argued that it was improper to baptize a believer who intended to join a non-Baptist denomination. In May 1878, another writer took aim at the Evangelical Alliance, asserting that "denominational distinctions are too important to be set aside." With regard to infant baptism, one contributor contended that "either the Baptists or the Pedobaptists are making a serious error in their interpretation and practice of the ordinance." Reporting on an associational meeting in Georgia, Jones himself weighed in on the push for nonsectarian "Union Sunday schools." While he disagreed with those who maintained that only Baptists were Christians (a position offered at the meeting), Jones did affirm that "we believe, of course, in *Baptist* Sunday schools."[32]

In 1873, Jones was still trying to loosen the Presbyterian hold on Washington and Lee University. He denied that the institution was a Presbyterian school, insisting that although Presbyterians had owned the academy that would become Washington College, the school had agreed to be "undenominational" in order to receive support from George Washington (an Episcopalian). Jones identified the hiring of Lee (also an Episcopalian) to be a continued effort to, in Jones's words, "unPrebyterianize" the college. The faculty, he maintained, agreed that the school was nonsectarian. He admitted that Presbyterians had earned their reputation for prizing education, but he rejected any denominational claim on Washington and Lee University.[33]

Jones's postwar scuffles with non-Baptists were not limited to Presbyterians. In early 1873, he criticized a Methodist congregation that had dedicated a church and thereafter announced that the church would be open to other denominations. He stated that many Baptists "gave liberally" for the church's construction, with the expressed understanding that the building would be "free to all the Evangelical denominations." Word got back to Jones, however, that a Baptist minister had been expelled from what the congregation was now calling an exclusively Methodist church. An irritated Jones responded that he had allowed Methodist ministers into the pulpit at Goshen Bridge Baptist Church, even though the church was not constructed under the premise that it would be free to other denominations. He then implied that the Methodist congregation in question was selectively open to other denominations and speculated that if a well-known non-Methodist minister came to town, the church would invite the speaker in order to draw a crowd. In other words, Jones continued, the congregation would be open to non-Methodists when the church needed money.[34] Jones's comments reveal that, on one hand, he maintained a friendly openness toward non-Baptist evangelicals and was even willing to share his pulpit. On the other hand, his remarks also suggest that he was coiled to strike when he sensed a threat to Baptists.

Jones went after the Methodists again in an 1874 letter to Broadus. Jones accused Methodists of spreading a rumor that Broadus had allowed his first child to be baptized as an infant. Not only had Broadus allowed the practice, the story went, but he had even carried his child to the font himself. Jones assured Broadus, "I have taken the liberty of denying it very emphatically."[35] Still, the rumor persisted, and Jones requested that Broadus publically deny the account.

Jones and Broadus held similar beliefs regarding Baptist particularities, and Jones likely would have echoed a sermon Broadus preached in 1881 entitled, "The Duty of Baptists to Teach their Distinctive Views." Broadus listed a number of these particularities, the first being that the only religious authority for the Christian was the Bible. Broadus held that the church could only consist of those "making a credible profession of conversion." He admitted that this number could include young children, but he denied the efficacy of infant baptism. He also demanded that church offices and ceremonies be rooted in the New Testament. With regard to baptism, Broadus endorsed no one mode, but noted that the ordinance represented the death, burial, and resurrection of Christ and symbolized the candidate's death to sin and resurrection to new life. He affirmed a Zwinglian understanding of the Lord's Supper and again took his cue from the New Testament in demanding that churches remain independent.[36]

Broadus also explained why Baptists should teach their distinctive views. First, he claimed that to do so was a "duty we owe to ourselves." He maintained that Baptists had no right to "stand apart" unless the theological distinctions had "real importance." Next, Broadus stated that teaching Baptist views was a duty Baptists owed to other Christians. With a decidedly sectarian bent, he offered the following:

Take the Roman Catholics. We are often told very earnestly that Baptists must make common cause with other Protestants against the aggression of Romanism. It is urged, especially in some localities, that we ought to push all our denominational differences into the background and stand shoulder to shoulder against Popery. Very well; but all the time it seems to us that the best way to meet and withstand Romanism is to take Baptist ground;

and if making common cause against it we abandon or slight our Baptist principles, have a care lest we do harm in both directions. Besides, ours is the best position, we think, for winning Romanists to evangelical truth.[37]

Broadus's position served as a glaring reminder that the coalition of nineteenth-century evangelicals in America and Europe was inherently anti-Catholic. (Recall Jones's emphasis in *Christ in the Camp* on the specifically evangelical nature of Confederate revivals.) Because evangelicals oriented their alliances in opposition to Roman Catholicism, wartime and postwar interdenominationalism was by nature a limited venture.

The anti-Catholicism of Broadus's sermon is not nearly as surprising as its depiction of evangelical relations. Particularly interesting is his allegation that other Protestants were "wonderfully ignorant" of Baptist views. As examples, he claimed that some non-Baptists thought Baptists performed triune immersion; other non-Baptists believed that Baptists were a subset of "Pedobaptists." If Broadus's characterizations were accurate, then another issue inhibiting evangelical collaboration was a general unfamiliarity with fellow Protestants' beliefs. In contrast to nineteenth-century efforts in the South to merge evangelical denominations, neither Broadus nor Jones—who until Broadus's death regularly relied on his mentor for vocational advice and spiritual guidance—suffered a compromise of distinctive Baptist beliefs. Jones would have affirmed unequivocally Broadus's conclusion, "Let us gladly cooperate with our fellow Christians of other persuasions in general Christian work, as far as we can without sacrificing our convictions."[38]

One year after the war, a writer to the *Religious Herald* discussed Northern efforts to unite denominations formally. The author observed that Northern leaders believed that their plans had hit the "nails" on the head. The two nails in mind were the "*comprehension* under the two ancient creeds, and *consolidation* of the nearest agreeing denominations." The *Herald* writer pessimistically judged that leaders were working in vain and would find that the "nails are quite too soft for driving."[39] Indeed, as was the case with the North, efforts for denominational union in the South ultimately faltered. Even ministers like Broadus and Jones—who both encouraged evangelical kinship in the context of revival and for the sake of evangelism—refused to yield their Baptist particularities. They were nails that could only be driven so far.

✣ ✣ ✣ ✣ ✣

The well-being of Southern Baptists was never far from Jones's mind, yet with the collapse of the Confederacy, another cause seized his attention. Although the battle for Southern independence was over, the battle for Southern memory was just beginning. Jones saw himself as first and foremost a Baptist minister, but also recognized and cultivated his stature as a former Confederate chaplain, and as one who had known Robert E. Lee and Stonewall Jackson personally. Eventually, Jones would befriend Jefferson Davis as well. When the fight over white Southern memory commenced, Jones was in the vanguard, tirelessly asserting his self-proclaimed authority as one uniquely qualified to tell the Confederacy's story. Because of his personal encounters with the Confederate triumvirate of Lee, Jackson, and Davis, and because of his bulldog determination to preserve and promulgate the "true story" of the Confederacy, Jones willingly accepted the mantle of Confederate apostle.

Less than two years after Lee's surrender, Jones was busy constructing the Confederacy's history. In January 1867, he asked *Religious Herald* readers for regimental records as well as records relating to the Confederate revivals. He anticipated dividing the proceeds from any publication of these records between the "education of soldiers' orphans" and "other benevolent purposes."[40] Publishing this ad in a religious periodical, Jones sensed no tension between the Lost Cause and "our cause" (by which he usually meant Baptist interests). Potential for conflict, however, was on the horizon.

While a traveling agent for SBTS, Jones occasionally lectured on Lost Cause staples, such as the righteousness of the Confederate Army or the virtuousness of Confederate leaders. In April 1872, he wrote to Boyce, chairman of the faculty at SBTS, heading off criticism that these engagements were hindering fundraising for the seminary. Jones insisted that he had only lectured on Lee five times from July 1871 to January 1872 and did not expect to give other addresses, "certainly not if any one thinks it injures the Seminary." That there could be complaints befuddled Jones:

"I am so fully satisfied that it has *not* had that effect that if the fact could be gotten at I would more cheerfully pay *twenty dollars for every one* lost in this way." He even suggested that the lectures *benefited* the seminary, claiming that the talks helped pay his expenses and thus relieved the seminary from doing so. When he discovered that he drew large crowds with free addresses but small crowds with paid speeches (an obvious enough observation), he suspended the lectures.[41]

Jones seldom missed an opportunity to assert his authority as a witness to the virtues of the Confederate Army and leaders. In the autumn of 1867, he charged into an imbroglio over the preaching of Confederate chaplains during the war. The debate centered on accusations that Lee and Jackson had instructed chaplains not to preach the particular doctrines of their denominations, but instead to deliver "moral lectures." These moral lectures, the rumors stated, were "wishy-washy" and did not convey the gospel to the soldiers. In essence, the argument hinged on the nature and practice of wartime interdenominationalism, a practice that purportedly produced watered-down sermons. Jones denied that there were any such orders to preach "moral lectures," and he backed his claim by appealing to his intimate knowledge of the Confederacy's officers and chaplains. He relayed that he had been with the Army of Northern Virginia from the war's beginning to the war's end, and that he was "in a position to know much of what concerned the religious interests of these noble men." With regard to the allegations, Jones relied on his apostolic authority, confidently pronouncing that it would have been "impossible that there could have been such a thing without my hearing of it."[42]

As with biblical apostles, though, Jones's authority did not go unchallenged. Winthrop Hartly Hopson, who had first leveled the criticism of "wishy-washy" moral lectures in the Confederate armies, fired back at Jones. In October 1868, he bristled at Jones's suggestion that Hopson should have left his "comfortable pastorate in Richmond," come to the army, and shown chaplains and soldiers "the more excellent way." In response, Hopson cut the callow Jones down to size: "[W]hen he has more age and experience," Hopson parried, "he will be less venturesome and more cautious in his statements." Hopson declared that he had indeed been commissioned as a chaplain and was even a prisoner. He rebuked

Jones for not following the Bible's injunction against speaking ill of a neighbor, and he accused Jones of "recklessly" misrepresenting him. Then came Hopson's coup-de-grâce: "His offense is too great to be overlooked on the plea of youthful indiscretion. My sympathy for the lost cause and my sacrifice for its success are matters about which I very seldom speak, and certainly have no disposition to write, particularly in the columns of a religious journal."[43] If Hopson's condescension did not affront Jones enough, his suggestion that "lost cause" narratives did not belong in a Baptist newspaper certainly cut Jones to the quick.

Not to be outdone, Jones desperately tried to right the ship. He admitted his mistake, acknowledging that Hopson was not a pastor in Richmond until *after* the war. He continued, "Those who know me will readily believe that I am one of the last persons who would rob a true Confederate of a single laurel to which he is justly entitled, and so far as Dr. Hopson labored or sacrificed for the 'lost cause,' I honor him for it." Even with his admission, Jones stood by his criticism of Hopson, maintaining that Hopson "made assertions seriously affecting the character of our noble chieftains—Lee and Jackson—and that of the chaplains of the army of Northern Virginia."[44]

Jones also remained suspicious of Hopson's military record, and he reiterated that if Hopson had possessed the pure gospel, he should have shared it with the supposedly misguided chaplains and soldiers. Even after committing an embarrassing oversight regarding Hopson's chaplaincy and subsequent pastorate, Jones made clear that Hopson's accusations not only besmirched the reputations of Confederate chaplains, but also committed the unpardonable sin of tarnishing the legacy of Lee and Jackson. From Jones's perspective, Lee, Jackson, and (later) Davis represented the very best of Confederate Christianity. In these icons resided the enduring reminder that Southern piety was and remained superior to Northern religion. For the remainder of the nineteenth century and beyond, not only would the apostle of the Confederacy preserve a faithful narrative of the Confederate Army's righteousness, but he would also deflect or redirect criticism of the Confederate trinity at any cost.

In April 1873, Jones wrote to the *Religious Herald*—again, in a story that would resurface in *Christ in the Camp*—of the eagerness of Confederate soldiers to attend camp revival services. By 1878, he was delivering at least four different lectures on Confederate history: "Jesus in the Camp or Religion in Lee's Army," "Stonewall Jackson the Christian Soldier," "Lee the Model Man," and "The Boys in Gray, or the Confederate Soldier as I Knew Him." At times, he would deliver his popular "The Boys in Gray" lecture in Baptist churches. On one occasion, he gave the speech in an opera house. The crowd numbered about one thousand, and admission was fifty cents.[45] Through his speaking tours and public correspondence, he garnered a reputation as the preeminent chronicler of the Confederacy's religious history.

As both gospel minister and Confederate apostle, Jones wielded considerable influence among Southern Baptists. At an associational meeting in August 1876, he exerted his growing influence when he spoke on the dangers of alcohol. Notably, he cited two authorities to back his warnings. First, he appealed to the scriptures. Second, he looked to Stonewall Jackson. According to Jones, Jackson confessed that he feared liquor more than he did the "bullets of the enemy."[46] Jones believed that, in addition their reliance on holy writ, Southern Baptists could take ethical and social cues from their Confederate archetypes.

Southern Baptists came to recognize that Jones's expertise extended beyond the pulpit and into Southern hagiography. On several occasions, Broadus encouraged Jones to write a second book on Lee, one dealing with the general's private life and correspondence. After hearing Jones lecture at the University of Virginia (UVA), one observer concluded, "What he, after his army experiences, and editing of the papers of the Southern Historical Society, does not know about the men and scenes of '61–'65, is hardly worth knowing." A writer for the *Religious Herald* held that "Dr. Jones owes it to the world to write a more extended account of the work of grace in the Confederate army than has yet appeared. He has the material, and before long we hope to see it in a book—a book which will be read with thrilling interest by good people in all sections of the country."[47] Roughly three years after the correspondent's plea, Jones heeded the call and published his opus, *Christ in the Camp*.

In private letters from the 1870s and 1880s, Jones reasoned that his devotion to the Lost Cause was a means of promoting the Baptist cause.

Communicating with Broadus, Jones wrote that he had accepted a temporary agency for the Lee Memorial Association and explained that such a position would allow him time to look for another pastorate. He was also in a better position financially because of the sale of his 1874 book on Lee. Jones also asked Broadus for a recommendation if a church position opened. In another letter to Broadus, Jones indicated that with his lectures on Lee, Jackson, and Confederate soldiers, he had hoped to raise money for the SBTS "students fund." To Boyce, Jones revealed his intention to use proceeds from *Christ in the Camp* in order to pay a note to the seminary. Minister George Boardman Taylor was under the impression that Jones also gave paid lectures on the Confederacy in order to support Jones's church.[48]

Back in 1872, Jones had assured SBTS leadership that his periodic lectures on Confederate history would not hinder fundraising for the seminary. Still, there lingered uneasiness in some colleagues' minds regarding how Jones was balancing his allegiance to the Lost Cause and to the Baptist cause. In 1887 Jones addressed the issue again, this time even more emphatically. He wrote to Broadus, "I expect to give my time, my talents, my energies, to the work of Home Missions. The great cause shall *always be first*, and I intend to let *nothing* interfere with my first duty to it." To reiterate his devotion, Jones resigned his post as Secretary of the SHS and began turning down lecture opportunities. He then resolved to "make no lectures which will interfere with my work." But Jones was by no means leaving the Lost Cause behind. He went on: "At the same time, I shall not think it wrong sometimes to put in a lecture, or to write an article, on Confederate themes of which my mind and heart have been so full. And while the staple of my conversation as I go around shall be about my work, I shall not consider it illegitimate (especially in a company of old Confederates) to sometimes 'Shoulder my crutch and fight my battles o'er again.'" Jones denied that he was stirring up bitter feelings toward the North and contended that he had done as much as anyone in his position to "promote real fraternity between the sections."[49]

Becoming increasingly passionate as his letter progressed, Jones continued, "But I am sure that you will agree with me, on the other hand, that I am not called on to do the dirt eating, cringing, and crawling, which some of our brethren have deemed proper, and which has, in my judgment, greatly retarded the cause of real fraternity." He rebuffed notions that he bore ill will toward the American Baptist Publication Society (ABPS) and admitted that the ABPS had published many fine works. Even so, he was disgusted with what he considered to be the ABPS's meddling in politics. "I did antagonize the idea that they were 'Nationals' at the time they were running a dirty, Negro-equality, Republican Campaign sheet," he wrote.[50]

Jones concluded his defense by thanking Broadus for his comments and critiques of *Christ in the Camp*. He reaffirmed to Broadus, "I mean to throw my whole soul into my work." Indeed, Jones did just that. Although he attempted to convince Broadus that the Baptist cause remained a top priority, the reality is that Jones saw no conflict between the denomination and the Confederacy. He drew on his Baptist background in order to provide white Southerners a religious lens through which to view Confederate history. Likewise, he harnessed his Confederate background in order to compel Baptists to venerate icons like Lee, Jackson, and Davis. Jones's faith animated his efforts, whether as pastor, missionary, chaplain, evangelist, or apostle. Perhaps God had not seen fit to send him overseas, but the postwar South would afford Jones an opportunity to cement his legacy as a bearer of the Confederate gospel.

✛ ✛ ✛ ✛ ✛

Before exploring Jones's role as Lost Cause advocate, it is important to appreciate the history and robustness of a Confederate mythology that had begun to take root in the postwar South well before Jones entered the scene. A number of prominent writers preceded or worked alongside him, and a brief survey of their work not only locates Jones in the literary landscape of the postwar South, but also throws light on Jones's unique contributions to the fabrication and dissemination of the Lost Cause mythology. Among the host of pro-Confederate partisans, three standouts include Edward Pollard, William Pendleton, and Jubal Early.

The self-proclaimed originator of the phrase "lost cause"—at least as it related to the Confederacy's fight for independence—was Richmond journalist Edward Alfred Pollard (1832–1872). Only a year after the war's conclusion, Pollard published a massive volume entitled *The Lost Cause*, in which he introduced many of the themes that would become fixtures in the works of Confederate apologists. One refrain concerned General Ulysses S. Grant. Pollard praised Grant's magnanimity in offering Lee gracious terms of surrender but utterly dismissed Grant's generalship. For Pollard, Grant knew nothing of military strategy, and he was content to hurl men at the enemy until superior odds won the day. In other words, Grant had "no conception of the battle beyond the momentum of numbers." Only with overwhelming numbers could Grant defeat the "consummate skill of Gen. Lee," Pollard determined. He also stressed that Grant was "overmatched by Lee, who showed himself his master in every art of war, and indeed left Grant not a single branch of generalship in which he might assert his reputation."[51]

Even though Pollard believed Grant could win battles only through superior numbers, Pollard did not attribute the South's loss to overwhelming odds. Instead, he traced defeat back to demoralization, which had resulted from an incompetent Confederate government. He launched a blistering attack on Jefferson Davis, accusing him of being obstinate, boastful, having a "mind intoxicated with conceit," a "singular fondness for erratic campaigns," and a scholarship that "smelt of the closet." Pollard went as far as to declare that Southern demoralization stemmed from "such a want of confidence in the administration of President Davis, as was never before exhibited between a people and its rulers in a time of revolution." Pollard wrote that of the manifold reasons one could proffer for the Confederacy's fall, with an "abler Government and more resolute spirit," the South might have won independence.[52]

Race and slavery occupied a disturbing place in Pollard's narrative. He preferred to use the phrase "negro servitude," believing that "slavery" was too harsh of a term to describe the South's "mild" system. He discussed the benefits of the institution and argued that this servitude "elevated the African, and was in the interest of human improvement." Pollard denied slavery's central place in the Civil War, maintaining that slavery "furnished a convenient line of battle" and that the North "found or imagined in slavery the leading cause of the distinctive civilization of the South, its higher sentimentalism, and its superior refinements of scholarship and manners." According to Pollard, even though slavery was incidental to the war, the Federal government harbored a racial agenda. He believed that the Republicans sought to make "blacks social and political equals to whites" and would encourage "intermingling of the races." In addition, he accused the "Black Republican party" of wanting to disenfranchise white Southerners while giving the vote to former slaves. Although conceding that the war had ended slavery, he categorically denied that the conflict had decided "negro equality" or "negro suffrage."[53]

Many of Pollard's views would resurface in Lost Cause writings for the remainder of the nineteenth century. At the same time, writers like Jones would jettison other themes. For example, Jones attacked Pollard for his treatment of Davis, commenting that as "histories" Pollard's works "were not worth the paper they are printed on" and that "the undisguised plagiarism of the author . . . and his malignant slanders of Ex-President Davis, should drive his books from our libraries." Still, Pollard articulated what was a common fear of most Lost Cause proponents: Southern extinction. Pollard and his ilk worried that conquered Southerners would lose their distinctiveness. His solution was for the South to "cultivate her superiority as a people." He summed up his point thusly: "There may not be a political South. Yet there may be a social and intellectual South."[54]

Two years after the publication of *The Lost Cause*, Pollard released a sequel — a la Milton — entitled *The Lost Cause Regained*. He began by claiming to have coined the phrase "lost cause" and then proceeded to reiterate themes from his previous book, including a criticism of the North's "cruel mechanical warfare of numbers" and an unsparing attack on Davis's "intellectual poverty." Yet what was truly jarring about *The Lost Cause Regained* — a work substantially shorter than its predecessor — was the attention it gave to race. Pollard admitted that the premise of white superiority was the sine qua non of his argument, and as a result, his tome dripped with racism. "The permanent, natural inferiority of the Negro was the true and *only* defense of Slavery," Pollard wrote. He went on to say, "[w]e believe, indeed, that the specific, permanent inferiority of the Negro, so far from being a mere disputation of the learned, a scholastic entertainment, is, as discovered and eviscerated by the past war, the most important question of modern times." He held that African Americans were a different species than whites and then attempted to prove African American inferiority scientifically, religiously, and historically. Pollard conceded that if African Americans were equal to whites, then slavery was indeed an evil. He therefore concluded, "We must do—what the South has never fairly done—meet the whole controversy at the minor premise, contending for the natural inferiourity of the Negro. It is from this inferiourity that we deduce all the benefits of Slavery in the past. It is from this inferiourity that we draw all our arguments with respect to future experiments on the Negro."[55]

For Pollard, a defense of white superiority was the only hope for the downtrodden South and the only means of staving off the "Negrophilism" that accompanied Reconstruction. Since assumptions of innate racial inferiority underpinned Pollard's work, *The Lost Cause Regained* complicates the assertion of some scholars that race, while important, was not foundational for the Lost Cause. Pollard's work demonstrates that, to the contrary, race was the fulcrum of some of the earliest Lost Cause claims.[56]

✢ ✢ ✢ ✢ ✢

William Nelson Pendleton (1809–1883), a former Confederate general who had served as Lee's chief of artillery, was more intentional than Pollard had been in cultivating and preserving a pristine image of Lee. When Lee died in the fall of 1870, Pendleton organized the Lee Memorial Association and began raising funds for a Lee statue and mausoleum. As did other Lost Cause advocates, Pendleton gave speaking tours and distributed literature in an attempt to coronate Lee as the perfect Christian soldier. In public addresses and in his memoirs, Pendleton echoed a number of Lost Cause motifs, and like Jones, he boasted of his intimate connection with Confederate notables. As was Lee, Pendleton was Episcopalian, and he relished serving a pastoral role for his champion. Their relationship preceded the war by many years, as the two had met at West Point. Pendleton was even delighted to observe that he and Lee resembled one another. With regard to Jackson, Pendleton testified to his rapport with the general. On at least one occasion, the two shared a blanket and discussed spiritual issues. Their relationship was apparently so close that Pendleton, upon seeing the wounded Jackson, nearly fainted.[57]

Pendleton's and Jones's works shared important elements. Both authors testified to their intimate acquaintances with Confederate leaders, and both exalted Lee's spiritual and martial renown. Pendleton wrote that Lee possessed an "unsurpassed greatness of soul," served as "model Christian, patriot, soldier," and was the "handsomest young man I ever saw." Pendleton acknowledged that Lee neither professed faith nor joined a church until after the Mexican-American War. Once a believer, however, Lee radiated a "Christian piety of purest quality" and excelled as "among the most perfect of men."[58]

Referring to Lee's refusal to accept a commission in the Union Army at the outset of the Civil War, Pendleton compared Lee to Moses. Like Moses, the prophets, and Paul (who was willing to be accursed for his people), Lee's overriding concern was for his people—his fellow Virginians. Like Jones, Pendleton portrayed Lee as open to all evangelical denominations. Although Lee was committed to the Episcopalian church, his mind and heart were "far too large and too thoroughly imbued with the blessed lessons of Revelation to be limited in his Christian sympathies by ecclesiastical boundaries, or any restrictions narrowing the divinely-ordained compass of human brotherhood."[59]

Pendleton and Jones also endorsed a particularly charged narrative of the battle of Gettysburg. One strategy for exonerating Lee for his disastrous defeat on the third day of the battle was to deflect blame onto Lee's subordinates. By far, the weight of this blame came to rest on General James Longstreet. Longstreet served as lieutenant general and as Lee's chief subordinate after Jackson's death in the spring of 1863. Pendleton, Jones, and former general Jubal A. Early vilified Longstreet for bungling Lee's orders during the battle. Longstreet was a convenient target for Lost Cause writers for a number of reasons, not the least of which were his postwar criticisms of Lee and his eventual alliance with the Republican Party. According to Pendleton, on the second day of Gettysburg, Longstreet commenced his attack later than ordered. The delay proved to be the "fatal failure of the entire occasion" and allowed a "golden opportunity" to slip away. Longstreet's mismanagement not only cost Confederates the battle, but ultimately led to the loss of "the cause of constitutional government."[60]

Pendleton's work also addressed race and reflected his entrenched hatred of Reconstruction policies. He blamed the onset of the war less on slavery and more on "slavery agitation." To Pendleton, not only were Northerners content in "supplanting reason and right by brute force," but they were also determined to make "the inferior African our equals and rulers." He quoted Lee as saying that slavery was a "moral and political evil," but that slaves were better off in America than in Africa, and that servitude would help them advance as a race. Pendleton himself conceded that the Bible "tends on the whole to ameliorate everywhere and ultimately abolish African slavery and all kinds of evils in society," but that "agitators" were not satisfied with this, and instead adopted the radical "new gospel" of immediate abolition. Dismissing African Americans as incapable of living "civilized" lives, he concluded disdainfully, "Poor creatures, they little dream of the difficulties freedom will bring them. They cherished the absurd idea that they would exchange places with us,—be gentlemen and ladies in our homes and have us for their negroes. To find themselves still black, with wooly heads, is to them an immense disappointment."[61]

Pendleton lashed out at the North as a conquering and occupying force, alleging that Southerners had been "shot down by German, Irish, negro, and Yankee wretches invading our home" and were now "exposed to insult and attack from the negroes let loose." The onslaught left him little choice but to take refuge in his faith, and he did so by drawing parallels between biblical archetypes and the Southern experience. He suggested that God had allowed the South to be defeated in order to abrogate their idolization of Virginia, and he reminded readers that Jesus, the apostles, and many Christian martyrs lived under "foreign domination."[62] Lost Cause writers commonly made such comparisons, often locating white Southerners in the exilic narratives of the Old Testament. Doing so enabled ministers like Pendleton and Jones to use religion both as salve and as subversion. Portraying white Southerners as God's chosen people in exile, pro-Confederate clergy kept the South central (and the North incidental) in the divine plan.

✣ ✣ ✣ ✣ ✣

While Pollard and Pendleton made their marks on the burgeoning mythology of the Lost Cause, few individuals wielded more direct sway than Jubal Anderson Early (1816–1894). During the war, Early rose to lieutenant general and led infantry in the Army of Northern Virginia until Lee removed him from command in the spring of 1865. Despite his dismissal, Early remained a staunch devotee of the general. Within months of the war's end, Lee contacted Early and asked him for materials related to the final campaign of the Army of Northern Virginia, a request that likely prompted Early to begin work on his memoirs. By publishing his 1866 *A Memoir of the Last Years of the War for Independence, in the Confederate States of America*, Early became the first major Civil War officer to complete a book-length reminiscence of the war. Early was also influential in his role as president of the SHS, a position he began in 1875. Through Early the SHS became "Virginia-centric" and committed to defending Lee from any criticism. Early and Jones worked closely together at the SHS, with Jones serving as the society's secretary-treasurer. When the SHS began the *Southern Historical Society Papers* (SHSP) in 1876, Jones served as editor until 1887.[63]

As did Jones and Pendleton, Early portrayed Lee as nearly superhuman. Also like Jones and Pendleton, Early assured his audiences that he was a personal witness to Lee's greatness. Early dedicated much of his attention to Lee's military acumen, which is unsurprising considering Early's rank in the Confederate Army. When discussing Lee's military exploits, he painted a Lee who was unconquered and unconquerable. "General Lee had not been conquered in battle," Early averred, "but surrendered because he had no longer any army with which to do battle." He denied that Lee's Maryland campaign—which had resulted in a Confederate withdrawal into Virginia after the Battle of Sharpsburg (Antietam)—had been a failure. Early also claimed that Richmond's fall was a result of Confederate setbacks in the west and southwest and was no fault of Lee's Army of Northern Virginia. Early testified that no military leader had been Lee's equal—be he Alexander the Great, Hannibal, Julius

Caesar, Gustavus Adolphus, Napoleon, or Wellington. A chief reason that no leader could compare to Lee was that the Confederate general had proven his greatness while negotiating the "new elements in the art of war."[64]

A prominent theme in Early's addresses was the numerical and technological advantages of the Union over the Confederacy. "It was genius and nerve, and valor, on the one side," he commented, "against numbers and mechanical power on the other." While Lee displayed remarkable skill in the face of overwhelming odds, there was only so much the Southern chieftain could do in the face of "mechanical arts," "physical science," and the North's "unlimited resources of men and money." Related to Early's "overwhelming odds" argument was his utter disregard for Grant's military competence. He determined that Grant's only strategy was to "hammer" Confederate forces with superior numbers until, as Early put it, the "unlimited resources of our enemies must finally prevail over all the genius and chivalric daring."[65]

Early was as resolute as any Lost Cause writer in shielding Lee from criticism. Early led the charge against Longstreet, blaming the general for the Confederate loss at Gettysburg. Even though Lee's "magnanimity" prevented him from blaming others, Early wanted a reckoning. He attested that Lee had ordered Longstreet to attack at dawn on the second day of Gettysburg, but that Longstreet's troops were not in position until four o'clock. Early was convinced that had Longstreet executed Lee's orders, the Confederates would have achieved a resounding victory. For Early, mistakes at Gettysburg, or any failures in the Army of Northern Virginia, were the fault of Lee's subordinates, not Lee himself.[66]

Early also disputed that slavery was the cause of the war. He argued that during the crisis "slavery was used as a catch-word to arouse the passions of a fanatical mob." As to African Americans, Early decreed that God had "stamped them, indelibly, with a different color and an inferior physical and mental organization." Early therefore concluded that an "amalgamation of the races was in contravention of His designs or He would not have made them so different." Furthermore, Early felt that "[r]eason, common sense, true humanity to the black, as well as the safety of the white race, required that the inferior race should be kept in a state of subordination." Not only was slavery—as practiced in the South—beneficial for the slaves morally and physically, but the institution had "furnished a class of laborers as happy and contented as any in the world, if not more so."[67] Through his writings, Early bolstered the chimera that masters were magnanimous, slaves were happy, and that chattel bondage was a testament to God's infinite wisdom.

Pollard, Pendleton, and Early represent only a small sampling of the Lost Cause writers with whom Jones dialogued, either in person or in print. Like Pollard, Jones tapped into postbellum anxiety concerning the loss of a distinctive (white) Southern identity. Like Pendleton, Jones emphasized the Christian character of Lee. Like Early, Jones guarded Lee from attack, even if this meant disparaging Lee's subordinates in the process. Unlike these figures, Jones was less overt in his discussion of slavery and race, a silence which itself spoke volumes. By avoiding such topics, Jones embraced Lost Cause tenets holding that slavery and the Civil War did not belong in the same discussion. In order to distance the Confederacy from slavery, Jones narrated Confederate history with only scant references to the South's peculiar institution.

Jones was also distinct from these figures in that he viewed himself as the spiritual authority on the South's three most prominent leaders: Lee, Jackson, and Davis. Of course, other ministers could have made similar claims, especially Episcopalian ministers in the case of Lee and Davis, or Presbyterian ministers in the case of Jackson. Nevertheless, Jones believed it his mission to burnish the images of the Confederacy's most treasured heroes. He widened his circle of influence beyond Baptists, carrying his message to all white Southerners, and even to Northerners. The way Jones, a Baptist, exerted his spiritual authority among white Southerners of various denominational stripes was by portraying his idols in a way that transcended sectarian squabbles. Such openness did not mean that Jones was receptive to Roman Catholicism, that he ceased viewing non-Baptist evangelicals as competition, or that he downplayed his own Baptist fidelity. Instead, Jones advocated interdenominationalism insofar as it served his apostolic mission to preserve a faithful narrative of the Confederacy, and to direct readers' attention to those he considered to be incarnations of Southern virtue.

✠ ✠ ✠ ✠ ✠

Jones's position within the Lost Cause movement was both representative and unique. In line with other Lost Cause advocates, he infused his rhetoric with religious undertones. More so than others, though, he interpreted the Lost Cause as organically and inextricably linked with evangelical Christianity. He also resembled fellow Lost Causers in his attempt to excise slavery from discussions of Confederate history. Unlike other writers, though, he did not take the issue of slavery head-on. Instead, he narrated the Confederacy's story as if slavery was so tangential to the war that the institution did not warrant mention.

As Jones rose to prominence, he held fast to his convictions for both the Baptist cause and the Lost Cause. His Confederate background enabled him to give Baptists firsthand accounts of the lives of paradigmatic Southern Christians. His Baptist background permitted him to give white Southerners religious insights into figures whose virtues extended beyond the battlefield. Animated by his apostolic mission, he brought religion to bear on the interpretation of Southern history. Through his editorship of the *SHSP*, and through his volumes on Confederate leaders and Confederate religion, Jones promised white Southerners unmitigated access to leaders like Lee, Jackson, and Davis—vessels of Christian piety, and enduring reminders that God remained immanently present with the Southern people.

J. William Jones. From J. William Jones, Christ in the Camp, or Religion in Lee's Army *(Richmond: B. F. Johnson and Company, 1887).*

Gen. Robert E. Lee. Library of Congress.

Last photograph of Thomas J. "Stonewall" Jackson, taken just two weeks before his death at Chancellorsville. National Archives at College Park.

Jefferson Davis. Brady-Handy Collection, Library of Congress.

Brig. Gen. William
Nelson Pendleton.
Reproduction of
drawing. Library
of Congress.

Lt. Gen. James
Longstreet.
Liljenquist Family
Collection of Civil
War Photographs,
Library of Congress.

*Father Abram Ryan,
likely shortly after
the war. Courtesy
of the Church of the
Immaculate Conception,
Knoxville, Tennessee.*

*John Albert Broadus.
Frontispiece of Archibald
Thomas Robertson,* Life
and Letters of John Albert
Broadus *(Philadelphia:
American Baptist
Publication Society, 1910).*

Jubal A. Early.
Library of Congress.

Seal of the Southern
Historical Society.

CHAPTER FOUR

Southern Hagiography: Jones and the Confederate Trinity

My comrades, I feel that I have given but a feeble picture of this grand period in
the history of this time of trial of our beloved South—a history which is a great
gift from God, and which we must hand down as a holy heritage to our children,
not to teach them to cherish a spirit of bitterness or a love for war, but to show
them that their fathers bore themselves worthily in the strife when to do battle
became a sacred duty. Heroic history is the living soul of a nation's renown.

—CHARLES S. VENABLE

"I wonder whether Dr. Jones has considered well what he is doing," wrote
a concerned *Religious Herald* reader in September 1886. The writer
referred to an August report Jones had sent to the *Herald* following
a recent visit with Jefferson Davis at his plantation home in Mississippi.
In the article, Jones described Davis as the "idol" of Southerners, and as
one who had "never lost his place in the hearts of his loving people." He
noted that Davis, almost eighty, accepted the outcome of the war, but
that the ex-president beseeched his people not to tell Southern children
that their fathers were "rebels" or "traitors."[1] Asserting apostolic privilege,
Jones noted that he could not divulge everything he and Davis had discussed. To do so would be to "invade the sacredness of the home circle,
or to betray the freely expressed opinions of private intercourse, or the
confidence of private friendship." He closed his account with a fitting
image: he joked that his Gulf Coast fishing trip would "settle his claim
to 'apostolic succession,'" placing him squarely in line with the fishermen
disciples of Galilee.

Jones's letter prompted a response from one *Herald* reader, who described Jones's "glowing reproduction and eulogy of Mr. Davis' underlying
secession views" as deeply troubling. To continue spreading such notions,

the writer continued, would lead Southern children into another war.[2] Jones responded to the letter without apology, assuring his critic that while secession had indeed been constitutional, by yielding to the North's overwhelming resources, Southerners had forfeited their right to secede again. Still, the incident conveyed to Jones that some Southerners were less than eager to fight another war, even a rhetorical one.

Critics notwithstanding, most white Southerners resonated with Jones's views, and they relished the firsthand accounts that Jones could provide. In the same issue as Jones's Davis article, one *Herald* reader wrote Jones from a sickbed. The writer thanked Jones for the first installment of the serial "Christ in the Camp," a column the correspondent read through "wet eyes." He then pled with Jones to turn the serial into a book.[3] While some Baptists balked at Jones dredging up the past, others clamored for Jones to preserve Southern memory, and to provide for them a window into the virtuous lives of their Confederate champions.

Jones concentrated his Lost Cause narratives on three leaders of the Confederacy: Robert E. Lee, Thomas J. "Stonewall" Jackson, and Jefferson Davis, all of whom Jones helped transform into paradigmatic and mythological heroes for white Southerners. For Jones, each of these men represented the quintessence of Southern virtue, and Jones felt it his mission both to testify to the greatness of these models and to encourage Southerners to follow their examples. As an apostle of the Confederacy, Jones pointed his readers toward Confederate icons who served as incarnations for white Southerners experiencing divine alienation in the wake of defeat. To Jones, the exemplars of Lee, Jackson, and Davis represented the best of Southern piety; they also reflected divine approval of the Southern people and the Confederate cause.

✝ ✝ ✝ ✝ ✝

By the time Jones published his *Personal Reminiscences, Anecdotes, and Letters of Gen. Robert E. Lee* in 1874, he had for years served as Southern Baptists' authority on Lee's spiritual life. When Lee died in October 1870, Jones gladly shared with Baptists his personal encounters with Lee. He printed glowing eulogies in the *Religious Herald* and the *Christian Index*, much of which he would reprise for his *Personal Reminiscences* and his 1887 *Christ in the Camp*. He recounted his first meeting with Lee and how eager the general was to comply with his and B. T. Lacy's request that military work be reduced on the Sabbath. He also took an opportunity to praise Jackson, comforting readers that both men "now walk the streets of the new Jerusalem, strike together golden harps, and bask in the sunshine of the Saviour's smiles." He was confident that Jackson had been "permitted to welcome his beloved chief to that 'rest' which 'remaineth for the people of God.'"[4]

Jones continued his encomium by insinuating his apostle-like status. For example, he told the story of looking through Lee's Bible while "the *writer sat alone* with his body." He also gave readers special insights into Lee's religious character. Jones noted that Lee seldom spoke of his religious feelings, but that when he did, Lee made clear his "reliance for salvation upon the merits of his personal Redeemer." Jones also began his habit of painting Confederate heroes as transcending denominational distinctions. He wrote that "General Lee was a member of the *Episcopal church*, and was sincerely attached to the church of his choice; but his large heart took in Christians of every name; he treated the ministers of all denominations with the most marked courtesy and respect."[5] In fact, Jones concurred with another minister that Lee's "brotherly kindness and charity" were "boundless," and that it would have seldom occurred to non-Episcopalians that Lee belonged to a different church than they. Jones also suggested that Lee's denominational particularities were unapparent, even to those closest to the general. In a postwar context of denominational rivalry, Jones avoided making much of Lee's "non-Baptistness." One of many ways to enshrine Lee in the hearts of white Southerners was to demonstrate that sectarian particularities in no way limited the general's magnanimity.

Jones's 1874 *Personal Reminiscences* represented a major extension of Jones's authority beyond Southern Baptists, and from the outset of the book, he asserted his apostolic standing. More than once in his preface, Jones alleged to have "intimate" knowledge of Lee. Even though much of this knowledge came after the war, Jones claimed to have had frequent contact with the general during the conflict. As Jones unfolded his pedigree for readers, his opening remarks resembled the preface of a biblical gospel. He attested that he "was on that band of living hearts whose sad privilege it was to bear him [Lee] to the tomb," and he proudly announced that Lee's wife, Mary Custis Lee, trusted no one more than he to complete the work at hand.[6]

The remainder of Jones's book, more than five hundred pages, consisted of one superlative after the other. First, Jones insisted that Lee's soldiership was incomparable. In so doing, Jones endorsed stock tenets of the Lost Cause. He cited John B. Gordon, former Confederate general and Lost Cause proponent, who stated that "Lee was never really beaten. Lee could not be beaten! Overpowered, foiled in his efforts, he might be, but never defeated until the props which supported him gave way." Jones quoted Confederate cavalryman and eventual South Carolina politician, Wade Hampton, who stressed that Grant's only hope for defeating Lee was through superior numbers. Jones contributed that Lee possessed "transcendent abilities," declaring that history had never produced a soldier who was Lee's equal.[7]

Jones continued by attributing to Lee a host of professional and personal accolades. Looking to Lee's postwar career, Jones wrote that Lee was "*the best college president,* whom this country has ever produced." Jones indicated that duty was the "controlling principle of General Lee's life," an attribute that led Lee to leave the Union even while opposing secession. Jones portrayed Lee as the epitome of humility and gentleness, and he exploited Lee's similarity to George Washington, reminding readers that Lee had married into the Washington family.[8]

For Jones, Lee was the picture of self-denial and kindness. According to Jones, the general bivouacked with his men and would not accept more rations than other soldiers. Lee never partook in tobacco or whiskey and only seldom drank wine. Jones concluded that a historian would search in vain to find a "nobler example of self-denial." He also wrote that Lee harbored no bitterness toward the North. The harshest monikers Lee would use for Union troops were "our friends across the river," "these people," or "General Grant's people." Lee even gave money to a former Union veteran who was in need, an act that Jones thought exemplified the biblical injunction to feed a hungry enemy. Jones lamented that despite the eminence of Lee's virtue, "this noble man dies a 'prisoner of war on parole'—his application for 'amnesty' was never granted, or even noticed—and the commonest privileges of citizenship which are accorded to the most ignorant negro were denied to this *king of men*."[9] Here Jones's tone conveyed not only sympathy, but also his bitterness toward Reconstruction, out of which came the fourteenth and fifteenth amendments, providing for African American citizenship (1868) and African American male suffrage (1870), respectively.

Jones also attempted to undercut prevalent myths, reminding readers that he received his information directly from the general. For example, Jones denied that Lee's discussion of surrender terms with Grant occurred under an apple tree (which had since been chopped down by "relic-hunters"). He also countered claims of Grant's "magnanimity" toward Lee at Appomattox. Grant did not return Lee's sword to him, Jones stressed, because Lee never offered his sword to Grant. While Jones did not dispute Grant's generous surrender terms, he reminded his audience that Grant offered Lee the only terms Lee would accept. Jones also reiterated that Lee's surrender was the result of "overwhelming numbers and resources."[10]

Even though the theme permeated his book, Jones dedicated a special chapter to Lee's "Christian character." Lee was faithful in church attendance and prayer, promoted chaplaincy and colportage, enforced Davis's many calls for national fast days, and "always expressed his preference for those sermons which presented most simply and earnestly the soul-saving truths of the Gospel." Effusive in his adulation, Jones concluded: "If I have ever come in contact with a sincere, devout Christian—one who, seeing himself to be a sinner, trusted alone in the merits of Christ, who humbly tried to walk the path of duty, 'looking unto Jesus' as the author and finisher of his faith, and whose piety constantly exhibited itself in his daily life—that man was General R. E. Lee."[11]

One of the most prominent features of Jones's 1874 book was his portrayal of Lee as a Christ figure. A number of historians have recognized this symbolism in Jones's work.[12] Indeed, Jones's Christ imagery was pervasive. He described Lee as humble enough to associate with the most common soldier. In one instance, Lee anonymously helped a wounded soldier put on a coat. When one household presented Lee with a grand meal, he only ate beef and bread, explaining that he could not feast while his soldiers were starving. When the war ended, Lee resolved to share the fate of all Southerners rather than flee into exile as did other prominent figures. Recognizing their general's greatness, Lee's soldiers responded with almost religious devotion. When Lee shook the hand of a one-armed soldier, the soldier departed "rejoicing that he had the privilege of suffering under such a leader." One evening, while soldiers were discussing the "tenets of atheism" (by which Jones meant evolution), a soldier proclaimed that while "the rest of us may have developed from monkeys . . . I tell you none less than a God could have made such a man as 'Marse Robert!'" For Jones, Lee was clearly the "idol of his soldiers."[13]

Lee not only demonstrated concern for his soldiers but for all of creation. When Lee witnessed a forest fire in the distance, he immediately expressed concern for the animals. On another occasion, he traversed a yard contested with enemy fire and picked up a small sparrow that had fallen from its nest. The symbolism was not lost on Jones: "That loving Father, without whose knowledge not even one sparrow falleth to the ground, gave to the stern warrior a heart so tender that he could pause amid the death-dealing missiles of the battle-field to care for a helpless little bird."[14] God never lost sight of a sparrow, and according to Jones, neither did Robert E. Lee.

Jones drew other parallels between Lee and Christ. He contended that Lee endured criticism when others (subordinates) deserved the blame. Jones cited former Confederate general John S. Preston as saying that "God gave him [Lee] to us, to sanctify our faith, and to show us and the world that, although we might fail, his chosen servant had made that cause forever holy." Jones quoted Paul H. Hayne, Confederate veteran and poet, who said that in "civil, social, and domestic relations" Lee "appears to have been perfect." Hayne continued, "We scarcely exaggerate in saying that, since the death of the last of the Evangelists, probably no mortal man has passed through life, 'walking habitually nearer to his God,' in thought, conversation, worship, sublime simplicity of faith, in action." Virginia politician James P. Holcombe likened Lee's decision to surrender to Christ's decision in Gethsemane: "[N]one could have been brought into contact with him [Lee] in that dark hour of the soul's crucifixion, and have beheld the majesty with which his spirit rose triumphant above the weakness of the flesh, the steadiness with which his gaze was bent all through the spectral gloom which enveloped the path of duty."[15]

Depicting Lee as the South's suffering servant, minister T. V. Moore opined that Lee received his "death-wound" at Appomattox and thereafter "died of a broken heart." Crucifixion, however, was not the end of the story. Moore continued, "Other men had conquered victory; it was his [Lee's] sublime preeminence to conquer defeat, and transform it into the grandest triumph."[16] Just as Christ had transformed his "defeat" on the cross into an act of divine redemption, so too had Lee achieved victory and vindication after Appomattox. Simply put, Lee "conquered" by being a better person—militaristically, personally, professionally, religiously—than anyone the North had produced. God had given Lee—the anointed one—to God's chosen people. Lee's virtuous life proved that the South remained central in God's plan. Yes, the verdict of the war had gone against the South, but Jones and others prophesied that God would once again use defeat for the purposes of redemption.

In order to preserve Lee's image as a Christ figure, Jones portrayed the general as stainless in every respect. In fact, Jones resolved to protect his hero's reputation, even if it meant editing Lee's own correspondence.[17] In *Personal Reminiscences*, Jones cited an 1858 letter from Lee to his son, William Henry Fitzhugh (Rooney) Lee. The letter included general encouragement from Lee to his son, as well as a strict warning to avoid the "universal balm" (whiskey). Jones finished his citation innocuously: "Then follows some interesting items about army movements, family matters, etc." Jones neglected to include, though, what exactly these "army movements" and "family matters" were. The army movements in question were directed at a Mormon disturbance in Utah. The family matters, on the other hand, involved insubordinate slaves at Arlington. In the actual 1858 letter, Lee complained of having trouble with some of the "people" (a euphemism Lee used to refer to slaves). Lee continued that three slaves "rebelled against my authority—refused to obey my orders, & said they were as free as I was." Lee reprimanded the servants by having them put in jail, where they "resisted until overpowered."[18]

Jones surgically cited another letter in *Personal Reminiscences*, this time an 1862 letter from Lee to Rooney. Again, Jones quoted a portion of the letter in which Lee encouraged and advised his son, but he ignored one of the major thrusts of the letter: what was to be done with Arlington's slaves. When Lee's father-in-law, George Washington Parke Custis, died in 1857, his will indicated that his slaves were to be emancipated no later than five years after his death. Lee had hoped that within that time period his inherited slaves would help make Arlington plantation—in disarray after Custis's death—solvent. With the outbreak of war, however, Lee was unsure as to the practicality of releasing the slaves. While acknowledging that the courts had upheld the provisions of Custis's will, and while resolving to release the slaves as soon as possible, he confessed that emancipation would be fiscally problematic under the present conditions.[19]

Although Jones's selective quoting of Lee is striking, one can only speculate as to how many of the general's letters Jones ignored altogether. For instance, Jones may have taken it upon himself to omit a particularly problematic correspondence of Lee's from 1860. In this post, again to Rooney, Lee wrote that he was happy to hear of the "good conduct of the people." Lee then grudgingly confessed his intention to buy a slave. "I fear I shall have to purchase a servant," he wrote. "I find it almost impossible to hire one, & nearly all the officers in the Dept. have been obliged to resort to purchase." Lee explained that he was currently paying twenty dollars a month to use the servant of a major. He reiterated his reluctance, concluding that "I would rather hire a white man than purchase if I could."[20] Since Jones made no citation of the letter in his books, whether or not he knew of the correspondence is uncertain. Judging by Jones's editing of other Lee letters, however, it is safe to assume that Jones would have left this letter unpublished.

Jones's determination to downplay Lee's connection to slavery revealed a perpetual tension in the writings of Lost Cause advocates. On the one hand, Lost Cause writers, along with most white Southerners, fiercely denied that slavery had been an immoral enterprise. On the other hand, these same ex-Confederates stressed that slavery was not a cause of the war. Jones's writings exhibit this tension, as he distanced

Lee from slavery as if the South's peculiar institution would somehow tarnish the great chieftain's character. Likely, Jones saw nothing suspect in his editing of Lee's correspondence. In Jones's mind, Lee owning slaves did not diminish his greatness; at the same time, Jones was aware of the charged environment in which he published. As far as he was concerned, the less race and slavery figured into historical accounts of the war or the war's leaders, the better. Readers who mistakenly associated slavery with immorality would by extension associate immorality with Lee. To Jones, compromising Lee's stainless reputation was simply not worth that risk.

Another factor that may have prompted Lost Cause writers like Jones to tamp down Lee's (and the South's) connection with slavery was, as odd as it may sound, the desire for reconciliation. When Jones published *Personal Reminiscences* in 1874, the nation was in the throes of a financial depression that had begun the previous year. The crisis sapped the enthusiasm of many white Northerners for Radical Reconstruction, and Northern businesses pressed for sectional harmony for the sake of financial stability. Furthermore, many white Northerners increasingly came to believe that ending Reconstruction would curtail political and racial discord in the South.[21]

As many white Northerners tempered their feelings toward the South, white Southerners painted ex-Confederates as valiant warriors who had fought for what they believed to be right—a narrative many white Northerners came to accept. Hence Jones's rhetorical acrobatics in severing Lee from slavery were part of a broader initiative of white Southerners to sidestep slavery and to narrate the Civil War in terms of courage and honor. That Confederates had martialed these virtues for the perpetuation of slavery was beside the point for Jones. Distancing the Confederacy from slavery facilitated reconciliation, and reconciliation would enable Jones to weave Lee into the tapestry of American heroism.

Jones's 1874 book depicted Lee as a model in virtually every facet of life. Unsurprisingly, Jones also made Lee the picture of denominational cooperation. Echoing much of what he wrote in the *Religious Herald* in 1870, Jones conveyed that while Lee was a committed member of the Episcopal Church, the general treated non-Episcopalians with the utmost respect. Jones revealed that Lee avoided theological questions and instead resolved to be a "humble, earnest Christian."[22]

Lee's respect for other faiths was not limited to evangelicals. Jones recorded more than one story about Lee's treatment of Jewish soldiers. In one case, when an officer refused to allow a Jewish soldier to attend synagogue, Lee overrode the order and encouraged the officer to "respect the religious views and feelings of others." Lee did not, however, honor a rabbi's request that Jewish soldiers be given a general furlough. Constrained by the necessities of war, Lee responded that Jewish soldiers had to apply for furlough individually, as did everyone else. Lee added, though, that in other circumstances he would have liked to grant the request.[23] Note that Lee's attitude here is better described as respectful, rather than ecumenical. By contrast, the fraternity of evangelical chaplains entailed not only cordial relationships, but also a spirit of cooperation for the sake of the Christian gospel. In this sense, to call Lee's attitude toward Jews ecumenical is inaccurate (although some scholars of the Lost Cause have used the term just this broadly).[24] Jones's purpose here was merely to say that Lee — as a paradigm of love — respected those with religious beliefs different from his own.

As president at Washington College, Lee allowed evangelical pastors of various denominations to lead chapel on a rotating basis. Baptist, Methodist, Presbyterian, and Episcopalian ministers shared the college's pulpit. When a new student entered the college, Lee would introduce the student to a minister of the same denomination.[25] As was the case with Broadus and Jones, the college setting invited interdenominational contact, and even friendliness. Such comradery did not demand a dismissal of denominational differences, but an honoring of them. Evangelical chaplains could cooperate for the sake of evangelizing a diverse student body, but they did not envision or encourage a blurring of doctrinal distinctions.

While Jones did not downplay Lee's Episcopalianism, neither did Jones emphasize the fact. Jones took for granted that denominational distinctions were important, but he also felt that he could give readers a Lee whose love was broad enough to rise above sectarian squabbles. Lee was a figure whose virtue demanded respect from all people, North or South, Baptist or not. In the aforementioned 1858 letter from Lee to

Rooney, Jones even removed a section in which Lee expressed harsh feelings toward Mormons.[26] Of course, by excluding Lee's comments about Mormons, Jones was not trying to show that Lee was open to Mormon beliefs. The vast majority of Jones's readership would have hardly objected to the general's anti-Mormon sentiments. The point was that Lee's love transcended all ill will, even ill will that readers would have found quite justified. For Jones, and for the rest of the white South, Lee had to rise above the pettiness and weaknesses of his contemporaries. In other words, Lee had to be more than human. By apotheosizing Lee, Lost Cause writers assured readers that God still favored the chosen people. Lee became for ex-Confederates the tangible assurance of God's continued presence. Through Lee, white Southerners felt close to God.

✢ ✢ ✢ ✢ ✢

For Jones, Lee remained unrivaled. This conviction did not prevent Jones, however, from exalting other Confederate luminaries, such as Stonewall Jackson. In fact, white Southerners began mythologizing the life and career of the general even before the war ended. John Esten Cooke, who served under both J. E. B. Stuart and William Pendleton, published his *Life of Stonewall Jackson* in 1863, the same year Jackson died. After the war, other prominent names venerated the fallen leader. Robert L. Dabney, a Presbyterian chaplain during the war, released his *Life and Campaigns of Lieut.-Gen. Thomas J. Jackson* in 1866. Eventually, even Jackson's widow, Mary Anna Jackson, would contribute volumes honoring her husband.[27]

If white Southerners were looking for heroes, Jackson was a natural choice. He espoused a nearly fanatical faith and represented to Southerners the perfect synthesis of Christianity and masculinity. Not only did his example demonstrate that Southerners were more pious than Northerners; it also indicated that Confederates were superior to Union soldiers. Killed soon after his successful flanking maneuver at the battle of Chancellorsville, Jackson had died in his prime. Furthermore, he had been cut down by his own men. While a cruel twist of fate in one respect, Jackson's death at the hands of his own people also meant that the enemy had not overcome him. Ex-Confederates could thus honor Jackson as the "only unconquered general."[28]

With Jackson's myth growing, some felt that Lee's reputation would necessarily suffer. After all, Jackson had been killed in the midst of victory; Lee, on the other hand, had surrendered. Some scholars have made much of the Jackson-Lee rivalry, proposing that Lee's followers downplayed Jackson's abilities in order to promote Lee.[29] These observations, however, can be misleading. Writers like Jones did redirect credit from Jackson to Lee from time to time, but Jones did not view the matter as a zero-sum game. Even in his 1874 book on Lee, Jones highlighted the supreme confidence that Lee placed in Jackson. Although Jones cited a letter from Lee asserting that Jackson had not conceived of the Chancellorsville maneuver in isolation, Jones commented, "Those who have attempted to institute comparisons between Lee and Jackson, or to exalt one at the expense of the other, have utterly misapprehended the character of both."[30] Indeed, Jones would come to portray both chieftains as embodiments of Christian virtue and martial brilliance.

Jones compiled no book-length work on Jackson (as he did with Lee and Davis), but he provided a 120-page appendix to John Esten Cooke's 1876 book, *Stonewall Jackson: A Military Biography*. Here again Jones stressed the deep affection Jackson and Lee had for one another, writing that "[t]he rising fame of Jackson excited no envy in the bosom of Lee; but the praises of the lieutenant were most heartily indorsed by the commander-in-chief, who gave him his full confidence and warm personal friendship." Jones quoted Lee as saying that the Confederates would have won the Battle of Gettysburg, and Southern independence by extension, had Jackson been there. Jones also quoted Jackson as saying that Lee was the only person he would follow blindfolded.[31]

Jones used the remainder of the Cooke appendix to laud a host of Jackson's personal and professional virtues. Jones highlighted the general's simplicity, humility, and modesty. Jackson was so "plain-looking" and "awkward" that Jones even failed to recognize the general at their first meeting. Jones did not overlook Jackson's eccentricities, such as the general's hypochondria, or his belief that one side of his body was heavier than the other (an unbalance Jackson corrected by keeping one arm lifted so that blood would distribute evenly). Jackson also believed in simple obedience to orders. On one occasion, he continued wearing a thick, wool uniform in the heat of the summer because he had not been ordered to wear anything else. Idiosyncrasies aside, Jackson was modest; he was quick to give credit to his men and to direct to God any glory that came from victory.[32]

Jones praised Jackson's military genius, boasting that the general could intuitively anticipate the moves of the enemy and that his forced marches were legendary. Jackson was the ideal blend of fight and faith, and Jones quoted Presbyterian minister Moses D. Hoge as stating that "[m]en cannot now think of Jackson without associating the prowess of the soldier with the piety of the man." Jones was still careful not to praise Jackson at Lee's expense, writing of Lee's "bold strategy" and Jackson's "splendid executive ability." As brilliant as Jackson was on the field of battle, Jones subtly reminded readers that Jackson carried out the orders he received from Lee.[33]

As Jackson had exemplified greatness in life, so did he in death. Jones cited the account of Hunter McGuire, a physician who attended the general and witnessed his last hours. McGuire insisted that Jackson maintained "complete control" of his mind after he was wounded. According to the doctor, Jackson was fully resigned to the divine will. Jackson saw his injuries as a blessing, believing that his wounding would work for his ultimate good. So confident was he in the wisdom of Providence, the general testified that if he had the power, he would not replace his amputated arm unless he was sure the restoration was God's will. As death drew near, a delirious Jackson shouted a military order and then composed himself enough to utter, "Let us cross over the river, and rest under the shade of the trees." Hunter's account of Jackson's death reflects the value nineteenth-century Americans placed on "dying well." The general epitomized the "good death" by facing his end with serenity and a sense of divine Providence.[34]

As was his practice with other Confederate icons, Jones singled out Jackson's Christian character. Jones described Jackson as dedicated both to Bible study and to prayer. A "diligent student of the Bible," the general would rise before dawn to consult the scriptures. So frequent was his Bible study that one minister mistook him for a chaplain. Jackson was also committed to a literal reading of the biblical injunction to pray without ceasing. Soldiers attested that they witnessed Jackson lifting his hands in the midst of battle and that those nearby could hear his "ejaculatory prayers." On other occasions, witnesses observed Jackson pacing in the woods and praying audibly. He prayed before meals, before drinking water, and even before mailing letters. When his pastor visited Jackson in camp, the minister confessed to having received more instruction than he imparted. Jones too admitted that he had to "lay aside my office of 'teacher in Israel,' and be content to 'sit at the feet' of the great warrior."[35]

Jones emphasized Jackson's care for African Americans, and thus echoed a common Lost Cause belief that slaves had been satisfied with their prewar status. Jones discussed Jackson's commitment to a "colored Sunday-school" and observed Jackson's concern for the "good of the negro children, whose true friend and benefactor he had always been." Jones continued: "Jackson was one of the most thoroughly conscientious masters who ever lived. He not only treated his negroes kindly, but he devoted himself most assiduously to their religious instruction. He was not only accustomed (as were Christian masters generally at the South) to invite his servants in to family prayers, but he also had a special meeting with them every Sunday afternoon in order to teach them the Scriptures."[36] Jones maintained that Jackson was influential over the African Americans of his region and that "to this day his memory is warmly cherished by them." Jones then told the story of a young African American boy, a member of the general's Sunday school, who placed a Confederate flag on his fallen teacher's grave. Hoge concluded that during a time when "political economists abandon the weaker races to the law of natural selection," Jackson "sought to place the gentle but strong and sustaining hand of Christianity beneath the African population of the South, and so arrest the operation of that law by developing them, if possible, into a self-sustaining people."[37]

For Jones, Jackson had been the model Christian. He "took Jesus as his Saviour, his guide, his great exemplar, 'the Captain of his salvation,' whom he followed with the unquestioning obedience of the true soldier." His life was emblematic of a "simple-hearted, earnest piety" and of one whose "entire trust was in the living God." He worshipped alongside the "humblest private" and was "content to share the hardships and privations of his men." Jackson also modeled denominational cooperation, a sentiment Jones endorsed by citing Hoge:

> Those who imagine that his [Jackson's] faith savored of bigotry do not know that one characteristic of his religion was its generous catholicity, as might well be inferred from the fact that the first spiritual guides whose instructions he sought were members of communions widely different in doctrine and polity; that when he connected himself with the church of his choice it was with doubts of the truth of some of its articles and doctrines . . . ; that nothing so rejoiced his heart, during the process of the war, as the harmony existing between the various denominations represented in the army; that in selecting his personal staff, and in recommending men for promotion, merit was the sole ground, and their ecclesiastical relations were never even considered; that, with a charity which embraced all who held the cardinal truths of revelation, he ardently desired such a unity of feeling and concert of action among all the followers of the same Divine Leader as would constitute one spiritual army, glorious and invincible.[38]

Interesting here is Hoge's implication that an army united in faith would be invincible. The circumstances of war prompted ministers of differing denominations to join hands for the sake of the Confederate cause. As Jackson's example demonstrated, a Christian army was a victorious army.

Regarding Jackson's death, Jones suggested that the general's "fatal disease" occurred the night *before* the battle of Chancellorsville and was the result of Jackson giving his only bed covering to a young staff officer who was sleeping near him.[39] By referring to Jackson's incipient pneumonia, Jones was tapping into a specific narrative of the general's death. While recovering from his wounds, Jackson had developed and died from pneumonia. Subsequently, some Southerners theorized that Jackson had developed pneumonia before being wounded. Such a story served a number of important functions for ex-Confederates. First, this narrative took the sting out of admitting that Jackson had been killed by his own men. Second, the story served a theological function. White

Southerners had to reconcile the idea that God had inscrutably allowed the chosen army to destroy its own leader. Many reasoned that Jackson's death was a divine chastisement on the Confederacy for making Jackson into an idol, and a reminder that God alone was the author of victory. Still, the idea that Jackson had agency in his own death was more palatable than the idea that Confederates had ironically destroyed their own object of worship. Third, the narrative protected Jackson from criticism. Jones defended Jackson for riding in front of Confederate lines under the cover of darkness, noting that such reconnaissance was not unusual. The story of Jackson forfeiting his only blanket imbued his death with an air of self-sacrifice. Even though Jackson was shot by his own troops, Southerners could still view him as a martyr. Of course, with or without such narratives, Southerners would have described their leaders as self-sacrificial. Jackson's story, however, was a clear example of a Christlike general who willingly laid down his life for those under his care. As was the case with Lee, Jackson's life imparted to white Southerners a godly example worthy of emulation.

✤ ✤ ✤ ✤ ✤

Along with Lee and Jackson, Jefferson Davis captured the imagination of postwar Southerners. Davis's canonization, however, was neither expeditious nor unchallenged. Federal troops captured the Confederate president in May 1865, and Davis served two years in prison. Upon his release, the Davis family moved to Canada and then to Tennessee. Davis also spent time in England before finally settling at the Beauvoir plantation in Biloxi, Mississippi in the late 1870s. Here Davis would complete his massive work, *The Rise and Fall of the Confederate Government* (1881). From Jones's position as secretary of the SHS, he was able to supply Davis with requested resources. Davis's postwar reputation had taken a severe hit as authors like E. A. Pollard placed blame for Confederate defeat largely on Davis's shoulders. In response, Jones was determined to rehabilitate the former president. In December 1877, Jones wrote to Davis: "I need not assure you again that your fame is dear to our Va people (whatever the few may say)—that the President of our Society, Gen. Early, and the members of the Executive Committee generally are your warm admirers—and that nothing will give us more pleasure than to do everything in our power to put right on the record that able statesman, gallant soldier, pure patriot, and accomplished gentleman who presided over the Confederacy."[40] In the spring of 1886, Davis's reputation received the boost it needed as he embarked on a tour of Southern states in order to speak at monument dedications. Crowds were overwhelmingly receptive to the ex-president.[41]

Four years before the 1886 tour, Jones had requested that Davis embark on a lecture circuit of the Southern states. While Jones may have seen the tour as an opportunity to raise funds for the struggling SHS,[42] there is no reason to believe that he did not attempt to foster a genuine friendship with Davis, much as Jones had done with Lee. Jones visited Beauvoir, and Winnie, Davis's daughter, made lengthy visits to the Jones family. Furthermore, Jones was open about his motivations, admitting to the ex-president that a speaking tour would be financially beneficial for the society. In addition to the "saving and establishing" of the SHS, though, Jones wanted Southerners to have an opportunity to give their former leader a "grand ovation."[43]

As far as Jones was concerned, he had cultivated an intimate relationship with Davis. For this reason, after Davis died in 1889, Jones felt particularly qualified to publish an opus on the leader's life and career. Many authors had been vying for the endorsement of Davis's wife, Varina, who herself anticipated publishing a volume on her husband. Jones convinced Varina that his book would not compete with her own and that he would make certain to divide the proceeds with her.[44] In 1889, Jones published the *Davis Memorial Volume*, informing readers that he had done so under the authority of Mrs. Davis.

Predictably, Jones began his more than six-hundred-page work by providing readers with his apostolic credentials. "Other pens will give detailed sketches of his [Davis's] eventful life," Jones wrote, "be it mine only to recall here some personal reminiscences of the *man* as I knew him, honored him, and loved him." Jones boasted of being a frequent visitor to Beauvoir and of possessing more than fifty letters from Davis—each marked "personal" or "confidential"—which Jones clung to as priceless relics.[45] Jones wrote, "I speak of my own personal knowledge and intimate intercourse with him when I say that Mr. Davis was one of the humblest, most intelligent, most decided evangelical Christians whom I have ever known." He spoke of Davis's private life at home, telling readers that "I had in my intimate personal intercourse with him the most abundant evidence that he took Christ as his personal Saviour; that he rested with child-like trust in the grand old doctrines of salvation by grace, justification by faith, and that he rejoiced in the sweet comforts and precious hope of the Gospel."[46] As he had done so often, Jones revealed to readers that he possessed a special knowledge of his subject, and that of all people, he could bear witness to God's presence in the life of the Confederacy's president.

Recounting Davis's life and career, Jones spared no superlative. In college, Davis was dedicated to duty and committed to study. He was an ideal soldier in the wars against Native Americans as well as a hero of the Mexican-American War. Jones also credited Davis for inventing both military tactics and weaponry. He was among the best senators, unrivaled as an orator, and the heir apparent to John C. Calhoun. In his service to the US government, he was the "greatest War Secretary the United States ever had." At every stage of his life, Davis had risen above all others. Jones reflected on the reasons behind Southerners' esteem for the ex-president, concluding that "the intelligent people of our Southland have long since repudiated the fallacy that 'success makes right,' and that *this* is the criterion by which to judge a cause."[47]

Much of Jones's book was an apology for Davis and the Confederacy. Jones cited one newspaper that expressed the matter thusly: "[H]istory—cold, calm, impartial, unbeclouded history—will do justice to the great dead." Jones demanded this justice by systematically refuting each rumor that had dogged the aging Davis. Jones dedicated an entire chapter—albeit one lacking in suspense—to the query, "Was Davis a Traitor?" Jones defended the right to secede, with one writer comparing secession to the Old Testament schism between the kingdoms of Israel and Judah. Just as Solomon's heavy taxation galvanized the ten northern tribes to secede, the argument went, so too had the US government's overreaching hand provoked the secession of the Southern states. Jones argued that his champion had been a Unionist, and he denied that Davis had advocated for secession in order seize the Confederate presidency. Jones also rebutted claims that Davis was responsible for the cruel treatment of Union soldiers, the onus of which fell on Grant, who had suspended prisoner exchange. At every point, Jones strove to exonerate Davis from guilt and to protect him from embarrassment. Jones even uprooted very specific rumors, such as one attesting that Davis had left church in a panic when he received Lee's message to evacuate Richmond. Another persistent rumor was that when Federal troops captured Davis, he had been wearing his wife's clothes. Jones went to great lengths to quash the story, even citing Union troops in order to do so.[48]

Even while Jones dismissed slavery as a fundamental cause of the war, his quotations of Davis and others were sometimes categorical defenses of the institution. Jones quoted Davis as saying that the rhetoric of equality in the Declaration of Independence had nothing to do with slaves. The ex-president was quick to point out that America's founders had not put slaves on the same level as whites, but instead considered each slave three-fifths of a person. Jones also cited a newspaper that complained of Davis's disenfranchisement while these privileges were given to "the millions of ignorant, irresponsible, and semi-barbarous negroes."[49]

Jones quoted a writer as saying that eighteenth-century England forced a reluctant Virginia to have slaves and that Northerners had resisted attempts to restrict slave traffic. Jones even cited his own work on the matter, arguing that it was a "slander alike upon the character of her [Virginia's] people and the motives which impelled her to secede and join the confederacy, to represent her as a cold, calculating, negro-trader, only influenced by the hope of gain in raising negroes for the Southern market." Calling into question the profitability of slavery, Jones continued, "The truth is that the average Virginia planter would mortgage his plantation and well nigh ruin his estate to support his negroes in comparative idleness before he would sell them." The idea that slaves were raised for the market, Jones maintained, was "a romance of abolition invention which fully served its purpose in the bitter controversies of the slavery agitation."[50]

Jones also quoted a revealing speech from Virginia Senator John W. Daniel. Daniel contended that "hatred to Union or love of slavery" had no more driven Southerners than "love of the negro" had animated Northerners. Instead, Daniel traced Northern motivations to "rivalry of cheap negro labor" and "aversion to the negro and to slavery alike." By contrast, Daniel declared that "race integrity" had roused Southerners, as did something Daniel called "free white dominion." Expounding on the concept of race integrity—the "predominant characteristic of the Anglo-Saxon race"—Daniel went on: "Fiercely did it sweep the red men before it; swiftly did it brush away the Chinese in the West and North, burning their homes, cutting their throats when they pressed too hard in rivalry, and then breaking treaties to hurl them back across the Pacific ocean to their native shores. Four million of black men lived in the South side by side with the white race; and race integrity now incensed the South to action."[51] If four million slaves were set free, Daniel asked, how could the South prevent racial "contamination"? The question precluding emancipation in Virginia, according to Daniel, was this: "Kill slavery—what will you do with the corpse?" Aside from Daniel's candid defense of white superiority, his speech was striking for its admission of slavery's central role in the war. Comparing the Civil War to the American Revolution, Daniel observed, "Each revolution concluded the question that induced it. Slavery was the cause of our civil war, and with the war its cause perished."[52] Although Jones avoided excessive talk of slavery and race in his panegyrics, Daniel's speech stood out for its blatant support of white hegemony and its admission that slavery had been a central factor in the onset of war.

For Jones, Davis was also the personification of virtue. He never gambled, was never intoxicated, and eschewed vices of every kind. Jones's admiration of Davis went beyond Davis's stainless life. Jones saw Davis, as did other white Southerners, as a Christ figure. Davis had suffered imprisonment for two years, enduring mistreatment in "ways such as only the refinement of cruelty could invent." Calling Davis a "noble martyr for his people," Jones proclaimed that Davis "suffered in the room of his people, went to prison for them, had indignity put upon him, and was hated, slandered, maltreated and ostracized in the land he had served so faithfully—all *for them*." Indeed, Davis had laid his "life on the altar of southern independence."[53]

Jones cited minister T. R. Markham, who spoke of the "crime" and "treason" of recanting one's dedication to the Confederate cause. Markham maintained that Southerners were not guilty of this crime, but had they been, Davis "would have expiated that crime by the shedding of his blood." Markham continued: "Never would he have stepped forth a free man from that fortress where they bound him in fetters of iron—fetters that we esteem anklets of gold, for he wore them for us. Chains whose clank makes music to our ears, for the sound has in it the martyr ring. Relics of his sufferings, which in our keeping would be held as Christians hold the wood of the cross."[54] Another speaker called Davis "a people's vicarious sufferer," while former Confederate general S. D. Lee announced that "[e]very shaft fell on his [Davis's] devoted and defenseless head, and nobly did he suffer for us all." As Davis had represented the South as president, another tribute testified, he also represented the South in suffering.[55]

By 1889, Jones had made his case that Lee, Jackson, and Davis had all given their lives for the Confederacy. Their virtues were worthy of imitation, Jones believed, and their memories were worthy of respect. Jones was fulfilling his mission to preserve the "name and fame" of Southern paragons and to prepare the way for future historians who might provide an "impartial" account of the war. Jones's charge, however, was not simply to preserve an accurate story. By lauding the virtues of the Confederate trinity, he tapped into some of the most deep-seated psychological needs of postwar white Southerners. Jones knew that in order for his narrative to touch Southerners, his story needed something more than abstract apologies; he needed to provide white Southerners with icons—tangible means of accessing the holy.

✣ ✣ ✣ ✣ ✣

A primary aspect of Jones's apostolic errand was to direct readers toward incarnations of Southern virtue. He executed this mission not just by venerating the Confederate cause, but by apotheosizing specific Confederate figures. Essentially, his works on Lee, Jackson, and Davis served a dual function. On one hand, Jones encouraged Southerners to emulate the

Christian merits of his Confederate heroes. In so doing, the defeated South—defined by its piety—could remain just as distinct as the prewar South. On the other hand, Jones's works were testaments to God's continued presence with white Southerners. By focusing on Southern leaders, Jones wrapped the Confederate cause in flesh. These incarnations served as proof that God had been immanently present with the Confederacy.

One way of appreciating the incarnational aspects of Jones's writing is by setting his work alongside another piece of Lost Cause literature. Jones's 1887 *Christ in the Camp* serves as a good case study. Jones published in the *Religious Herald* large portions of what would become *Christ in the Camp*, and only after readers of the periodical pled with Jones did he agree to transform his serial into a full-length book.[56] When he published his volume in 1887, readers embraced it. Finally, white Southerners had a substantial volume that focused on the Confederate revivals and provided yet another proof that God had been present with the Southern people and sympathetic with the Southern cause. Jones's work, however, was not the first of its kind. A decade earlier, another Confederate chaplain, William W. Bennett, had published a very similar work. Yet Jones's book resonated with white Southerners in a way that Bennett's did not. The reason why revolves around Jones's employment of incarnational hagiography.

William W. Bennett published *A Narrative of the Great Revival* in 1877, ten years before Jones released *Christ in the Camp*. Bennett's background was similar to Jones's. Bennett was a native Virginian and had been ordained as a Methodist minister prior to the war. During the conflict, Bennett served as Confederate chaplain and as superintendent of the Soldiers'Tract Association. After the war, Bennett ministered through circuit preaching, and in 1867, he became editor of the *Christian Advocate* in Richmond. In 1877, Bennett became president of Randolph Macon College in Ashland, Virginia, a position he held for nearly ten years. That same year he composed *A Narrative of the Great Revival*. He died on June 9, 1887 and was buried in Richmond, Virginia.[57]

At first glance, Bennett's *A Narrative of the Great Revival* is remarkably similar to Jones's *Christ in the Camp*. For instance, both books begin on a "conciliatory" note. Bennett's tone was surprisingly mollifying when he wrote that "the people of the North and of the South fought with equal earnestness for principles regarded by each as essential to the well-being of the American people." Similarly, Jones extended his olive branch, writing, "Let its [the war's] stormy passions, its animosities, its bitter memories be buried forever beneath the wave of forgetfulness. And let us thank God that men who 'wore the blue' and men who 'wore the gray' may meet once more in friendly reunion." Perhaps many white Southerners were hungry for a work light on reconciliation and heavy on defense. But in terms of tentative bridge-mending, the opening pages of Bennett's and Jones's books were very much alike.[58]

Not surprisingly, what Bennett and Jones gave with one hand, they took away with another. Acknowledging that the North fought "to maintain the Union" while the South fought for the "right of self-government," Bennett avowed that the North was the aggressor in the war. He continued by defending the South's treatment of slaves, by declaring that state sovereignty was the vision of the "fathers of the Republic," by deeming Union forces an invading army, and by implying that Northerners trusted in superior numbers while Southerners trusted in God.[59]

Jones's defense of the South resembled Bennett's. In the introduction to *Christ in the Camp*, former Confederate chaplain J. C. Granberry wrote, "Some narrow and prejudiced Federals may not be able to understand how it was possible for those men to be saved without repenting of 'the sin of rebellion.' We cannot waste time on them." Though trying to restrain his bias, Jones too betrayed the cracks in his objectivity, noting that Southerners were fully justified in "resisting the invasion of their soil." Jones was equally bitter about Reconstruction. He bemoaned what he called the "'carpet bag' and 'negro rule' of the Southern States," which he judged to be a "blot upon our history, at which every true American should blush." Like Bennett, Jones harbored noticeable resentment about the war and its aftermath. Yet between the two books, neither defended the South more stridently than the other. Both pieces carried a conciliatory tone, and both works subsequently undercut this tone by exonerating the South and demonizing the North. As neither work stood head and shoulders above the other in terms of a Southern apologia, one must look elsewhere to determine what exactly set these two volumes apart.[60]

Another explanation for the books' disparate popularity could be that one of the authors portrayed Confederate troops in a more positive light. Both men, however, were equally critical of improprieties in the Confederate ranks, and both described pre-revival camp life as fraught with moral danger. Bennett griped over the "example of wicked and licentious officers and men." Likewise, Jones admitted that vice ran rampant in the Confederate camps. Neither author gave a glowing review of pre-revival soldiers.[61]

Although both opuses were popular with white Southern readership, Jones's book found more traction than did Bennett's. As a result, Jones's text was reprinted multiple times in his lifetime (1887, 1888, 1893, and 1904). By contrast, Bennett's 1877 work was not reprinted again until 1957.[62] There are a number of reasons that Jones's book thrived in a way that Bennett's did not, many of these reasons being external to the texts of the books themselves. Scholars have recognized that it was not until the late 1880s that Lost Cause activities (such as involvement with Confederate veterans' associations) grew in popularity.[63] Jones's 1887 work was thus part of this late 1880s wave of Lost Cause sentiment. Still, a spike in Lost Cause sentiment only explains why Jones's work was popular, not why Bennett's work was not resurrected to enjoy similar popularity.

Another explanation for the reception of *Christ in the Camp* could be that Jones simply wrote a *better book*. The problem with this theory is that historians disagree over which book is better![64] Thus style and scope only partially account for the success of *Christ in the Camp*. A more likely explanation for the popularity of Jones's work was the popularity of Jones himself. By the time Jones published his book, he was already well established as an author of the Lost Cause.[65] As secretary of the shs, he kept his finger on the pulse of Southern sentiment. Indeed, many white Southerners gravitated to Jones's work simply because of his name. But Jones's fame alone does not explain why his book—so similar to Bennett's—provoked such an enthusiastic response. Neither does Jones's reputation illuminate why he felt it necessary to contribute yet another lengthy volume on religion in the Confederate Army. He was fully aware of Bennett's work—even praising Bennett's book in *Christ in the Camp*—yet Jones felt that there was still a significant contribution to be made and that only someone with his apostolic status could make it.

Although he published his manuscript ten years after Bennett, Jones insisted that he had begun his book as soon as the war ended. In his preface he wrote, "In 1865 I was solicited by many of my fellow-chaplains and old comrades, and by General Lee himself, to prepare this chapter of our history." While Jones did not directly compare his work to Bennett's, he did note that any account of the Confederate Army that omitted a discussion of religion or the "humble piety and evangelical zeal of many of its officers and men" was both "incomplete and unsatisfactory."[66] Jones's narrative would be different. He would testify to the virtue not only of the Confederate rank-and-file but of the South's most beloved officers. He would also assure readers that Lee had personally charged him to complete such a work. As Christ had commissioned his apostles to spread the Christian gospel, the South's great chief had commissioned Jones to preserve and promulgate the Confederate gospel. Jones would do just that. His book, unlike Bennett's, would focus on the pious lives of Confederate leaders. By giving his readers incarnations of Christian virtue, Jones would remind a dispirited South that God remained near.

For Bennett, the Confederate brass were flawed and thoroughly human. By the time he published his narrative, he had become perturbed with the memorial movement of the 1870s.[67] His book reflected as much, arguing that the piety of chaplains and soldiers had exceeded that of their leaders. In this respect, Jones's work stood in sharp contrast. For Jones, the power of the officers' morality had spread throughout the army. To drive home the point, Jones dedicated three chapters to the Christian example of Confederate officers. Bennett included no such chapter.

Jones spent nearly one-fifth of his book lauding Southern leaders, citing Jackson and Davis almost twice as many times as did Bennett.[68] Jones described Lee as the "idol of his people and the admiration of the world," calling him "one of the noblest specimens of the Christian sol- dier that the world ever saw." According to Jones, Lee regularly attended church, supported churches financially, was a man of prayer, encouraged Bible distribution among the troops, and respected the religious views of others. Concerning Jackson, Jones wrote that the general's piety "seemed to brighten as the pure gold is refined by the furnace." As he had done in other works, Jones again illustrated Jackson's almost fanatical dedication to "ceaseless prayer." Jones also heaped praise upon the one he called the Confederacy's "Christian President." He claimed that Davis was an ardent supporter of colportage, that he credited God with Confederate victories, and that he exemplified a "humble, devout piety." By focusing intently and intimately on Lee, Jackson, and Davis, Jones provided white Southerners unparalleled access to the Confederate triumvirate.[69]

Robert Penn Warren once noted Southerners' "instinctive fear ... that the massiveness of experience, the concreteness of life, will be violated; the fear of abstraction."[70] Indeed, the postwar South labored under the burden of abstraction. The flame of their inchoate nation now extinguished, white Southerners grappled with the idea of a South without a Confederacy. The prominent Lee historian, Douglas Southall Freeman, observed, "[i]t is impossible to realize now what the death of the Confederacy meant to the South. . . . [S]uddenly, the South found itself eleven conquered States — each one of which felt itself in a strange manner the guardian of a disembodied Confederacy and the defender of its history."[71] Disembodiment was not the only affliction of the postwar South; white Southerners also wrestled with spiritual alienation, or in the words of historians Thomas Connelly and Barbara Bellows, an "*estrangement* from their Creator."[72] Orphaned postwar Southerners needed concrete affirmation of God's continued presence.

To Jones, only incarnations of Southern virtue could bridge the gap between God and a disembodied South. An apostle — one who had personally encountered the greatness of these incarnations — could give white Southerners access to the tangible assurance that God favored the Southern people and the Confederate cause. Viewed in isolation from this mission, Jones could come across as merely an obsequious, star-struck ex-Confederate who dropped names in order to establish credibility and enhance his own reputation.[73] While Jones was certainly not immune to sycophancy, what is vital to recognize is the inescapably religious underpinning of his claims. What modern-day readers might dismiss as name-dropping, Jones understood to be a record of apostolic pedigree. By testifying to his personal interaction with Confederate leaders, he bore witness to what he had heard, what he had seen with his eyes, and what he had touched with his hands.[74]

Jones's use of incarnational hagiography was the chief reason his book resonated with postwar white Southerners in a way that Bennett's work did not. In general, white Southerners navigated their spiritual alienation in two ways. One approach — induced by the desire to reconcile a loving and all-powerful God with the carnage of the war — was to stress the inscrutability of the divine purpose.[75] A second approach, heralded particularly by Lost Cause advocates, was to locate the divine presence in Confederate "saints." Here is where works like Jones's became so indispensable. Whereas the war had made God seem distant, mysterious, and unapproachable, the revivals — as recorded by Jones — portrayed God's presence as immanent and pervasive.

In essence, Jones's hagiographical treatment of Confederate officers gave white Southerners access to the holy. By describing each of his subjects with Christlike imagery, Jones enabled Southerners to trust that Confederate leaders had suffered vicariously for them. Lee had endured the humiliation of Appomattox; Jackson had forfeited his life; Davis had suffered the indignity of imprisonment. Though all Southerners suffered in the wake of defeat, these three bore the brunt of Northern aggression. And Jones believed that, like Christ, they would one day be vindicated.[76]

The Confederate leaders of Jones's *Christ in the Camp* were not merely exemplars of Southern virtue, but incarnations of it. Bennett painted a somber picture of his Confederate leaders sleeping in "lonely graves" on the field of battle.[77] Jones, on the other hand, celebrated Confederate officers as vibrant and victorious. More importantly, Jones's heroes gave a face to the revivals he recounted. Bennett's record of the revivals was thorough, but it remained abstract and disembodied. For Jones, God's presence was tangible; one needed only to look at the virtuous lives of his Confederate icons, the embodiments of Southern piety and divine presence.

Jones felt that his interactions with Confederate leaders placed him in a unique position. He reminded readers that he had followed the army throughout the war's duration and that he was confident in his ability to provide an accurate history of the Confederate Army. "For such a work," he wrote, "I think that I may (without improper egotism)

claim some special qualifications."[78] For Jones, these special qualifications included his status as an apostle of the Confederacy. He had
known his heroes, spoken with them, fought with them, prayed with
them, and received a personal commission to tell their story. His work
would thus spread the Confederate gospel and direct white Southerners
to Confederate saints who were accessible in a time when God's plan
remained painfully mysterious.

✟ ✟ ✟ ✟ ✟

Just as Jones's incarnational hagiography brought Southerners close to
God, Jones's emphasis on interdenominational cooperation brought
Southerners close to one another. Of course, even Christian cooperation
had its limits, as Jones held no real affinity for Roman Catholics and continued to view non-Baptist denominations as competitors. Still, Jones was
willing to network with various denominations in service to his apostolic
mission. Far from necessitating that Jones mute his Baptist particularities, this collaboration enabled him to craft works with broad appeal
among white Southerners. Key was that Jones's Confederate paradigms
exhibit virtues that transcended denominational boundaries. Through his
sweeping panegyrics, Jones fabricated what historian Zachary Dresser has
described as a "common southern mode of piety."[79]

There was an identifiable pattern in Jones's hagiographies. In his
major works on Lee, Jackson, and Davis, Jones constructed a common
mode of piety by highlighting similar qualities in each of his three models.
According to Jones, all three were avid students of the Bible, devoted to
prayer, and regular church attendees. Jones maintained that each leader
also wanted religion to play a more significant role in the Confederate
armies. For example, Lee ordered his soldiers to observe fast days, and
upon Jones's recommendation, Lee decreased the amount of work allowed
on the Sabbath. Jackson valued preaching in his ranks, and Jones boasted
that Jackson's corps was the best supplied with it.[80] Jones also described
Davis as a strong advocate of colportage.

Jones praised all three figures as peace-loving and adamantly against
a war with the North. He asserted that Lee would have surrendered

all the slaves to avoid bloodshed and that Jackson too had pled to God for peace. Davis also exhausted efforts to avert war, and for Jones, the North was ultimately guilty for instigating armed conflict. Davis had the US Constitution on his side, Jones reasoned. By attacking the South for "peaceably" exercising its constitutional right to secede from the Union, the North—not Davis—was the "rebel" against the law and the "traitor" to the Constitution.[81]

Jones also placed a high premium on character. He claimed to possess a personal and intimate knowledge of his leaders, and he made a point to highlight their humility and simplicity. Jones stated that Lee was humble in spirit and simple in dress. Jackson was so humble, Jones maintained, that at first he was struck at how inelegant and ordinary the general appeared. As to Davis, the Confederate president was one of the humblest men Jones ever knew. Important for Jones was that his readers not only admire the superior character of Lee, Jackson, and Davis, but that they imitate it as well. Jones emphasized that Lee refrained from tobacco and strong drink. Jackson too was the picture of abstinence. Jones wrote that the "young men of the country who think that it is *manly* to drink, and cowardly to refuse, would do well to study and imitate the example" of leaders like Jackson. Jones also cited sources testifying that Davis had never been under the influence of liquor. In Jones's mind, these archetypes of Christian goodness served as vehicles for championing those virtues most essential for postbellum Southerners.[82]

Jones also described his three paragons as self-sacrificial, going as far as to declare them martyrs. Content to eat meager meals when his men ran short of rations, Lee embodied a spirit of self-denial. Jackson's concern for his men ran just as deep (recall that by sharing his blanket with a subordinate, the general may have contracted the pneumonia that would ultimately take his life). Jones's martyr imagery was most blatant in his description of Davis. Injecting messianic overtones, Jones affirmed that Davis had suffered vicariously for the Southern people.[83]

There were a number of reasons that Jones's accounts of Lee, Jackson, and Davis bore such striking similarities. First of all, Jones returned time and again to those qualities by which postwar Southerners, regardless of denominational loyalties, could pattern their lives. He challenged his readers to imitate his heroes' dedication to the Bible, church, prayer, peace, humility, genuineness, and self-sacrifice.[84] The efficacy of these virtues extended beyond individual edification; Jones felt that by adopting these qualities, white Southerners could maintain a separate identity. Lee, Jackson, and Davis represented the paradigms of Southern holiness; to model these leaders was to remain distinctive — or, one might say, "Southern." By espousing the common mode of piety that Jones set forth, white Southerners of every evangelical denomination not only exalted the Confederate trinity, but mirrored their examples.

A second reason that Jones stressed certain values was because he felt they characterized the life of Christ. Appealing to Christ's example was yet another means of promoting a list of core virtues specific to no one denomination. By following the examples of Lee, Jackson, and Davis, Southerners followed the example of Christ. Jones deemed Lee's life "spotless," and readers needed little reminder that Jackson had literally forfeited his life for the Southern people. Likewise, Jones compared Davis's death to Christ's, using terms like "stainless" or "incorruptible" to describe the martyr president.[85]

Another reason that Jones compared his heroes to Christ was because he felt that Confederate leaders, like Christ, would one day be vindicated. This feature of Jones's work had less to do with providing a common mode of piety and more to do with preserving an accurate narrative of the Confederacy. Specifically, Jones foretold Confederate vindication by using "crown" imagery in his biographical works. These metaphors usually entailed Lee, Jackson, and Davis receiving a heavenly crown as a reward for their earthly faithfulness. Lee, a "faithful Soldier of the Cross," received a "crown of rejoicing." In death, Jackson "won the victory" and earned the "crown of rejoicing." Reacting to a description of Davis as "the uncrowned king of his people," Jones praised: "Thank God, he is no longer 'uncrowned.' His people have crowned him with loving hearts, and redeemed by the blood of that Saviour in whom he humbly trusted, he has come off 'conqueror — aye, more than conqueror,' and the Captain of our salvation has given him 'palms of victory' and a 'crown of rejoicing.'"[86] Directing his comments to Davis himself, Jones wrote: "[T]hou hast won thy last great victory . . . thou dost now 'rest from thy labours' and wear thy fadeless crown." For Jones, the coronation of Lee, Jackson, and Davis revealed that the South had produced morally superior leaders compared with the North. Jones included both "North as well as South" in the company of those crowning Lee. Jackson's crown was likewise associated with victory. When reflecting on Davis's crown, Jones declared that God had made Davis a "conqueror" and had given him "palms of victory."[87]

To cap off the matter, Jones dovetailed a subversive doxology with his crown metaphors. Whether eulogizing Lee, Jackson, or Davis, he included with his crown imagery the following stanza:

> That crown with peerless glories bright,
> Which shall now luster boast,
> When victors' wreaths and monarchs' gems
> Shall blend in common dust.[88]

This verse came from a hymn by Philip Doddridge, published in 1755, entitled "Awake, My Soul, Stretch Every Nerve." In the first line, Jones replaced the word "prize" with the word "crown." The change is curious, since he could have easily used the first stanza of the hymn, which referred to an "immortal crown." Instead, Jones was attracted to the fourth stanza, not as much for its reference to a crown, but for its reference to the "victors' wreaths." Since he believed the crowns of his leaders to be "fadeless," this fourth verse was a logical choice. In it the "victors' wreaths" (read "Northerners' crowns") would one day fade to dust. Jones's subversive doxology represented a dismissal of the North's ephemeral crowns, which stood in stark contrast to the enduring crowns of Lee, Jackson, and Davis. Earthly "crowns of victory" were unimportant, Jones reminded his fellow Southerners, since it was fallacious to associate might with right.[89] Instead, Jones encouraged his readers to take comfort in the Confederacy's motto, *Deo Vindice*—a testament and prophesy for those seeking divine vindication. Just as white Southerners could rally around a common core of Christian virtues, so too could they find consolation in the quiet assurance of a future reckoning.

✦ ✦ ✦ ✦ ✦

Through his incarnational hagiography, Jones provided readers with tangible assurances of God's presence with Southerners. Through his transdenominational encomiums to the Confederacy's finest, Jones provided Southerners with a common mode of piety through which they could preserve their distinctive identity as God's chosen people. Testifying to incarnations of Southern virtue was but one aspect of Jones's two-pronged apostolic mission. He also resolved to preserve a faithful narrative of the Confederacy — a narrative that could be handed down to coming generations and confirmed by future historians. As Jones saw the matter, he had been commissioned by Robert E. Lee much as biblical apostles had been commissioned by Christ. Because of Jones's intimate connection with Confederate leaders, he boasted in the special access and insight he could provide his readers. In a postwar context of competing narratives, Jones believed that his story would rise above the others, and that in the end, truth would prevail, and the Confederate gospel would save the South.

CHAPTER FIVE

Quest for a Faithful Narrative: Jones and the Battle for Southern History

It is doubtless true, that an accepted history can never be written in the midst of the stormy events of which that history is composed, nor by the agents through whose efficiency they were wrought. The strong passions which are evoked in every human conflict disturb the vision and warp the judgment, in the scales of whose criticism the necessary facts are to be weighed—even the relative importance of these facts cannot be measured by those who are in too close proximity. Scope must be afforded for the development of the remote issues before they can be brought under the range of a philosophical apprehension; and the secret thread be discovered, running through all history, upon which its single facts crystalize in the unity of some great Providential plan.

—"Official Circular, Southern Historical Society,"
Southern Historical Society Files, Museum of the Confederacy

When one day J. William Jones's school-age son came home with his history class textbook, Jones knew immediately that something was amiss. For Jones, "only a glance was required to show that it was not the truth." Abhorred at the book's calumnious treatment of the Confederacy, Jones determined that the text was unfit for any self-respecting Southerner. He flipped through the textbook and then pulled out his knife. Summarily, he cut out every reference he could find that related to the Civil War. Returning the book to his son, he said, "Give my love to your teacher, and say to him if it is necessary for you to study that book you can quit that school."[1] For Jones, Southern history was a battlefield, and only knife-wielding ex-Confederates like he could ensure that truth won the day.

Jones's acute concern for Southern history was an extension of his apostolic mission, as he set about to preserve a faithful Confederate narrative for future generations. Such a testament would not only vindicate the Confederacy, but would serve as a means by which white Southerners could define and guard their distinctive identity vis-à-vis Northerners. This chapter explores three of Jones's most widespread and influential efforts to craft a distinctive Southern narrative.

First, Jones disseminated the Lost Cause narrative through his editorship of the *Southern Historical Society Papers* (*shsp*). During his tenure with the *shsp*, Jones exerted tremendous influence over the shaping of Confederate memory. For more than a decade, he idolized Confederate leaders, exalted Confederate soldiers, endorsed Lost Cause tenets, and suppressed historical heterodoxy. Second, Jones forged a particular narrative of race as he outlined the relationship between white Baptists and African Americans. Here he downplayed the atrocities of slavery, idealized the master-slave relationship, and encouraged paternalism as a means of guiding heresy-prone African Americans. Third, Jones shaped a Lost Cause narrative for Southern youth. In 1896 he published his very own textbook for children, and in so doing, passed down to the next generation a distinctly white, pro-Confederate account of American history. The hope, of course, was that that these young white Southerners would in turn embody the Lost Cause tradition and hold in pristine memory the virtues and valor of their Confederate forbearers.

Scholars generally agree that Jones's narratives left an indelible imprint on the postwar South. Some historians, however, have contended that Jones's work—specifically while editor of the *shsp*—was predominantly a future-oriented enterprise. In other words, Jones was less interested in developing a definitive history of the Confederacy, and more concerned with exposing multiple narratives to the light of day, in the hopes that a future historian would sift through the material and thereafter write an authoritative history of the conflict. Indeed, this was the stated purpose of the Southern Historical Society (*shs*), which began publishing the *shsp* in 1876.

For the *shsp*, however, purpose and practice differed greatly. Under Jones's watchful eye, there was little chance that the *Papers* would remain merely a source-gathering enterprise. At least in print, leaders of the SHS conceded that combatants could at best compose a slanted history. No one emerged from the crucible of war as an objective arbiter of truth. Even so, this admission belied the purposes of the *SHSP* and perpetuated the illusion that the collection and presentation of sources was not in itself a highly redactive process. Jones spearheaded this redaction, and by strategically arranging the articles of prominent ex-Confederates, he fashioned a mosaic of white Southern history. Far from being a "rough draft" of history, his work was no less than a calculated reification of Confederacy memory.

For all the SHS's rhetoric of collecting resources for future historians—who presumably would approach the war with a perspective lacking in the conflict's participants—Jones did not doubt his own objectivity. Furthermore, he did not believe that anyone—present or future—was more qualified than he to preserve a faithful narrative of the Confederacy. This narrative was a matter of apostolic succession for Jones, and his mission was not to leave behind an inchoate account of the war, but to hand down the Confederate gospel.

✠ ✠ ✠ ✠ ✠

In his position as editor of the *SHSP*, Jones wielded the most powerful arm of Lost Cause dissemination. Before serving as editor—a role he began in 1876—Jones had functioned as the secretary-treasurer of the SHS. As editor, however, Jones was given an unprecedented opportunity to sculpt and deploy the Lost Cause message. His influence in this capacity is difficult to exaggerate and impossible to ignore. In fact, historian Gardiner Shattuck goes as far as to claim that, during Jones's tenure with the SHS (1873–1887), he "literally controlled the shape of the Lost Cause."[2] For Jones, the *SHSP* was the most effective vehicle for preserving a truthful Confederate narrative. Through the *Papers*, he would guard, defend, and pass down a sacred account of Southern history, and he would do so at any cost.

In May 1869, a core of ex-Confederate notables like P. G. T. Beauregard, Richard Taylor, Braxton Bragg, and Dabney H. Maury met in New Orleans and founded the SHS. A well-known Presbyterian orator from Louisiana, Benjamin Morgan Palmer, served as the group's first president. The SHS initially and unsuccessfully tried to organize a system of branches throughout the Southern states, the hope being that each former Confederate state (and the District of Columbia) would have its own vice president. One reason for the lackluster branch system, later SHS leaders reasoned, was that New Orleans was not an ideal location for a parent society. Eventually, these same leaders would lobby for a Richmond headquarters instead, a move that portended a Virginia-centric shift in the SHS's focus.[3]

Early on, the society expressed its intent to preserve an accurate account of the war. During the war, Federal troops had confiscated Confederate archives. Many ex-Confederates feared that Southern history was being held hostage, and they resolved to publish the Southern side of the story before Northern accounts of the struggle won the day. The society's first attempts to publish were non-centralized. The SHS began publishing reports in journals such as *The Pecayune* and *The Land We Love*, the former published out of New Orleans, and the latter headed by former Confederate general, Daniel Harvey (D. H.) Hill.[4]

The SHS suffered from financial difficulties in the early 1870s, a malady from which the society would seldom be free for the next decade. The Panic of 1873 exacerbated problems for the young society, which had still not found its footing in either organization or publication. In August 1873, the SHS met at White Sulphur Springs in Virginia. Here the society reorganized, charting a course that would thereafter alter the SHS's focus and also occasion Jones's rise to prominence. In short, the 1873 meeting opened the door for ex-Confederate Virginians to take control of the SHS. At the behest of the Virginians, the SHS decided to move the society's headquarters to Richmond. With the physical move to Richmond came a conceptual shift as well. The society resolved that only Virginians could serve as officers in the newly reorganized SHS, and they then elected former Confederate general Jubal Early as president. At the same meeting, the society also elected Jones as temporary secretary (he would become permanent secretary in 1875). Through Early and Jones, Virginia would take center stage in the Lost Cause mythology. Furthermore, with

Virginians now at the helm of the SHS, the myth of the invincible and inviolable Robert E. Lee would reach stratospheric heights.[5] A society circular laid out the group's aims. Objectives included the "collection, classification, preservation, and final publication, in some form hereafter determined, of all the documents and facts bearing upon the eventual history of the past, illustrating the natures of the struggle from which the country has just emerged, defining and vindicating the principle which lay beneath it, and marking the stages through which it was conducted to its issues."[6] Officially, the SHS was not to be "purely sectional" or of a "partisan character": "Everything which relates to this critical period of our national history, pending the conflict, antecedent or subsequent to it, from the point of view of either, or of both the contestants; everything in short, which shall vindicate the truth of history is to be industriously collated and filled."[7] The reorganized society would negotiate a number of challenges over the next decade and a half. One would concern just how nonpartisan the SHS could remain. Another concerned the issue of publication. The SHS had decided to publish material "in some form hereafter determined," but even the revamped society continued to farm out reports to other journals.

In the mid-1870s, the SHS published items in *The New Eclectic* out of Baltimore, which had recently taken over Hill's *The Land We Love*. The *New Eclectic* itself would soon thereafter become the *Southern Magazine*. Finally, in the mid-1870s, society members saw an opportunity for change. William W. Corcoran, a Washington banker who was interested in the work of the society, donated five hundred dollars to the SHS, and leaders used the money to fund their own publication. The result was the *Southern Historical Society Papers*, which began in 1876. As secretary-treasurer of the society, Jones oversaw the printing and publication of the *SHSP*.[8]

The society's experiment was successful long-term, considering that the *SHSP* survived as a stand-alone publication (in some form) until the 1950s. Nevertheless, the 1870s and 1880s were tumultuous times for the *Papers*. Though head of the "nonpartisan" *SHSP*, Jones made clear enough his contempt for Northern accounts of the war. Attacks from the North, though, would not be his only concern. He also had to perform a precarious balancing act when including conflicting accounts from Confederate officers. Contradictory reports from Southern leaders sometimes ignited bitter and libelous feuds. In addition, some of the *SHSP*'s Southern readership balked at the disproportionate attention that Jones gave to the Army of Northern Virginia. When veterans of the Western theater contemplated starting their own journal, Jones responded by printing more articles on Confederate armies in the west.[9]

By far the most debilitating challenges during Jones's time as editor were financial. Annual membership fees for the SHS were three dollars (one could be a lifetime member for fifty), yet Jones was often unable to collect dues. Debts hounded him, and he pled incessantly for more subscribers to the *Papers*. The debts accrued by the SHS came mostly from printing, since the Virginia legislature had provided rent-free office space to the society in the Virginia State House. Jones also envisioned purchasing a fireproof building in which the society could store records. With the society's coffers empty, Jones soon realized that drastic measures would be needed to keep the SHS solvent.[10]

In October 1879, Jones made his move, asking the SHS executive committee to turn over the *Papers* to him. He insisted that his request was offered with "no view to self-interest, or pecuniary advantage of any sort," and that his primary aim was to reduce the debt of the SHS. The desperate executive committee agreed to the proposal, handing over to Jones "the entire business management and control of the Papers."[11] By November of that year, Jones had unrivaled control of the most wide-reaching and influential instrument of the Lost Cause.

One of Jones's strategies for reducing the society's debt was entreating former Confederates to do speaking tours. Even though Fitz Lee — Confederate general, Robert E. Lee's nephew, and eventual governor of Virginia — embarked on tours for the SHS, financial problems persisted. For one thing, there was confusion between Lee and the SHS concerning the proceeds of such tours. The society seemed surprised at the payment Lee requested for his "fundraising" endeavors, and Jones set about to clarify the issue and reconcile with the general.[12]

Creditors and testy ex-Confederates were not Jones's only woes, however; at times he himself ran afoul with the SHS. When in July 1883 the executive committee voted that all the society's monies should be handed over to a treasurer (instead of Jones), Jones protested, reminding the committee that his official title was that of secretary *and* treasurer. He maintained that the committee could not change his title without amending the society's constitution. Furthermore, he declared that he had always kept his books open to review, lest anyone suspect impropriety on his part. Also in the summer of 1883, there was a misunderstanding between Jones and the SHS concerning his salary. Jones contended that his salary was not contingent upon the society making expenses. He had already taken salary during years when expenses had not been met, and he complained that he had been forced to make decisions without the executive committee's prior approval. Had the committee met as often as it should have, he concluded, the whole issue might have been avoided.[13]

Problems continued in August 1883, when the SHS audited Jones's books and found discrepancies. Responding with a backhanded apology and a reminder of his more than competent work, Jones testified: "I will only add that if I have managed badly the affairs of the Society, my management has at least paid off a debt which threatened our very existence, put into the treasury of our special fund over $4400, and given the Society a wider hold on the people of the South than we ever had before."[14] Then, with a hint of contrition, Jones conceded, "[i]f I have made mistakes, as God is my witness, they have been born of a conscientious desire to promote the interests of the Society and from no personal or selfish motives."[15] When the dust settled, Jones was still heading the *SHSP*. The verdict was unsurprising. After all, despite its punishing debt, the society still enjoyed exceptional sway over white Southerners. This "wider hold," the executive committee well knew, was largely owed to Jones's efforts.

Burgeoning influence aside, the SHS could not claw its way out of debt. In February 1885, the executive committee recommended suspending publication of the *SHSP*. With the sting of the 1883 audit in the back of his mind, and anxious that the most valuable tool for preserving Confederate memory not fold, Jones offered to print the *Papers* without drawing a salary. Anticipating that the SHS would pay him back salary when the society had the means, Jones worked without a salary during 1885 and 1886. Despite his efforts, cuts were necessary. As his tenure at the SHS wound down, Jones tried to save money by combining multiple issues into one printing. By the summer of 1887, Jones felt he had run his course at the SHS. On June 25, he resigned his post with the society. He had served the SHS for more than a decade, and he had edited fourteen volumes of the *Papers*. As editor of the *SHSP* from 1876 until 1887, he had done as much as anyone else to shape white Southern memory of the war. In Jones's mind, he had also been true to his apostolic mission of preserving for future generations a truthful narrative of the virtuous South.[16]

✠ ✠ ✠ ✠ ✠

Most of the *SHSP*'s themes during Jones's time as secretary echoed common Lost Cause tropes. One of these themes concerned the origins of the war and the justification of secession. In the *SHSP*'s first issue, Congressman R. M. T. Hunter insisted that slavery had been protected by the US Constitution. Another writer compared the United States to ancient Israel, noting that just as Solomon's push toward centralization had led to the northern kingdom's succession, so too had the North's meddling prompted the South to leave the union. The writer continued by blaming the North for "inciting the negroes to revolt" and to "murder their owners." In 1884, the *SHSP* printed an elaborate discussion of the US Constitution—one that was largely sympathetic to state sovereignty.[17]

Another stock theme of the *SHSP* was that the Confederate Army had not been defeated by the Federals, but simply "overwhelmed" by superior numbers and resources. Hunter maintained that the South had stopped fighting out of "physical exhaustion—the want of food, clothes and the munitions of war." He asserted that the South had yielded to "no superiority of valor or of skill, but to the mere avoirdupois of numbers."[18] Writers to the *SHSP* groused that Northern accounts of the war had overestimated the numbers of Southern troops. Jones wrote, "[e]ven our own people are in profound ignorance of the great odds against which we fought, while Northern writers have persistently misrepresented the facts."[19] Oftentimes the disputes over troop numbers were tedious, but for Jones and his ilk, they were necessary. For these veterans, chivalry demanded that two equals meet on the field of battle. Not only was the numerical superiority of the North overwhelming, but it was, at root, dishonorable.

Writers for the *SHSP* seldom missed opportunities to denounce the Union Army. The first issue of the *Papers* printed an excoriating wartime address from the Confederate Congress. Congressmen declared that the "atrocities" of Northern soldiers were "too incredible for narration": "Houses are pillaged and burned; churches are defaced; towns are ransacked; clothing of women and infants is stripped from their persons; jewelry and mementoes of the dead are stolen." Southerners were forced to choose between taking an oath of allegiance to "a hated government" or watching their children starve. Prisoners were maltreated, the wounded left to die, and the women "exposed to the most cruel outrages and to that dishonor which is infinitely worse than death."[20] The context of war doubtless fueled the document's heated rhetoric. That said, Jones printed the report more than a decade after the war's end, a move that contradicted his alleged commitment to exclude incendiary articles from the *SHSP*.

In particular, writers took dead aim at Ulysses S. Grant. Dabney H. Maury, former Confederate general and one of the founders of the SHS, downgraded Grant's generalship and harangued that "history will arraign Grant for the recklessness with which he dashed his men to death." He lambasted Grant for ceasing prisoner exchange, a "crime against humanity" that Maury claimed had no equal. He credited Grant with courage, and for honoring the paroles of former Confederates, but believed Grant's military strategies exposed the general's deep moral flaws.[21]

Another common refrain of the *SHSP* was the superiority of the Confederate soldier over the Union soldier. D. H. Hill, for example, argued that the South had an unrivaled military pedigree. He reminded readers that the South had come to the North's aid in the American Revolution, losing more men and producing the likes of George Washington. Hill even claimed that many of the Union Army's finest officers had come from Southern states.[22] Southern minister J. B. Hawthorne applauded that Confederate soldiers had fought to suppress "political heresy" and had striven for "political truth, wisdom, and justice." Hawthorne then compared the courage of Southern and Northern troops, writing, "Of mere brute courage the savage has more than the civilized man; the drunken man more than the sober man; and the villain more than the virtuous man. Of this courage the army of Grant had more than the army of Lee."[23] As Hawthorne demonstrated, ex-Confederates who could bring themselves to "praise" the enemy's bravery often did so through clenched teeth.

While Jones filled the *Papers* with typical Lost Cause doctrines, there are a few important themes that deserve detailed treatment, not only for what they indicate about the *SHSP*, but for what they reveal about Jones. For instance, one of Jones's primary goals as Confederate apostle was the glorification of Robert E. Lee, Stonewall Jackson, and Jefferson Davis. That the Confederate trinity would factor largely into the *SHSP* is thus predictable. The *SHSP*'s primary focus, however, remained on Lee. The chieftain's gravitational pull was at times overwhelming, as authors felt compelled to downplay the achievements of other Confederate leaders in order to afford Lee due respect. The matter was a sensitive one, since if any Confederate icon was a perceived threat to Lee's preeminence, it was Stonewall Jackson. A contributing factor to what would become a "Lee-Jackson rivalry" was Robert L. Dabney's 1866 biography of Jackson, which Lee admirers (and even Lee himself) felt elevated Jackson at Lee's expense.[24]

Particular sticking points with Jackson included his roles at the Battles of Seven Days and Chancellorsville. The Battle of Seven Days had included numerous Confederate missteps. In order to protect Lee from criticism, Jones employed a familiar strategy of blaming Lee's subordinates. Key here, though, was that one of Lee's bungling subordinates was Jackson. Concerning Seven Days, Jones wrote that Jackson—who was tardy in his attacks and confused by Lee's orders—had committed a "great blunder." Jackson was not "infallible," but Lee's plans were, had they been properly executed. Furthermore, when printing a piece by Dabney that extolled the great Jackson, Jones offered the caveat that all his readers might not agree with Dabney's assessment. Jones and Dabney would have run-ins even after the former's time as editor, with Dabney taking exception to what Jones wrote about him in *Christ in the Camp*.[25]

The Jones-Dabney rivalry notwithstanding, the *SHSP* still included numerous articles acclaiming Jackson. Even in a Fitz Lee article that credited Robert E. Lee (not Jackson) with the legendary flanking maneuver at Chancellorsville, the author still noted that the battle was "inseparably connected in its glory and gloom with Stonewall Jackson," whose "pure military genius" was like that of Caesar and Napoleon.[26] In addition, and beyond the pages of the *SHSP*, Jones spared few plaudits in his own writings on Jackson. For example, Jones contributed more than one hundred pages of panegyric to Jackson in John Esten Cooke's 1876 book on the general. Likewise, Jones celebrated Jackson's military brilliance in his 1887 *Christ in the Camp*. Jones was eager to burnish the image of Jackson, as long as that image did not outshine Lee's.

Regarding Davis, Jones used the *Papers* to douse postwar rumors that had arisen about the ex-president. Articles hammered on the oft-cited story of Union troops capturing Davis while the Confederate president was wearing his wife's clothing. Contributors also countered the story of Davis leaving church in a panic when he received word from Lee that Richmond should be evacuated. More serious rumors concerned the accusation that Davis had played a role in Lincoln's assassination. Writers dismissed defamations about a leader whose reputation the *Papers* was working diligently to rehabilitate. Still, Davis was not oblivious to the lopsided attention the *SHSP* gave to Lee. In an 1883 letter to Jones, he wrote that while Lee's qualities were admirable, they required no "ornamentation" from the *Papers*. He expressed particular annoyance that Lee was being praised at the expense of others (presumably himself).[27] Davis saw as clearly as anyone that Jones, while willing to commend other leaders, ensured that those leaders be safely tucked in Lee's shadow. Indeed, Jones was a disciple of the Confederate trinity. He was also a subordinationist.

Still a committed Baptist, at times Jones struck a cooperative chord in the *Papers*. One intriguing demonstration concerned his treatment of Father Abram J. Ryan. Jones printed a poem of Ryan's that had been intended for the SHS meeting in the spring of 1882 (the poem had not reached the committee in time and was not read). Jones wrote admirably of Ryan, extending "warm gratitude" to him on behalf of all Confederates. As far as the poem was concerned, Ryan infused the work with religious imagery, comparing the South's future vindication to Christ's resurrection: "When Wrong's rock shall roll away / From the sepulchre of Right, / And the Right shall rise again / In the brightness of a light, / that shall never fade away." Here Ryan's sentiments seemed largely in line with Jones's. In fact, Jones printed a number of other Ryan poems in the *SHSP*.[28]

Ryan was a well-known figure in the postwar South. In 1879, Early invited him to give an address before the SHS. Recognizing the priest's immense popularity, Early suggested to Jones that the society might need a larger venue for the event. In 1883, at the unveiling of Lee's recumbent statue at Washington and Lee University, Ryan was there. Before Ryan read one of his well-known poems, "The Sword of Lee," the grateful crowd greeted him with "enthusiastic applause." Jones printed a letter from Ryan describing the event.[29]

Jones's inclusion of Ryan's poetry in the *Papers* was yet another example of his willingness to reach across sectarian boundaries, at least in the sense of allowing various religious groups to participate in the common cause of preserving the culture and memory of the white South. He was not open, however, to an ecumenism that muted doctrinal distinctions and envisioned organic unity. Put another way, Jones's openness to non-Baptists was pragmatic, not theological. True, Ryan's poetry displayed a general religious tone to which both Roman Catholics and evangelicals could ascribe; yet in the same issue as one of Ryan's poems, Jones printed an address from Rabbi J. K. Gutheim. Gutheim's speech was also thoroughly religious—he compared the SHS to the "rival" altar erected by the tribes of Reuben, Gad, and the half-tribe of Manasseh in Joshua 22.[30] Still, the inclusion of the rabbi's speech was not an indication that Jones or other Lost Causers endorsed any sort of doctrinal move toward Judaism. Like Roman Catholics, Jews could participate in the Lost Cause in spite of their faith, not because of it.

Important to note here is that Jones was drawn to Ryan's poetry, not to Ryan's Catholicism. No matter how innocuously Ryan expressed his faith in verse, Jones remained convinced that God prized evangelical faith over all others. In short, Jones viewed the Lost Cause through a religious lens. Because evangelical faith made the South unique, evangelical religion was part and parcel of his Lost Cause vision. While Roman Catholics could participate in the general mission of vindicating the South and apotheosizing Confederate leaders, their faith relegated them to the fringes of a South whose identity was inextricably linked with evangelical religion.

Another theme that dominated early issues of the *SHSP* was the treatment of prisoners during the war. The discussion was not merely academic; Jones and the SHS determined to portray Southerners as more virtuous than Northerners. In order to do this, Jones had to neutralize accusations—such as those leveled by Maine senator, James G. Blaine—that Confederates had deliberately abused Union prisoners. In February 1876, Jones outlined the case *SHSP* contributors would make in the coming months. The points were as follows: that Confederate officers had ordered the kind treatment of Union prisoners, that Union prisoners received the same rations as their Confederate guards, that prisoner hospitals were no worse than other Confederate hospitals, that diseases that killed Union prisoners were unpreventable and also affected Confederate guards, that Union prisons were guilty of the same crimes of which they accused Confederate prisons, that poor prison conditions were owed primarily to the Union's decision to cease prisoner exchange with the Confederacy, and that more Confederate soldiers died in Northern prisons than Union soldiers in Southern prisons. Jones was confident that the forthcoming discussion would produce "a complete vindication of our long slandered people."[31]

In March 1876, Jones cited prominent Southerners such as Lee, Davis, and Confederate vice president, Alexander Stephens, in order to ward off accusations of war atrocities in Confederate prisons. Jones systematically refuted rumors about intentional starvation and shooting prisoners. Then, Jones turned to the infamous Andersonville, widely known as the most appalling of Confederate prisons. First, Jones alleged that many of the problems at Andersonville originated with Union prisoners themselves. They fought each other, he maintained, and had they abided by the "discipline and sanitary regulations" of the prison, their suffering would have been greatly mitigated. He then blamed the North for not trading with the South, noting that if Northerners had accepted Southerners' cotton in exchange for medicine, Union prisoners could have received proper care.[32]

In the April 1876 issue, Jones turned the tables and condemned Union prisons for the treatment of Confederate soldiers. He printed articles demonstrating that Confederate prisoners had been tortured. One medieval-like practice involved captives being bound and hoisted by their thumbs until they turned "black in the face." Many writers discussed their fear of "dead lines"—ditches dug approximately fifteen to twenty feet inside prison walls. If prisoners crossed the dead line, they could be shot. An article observed that on one occasion a "man's brains were blown out and scattered on the walls, where they remained for many days, for no offence other than looking over the bounds, unconsciously." For water, prisoners had to drink near latrines; for food, detainees resorted to eating cats.[33]

Articles in the SHSP also charged Union soldiers with the most heinous of crimes, including the rape of Southern women. One writer alleged that Union troops had thrown fifteen African American children into the river because the soldiers could find no family to take them. Writers to the *Papers* also believed that there had been a racial element to prison abuses. Because African American soldiers were mistreated by their white Northern officers, the narrative went, the troops unleashed their frustrations on white Southern prisoners. Articles reported that African American guards would commonly shoot prisoners for no apparent reason. After discussing a host of brutalities, one writer was paralyzed with revulsion: "Through disgust, horror and shame, I cast my pen aside, and sit in amazement, that for crimes like these an angry God has not, by His breath, cursed the earth, and sent it as a floating pandemonium throughout the immensity of space, as a warning to other worlds, if other worlds be so depraved, corrupted and lost to the charities of life and the mercies of God."[34]

As far as Jones was concerned, the North was to blame for the condition of prisons in both sections. He asserted that the Union was at fault for stopping prisoner exchange and that this was the "real gist of the whole matter." Simply put, Southerners lacked the resources to care for Federal prisoners; still the Union had refused to exchange Confederate prisoners for them (one strategy of Grant's "war of attrition"). Furthermore, the Union had rejected the South's request for medicines that would have prevented Union prison deaths. As for the barbarities in Federal prisons, they were owed to the hatred and spite of Union guards. The Federal government had more than enough resources to care for Southern prisoners; they had simply refused to do it. For this and other outrages, Jones believed that the "verdict of history" would fully indict the Union for its "system of cold-blooded cruelty." The *SHSP* readership was largely convinced with Jones's interpretation of prisoner treatment, and his narrative would become the standard view of the white South.[35]

If Jones's preoccupation with prisoner treatment was an attempt to preserve the image of the virtuous South, his preoccupation with the battle of Gettysburg was an attempt to preserve the image of Lee as a supreme and flawless military mind. In 1877, Louis Philippe Albert d'Orléans (Comte de Paris)—who had served on General George McClellan's staff, and was now working on a multi-volume history of the war—sent Jones a letter requesting details about Gettysburg. In private correspondence, Jones was cordial with the Comte, advertising his publications, and even allowing him to become a lifetime member of the SHS. Jones did not hide, however, that he disagreed with the Comte on many points. In March 1877, Early wrote a scathing review of the Comte's first volume on the history of the Civil War. Early criticized the Comte for culling his information about slavery from *Uncle Tom's Cabin* and for portraying the South worse than could the "most embittered partisan of the North." To highlight all the Comte's errors, Early continued, would be an "interminable task." His suggestion: burn the first volume and begin again.[36]

Even though neither Jones nor Early agreed with the Comte, his letter afforded them an opportunity to set the record straight on Gettysburg. The Comte had presented five points for discussion. First, was Lee's invasion of the North a mistake? Second, why did Lee not utilize raiding parties in his attack? Third, why did the second day of battle at Gettysburg lack coordination? Fourth, why did Lee not attack Union forces from the south? Fifth, why did Lee attack at all on the third day (the infamous "Pickett's charge")? In order to answer these questions, Jones sent copies of the inquiries to around twenty-five Confederate officers. He then printed their responses in the *SHSP*.[37] Some writers specifically confronted the five disputed points, and opinions were especially passionate concerning the third question—why the July 2 attacks had lacked the coordination of previous Confederate battles. One by one, writers began to assign blame, most of them sharpening their knives for General James Longstreet.

Though he had been Lee's most trusted subordinate after the death of Stonewall Jackson in the spring of 1863, many postwar Southerners saw

Longstreet as a turncoat. After the war, Longstreet had committed the unpardonable offense of joining the Republican Party, and Southerners were appalled that he had dared to criticize Lee in print. In 1877, Jones and Early set about in a methodical attempt to dismantle Longstreet's reputation. In Early's response to the Comte's inquiries, Early blamed Longstreet for not carrying out Lee's orders on the second day of battle — orders that allegedly instructed Longstreet to attack Union forces at dawn. Instead, Longstreet had commenced his attack in the late afternoon. The delay had proved costly, Early maintained, since with an early enough attack on July 2, the South would have carried the day, and the battle. Even though Early admitted that Longstreet could at times be a "brilliant" fighter, he believed that Longstreet lacked confidence in Lee's strategies, and that this "constitutional inertia" had undermined Confederate efforts at Gettysburg.[38]

Other contributors to the Gettysburg series concurred with Early. Generals C. M. Wilcox and A. L. Long, along with Colonel Walter H. Taylor, all held Longstreet culpable for the Gettysburg defeat. Some letters were not as blatant in their criticism of Longstreet. For example, General John B. Hood explained that Longstreet delayed because he was waiting for General George Pickett. Without Picket, Hood explained, Longstreet would have felt that he was fighting with "one boot off." In his letter, General Henry Heth, while not absolving Longstreet, cast the onus of the defeat on J. E. B. Stuart, whose cavalry had not been available to provide Lee with proper intelligence. Even with letters like those of Hood and Heth, Early was confident that he had made his point. "I think I have demonstrated that he [Longstreet] was responsible for the loss of the Battle of Gettysburg," he wrote Jones in October 1877. "I don't see how he can introduce anything new into the question."[39]

In December 1877, Jones prefaced the Gettysburg discussion by printing material "without comment and without endorsement." Even so, the SHSP's position was abundantly clear. When Longstreet accused Early of unfair criticism, Early went on the attack again. With Jones arbitrating the debate, he ensured that Early had the last word. In early 1878, Jones printed an interview that Longstreet had given to the Philadelphia *Times* the previous November. In the article, Longstreet not only defended his actions on July 2, but avowed that he had tried to convince Lee not to attack on the third day of Gettysburg. He went further by revealing that Lee had later agreed with him. Jones printed the article not in the interest of fairness, but with the full expectation that Early would continue eviscerating the general. In a March 1878 letter, Jones wrote Early, "Of course *I* am anxious for you to slice up what is left of Longstreet."[40]

The bombardment continued in April 1878, when Fitz Lee responded directly to Longstreet and censured his delay at Gettysburg. In June, Jones printed another report by Longstreet in which the general denied receiving orders to attack early on July 2. Longstreet then criticized what he felt was the flawed strategy of Gettysburg. Once again, Early pounced. He claimed that if Longstreet had let the matter rest, no one would have blamed him for the loss at Gettysburg. Since Longstreet had the "overweening vanity and egotism" to denigrate Lee, however, Longstreet must take full responsibility for his (in)actions on the second day of battle. As far as Early was concerned, Longstreet himself had provoked the fracas that had now drug out for over a year. The battle would actually continue long after. Gettysburg material—whether or not dealing with Longstreet specifically—surfaced in nearly every issue of the *Papers* during Jones's time as editor. Finally, in 1884, Jones blatantly showed his cards, pronouncing that if Lee had won Gettysburg, England would have recognized the Confederacy, and the South would have won the war. He concluded, "We verily believe that the verdict of impartial History will be that the Confederates would have won Gettysburg, and Independence, but for the failure of *one man*."[41]

The Jones-Early assault on Longstreet—a campaign historian Thomas Connelly has judged to be "most cynical manipulation that ever occurred in the writing of Civil War history"[42]—revealed the lengths to which Jones and Lost Causers would go in order to sanitize Lee's legacy. Jones's apostolic zeal made him an eager participant in the character assassination of Longstreet. For Jones, Lee's iconic status had to be preserved at any cost. Lee was not only the incarnation of Southern virtue; he was also the paragon of martial acumen. Lee's apparent defeat was not defeat at all; instead, it was the betrayal of those closest to him. Inasmuch as Lee was Christ, Longstreet was Judas.[43] In addition to his role as the Confederacy's apostle, Jones donned the mantle of apologist, and he countered any narrative that cast the great chieftain in an unsympathetic light. Jones well knew that the postwar South was a battlefield of competing stories. For him, Longstreet would just have to be one of the casualties.

Other weighty issues surfacing in the periodical included slavery. Ironically, however, many Lost Cause writers brought up the South's peculiar institution in order not to talk about it. In the first issue of the SHSP, R. M. T. Hunter began his discussion of the war's origins by steering away from a detailed treatment of slavery. Interestingly, though, Hunter conceded the weight of the emancipation narrative, writing that "[w]hen we consider how deeply the institution of southern society and the operations of southern industry were founded in slavery, we must admit that this was cause enough to have produced such a result [war]."[44] The importance of slavery and race surfaced in other articles as well, despite most writers' attempts to avoid the topics. Again in the first issue of the *Papers*, Jones printed an undated wartime address from the Confederate Congress that warned Southerners that Confederate defeat would lead to, among other things, "equalization of whites and blacks." In his defense of the South, particularly Virginia, one contributor echoed the common argument that England had forced colonial Virginia to have slaves. When Virginia tried to stop the slave trade, Northerners, who profited from selling slaves to Southerners, objected.[45]

Another article, this one from former Confederate private and eventual mayor of Richmond, Carlton McCarthy, pined for an antebellum South complete with amiable, satisfied servants:

> Quite a large number [of soldiers] had a "boy" along to do the cooking and washing. Think of it? a Confederate soldier with a body servant all his own, to bring him a drink of water, black his boots, dust his clothes, cook his corn bread and bacon, and put wood on his fire. Never was their fonder admiration than these darkies displayed for their masters.
>
> Their chief delight and glory was to praise the courage and good looks of "Mahse Tom," and prophesy great things about his future. Many a ringing laugh and shout of fun originated in the queer remarks, shining countenance and glistening teeth of this now forever departed character.[46]

Not only was McCarthy's piece replete with racial stereotypes, but the article also depicted slaves as happy with their stations in life. McCarthy also betrayed a belief common among lower-class white Southerners—a sentiment coined by sociologist Pierre L. van den Berghe as "Herrenvolk democracy." This was the assumption that there existed a "master race," and that whites, even if destitute, remained superior to African Americans. As historians James McPherson and James Hogue observe, the Herrenvolk democracy represented "the central paradox of American history: slavery became for many whites the foundation of liberty and equality." Slaveholders and nonslaveholders alike "feared emancipation because it would render their whiteness meaningless."[47] The Herrenvolk mindset thus sheds light on the reasons white Southerners—even those who did not own slaves and who resented the planter class—would fight and die in order to preserve slavery as an institution and racial hierarchy as an ideal. McCarthy's portrayal of the idyllic days of slavery was not just yearning for lost friendships, but mourning for a society that had lost its proper order.

In an article from the fall of 1879, former Confederate general James R. Chalmers made a provocative admission, stating that Southern greats like Lee, Davis, and Albert Sydney Johnston had not left the Union lightly: "They seceded not, as falsely charged, 'to shoot the Union to death,' but mainly to preserve alive the institution of slavery, guaranteed by the constitution of the United States, and which they feared would be destroyed by the Republican party. Time has proved that their fears were not without foundation. Mr. Lincoln and two-thirds of his party in Congress then denied any purpose to destroy slavery, but every Republican leader now shamelessly boast[s] that this was the great object of the war."[48] Chalmers did not deny that the South had seceded over the issue of slavery. In fact, he defended Lee, Davis, and Johnston by asserting that slavery was *precisely* why the South had seceded. Chalmers's criticism was not that Northerners had falsely accused the South of fighting to preserve slavery, but that Northerners had—unlike Southerners—pretended as if slavery was not at the heart of the conflict.

Chalmers then imbued his argument with religious rhetoric, declaring that slavery's "destruction was perhaps as necessary to the preservation of the Union as the death of Christ was necessary to the salvation of man." Lest this sentiment be confused with implicating the South, Chalmers continued: "But while we rejoice that the plan of salvation was accomplished, no Christian loves the Judas who for money betrayed Him with a kiss, nor the Pontius Pilate who dared not resist the clamor of the mob, crying for his crucifixion, nor the fierce fanatics who drove the nails into his flesh."[49] Chalmers's religious imagery enabled him to perform important rhetorical functions. He could admit that the end of slavery was a good thing, and at the same time liken Northerners to Judas, Pilate, and the crowds who crucified Christ. Here Chalmers exemplified a common approach of Southerners to use the Bible simultaneously as a tool of reconciliation and subversion.[50]

Jones was often unsubtle with his opinions on contentious matters. In 1885, he printed and endorsed an article by Dabney. Dabney's piece was a scalding critique of Southern novelist, George Washington Cable, whose publication in New York's *The Century* had denounced slavery and lobbied for freedmen equality. Dabney skewered Cable for arguing that slavery had been the cause of the war instead of properly grasping the difference between what was the "occasion" for war (slavery) and what was the "cause" of war (Southern rights). Jones made his opinions apparent, castigating what he considered to be the "cringing, crawling, dirt-eating" spirit of Cable's work.[51] While *SHSP* writers often dismissed issues of slavery and race as irrelevant to discussions of the war, at times they did touch on such matters. When they did, the tenor of their articles varied. Some writers ensconced their articles in racial stereotypes and an idealized past. Others wrote with more agitation, their articles betraying a bitter, penetrating fear that white hegemony was being lost forever.

As strange as the idea may appear on the surface, many contributors to the *Papers* used the periodical in order to foster reconciliation between white Northerners and white Southerners. This South-North "reconciliation," however, was not one dimensional. Such articles were alloyed with subversive undertones, admitted no wrongdoing on the part of the South, stymied racial reconciliation, and laid the foundation for Lost Cause dogmas that have persisted into the twenty-first century.

One way in which *SHSP* writers gestured toward reconciliation while honoring the Confederate cause was through their treatment of Confederate flags. Jones printed a wartime article that gave the history of the Confederate seal, the Confederate national flag, and the battle flag for the Army of Northern Virginia. Reflecting on the Confederate banners was a crucial move for white Southerners, as it allowed them an opportunity to cultivate a national mythology in the absence of an organized state. Unsurprisingly, postwar Southerners mounted tenacious and creative defenses of their sacred symbols. In one Confederate flag article, a soldier signing only "Turkey-Foot" proclaimed that he would fight under his "lady's handkerchief" if the Confederate government dared change the "azure cross."[52]

In 1880, a Carlton McCarthy article—based on a speech by P. G. T. Beauregard—articulated a defense of the Confederate battle flag that has found purchase among Confederate apologists ever since. McCarthy, who fancied himself an expert on the lives of private soldiers, drew a sharp distinction between the Confederate national flags and the Confederate battle flag for Lee's army. McCarthy argued that the St. Andrew's cross was "not the flag of the Confederacy, but simply the banner—the battle flag—of the Confederate soldier." He continued, "As such it should not share in the condemnation which our *cause* received, or suffer from its downfall. The whole world can unite in a chorus of praise to the gallantry of the men who followed where this banner led."[53]

McCarthy was transparent in his intentions to strip the battle flag of all political baggage. Yet McCarthy couched his argument in conciliatory language. The entire nation could respect the principles that the battle flag signified, McCarthy reasoned, since the banner represented the courage of the common soldier, not the politics of secession and slavery. Here McCarthy's move was indicative of a larger movement among white Southerners to reconcile with Northerners on the basis of mutual respect among soldiers. Preservation of the battle flag—and by extension, Southern identity—was reconciliation on the South's terms and an attempt to craft a narrative that honored the valor of Southern soldiers. This narrative also redirected memory away from thorny political questions, like slavery.

In 1881, the reconciliationist attitude surfaced again in an article by J. B. Hawthorne. Hawthorne avoided value judgments of the Union cause and instead offered cautious praise for those who had believed they fought for right. He encouraged readers, "Let us have the magnanimity to own that among our foes there were thousands who fought for what they believed to be truth and justice."[54] Then, with a subversive barb, Hawthorne compared the "courage" of Grant to that of a drunken man who had lost all inhibitions. Hawthorne's dig was reminiscent of James Chalmers's admission in 1879 that slavery's abolition was a good outcome of the war. Chalmers endorsed the mutual pride of postwar Northerners and Southerners, only then to compare Northerners to Pontius Pilate and Judas Iscariot.[55] Even seemingly conciliatory articles in the *SHSP* took opportune jabs at Northerners.

There was a dark side to the *SHSP*'s conciliatory rhetoric, one that went well beyond veiled insults. Historian Gary Gallagher has identified four strains of memory that emerged after the Civil War: the Lost Cause, the Union Cause, the Emancipation Cause, and the Reconciliation Cause. While freed slaves interpreted the conflict as a war of liberation (Emancipation Cause), the Reconciliation Cause "represented an attempt by white people North and South to extol the *American* virtues both sides manifested during the war, to exalt the restored nation that emerged from the conflict, and to mute the role of African Americans."[56] The Reconciliation Cause was not merely an ex-Confederate construction, as the last quarter of the nineteenth century saw most white Northerners eager to leave behind sectional animosities and to reunite with their white Southern brethren. This reunion, however, was largely on the South's terms. Much like the family that preserves a tenuous peace by avoiding discussions of religion and politics at the dinner table, whites in the North and South honored an unwritten agreement to muffle discussions of race and slavery. Such a pact carried enormous ramifications. Politically, the gains of Reconstruction — which afforded African Americans unprecedented liberties in the civil and political arena — became, in the words of historian David Blight, "sacrificial offerings on the altar of reunion."[57] Ideologically, narratives of reconciliation took precedence over narratives of emancipation, as Northerners and Southerners dismissed calls for African American justice amidst the deafening white noise of reunion.

Conciliatory articles that praised the virtues of the common soldier—North and South—excluded African Americans from the postwar narrative. This had already been a staple approach of Lost Causers who vehemently denied that the South had fought to preserve slavery. Now, mutual respect among soldiers would prove even more effective in whitewashing the memories of both Northerners and Southerners. Even as a bastion of the Lost Cause, the *SHSP* interwove both reconciliationist and Lost Cause strands of postwar memory.[58] In so doing, white Southern writers continued to downplay or ignore that slavery had been a fundamental cause of the war.

In many ways, the firestorms surrounding race, slavery, prisoner treatment, or Lee's legacy centered on how white Southerners wanted to remember and be remembered. Jones, the SHS, and *SHSP* contributors were all intently concerned with how future historians would assess their work. Some scholars have emphasized the role of the *SHSP* as largely a source-collecting endeavor—a repository for eyewitness accounts that later historians could critique or vindicate.[59] In this line of thinking, *SHSP* writers recognized that no contemporary could view the war with the requisite objectivity to write its history. Thus the *Papers* did not shy away from biased accounts, but welcomed them with the full knowledge that historians would one day weigh and sift those narratives in order to find the truth.

There is some credence to the argument that Jones allowed competing narratives into the *Papers* under the assumption that a dispassionate historian would one day sort through the stories, gleaning the wheat and discarding the chaff. This appeared to be one of the animating principles of the nascent SHS. As an official SHS circular stated:

> It is doubtless true, that an accepted history can never be written in the midst of the stormy events of which that history is composed, nor by the agents through whose efficiency they were wrought. The strong passions which are evoked in every human conflict disturb the vision and warp the judgment, in the scales of whose criticism the necessary facts are to be weighed.... Scope

must be afforded for the development of the remote issues before they can
be brought under the range of a philosophical apprehension; and the secret
thread be discovered, running through all history, upon which its single facts
crystalize in the unity of some great Providential plan.[60]

Indeed, Jones confessed on numerous occasions that the *SHSP* did not endorse all the articles the journal printed. Jones justified doing so, writing that "we may sometimes publish what we differ from, on the principle that if errors endorsed by responsible names creep into our archives, they had better be published now while men competent to correct them are living, than to turn up in future years when probably no one will be able to refute them."[61] For Jones, the goal of the *SHSP* was to expose competing narratives to peer critique, trusting that the true story would rise to the top. He was also wary of printing articles of some veterans and not others, especially when those veterans were prominent Confederates.[62]

Before Jones was even editor of the *SHSP*, he believed the SHS's purpose was to prepare the ground for later historians. He wrote to Union general Andrew A. Humphreys that the society was collecting material for future historians so that a "true history of the great struggle" would "shed lustre on the <u>American</u> name." Hopefully, Jones continued, the SHS could hasten the day when the blue and the gray would do one another justice. Jones actually engaged in extensive correspondence with the US War Department in order to arrange an exchange of records, believing that such reciprocation would benefit both Northern and Southern accounts of the conflict.[63]

Jones did anticipate exoneration from future historians, but arguments stressing the *SHSP*'s quasi-neutrality can be exaggerated. True, the SHS welcomed biased accounts of the war, expressing the society's intention of printing conflicting accounts over contentious matters. Yet what can be lost in the discussion, and what is so crucial to remember, is that Jones served as final redactor of these accounts. Even if he did not edit the articles' wording, his strategic use of these pieces spoke volumes concerning his own biases. His arrangements set the parameters for discourse and instilled in Jones more power to shape white Southern memory than even *SHSP* writers themselves possessed.

In one editorial paragraph, Jones wrote of the impropriety of arbitrating controversial issues, or siding with one contributor over another. Instead, the *Papers* would print "impartially and without comment, *both* sides."[64] What Jones meant by "both sides," however, was not both sides of the Mason-Dixon. Jones meant both sides of issues on which two Confederates disagreed. Regardless of the society's stated purpose, the goal of the SHS was not to construct an objective account of the war, or even to till the soil for future objective accounts; the goal of Jones and the society was to narrate a specifically *Southern* account of the war. Jones could have admitted as much, since he remained thoroughly convinced that Northern accounts of the war were far too corrupt to be trusted.

Even in his pursuit of a specifically Southern narrative, Jones did not extract himself from the fray. He printed a disproportionate amount of material on what he believed was the heart of the Confederacy: the Army of Northern Virginia. When veterans of the western theater protested, Jones responded that he had concentrated on Lee's army only because he had access to the material. If westerners would send in their accounts, he would gladly publish them.[65] Jones also ensured that the *Papers* revolved around Lee, taking care to check potential rivals (like Jackson). Jones was quick to print articles crucifying Longstreet, and when publishing rebuttals from the general, Jones made sure to provide Early's rejoinders.

Jones shrugged off criticisms that the *Papers* were stirring up bitter feelings between the North and South. He wrote that if his treatment of the prisoner issue offended Northerners and hampered reconciliation, then "it will only prove that their friendship is bound to us by so brittle a thread that it is scarcely worth an effort to preserve it." He was willing to print anti-South articles, but did not do so out of a sense of evenhandedness. Instead, he published them in order to expose the absurdity of "so called 'history'" and to advance his claim that the North was intent on shaming the South.[66]

Jones's modus operandi was often to let critics have just enough rope to hang themselves. In the summer of 1881, he printed selections of an article by New York author Rossiter Johnson. But Jones did not publish the original piece (from *The North American Review*); the article was actually a reprint of a reprint—a truncated version he pulled from the *Army and*

Navy Journal. He included comments from the *Army and Navy* editor, who dismissed Johnson's claims that Lee had never won an offensive battle, or that the SHS exemplified the deliberate "falsification of history."[67]

The Johnson article is intriguing for a number of reasons, not the least of which is its systematic assault on Lost Cause attitudes. Johnson's article demonstrates that while many Northerners would accept, or at least tolerate, certain tenets of the Lost Cause, there were many like Johnson who were determined to demolish the mythology. Johnson delivered a blistering attack on Lost Causers, arguing that there was "nothing heroic in their struggle" aside from the courage to fight. He criticized the South's "ludicrous definition of chivalry" and expounded on atrocities he felt made the "lost cause" the epitome of "vulgarity."[68]

Beyond his revulsion at alleged war crimes, Johnson delivered a penetrating assessment of white Southern memory. He derided how Southerners had remembered the war, ridiculing their "preposterous school-books" and their falsification of battle reports. He called out the "literary conspiracy" that had transformed ex-Confederates into heroes and had set about "to glorify the achievements which they didn't achieve, to change the apparent motive of the war, to magnify the genius of the rebel generals, and belittle their conquerors—an endeavor to write into respectability the meanest of causes, and invest with a glamour of heroism the most inexcusable of crimes."[69]

For Johnson, the Lost Cause ploy was transparent. He objected to Southerners for not using the descriptor "Civil War" and for reassessing troop numbers in order to make it appear that Confederate armies had even less and the Union armies even more. He decried the glorification of Lee, saying that Southerners believed "Lee, who never won an offensive battle, was the great general of the war. Grant was a blunderer—always blundering into success."[70]

Johnson specifically charged the "historical society at Richmond" as being a "bureau for the falsification of history." He astutely noted the SHS's strategy of misdirection: by focusing on "inessential accuracies"—such as troop numbers and casualties—the society avoided questions of real consequence. Northerners could not allow Southerners to write the history of the war, he contended; that privilege belonged to the Union. "The field is theirs, for they won it," he wrote, "and it will be a ghastly solecism if the philosophy of their inspiration and the records of their valor are to be at the mercy of the same murderous hands that sent them to the grave."[71]

Johnson's vitriolic criticism of the SHS likely left Jones unfazed. In fact, Jones believed that such caustic language played right into his hands. The more libelous Johnson's attacks appeared, the more justification there was for the SHS to right the ship of history. By the time Jones left his post as editor of the *Papers*, he felt he had done just that. But his battle for Southern history was not yet over, and his determination to preserve a faithful narrative had not yet faded. Within four years of his *SHSP* resignation, Jones was narrating white Southern Baptists' history vis-à-vis African Americans. Within nine years of his resignation he had written a school textbook, trusting that such a work would do for Southern children what the *Papers* had done for their parents. Through this primer, Jones would equip the next generation with carefully forged spectacles through which to view rightly both the Civil War and their own Southern identity.

✣ ✣ ✣ ✣ ✣

While not a well-known work of his, Jones's 1891 pamphlet, "Work Among the Negroes of the South," offers special insight into his views of race.[72] Furthermore, the piece demonstrates yet another attempt of Jones to craft and to preserve a particular narrative of the white South. He composed and distributed the pamphlet while serving as assistant secretary of the Home Mission Board of the Southern Baptist Convention. The goal of the tract was to provide a historical overview of white Southern Baptists' relationship with African Americans and to chart a course forward as the nineteenth century drew to a close.

Jones began the work with a disclaimer. He would not, he stressed, discuss any of the "'buried issues' connected with the negro race." Instead, he acknowledged, "The negro is here. He is here a freedman, and he is here to stay, and to exert no inconsiderable influence upon the destiny of the Republic." He then asked, "What will we do with him? What shall we do for his further enlightenment? What shall we do to Christianize him?" Such questions, Jones felt, were "*practical* questions connected with the 'negro problem.'"[73] Before addressing any of these inquiries, Jones had already revealed important presuppositions, many of which he shared with the majority of nineteenth-century white Southerners. Jones espoused a decidedly paternalistic attitude toward African Americans, assuming that they were naturally unenlightened and in need of white tutelage. Furthermore, despite his past contact with African American congregations, Jones portrayed African Americans as largely unchristianized. By equating emancipation with the "negro problem," he revealed his belief that white Christians were burdened with the education and evangelization of African Americans, even a quarter century after the war's end.

Drawing on stock themes of the Lost Cause, Jones tried to soften slavery's image. While admitting that some slave-owners had not performed their "full duty" to their servants regarding Christian education, he maintained that "no laboring class in the world was ever better provided with religious instruction by their employers." Just as Lost Causers idealized the master-slave relationship, Jones idealized the relationship between former masters and former slaves. Even in the "dark days" of Reconstruction there existed the "kindliest feeling between the freedmen and their former owners, many touching scenes were enacted between them, and much was done by our white people for the good of 'our brother in black.'"[74]

Jones recognized the past work of other "evangelical Christians," but he emphasized the role of Baptists in the evangelization of slaves. Still, he could not resist invoking the name of the great (non-Baptist) Stonewall Jackson. Jones admired the general's dedication to a "colored Sunday-school," and he included an oft-cited Jackson anecdote to prove the point. As Jones had done for so many years for the *Religious Herald*, he drew on his intimate and apostolic connection with Confederate leaders in order to inspire Baptists to greatness.

Jones also used his tract to correct what he believed to be specious narratives. He noted that while Reconstruction had indeed brought "considerable alienation between the races," Southern whites were still the ones funding African American churches. He also disputed the claim that the education of former slaves was owed solely to Northern initiative. He stressed that he did not share the pessimistic attitude of some concerning the religious education of former slaves, writing that African Americans were neither "black angels" nor "black demons." Believing that African American churches would grow with or without white aid, he still worried about "ignorance and vice" as well as "corrupt doctrines and practices in some of their churches."[75]

Jones made clear that the religious education of former slaves remained the responsibility of white Southerners. "They are our 'neighbors,' our friends, and have peculiar claims upon us which we dare not evade, ignore, or neglect," he wrote. He then appealed to white self-interest in observing, "If there were no higher motive, we should be stirred by the consideration that these millions of negroes are held in our midst — that they are *here to stay* — and *that if we do not raise them up by the power of the gospel they will most assuredly drag us down.*"[76] Apparently, Jones believed that the best method for prodding his readers toward action was to fuse paternalism with practicality.

Jones's tract revealed that he had adopted a number of widespread and stereotypical narratives. He blunted the image of slavery; he idealized the relationship between whites and African Americans in the antebellum and postwar South; he lamented the Reconstruction period; and he asserted that African Americans needed white instruction, believing that if left to themselves, African Americans were prone to immorality and false teaching.

At the same time, Jones grafted into these narratives distinctive mythologies that were characteristic of his postwar work. First, Jones emphasized the roles of Baptists. Such an emphasis is unsurprising in a pamphlet published by and for Baptists. That said, the pamphlet was further proof that while acknowledging the contributions of non-Baptist evangelicals, Jones was proud of and firmly committed to his denomination. Second, Jones emphasized the roles of Confederates. Not only citing Jackson, he referenced multiple Confederate officers who had shown unyielding dedication to Sunday school and African American education. In what had become his signature since the war's end, Jones effortlessly merged the Baptist cause with the Lost Cause. As the nineteenth century drew to a close, Jones felt that both of these causes spoke to what he considered to be "the negro problem."

✣ ✣ ✣ ✣ ✣

A driving force behind Jones's battle for Southern history was his fear that the conquering North would propagate a definitive and one-sided narrative of the Civil War. This fear prompted Jones at times to take extreme measures, such as performing an impromptu surgery on his son's schoolbook. As historian James McPherson writes, ex-Confederates saw Northern textbooks as "the serpent in the garden"; these books would expose "innocent Southern children to the knowledge of good and evil—mostly Northern good and Southern evil."[77] By the 1870s, Jones had resolved to expel the serpent, and after two decades of gathering sources, in 1896 he produced his *School History of the United States.*

He began his work with a classic Jones introduction—one that proclaimed his apostolic status: "Born, reared and educated on Southern soil, following for four years with youthful devotion the battle-flag of the Southern Confederacy, for twelve years secretary of the Southern Historical Society, and during all of these years devoting time and close attention to American history, I may modestly claim that I have had some facilities for knowing, and some qualifications for preparing, a history of the United States which shall be acceptable to the South and fit to be taught in her schools."[78]

As to the presuppositions he brought to the study of American history, Jones's message was divided. On the one hand, he claimed to have left out "sectional and partisan bias." On the other hand, his work was directed toward Southerners, and he critiqued Southern authors who had attempted to remain "neutral" in their textbooks, thereby producing works that were "colorless on the great questions that have divided the sections." He also anticipated concerns that his book gave too much space to the Civil War, and he comforted readers with the knowledge that if too much attention had been spent in one section, that was only because there were so many errors of others that needed to be corrected.[79]

Jones's work was largely a Civil War textbook with a lengthy introduction. Even though he began his history with the discovery and exploration of what would become America, he gave the most space to a section he entitled, "The War for Southern Independence." Here he dedicated more pages to the first year of the war than he did the entire American Revolution. Jones knew that his textbook afforded him a unique opportunity to influence the next generation of Southerners. By focusing by and large on the war, Jones articulated themes for children that he had long promoted during his time as editor of the *SHSP*.

As to the origin of the war, Jones placed the responsibility squarely on the North. He wrote of Lincoln's "coercion" of Southerners who were only exercising their "inalienable rights." He denied that Southerners had fired the first shot of the war, agreeing with another writer that the aggressor was not the first to shoot, but the one who first made shooting necessary. In this regard, John Brown's raid was "the first gun," and Sumter was "as pure an act of self-defense, as simple a repelling of invasion, as is to be found in history." "The policy of the Confederacy was peace," he argued, and "the war was begun by the Federal Government, and that government alone is responsible for all the horrors which ensued."[80]

Jones was generally unsparing in his treatment of Northerners. He portrayed Southerners as more religious, noting that the South had invoked God in the Confederate Constitution, while in response to President James Buchanan's call for a fast day, many Republicans reacted with "ridicule and ribald jest." Addressing religion in the Confederate Army, he affirmed that "in no armies in the world's history has there been so much of evangelical religion, genuine piety or active effort for the salvation of others." Concerning Union officers, he called Sherman's burning of Atlanta "a most unjustifiable act of vandalism," and he condemned Sherman's actions as a "blot upon the American name and upon the civilization of the nineteenth century."[81]

As he had done before, Jones tempered his treatment of Grant. Regarding Lee's surrender, Grant's terms were "generous" and his actions "chivalric." Jones praised the Union Army for not gloating at Appomattox, an indication to Jones that the Federals respected their valiant adversaries. Of course, Jones's emphasis on Grant's generous terms may have had a self-serving function. By insisting that the terms were attractive, he was implicitly justifying why Southerners had not fought to the death. Likewise, a focus on the magnanimous terms reminded readers that although Lee and his armies had forfeited their arms, they had kept their dignity and honor. Jones's treatment of Lincoln also served a dual purpose. He called Lincoln "one of the most remarkable men in history." He also mourned the president's death, declaring that postwar Southerners would much rather have dealt with Lincoln than with Andrew Johnson.[82] Couched in Jones's lukewarm nod toward Lincoln, Jones bemoaned what he considered to be the bleak and brutal days of Reconstruction.

Jones's book paid keen attention to Lee, Jackson, and Davis, and he deployed his characteristic superlatives to exalt the triumvirate. He dedicated disproportionate space to Davis, proclaiming that the Confederate president's "undaunted courage and chivalric bearing" was unsurpassed "in all history." There was little hint of the Lee-Jackson rivalry that had surfaced from time to time in the *Papers*; instead, Jackson was "one of the greatest military geniuses," and Jones encouraged his young readers to consult Dabney's work on the general. He lavished praise on Lee, and as was Jones's custom, he buffed away any blemish on the general's record. Jones refrained from attacking Longstreet with the ferocity of earlier publications, but still made clear that Lee's subordinates, not Lee, failed at Gettysburg. Jones spoke of Longstreet's "superb fight" on the second day, but concluded that the general "failed in the main object of the attack." Jones also echoed his earlier sentiment that a victory at Gettysburg would have led to Southern independence.[83]

When matters turned to slavery and race, Jones once again blamed the North. Virginia resisted the slave trade, he wrote, but slave traders from England and the Northern colonies found the enterprise too profitable to abolish. Implicating the North, he observed that "New England's history on this question is one of sordid self-interest and meddlesome interference, instead of philanthropy." Regarding race, he called the Dred Scott decision of 1857 "manifestly just" and "entirely in accord with the fundamental principles of the Constitution." Of the Emancipation Proclamation, Jones asserted that the "final consummation of the edict, by a triumph of force over justice and right, was as bold a piece of wholesale robbery as ever the conqueror inflicted upon the conquered."[84]

Even though he had taken ample opportunities to condemn the North, Jones ended his textbook on a conciliatory note. He lauded the military leadership of the war, even installing select Federal officers in the pantheon of those whose greatness had neither precedent nor parallel. Along with his photographs of Confederate officers, he included in the textbook a number of Union officers (though not nearly as many).[85] In his final assessment of the postwar union, Jones wrote: "[A]nd if for four years we did fight against it [the nation] because we believed that sacred rights had been violated, and the principles of the Constitution set at naught, yet since the decision went against us, and it has been decreed that there shall be henceforth one general government, one flag and one country, let us not only 'accept the situation,' as our people have cheerfully done, but vie with our brethren across the old border in making our common country indeed the freest, most enlightened, the purest and the happiest land on which the sun shines."[86] Along with this irenic closing, Jones made a final plea for the sections to show one another justice. This justice would include a mutual respect between Union and Confederate veterans who had fought and died honorably on the field of battle. Of course, Southern reincorporation into the national narrative did not come cheaply. What conciliatory white Southerners understood as due justice, former slaves would experience as profound injustice, as white memory marched on unabated, and the drums of valor slowly drowned out the songs of freedom.

✠ ✠ ✠ ✠ ✠

Through his work with the *SHSP*, his tract on Baptists and African Americans, or his textbook on American history, Jones fulfilled the second point of his two-pronged apostolic mission: to preserve a faithful narrative. While Jones edited and wrote with one eye on the future, he did not leave exoneration to chance. He and the SHS trusted that future historians would vindicate the South, but in Jones's mind, he had already drawn the contours of Confederate history. He carefully edited the *Papers* in order to support and spread the message he desired. The differing opinions that he boasted of publishing did not delve into the mire of North-South relations or foster actual dialogue on matters of secession or slavery. Despite the host of temperamental and easily offended ex-Confederate contributors who bickered over troop numbers and movements, the SHSP remained a largely controlled environment for the dissemination of the Lost Cause.

By directing readers toward the virtues of the Confederate trinity, Jones had inspired Southerners to emulate moral icons, and in so doing, to sustain a distinctly Southern identity. Now, by handing down a Confederate account of the war, Jones entrusted to readers a Southern mythology. Far from being a mere reporting of the past, this mythology was, in the purest sense, a story through which white Southerners understood themselves. Through this mythology white Southerners could interpret their trials and cultivate their identity, and by bestowing this mythology onto future generations, they empowered their children to sing the songs of Zion in a foreign land.

CHAPTER SIX

Finishing the Course:
Jones and the Changing Landscape
of the Lost Cause

Though men deserve, they may not win, success.
The brave will honour the brave, vanquished none the less.

— Confederate Veteran

As he delivered a sermon before a roomful of wizened Confederate veterans in the spring of 1901, J. William Jones may have felt as though his Southern champions were looking approvingly over his shoulder. Jones's text was Hebrews 12:1–2. His focus: the "cloud of witnesses" whose pious lives and resilient faith inspired Christians to persevere to the end. "Are you prepared when your summons comes joyfully to 'cross over the river and rest under the shade of the trees' with Davis and Lee, and Jackson, and other Christian comrades who wait and watch for your coming?" he asked his fellow Confederates. "Patriotism is not religion," he continued, "and to have been a true soldier of your country does not constitute you a soldier of the Cross."[1] The years were waning fast, and Jones knew it. Swiftly and surely, ex-Confederates were fading from the scene. Jones beseeched veterans who had followed their cherished leaders into the inferno of war to follow them now into paradise. Jones's message was evolving. So too was the Lost Cause.

Although Jones professed a clear demarcation between patriotism and religion, the line he drew between the two was often too faint to see. He tapped into patriotic ardor in order to further the Christian gospel, beckoning ex-Confederates to mirror the faith of Lee, Jackson, and Davis. In fact, Jones's entire postwar career exhibited an inextricable link between patriotism and religion. As much as anyone, he transformed political and military figures into Christ-figures. Believing that his work had been blessed by three icons of Southern virtue, Jones defended the Southern story and disseminated the Confederate gospel until the end of his days.

In the last two decades of his life, Jones was unswerving in the execution of his apostolic mission to direct audiences toward incarnations of Southern virtue and to preserve an enduring Confederate narrative. Committed to this vision as he was, Jones also served as a transitional figure in the history of the Lost Cause. Some historians have highlighted that with the passing of Confederate veterans, the Lost Cause took on a new shape. Whereas first-generation Lost Causers focused on the superiority of Confederates, second-generation (and later) Lost Causers sought to situate the South in the united nation, paradoxically casting the South as defeated yet victorious, tragic yet romantic, Southern yet American.[2]

Jones's career reflected the traditions of both first- and second-generation white Southerners. On one hand, he portrayed Confederate soldiers as morally and martially superior to their Federal counterparts. On the other hand, he also cast white Southerners as the very embodiment of the American spirit. For Jones, since Southerners held the strongest claim to American history, they could willingly reunite with Northerners. Serving as a bridge between two iterations of the Lost Cause meant that Jones was not only committed to defending Southern identity in the wake of defeat; he was also determined to reincorporate the South into the American narrative and to reclaim the South's proud standing in the American nation.

✠ ✠ ✠ ✠ ✠

After helming one of the most powerful instruments of Lost Cause propagation, Jones resigned as secretary of the SHS in 1887. He then accepted a position as the assistant corresponding secretary of the Home Mission Board (HMB) of the Southern Baptist Convention in Atlanta, where he remained until 1893. His work with the HMB took him all over the South and as far west as Texas and Native American territories, where he helped to found mission churches.[3] The same year he began his work with the HMB, Jones published one of his most successful works, *Christ in the Camp*, a text that solidified his reputation in the South as the preeminent authority on Confederate religion. The timing of the publication is a fitting description of the way in which Jones felt denominational identity related to the Lost Cause. At the same time he was publishing a book that lauded the interdenominationalism of Confederate revivals—circumstantial and limited as that collaboration was—he reaffirmed his denominational loyalty by leaving the SHS for the HMB. The move was not a surprising one; as was the case throughout his postwar career, Jones kept one foot in the Baptist church and one foot in the Confederate camp.

At the HMB, Jones served under corresponding secretary Isaac Taylor Tichenor. By the time Jones arrived at the HMB, Tichenor—widely credited with righting the ship of a foundering HMB—had been searching for new and creative ways to expand the mission and influence of Southern Baptists. By the late 1880s, Tichenor had set his sights on Cuba. That the HMB should consider a foreign nation within its purview sparked no small controversy. For Tichenor, the mission made perfect sense, as he assumed the United States would eventually annex Cuba, thus bringing the country into Baptists' "home field." There were a number of unsavory aspects of the Cuban mission; aside from being imperialistic, the mission was also paternalistic, working under the assumption that Cubans were incapable of taking care of themselves.[4]

While the mission in Cuba began more than a year before Jones joined the HMB, he heartily embraced the venture. In 1888, he became the editor of a new HMB publication, *Our Home Field*. The periodical enjoyed a circulation of about ten thousand, and Jones took ample opportunity in the paper to promote the HMB's efforts in Cuba. Quite accustomed by now to soliciting donations from Southern Baptists, Jones took to the newspapers in order to raise funds for the HMB and for the Cuban mission in particular. Specifically, he and the HMB wanted money for the Havana House. The Havana House had once been an old theater, but A. J. Diaz, Baptist minister and head of Baptist work in Cuba, converted the space into a church. The anemic Southern economy troubled Jones, and he confessed that financial strains were hampering the HMB's mission and that the Board was having a difficult time making payments on the Havana House.[5]

If Jones was familiar with fundraising, he was equally acquainted with controversy. One dispute centered on the work of Diaz, the Board's primary representative in Cuba. Diaz had become increasingly dissatisfied with the HMB's control of the mission, believing that the board's power over local churches in Cuba was compromising Baptist polity. When Tichenor fell ill and was absent from his post, Jones took it upon himself to correspond with the disgruntled Diaz. Jones affirmed the autonomy of the local Baptist church, but reminded Diaz that if the Cuban churches wished to be independent, they would be cut off from HMB support. Jones's heavy-handed approach did not sit well with Diaz, and it was up to Tichenor to ameliorate the situation when he returned.[6]

While at the HMB, Jones continued his close relationship with his mentor, John Albert Broadus. He wrote Broadus often, requesting advice on both professional and personal matters. Confiding in Broadus, Jones frequently expressed worry over his sons' academic careers, and not without reason. His second son, Pendleton, had contracted a lengthy illness while at Southern Baptist Theological Seminary (SBTS), and Jones contemplated withdrawing him from school. Jones's youngest son, Howard, attended Wake Forest College, but did not fare much better. He missed classes due to sickness, and then joined a fraternity (which was prohibited). Seminary officials asked him not to return. But academics were not Jones's only concern; he admitted to Broadus that both Howard and Ashby (Jones's fourth son) had been "careless in their religious duties." Fortunately for Jones, his oldest son, Carter Helm, preached the two brothers under conviction, and they were "thoroughly 'converted again.'"[7]

Four of Jones's sons anticipated entering the ministry, and they seemed destined to follow in their father's footsteps until Ashby failed to graduate from SBTS. Jones was distraught and expressed his belief to Broadus that a grudge-holding faculty member had "fixed the record" to ensure Ashby's failure. Jones identified the professor as "Dr. Sampey"—likely John R. Sampey, who served as professor of Old Testament at the time and eventually as president of SBTS (1929–1942). As matters would have it, Sampey was well known for his adoration of Lee, but his and Jones's mutual admiration for the general did not prevent Jones from theorizing that Sampey had targeted Ashby. Jones confessed that he could not trust himself to talk about the circumstances and that he had instructed his other sons to "suffer in silence" instead of disparaging SBTS — a seminary Jones proclaimed he had "loved and served with almost idolatrous devotion."[8] The stumble notwithstanding, Ashby joined three of his brothers in becoming Baptist ministers (Jones's third son, Frank, became a lawyer in New York). Just as Jones's Lost Cause legacy endured through his writings, Jones's Baptist legacy survived through his sons.

With Tichenor's frequent absences due to illness, Jones's work with the HMB was demanding. Still, he remained dedicated to his apostolic duties. When Jefferson Davis died in 1889, Jones soon after published *The Davis Memorial Volume.* Through his superlative-laden opus, he confirmed once again his intimate acquaintance with the Confederate's finest, giving readers rare insight into the Christian character of the Confederacy's president. Jones's testament also served as a counterbalance to the works of Lost Cause writers like E. A. Pollard, who had mercilessly criticized Davis in the wake of the Confederacy's defeat.

In 1893, the University of Virginia (UVA) offered Jones a two-year chaplaincy. Leaving the HMB was a difficult decision. "If I know my own heart at all," he wrote Broadus, "I want to do *what is my duty* regardless of personal interest, convenience, or inclination."[9] As if echoing Lee himself, Jones recognized duty as the supreme motivator. Admitting that the UVA chaplaincy would allow him more time to publish books, Jones decided to accept the position. The duty animating Jones was not just a calling to college ministry, but a responsibility to continue his work of crafting and defending white Southern memory.

A UVA chaplain's responsibilities were time consuming. A typical Sunday involved Bible class at 9:00 a.m., a sermon at 11:00 a.m., meetings in the afternoon, and then an evening sermon. On weekdays there were morning prayers and a variety of meetings and visitations. Jones presided over a student body that was denominationally diverse, including not only evangelical denominations, but also Roman Catholics and Jews. Since a characteristic feature of Jones's ministry was an openness to worship with other denominations, he was well suited for college chaplaincy. At the same time, he was dissatisfied that there were fewer Baptist students than Episcopalian and Presbyterian students. In December 1893, he asked Broadus to come speak at the university, noting that Broadus's message would "be so valuable to the cause of Truth in general, and to our Denomination in particular."[10]

Jones envisioned a spiritual renewal on the campus of UVA, writing to the *Religious Herald* in the summer of 1894 that he coveted a revival of "old-time religion." He invited preachers from several denominations and even had two of his sons — Carter Helm and Pendleton — fill the pulpit. In the fall of 1894, an organized "week of prayer" had the intended consequences, and Jones rejoiced that his chaplain's study thereafter had "almost a constant stream of students coming to talk on the subject of personal religion." In his fervor for student chaplaincy, or perhaps in preparation for the end of his two-year stint at UVA, Jones also began serving as a chaplain for the Miller School of Albemarle, in Charlottesville.[11]

The years 1894–1897 were for Jones a time of transition, loss, and accomplishment. In the spring of 1894, Jones became one of four vice presidents for the SBC. He ended his chaplaincy at UVA in 1895. That year also saw the death of Broadus. Jones mourned the loss of his dear friend, and in the spring, he led a memorial service at the university. In April 1895, he completed his *School History of the United States*.[12] Published in 1896, the textbook would become one of Jones's most well-known works. Many Southern schools had been clamoring for history books that were void of Northern bias, and Jones's work provided what he believed was an essential corrective to the Northern narrative of history in general, and of the Civil War in particular.

Jones ended his chaplaincy at the Miller School in late 1897. He moved to Richmond once more and began attending Leigh Baptist Church, where his son Ashby served as pastor. In 1900, Jones left Virginia and became pastor of Chapel Hill Baptist Church in North Carolina. Now in his sixties, he admitted the difficulty of leaving his home state, but vowed to do all he could for "Baptist interests" in the Old North State. While pastoring, Jones — who retained a perennial concern for the religious education of college-age men — also served as chaplain at the University of North Carolina. On at least one occasion, he delivered his popular lecture, "The Boys in Gray," at the university, and the proceeds went to the school's YMCA. In 1902, he left his pastorate and chaplain duties in Chapel Hill, took a position as the Secretary and Superintendent of the Confederate Memorial Association, and moved back to Richmond.[13]

With his health declining, Jones retired from pastoring in 1903. His passion for ministry and the Lost Cause, however, had not diminished. He was a regular at Confederate reunions and remained active in the Confederate Memorial Association. As part of his work with the association, Jones served as a trustee for fundraising efforts to found Battle Abbey, in Richmond. The purpose of Battle Abbey, which did not begin construction until after Jones's death, was both to memorialize Confederate soldiers and to preserve Confederate archives of the war. Jones also continued in his role as chaplain-general of the United Confederate Veterans (UCV), a position he had held since 1890.[14] In 1906, he ended his book-writing career the same way he had begun it: by venerating the life, career, and character of the South's greatest hero, Robert E. Lee. Jones's *Life and Letters of Robert Edward Lee: Soldier and Man* was in many ways a new edition of his 1874 book on Lee. While Jones included Lee correspondence that had never before been published, the thrust of the book was precisely what white Southern readers had come to expect from the Confederacy's apostle: a sweeping panegyric of the immortal Lee—an icon as incomparable in Christian virtue as he was in military genius.

As his career came to an end, Jones was satisfied that he had been true to his calling. He had honored the Confederate trinity by directing Southerners toward personifications of Christian virtue. He had also preserved a Confederate narrative, providing not only an accurate account of the war, but a legacy in which defeated white Southerners could find distinctiveness and take pride. And while Jones shaped and was shaped by Lost Cause attitudes of the late nineteenth and early twentieth centuries, he never diverged from his mission. As any great apostle, he was resolved to fight a good fight, to finish the course, and to keep the faith.

✠ ✠ ✠ ✠ ✠

Up until the end of his life, Jones stayed keenly aware of his mission. At an 1895 reunion of the UCV, he prayed: "Oh God! Our God, our help in years gone by, our hope for years to come—God of Abraham, Isaac and Jacob, God of Israel, God of the centuries, God of our fathers, God of Jefferson Davis, Robert Edward Lee, and Stonewall Jackson."[15] Hearers no doubt detected the Trinitarian structure of Jones's prayer. Even though he would at times add the names of other leaders to his UCV prayers, Jones's heart and mind revolved around the triumvirate of Lee, Jackson, and Davis.

Jones's admiration of Lee only grew with time. In 1893, Jones delivered an address on the general at UVA. As was Jones's custom, he blamed any supposed failures of Lee on "causes beyond his control," including subordinates who could not follow orders. Jones harped on the overwhelming numbers of the North, and he declared that prior to Petersburg Lee had "outgeneraled Grant at every point and defeated him in every battle." For Jones, Lee endured as the "greatest soldier," the "noblest gentleman," the "truest patriot," and the "purest man that ever figured in American history." In an 1899 article, Jones reiterated that Lee "completely outgeneraled Grant, whipped him in every battle, and foiled him at every point." Lee's mastery over Grant had long been a stock theme for Jones, and he buttressed the storyline whenever possible. Throughout the final two decades of his life, Jones continued to publish on Lee, often using anecdotes found in earlier Jones material.[16]

Thanks to Jones and other die-hard Lee admirers, Lee's possessions took on an almost relic-like quality. In 1899, Jones published an article that simply described Lee's office at Washington and Lee University. Jones hoped that for the sake of visitors the space would be preserved just as Lee had left the office. Jones extolled Lexington—the final resting place of both Lee and Jackson—as the "Mecca of our Southland," and he anticipated that pilgrims would flock to the university to lay eyes on the pew where Lee had sat and the chapel where Lee had worshiped.[17]

In 1906, Jones issued a second book on Lee. Jones's *Life and Letters of Robert Edward Lee: Soldier and Man*—a hulking work of nearly five hundred pages—was Jones's final book, and an ultimate testament to the South's most hallowed general. Jones attested to his intimate association with the former college president, promising readers both exhaustive research and unparalleled access to the general's correspondence. Jones's book would not indulge in bitter memories, he stated, and would appeal to "all lovers of true Christian manhood."[18] Just as white Northerners and Southerners could reunite on the basis of soldierly courage, they could also agree that Lee represented all that was pure and good in the American spirit.

Jones's book provided a detailed treatment of Lee's early life, including his lineage, childhood, and stellar military career at West Point. Jones portrayed Lee as one wholly committed to the preservation of the Union, but also as one duty-bound to his native Virginia. As for slavery, Jones quoted Lee as admitting that the institution was a "moral and political evil in any country." Even so, Lee acknowledged that slaves were better off in America than in Africa, and that only Providence could determine when the institution should come to an end. Jones hammered on Lost Cause themes that he had worked for over four decades to engrain into white Southern consciousness: the constitutionality of secession, the inexhaustible resources of the Federals, and the failure of Lee's subordinates.[19]

What was truly remarkable about Jones's book was that so much of the text was unremarkable. While the book contained numerous never-before-published letters of Lee, much of the correspondence revolved around mundane aspects of Lee's life. These seemingly trivial details, however, were important for Jones. First of all, such material reinforced Jones's claim that he had unprecedented access to Lee the man. As Jones testified in the book's introduction, "I think I may, without improper egotism, claim some qualifications for writing of him as he really was." Second of all, Jones's use of commonplace letters indicated the relic-like status of Lee's correspondence. If Lee's office was sacred space for Lost Causers, Lee's letters were holy writ. Little mind that many of the letters recounted the humdrum minutiae of Lee's life; heretofore unpublished letters were new revelations into the spirit of one Jones "conservatively" deemed as the "greatest soldier of the war, if not of history."[20]

As for Stonewall Jackson, Jones published numerous articles praising Lee's most trusted subordinate. Jones's pieces on Jackson — while acknowledging certain flaws in the general — were nearly as saccharine as Jones's books on Lee. Jones conceded that at times Jackson could be "too severe" and "not always just," but that many other Confederate generals would have benefited from being likeminded disciplinarians. Jones praised Jackson's military legacy, decreeing that "the world had never seen an uninspired man who deserves higher rank as a true Christian." Jones frequently contributed anecdotes about Jackson, and the general was a regular topic of Jones's lectures.[21]

Jones never let Jackson overshadow Lee, but neither did Jones go to great lengths to diminish Jackson's greatness. In 1881 Jones had critiqued Jackson's gaffes at the Battle of Seven Days. When publishing the 1906 book on Lee, however, Jones cited authorities like Robert Lewis Dabney and Jefferson Davis in order to exonerate Jackson. In 1901, Jackson's faults were the last things on Jones's mind. He referred to Jackson as "one of the immortals," calling him the "personification of the genius of battle" and "one of the greatest soldiers of all history."[22]

Although his work on Jackson suggested that Jones saw no incompatibility between the Christian message and the Lost Cause message, Jones did draw a line when matters involved incorporating military history into his sermons. In response to one inquirer who wondered if Jones had lectured on Jackson's military record from the pulpit, Jones responded: "I did not lecture, but preached as earnest a gospel sermon as I am capable of preaching on the 'Christian character' of this soldier of the cross. At proper times and places I am in the habit of discussing the military career of this wonderful genius, and I make no apology to mortal man for doing so; but in the pulpit, and on Sunday, I never speak on such themes."[23] Even though Jones did not feel as if he had conflated Christianity and the Lost Cause, his nuanced distinction between the two was often undetectable.

As he had done with Lee and Jackson, Jones maintained unwavering allegiance to Jefferson Davis. Jones continued to think that Davis had been maligned by Northerners and scapegoated by Southerners after the war. In an 1899 letter, Jones reminded a colleague, "I . . . was loyal to our grand President during all of the inexcusable, and malicious fight made on him, and am loyal to him still." The day after Davis died, Jones wrote a letter to Davis's widow, Varina. Jones offered his condolences and included a poem that his wife, Judith, had composed about the fallen president. Entitled "Our Dead Chief," the poem anticipated language that Jones would employ in his soon-to-follow *Davis Memorial Volume*. For example, Judith professed that Davis had sacrificed himself for the South: "A martyr for a glorious cause, // For us his heart has bled." Describing Davis's "broken heart," Judith also bemoaned the way in which postwar writers had attacked the president: "The target of a hundred pens, // Aflame with hate their arrow sends // Full many a poison dart."[24] The Joneses trusted that Davis would find in death a vindication he had been denied in life.

In January 1890, while serving as editor of *Our Home Field*, Jones included a tribute to Davis. Notably, Jones had for months prior featured the portraits of prominent Baptists on the front page of the paper. Now, he included a picture of Davis. For Jones, there was nothing unusual about recognizing a Baptist turned Episcopalian ex-president on the front page of a periodical dedicated to Baptist home missions. Here again Jones exhibited his confidence in the seamlessness of the Lost Cause and the Baptist cause. Ever ready to assert apostolic privilege, he guaranteed his fellow Baptists the he had known Davis "intimately" and that the president had called him "Friend." Jones named Davis "one of the truest, noblest Christian gentlemen whom the wondrous country, or this marvelous century, has produced." Jones then noted—based on his "most intimate association and freest conversation" with Davis—that the president "cordially accepted the grand old doctrine of salvation by grace and justification by faith."[25] In case any of his readers were in doubt, Jones confirmed that ex-Confederates could not have asked for a more spiritually enlightened leader.

With Davis's death, the last member of the Confederate trinity had crossed over the river. For Jones, however, Confederate heroes deserved more than mourning; in fact, they demanded emulation. He believed that Lee, Jackson, and Davis remained models for holy living, and he continued to direct white Southerners toward these incarnations of Christian virtue. The Confederate nation was no more, but inasmuch as Southerners followed the examples of their Confederate exemplars, the South would endure.

✝ ✝ ✝ ✝ ✝

The graying Jones never forgot his aim to preserve a true and lasting narrative of the Confederacy. His writings throughout the 1890s and into the twentieth century rehashed many of the Lost Cause tropes he had defended so enthusiastically in his younger days. Yet even while the core of his message remained largely unchanged, Jones expounded on certain themes, such as his focus on the rank-and-file soldiers of the South. In 1899, he contributed an article to *Confederate Military History*, a book of essays compiled by former Confederate general, Clement Anselm Evans. Writing on "The Morale of the Confederate Army," Jones aggrandized not just the leaders of the Confederacy, but the common soldier as well. He argued that the Confederate Army was equal or superior to any military in history, and he described the troops as the "very flower of our Southern chivalry, the bone and sinew, the brain and brawn, the wealth, education, social position and moral worth of our Southern manhood."[26]

The Evans essay was not the first or last time Jones would concentrate on the virtues of workaday Confederates. In 1894, he gave an address on "The Private Soldier"; in 1902, he returned to the same theme in a Confederate reunion address. Ironically, his preoccupation with Confederate leadership may have led him to emphasize the role of the homespun soldier. According to Jones, Lee himself had called those troops the true heroes of the war.[27] If true, then Jones diverted his gaze from Confederate leaders only because Lee had essentially given him permission to do so.

Whereas Jones's emphasis on common soldiers demonstrated his willingness to move beyond apotheosizing leaders, he seldom strayed from his traditional narratives. In the Evans essay, Jones continued to showcase the overwhelming odds against which the South fought, and he still accused Union soldiers of committing heinous acts toward women and children. He also condemned the treatment of Confederate troops in Northern prisons. Finally, and expectedly, he stressed the religious nature of the Confederate Army, to which he credited the highest proportion of "active, Christian men" and more revivals and conversions than in any army in history.[28]

Jones was a fixture in Southern periodicals, trumpeting the Lost Cause melody in journals such as the *Confederate Veteran*. There he insisted that Southerners had gone to war over the issue of constitutional freedom, unlike Northerners who had "trampled under foot the Constitution of our country and the liberties bequeathed to us by our fathers." He stood by his estimations of troop numbers, mocking Northern authors who had "exhausted their ingenuity and skill in seeking to lessen Grant's numbers, and increase Lee's."[29] Like many Lost Causers, Jones poured over the tedium of such figures. The "overwhelming odds" narrative was a keystone of the Lost Cause mythology—the most effective way of warding off criticisms that Confederates had been deficient in strength, skill, courage, or honor.

Jones carried on battles he thought he had won as editor of the *SHSP*. For example, he pounced whenever there surfaced a discussion of wartime prisoners. As late as 1905, he was still decrying the treatment of Confederate troops in Federal prisons. Recalling how thoroughly authors had treated the matter in the *SHSP*, Jones felt that there was little more for objectors to say. As far as he was concerned, no one had yet been able to discredit *SHSP* accounts of Union war atrocities, and disputing such indisputable truths could only impede efforts at reconciliation. Despite the lip service to sectional harmony, Jones charged back into the fray of the infamous Gettysburg controversy. Of course, he reminded readers that Longstreet had not only lost the battle of Gettysburg, but had alone ignited the debate over culpability. As readers surely recognized by now, Jones was unrelenting until he had the last word.[30]

White Southerners considered Jones an authority on Confederate history even before he published his *School History of the United States*. With the 1896 release, however, Jones reasserted himself as—in historian Charles Reagan Wilson's apt description—a "self-appointed truth squad." Groups like the United Daughters of the Confederacy (UDC) endorsed his work for use in schools, and Jones began reviewing the textbooks of other authors. After assessing a publication he would either give his stamp of approval or discard the text as yet another of the "Yankee books" bent on spreading noxious rumors about the South.[31]

When writers disputed any of Jones's historical claims, his rebuttals were swift and firm. In 1897, reviewer H. L. Wayland questioned a number of Jones's assertions in *School History*. Specifically, Wayland accused Jones of reading secession into colonial and antebellum history, as if to suggest that the South had precedent for leaving the Union in 1861. Wayland also quarreled with Jones's numbers regarding prisoner deaths. "I do not charge Dr. Jones with conscious misrepresentation," Wayland commented. "He is so passionately devoted to his old commander, General Lee, and to the cause which General Lee represented, that it is altogether likely that he is unfitted for taking a judicial view of the facts." Even though Jones often did not take criticism well, he responded to Wayland's remarks point by point. Unfazed and systematic, Jones detailed his rationale and his research.[32] Over the course of his postwar career, Jones had become accustomed to the scrutiny, and he exerted great effort in picking apart the arguments of his detractors.

While he remained collected in his reply to Wayland, Jones could at times respond sternly to critics. E. C. Dargan, professor of homiletics at SBTS, knew this all too well. In 1896, Dargan wrote a review of Jones's *School History* for the *Christian Index*. "It is one-sided," Dargan opined. "In matter and method it is too evidently a piece of special pleading to be ever regarded as a good, all round, comprehensive history." One of Dargan's chief critiques was that Jones's book did not provide "sufficient consideration to the Northern point of view." Dargan observed the clearly disproportionate space that Jones allowed for the Civil War and then drew attention to a host of typographical errors in the text. Dargan committed the ultimate transgression, though, when he corrected Jones's knowledge of the war, calling out Jones for an anachronistic reference to the "Stars and Bars."[33]

Although Dargan's evaluation of Jones's book was highly complimentary in places, Jones failed to notice. Soon after the review appeared, Jones sent Dargan a personal and cutting response, writing, "I want to say to you privately, kindly but emphatically, that I regard your notice as one of the best specimens of 'damning with faint praise', and killing with hyper-criticism that I have ever seen, and that if your object had been (as I have no idea it was) to prevent any one from reading the book, I do not see how you could more effectively promote that object." He chastised Dargan for publicly enumerating typographical errors, feeling that the professor should have instead relayed this informing through private correspondence. Likening Dargan's criticism to "wounding a man in the dark," Jones took particular issue with Dargan's patronization: "Did you not think while penning these petty criticisms upon my style that you were correcting the essay of some unfledged student in the Homiletics class, instead of the book of a man who has published *thousands* of pages, whose style has passed muster before the best critics of the country, whose books have had a very wide circulation and reading, and whose present book was read and revised in ms. by Noah K. Davis, W. E. Peters, and J. C. Hiden?" For Jones, the wound was a deep one, not only because the critique reflected poorly on an alumnus of SBTS, but because the criticism had come from a fellow Southerner: "I confess that I have been utterly amazed that Southern men—and *South Carolinians* at that—should pronounce 'one-sided,' and 'partisan' a book which tells the 'truth, the whole truth, and nothing but the truth,' concerning our country's history."[34]

Jones believed that he shouldered the supreme duty to preserve a faithful narrative of the South, and his letter to Dargan put this mission on full display. Faintly echoing the apostle Paul's astonishment in the book of Galatians, Jones's letter to Dargan was in many ways a denouncement of Southerners who had turned to a false gospel. Jones tolerated no such heresy, and he allowed for no such questioning of his apostolic authority. Spurred by an errand as spiritual as it was historical, Jones's closing words to Dargan were oddly appropriate: "But pardon me for writing so much," Jones concluded, "I had not intended to inflict on you so lengthy an epistle."[35]

✠ ✠ ✠ ✠ ✠

Throughout his ministry, Jones had learned how to rally with non-Baptists for the sake of revival. Along the way, he discovered that the same trans-denominational approach was effective in propagating the Lost Cause. He delivered Lost Cause lectures in non-Baptist churches, and he continued to respect the work and advocacy of Father Abram J. Ryan, to whom Jones's wife, Judith, even dedicated a poem. Yet Jones's public and private correspondence left little doubt that he remained steadfastly Baptist. He expressed untiring gratitude and fierce dedication to SBTS, even describing his loyalty to the seminary as an "almost idolatrous devotion." In a letter to Broadus, Jones admitted his desire that his sons attend a school with a "Baptist atmosphere." He also concurred with sentiments that authors such as he "could do a great deal for the Baptist cause by preparing books outside of denominational lines."[36] Almost counterintuitively, here Jones interpreted interdenominationalism as a means of furthering Baptist interests. The nonsectarian nature of his writings was not intended to negate the need for denominations, but represented, at least in part, an effort to acquire as broad an appeal as possible, and thereby reflect well on Baptists.

Despite his support for Lost Cause partisans from non-Baptist denominations, there persisted an undercurrent of anti-Catholicism in Jones's work, in deed if not by word. An inherently anti-Catholic agenda drove his and Tichenor's work at the HMB, as many viewed the board's mission in Cuba as a Baptist challenge to the hegemony of Latin American Catholicism.[37] True, Jones was willing to celebrate a priest like Father Ryan, who conspicuously toed the line of Lost Cause orthodoxy. Jones's affirmation of Ryan, however, was in spite of the poet's Catholicism. In the mission field, Roman Catholics were competitors. In the world of the Lost Cause, matters were different, but not much so. For Jones—and for all those who interpreted the Lost Cause through the lens of divine (evangelical) chosenness—Roman Catholics essentially remained outsiders.

With regard to non-Baptist evangelicals, Jones made common cause with them when possible, but he was unwilling to suffer their doctrinal errors. In the summer of 1901, he wrote to the *Biblical Recorder* in order to defend baptism by immersion. In the article, he refuted claims that between Jerusalem and Gaza there existed too little water in which to immerse a candidate. "[W]e ought not to be too hard on our Pedobaptist brethren," he wrote. "They are very hard run for 'arguments' to sustain their position, and must be excused if they resort to very flimsy ones." He even cited a "'Low Church' Episcopalian" who agreed with his position. He then closed with an anecdote. When someone asked an African American pastor why so many African Americans were Baptist, the minister responded that unscholarly folk simply could not "explain away the Bible."[38] Jones's closing was less a statement on African American Baptists and more of a commentary on the proclivities of non-Baptists to avoid literal, common sense readings of scripture.

Jones stayed active in Baptist politics, both on the state and the national level. He took a special interest in the "Whitsitt controversy" of the 1890s. William H. Whitsitt, church historian and president of SBTS, had run afoul of many Baptists—Landmarkers especially—when he argued that Baptists had originated in the seventeenth century. Jones, who felt as though Whitsitt's potential resignation as president would hurt the seminary, urged Whitsitt to remain at his post. Sensing that Whitsitt's enemies were getting more press than Whitsitt's supporters, Jones came out in favor of the embattled president. Writing the *Religious Herald* in August 1897, Jones recalled the show of support that Whitsitt had received at the SBC meeting in Wilmington, North Carolina. There delegates gave Whitsitt a rousing ovation and, as far as Jones was concerned, exoneration: "If that was not a triumphant vindication of Dr. Whitsitt, a glorious victory, not for his historical opinions, but for his standing as a Baptist scholar, his competence to preside over the Seminary, and the principles of free investigation, free thought, and free speech, within the limits of the articles of faith of the Seminary—then what was it?"[39] Without officially endorsing Whitsitt's historical views, Jones defended Whitsitt's right to publish them.

Less than a month after his first article, Jones wrote another defense of Whitsitt, this time indicting those who were refusing to let the matter rest. In Jones's mind, the Wilmington meeting had all but settled the issue. "But, alas!" he wrote, "the truce was soon broken; the bugle call to battle was soon heard in the ranks of the opponents of Dr. Whitsitt, and it was soon found out that, instead of peace, we were to have more relentless war than ever before." Jones criticized colleagues who, in fear of a convention split or the founding of a rival seminary, felt that "we must sacrifice Whitsitt for the good of the cause." For Jones, this was unthinkable. To do so would be to "accept the new test of Baptist orthodoxy, 'baptismal succession,' traditionalism, and church history, instead of the old standard of our fathers—the Word of God, and Word of God alone, as the rule of our faith and the standard of our practice." Jones's response was unequivocal: "Can we afford to purchase peace at such a cost? For one, I say: No! a thousand times, No! Better, if it comes to that, let the Convention divide than that we should abandon the cherished principles of our faith."[40]

Perhaps more than any other event in Jones's life, the Whitsitt controversy established that Jones was against forfeiting for the sake of unity what he believed to be core Baptist principles. In fact, he had long held this attitude. Whether in his seminary days, wartime revivals, or postwar pastorates, he rejected any unity that required a dilution of his Baptist particularities. Fortunately for Jones, friendly cooperation with other denominations did not make these demands. Likewise, his participation in the Lost Cause did not compel him to hide his Baptistness. If the price of solidarity was a surrendering of denominational fidelity, he—as any good Baptist—would have dissented.

✟ ✟ ✟ ✟ ✟

Although Jones was one of the earliest purveyors of the Lost Cause message, the landscape of white Southern memory was beginning to shift by the end of his career. As Confederate veterans faded from the scene, second-generation writers took up the Lost Cause mantle. Understanding the developments and vicissitudes of the mythology during this time period is an unwieldy task. To address the challenge, historians Thomas Connelly and Barbara Bellows categorize two Lost Causes: an "Inner Lost Cause," which entailed a literary movement by "diehard" Confederates in the first three decades after the war, and a "National Lost Cause," which included second-generation efforts to come to terms with the South's place in the united nation. For Connelly and Bellows, the efforts of Inner Lost Causers such as Jones, Jubal Early, and Daniel Harvey Hill were well organized and had an "emotional drive"; by contrast, the National Lost Cause was headed by "pragmatic reunion-oriented authors" who came to see the South as a paradox of victory and defeat, romance and tragedy.[41]

Jones's career tends to blur the lines between the Inner and the National Lost Causes. For example, since Connelly and Bellows assert that a key element of the Inner Lost Cause was that authors "did not expect exculpation in *their* time,"[42] rooting Jones firmly in this camp is difficult. While he alleged that his work with the SHSP was a means of sowing seeds for the vindication he was sure future "objective" historians would reap, Jones's labors with the SHSP extended well beyond source gathering. Instead, he forged a distinctly white Southern narrative of the war. He did not wait for future historians to justify his findings; to the contrary, he crafted in his books and articles arguments that he believed were so airtight that future historians would have no choice but to agree with him.

Another way that Jones confuses the Inner-National Lost Cause distinctions is through his focus on reunion, a characteristic of National Lost Causers. This is not to say that Jones's move toward reconciliation was dramatic, or that he in any significant sense could be labeled "reconstructed." Still, a chief feature of his career in last two decades of the nineteenth century, and into the twentieth, was his efforts to reintegrate the South into America's national narrative. The way he did so carried heavy Lost Cause undertones, but this again exposes the danger of too cleanly separating supposedly intransigent Confederate veterans from second-generation reunionists. Jones did emphasize reunion, albeit an Anglo-centric reconciliationist one. He also focused on the South's place in a united America, even using the South's story to redefine what a true American was.

At times, Jones seemed reticent to dredge up memories of the past. In 1888, two West Virginians commented on his anticipated visit to the state. One wanted Jones to raise the "Confederate yell" in support of home missions; the other feared that Jones would lace his speeches with animosity toward the North. To the first individual, Jones responded, "I shall have to disappoint him about the 'Confederate yell.' I do not see just where I could put *that* into a Home Mission speech." To the second contributor, Jones assured that his talks would not foster division. Instead of dwelling on "bitter memories of a stormy past," he celebrated the "returning goodwill between once belligerent but now fraternal sections of our common country." He would also do all in his power "to cement the ties which should bind together our common Baptist brotherhood."[43] Here Jones was hesitant to conjure up ghosts of the past, even suggesting that denominational identity might bridge the postwar chasm between Northern and Southern Baptists.

For Jones, the Confederacy was not a blemish on American history, but actually a source of pride for both Northerners and Southerners. He wrote in 1899: "It is not a boast to declare that in fact the spirit of the South was never broken, the courage of the South never qualified, the conviction of the South was never deserted, and the manhood of the South was never surrendered. It is also the gratification of every patriot in the United States that the Union was not a conqueror, and the free citizenship of our country was never conquered." He also reminded readers that Confederate veterans were serving the US government, filling such posts as secretary of the navy, postmaster general, or speaker of the House of Representatives.[44] For Jones, ex-Confederates were not merely rehabilitated Americans; they were some of the best Americans the nation could hope to produce.

While editor of the *SHSP*, Jones had relished in the letter of a certain unnamed Union colonel who admitted that Northerners could admire Confederates as fellow Americans fighting for their rights. The colonel went on to praise the Confederates' stand against staggering odds, taking pride that the "Southern army, composed almost entirely of Americans, were able, under the ablest American chieftains, to defeat so often the overwhelming hosts of the North, which were composed largely of foreigners to our soil."[45] The officer's correspondence not only displayed the inroads the Lost Cause had made in the North, but articulated for the *SHSP* audience something that Jones would later argue himself: that Confederates had not fought the Civil War because they were bad Americans, but precisely because they were the quintessential Americans.

As his reaction to the colonel's letter had shown, Jones was open to amicable communication with Northerners on matters of the war, as long as the dialogue was on Southern terms. In May 1907, an aging Jones traveled to Boston to give a lecture on Stonewall Jackson. He spoke before the Massachusetts Military Historical Society, whose ranks included many Union veterans. There he received a warm reception, including "enthusiastic applause from start to finish." Jones fully expected that despite lingering resentments between the sections, Northerners could appreciate the military genius of Confederate leaders like Jackson and Lee. He conveyed as much in the conclusion to his 1906 book on Lee: "But the day will come—nay now is—when at the North as well as at the South Robert Edward Lee of Virginia, of America, will be recognized as one of the finest specimens of the soldier and the man whom God ever gave to bless the world."[46]

Jones's invocations as chaplain-general of the UCV evinced both his openness to pray for Northerners and his eagerness to find the South's place in the united nation. During the Spanish-American War, he prayed to the "God of our reunited country" and thanked God for the "signal victories that Thou has recently given to American arms on the sea and on the land." At other times, Jones included the US president in his UCV prayers. On one occasion, Jones asked God to bless "our entire country" and longed for the day when the South would "take her old place in leading the councils of this great country."[47]

One of Jones's clearest statement on matters of reunion came in 1896, when he spoke at an American flag raising in Chattanooga, Tennessee. He recounted the event: "And why should I not feel the profoundest interest in, the deepest loyalty to, and the warmest love for the old flag?" He continued, "Born, and reared, and educated on the soil of old Virginia — proud of her hallowed memories, her cherished traditions, her glorious history — I know of no one who has a better right to hurrah for the 'starry banner' than a son of 'Old Dominion.'"[48] He even boasted that Virginians had supplied more troops for the American Revolution than had any other colony.

Jones also appealed to the oft-cited (but undocumented) nineteenth-century myth that the American flag had been based on the coat of arms of George Washington, a Virginian. Jones recalled that Francis Scott Key, author of the "Star-Spangled Banner," was himself a Southerner. Furthermore, Jones reminded readers that Virginia had given to the US government — laying a "free gift on the altar of the nation" — Northwest territory that by charter had belonged to Virginia. Out of this territory came the states of Ohio, Illinois, Indiana, Michigan, Wisconsin, and sections of Minnesota.[49] In a shrewd move, Jones had essentially argued that the South had given the North much of the North!

In the same article, Jones acknowledged that the South had fought against the American flag, since at the time the banner "represented just the opposite of what our fathers fought for in '76." For that, Jones made no apologies, declaring that Southerners "thought then, and know now, that they were right." Yet when the Confederacy buckled under "overwhelming numbers and resources," Southerners reunited with the Union in good faith. Jones vowed that if a foreign war were to occur, Southerners would do their part. For him, Southerners had come to the nation's rescue in the War of 1812 and the Mexican-American War, and another conflict would afford them the opportunity to do so again.[50]

Even though Jones's piece on the American flag was ostensibly conciliatory, not every reader interpreted it as such. The opening volley came from John D. Billings, a Union veteran writing from Massachusetts. Billings disputed many of Jones's claims, writing that Jones's article had infused the American flag with sectional bias and had suggested that "whatever honor and distinction this country has achieved belongs almost exclusively to Virginia and the South."[51] Responding to Billings, Jones defended the facts and figures from his article. Then, as was so often his habit, he injected the discussion with biblical imagery:

> [T]his tongue of mine shall cleave to the roof of my mouth—this right hand of mine shall forget its cunning with the pen—ere I cease to maintain, on every proper platform and against all comers, that no section of our common country contributed more to establish and build up the Union, and to promote the prosperity of the country, or has done more to add lustre to the stars that glitter on "Old Glory," and no section has a better right to be proud of our country's history, or to labor for its future prosperity, greatness, honor and glory, than our Southland—the home of Washington, Jefferson, Jackson, Davis, and Lee.[52]

Through his rhetoric Jones was attempting to realize something the Confederate Army had never fully accomplished: a successful invasion of the North. Instead of conquering the North—which had never been the goal of secession in the first place—Jones would recast national memory in a Southern mold. He would move beyond defending Southern identity from a Northern onslaught; now he would claim the North for the Southern people.

Billings did not let the subject rest. He opposed Jones once more, denying that the American flag had been based on Washington's coat of arms and noting that Connecticut and Massachusetts—not just Virginia—had donated Northwest territory for the good of the country. Once again Jones mounted a defense. Then, a month after that, Jones published an even more extensive article directed at Billings's criticisms, this one focusing on issues of nullification and secession. Jones contended that historians were wrong to blame the South for birthing the idea of nullification—an issue that raged in 1832–1833, when South Carolina balked at federal tariffs. Instead, Jones held, Massachusetts had evidenced the nullification instinct much earlier than did South Carolina. The people of Massachusetts, in their 1780 convention, defended the "sole and exclusive right of governing themselves as a free, sovereign, and independent state." In that declaration, Jones continued, was the "germ of both nullification and secession—the doctrine of state sovereignty."[53]

Strikingly, Jones named Northern states as responsible for "nullifying the Constitution of the United States, the laws of Congress, and the decisions of the Supreme Court by their 'personal liberty' bills and other legislation designated to defeat the rendition of fugitive slaves." In other words, before Southern states had seceded from the Union, Northern states had effected nullification by refusing to abide by the Fugitive Slave Act of 1850. With this history in mind, Jones was flabbergasted that New Englanders could use terms such as "traitors" or "rebels" to describe Southerners.[54] For Jones, the case was plain: Southern states had but claimed in 1861 what Northern states had defended roughly four scores earlier.

One way of summing up Jones's concept of Southerners as the truest Americans is to study an 1895 speech by Clement A. Evans. A former Confederate general, Evans delivered to the Association of the Army of Northern Virginia an address on the many contributions the South had made to the American nation. Jones attended the association's meeting and endorsed the address. Evans's speech included lofty visions not only of the South's history, but of America's future:

> The South possessed in affluence the true American spirit,—that pride
> in the grandeur of our country, that hospitality which keeps open house
> for the worthies of all the world, that glorying in our free institutions,
> that faith in our Nation's power to maintain its place among the earth's

greatest governments, and the profound conviction that in the constitutional union of all the States, we shall achieve a national greatness never equaled in the history of the world. The South says let the decayed corpse of long gone, lurid, sectional strife lie like John Brown's body mouldering in the grave, while the American soul shall go marching on—marching on forever,—under the flag of the Union, keeping step to the music of Hail Columbia, Yankee Doodle and Dixie, harmonized into one national air.

Evans promoted a key tenet of reconciliationist memory when declaring, "The hour then has come and now is for mutual honors to be awarded to all true defenders of their respective convictions."[55] As did many postwar white Southerners, Evans felt that the path to national healing involved respecting the valor of soldiers, North and South. As Jones himself had attempted, Evans detailed innumerable Southern accomplishments, making evident that America owed much of its "true American spirit" to the Southern states.

Evans stirred his listeners to take pride in their home states but also to "declare with one common voice to the nations of the earth, 'We are all Americans!'" His speech exemplified the efforts of postwar Southerners to hold in tension Confederate pride and American patriotism. In fact, Evans concluded his address by defending the flags of both the United States and the Confederacy. Referring to the Confederate battle flag, he rallied his fellow veterans: "Your battle banner, stripped of all gory significance and meaning only the memory of a comradeship in arms, although radiant yet with stars that bejewel the red cross, signifies the luster shed upon the whole American name by the intrepid courage of the brave young Southerners who bore it aloft through storms of fire. That emblem need not be furled, for it has no honorable foe who demands its disgrace; shows no stain upon its bullet-riven folds, means no fight, frightens no man of sense, and only inspires the Southern patriot to love, follow and defend the star-spangled banner of his country."[56] For Evans, the battle flag represented the transcendent values of honor and courage—virtues that Northerners both respected and shared. As did so many ex-Confederates, Evans stripped the battle flag of any connections to race, slavery, or even rebellion. Those who had hoisted the banner had been fighting for independence, pure and simple. What could be more quint-essentially American than that?

Two interrelated factors motivated white Southerners like Evans and Jones to reconcile with the North: pragmatism and survival. Late nineteenth-century white authors wanted to equip Southerners with the tools necessary to preserve a distinctive identity in the twentieth century. Even if postwar Southerners continued to view themselves as a nation within a nation, the fact of the matter was that the South remained part of the Union. Once Confederate veterans and the rest of the wartime gener-ation were no more, Southerners who had never experienced the crucible of war would need guidance. Jones could continue fighting the war rhe-torically, but in order for his work to remain relevant, he had to chart a course forward. He did so by crafting a mythology that encompassed not only the Civil War, but all of American history. The result—as Connelly and Bellows have observed—was that second-generation Lost Causers could interpret the place of the South in the united nation. By reading all of American history through a white Southern lens, Jones enabled the next generation to identify as fully American and yet fully Southern.

Confederate personalities such as Evans and Jones compelled white Southerners to reintegrate into America, not by shunning their Confederate past, but by embracing that past more than ever. By glorify-ing the South's role in American history, Evans and Jones justified—and even demanded—allegiance to the American flag. While that flag had for four years symbolized a rejection of the nation's founding principles, now Americans could redeem the stars and stripes. Now, Southerners could reclaim their status as the country's truest Americans. Now, over the cacophony of sectionalism and lingering animosity, the harmony of Yankee Doodle and Dixie might ring out once more.

✣ ✣ ✣ ✣ ✣

To say that Jones lobbied for Southern reincorporation into the Union is not to say that he left the past in the past. As the Confederacy's apos-tle, he could deign to be forgiving; he could not, however, afford to be forgetful. In fact, the late nineteenth century saw Jones spewing some of the harshest vitriol of his career. He directed his fury not only toward Union veterans, but also toward Northern Baptists. At a time when many Union and Confederate veterans cultivated friendship on the basis of mutual respect amongst soldiers, Jones was suspicious of reunion efforts. When many Northern and Southern Baptists cooperated on the basis of denominational fidelity, Jones derided the work of Northern Baptists. His ambition to interpret the South's position in a united America on one hand, combined with his reticence to let go of the Confederate story on the other, made him a transitional figure. He had lived and worked long enough to observe shifting attitudes toward white Southern memory, but in the end, he could only move so far.

Although he paraded that he had attended gatherings of Northern and Southern veterans, Jones was just as likely to stymie reunion efforts. In the spring of 1892, UCV members motioned that the group visit the World's Fair in Chicago as a means to "promote a fraternal feeling among the people of our common country." Jones objected, stating, "I do not believe in Confederate veterans visiting any place where they cannot carry the battle flag of the Confederacy unfurled to the breeze and at the head of their columns." In 1894, when the UCV considered inviting the Grand Army of the Republic (GAR) — the Northern equivalent of the UCV — to hold their annual reunion in Atlanta, Jones "opposed most decidedly."[57] The motion passed nonetheless.

Even some of Jones's colleagues felt he had gone too far in protesting the GAR invitation, and the incident led Jones to publish an explanation the next month. He alleged that he had only disapproved the invitation because he thought the location of GAR meetings had nothing to do with UCV business. He said that he did not mind meeting with Union veterans — and had even done so — but that he was against gathering with members of the GAR who had not fought in battle. "I would be glad to welcome and fraternize with the true soldiers who wore the blue," he wrote. At the same time, he had little use for those who had "never smelt gun powder" or who had joined the army merely to acquire a soldier's pension.[58]

At the 1894 UCV reunion, Jones struck a conciliatory note: "Yes; we are loyal citizens of these United States, ready to unite with our brethren of every section to make our common country the grandest, freest, the most prosperous that the sun shines upon." He even urged his audience to honor the US national anthem. Lest listeners misinterpret his sentiments, however, he continued: "[L]et it be distinctly understood that we are not going around with our fingers in our mouths, whimpering and whining and asking pardon, and promising to do so no more. No, sirs; with head erect, we look the world squarely in the eyes, and say: 'We thought we were right in the brave old days, when to do battle was a sacred duty; but now, in light of subsequent events, we *know* we were right; and with malice toward none and charity for all, we are asking pardon of no living man.'"[59] Here again, Jones pushed for reconciliation on the South's terms. Southerners would be loyal to America, he assured, but they would never apologize for trying to leave the Union.

As much as Jones was a bastion of Confederate orthodoxy, he was nearly as fervent in his devotion to Southern Baptists. In defense of Southern Baptists, he took a keen disliking toward the American Baptist Publication Society (ABPS). During Jones's tenure with the HMB, he found the work of J. S. Murrow, an HMB missionary in "Indian territory," to be especially disturbing. The controversy ignited when Murrow expressed a desire to align himself with both the HMB and the Northern-based Home Mission Society (HMS). "I am in favor of preserving the most friendly and fraternal relations with our Northern brethren, and bidding them God speed in all their legitimate work," Jones wrote in 1890. Nevertheless, he concluded that the SBC should not join with Northern Baptists in their endeavors, convinced as he was that "we must do our own work in our own way." As for Murrow's mission, Jones wrote that he had "no sympathy whatever with its mongrel composition." As time progressed, Jones's comments toward the ABPS became increasingly acerbic. In an 1897 letter to J. M. Frost—founder of the Sunday School Board for the SBC—Jones declared, "I shall not die happy until I get a chance to fully expose the cool, imprudence, the persevering cheek, and the monumental humbug and fraud of the A. B. P. Society and their henchmen."[60]

In another letter to Frost, Jones expressed pride that his son, Ashby, had given a "decent drubbing" to someone who had praised the ABPS's "benevolence" to the South. When Jones became pastor at Chapel Hill

Baptist Church and realized that the congregation had been using ABPS material, he immediately changed the literature. He described the ABPS as "interlopers," accusing them of turning a profit in the South. They gave Southerners no voice in their own affairs, he complained, and their motivations were anything but altruistic. Worse yet, the ABPS was sectional and pro-Republican, according to Jones. To him, these sins were intolerable, and in a letter to Frost, Jones confessed that he was gathering "ammunition" for future attacks on the ABPS. He sought out articles on the ABPS that offered "some of the bitterest things about the A. B. P. Society which have ever been published," and these he added to his "arsenal."[61]

A number of factors contributed to Jones's antipathy toward the ABPS. Both Jones and Tichenor viewed the ABPS as competing with the HMB for the loyalty of Southerners. The ABPS enjoyed a large Southern readership, and Jones and Tichenor were determined to break up the monopoly. As a result, the HMB published its own Sunday school literature, *Kind Words*—a publication to which all loyal Southern Baptist churches were expected to subscribe. Largely due to the work of Tichenor, the SBC revived the hitherto defunct Sunday School Board (SSB) in the early 1890s. With the HMB and the SSB at Southerners' disposal, the reasoning went, Southern congregations would soon jettison ABPS material. Likely another reason behind Jones's revulsion of the ABPS was the society's practice of hiring African American writers, even though he and Tichenor agreed that the HMB should print no official statement about the "appointment of these negroes by the A. B. P. Society."[62]

Jones surely voiced the attitudes of some Southern Baptists, but many others believed that he was overzealous in his attacks on the ABPS. He inadvertently set off a firestorm when in 1888 he printed what many thought was an inflammatory circular about the ABPS. To make matters worse, the publisher for HMB distributed two anti-ABPS tracts (one from Jones), leading many to think that the circulars gave the official position of the board. Tichenor and Jones desperately tried to mitigate the damage, avowing that the "Board had sent neither circular." Jones admitted to having sent one, but denied that he had done so in his official capacity with the HMB.[63]

The circular incident reflected badly on the HMB. That Jones acknowledged writing one of the pieces—whether or not in his official role with the HMB—did not help the situation. Some wanted to give Jones the benefit of the doubt. One writer observed that while Jones was "[u]tterly incapable of intrigue or double dealing," he was also fallible, impulsive, and "liable to 'go off half cocked.'" Other Baptists gave Jones no quarter. One North Carolinian reported that Jones had almost single-handedly turned the state convention against the ABPS. According to the author, after the convention had adopted a measure to use ABPS material,

> Dr. J. Wm. Jones took the floor and made a very bitter speech against the Society and its periodicals—said, in the course of his remarks, that they taught "falling from grace and baptismal regeneration, and went out of their way to do so"; criticized the Society's liberality, and said that for every dollar they had given to the South, they had received fifty dollars in return. His speech made such a complete revolution in the minds of the brethren that the motion to strike out the recommendation was carried almost unanimously, and one good brother went so far as to offer a resolution prohibiting our Supply Store from keeping those periodicals in stock.[64]

Even while he spoke of "fraternal relations" with Northern Baptists, Jones actively frustrated attempts for Southern and Northern Baptists to unite in any meaningful way. He distrusted the motives and ministry of the ABPS, and he tried at every turn to discredit the organization. Although other Baptists attributed Jones's actions to rashness, Jones himself never apologized for his contempt of the ABPS. For him, the society was an embodiment of the Yankee impulse to patronize and exploit Southerners—a galling reminder that the postwar South was still under invasion.

✢ ✢ ✢ ✢ ✢

At the annual reunion of the UCV in the spring of 1906, attendees took time to honor their faithful chaplain-general. They presented Jones with a commemorative cup and gave glowing testimonies of his postwar career.

One former Confederate general even called Jones "the greatest living Confederate to-day," announcing that Jones had "done more, prayed harder and preached longer and more about the Confederacy than any man since the war." Jones was nearly overcome with emotion: here was yet another affirmation that he had been true to his apostolic calling.[65]

By the 1906 meeting, Jones had been laboring for the Confederate cause for more than four decades. During that time he remained devoted to his mission, providing white Southerners with icons to follow, and with a story to tell. He was also willing to adjust to the changing landscape of Lost Cause mythology. Like Lost Cause writers who would follow, he was dedicated to finding the South's place in twentieth-century America. For Jones, the most effective way of reintegrating the South into the American narrative was by portraying Southerners not as rebels, but as the truest, most patriotic Americans in the nation's history. Through his work, white Southerners learned that the past could not be changed—except when it could. With each re-articulation of the South's story, Jones altered the past. By doing so, he equipped white Southerners with the examples and narratives they needed to preserve a distinct identity in a new century.

Conclusion

My dear old comrades, brothers beloved, we are passing away...
Are we ready for our summons?

— "Reunion Memorial Services:
Address of Chaplain General J. Wm. Jones,"
Confederate Veteran

At around five o'clock on March 17, 1909, while visiting his son Ashby in Columbus, Georgia, J. William Jones died. His family had the body taken back to Richmond and held his funeral at Calvary Baptist Church.[1] He was interred in the hallowed ground of Hollywood Cemetery, his headstone humbly tucked away amidst the graves of Confederate giants such as Jefferson Davis and J. E. B. Stuart. For more than four decades he had followed Lee, Jackson, and Davis with unremitting zeal. Prepared to follow the triumvirate one last time, he remained confident until the end that he had fulfilled his apostolic duty and that he had born a faithful witness for his beloved Southland.

Many white Southerners seemed to sense that with Jones's passing an era had ended. The *Confederate Veteran* described him as "perhaps the most tireless advocate of the merits of the Southern people that the South had." His former professor at the University of Virginia, Edward S. Joynes, spoke affectionately of his former student. Joynes—who stopped shy of saying that Jones had "worshiped" Lee—noted the deep trust that Lee and Lee's family had placed in Jones's ministry and writing. One professor from Southern Baptist Theological Seminary (SBTS) hailed Jones's role in helping ignite a "revolution in the thinking and writing of Northern historians and publicists." Due to the efforts of Jones and other Lee devotees, Northerners had not only come to see Lee as a "national hero," but had finally recognized the "valor and sacrifices" of Confederate soldiers.[2] Having furthered the reconciliationist strain of memory—which promoted a mutual respect among white Union and Confederate veterans—Jones willed to the defeated South a final victory.

In the decade following Jones's death, stories of his fealty to the South loomed large, even among Confederate organizations. One veterans' chapter observed of Jones, "[s]o uncompromising was his devotion to the cause espoused by Lee and Jackson (the realized ideals by which he measured all human excellence), and so bold his spoken and written words, that he became a national example of fidelity unreconstructed and unreconstructable. Pathetic it may have been, but sublimely loyal."[3] For white Southerners, the "unreconstructable" Jones was part legend, part tragic hero. As unrivaled as his allegiance to the Confederacy was his inability to grasp when a cause was truly lost.

Jones provided white Southerners a religious lens through which to view their Confederate past. Crucial to remember, however, is that this interpretation was linked to, and refracted through, Jones's denominational identity. Even his experience with Confederate revivals—so foundational for his understanding of the South's divine chosenness—demonstrated that camp interdenominationalism was circumstantial, inextricably tied to the exigencies of war and the specter of imminent death. Jones's narrative also revealed that Christian fraternity had boundaries, as there persisted an underlying anti-Catholicism that both catalyzed and constrained evangelical unity.

In the postwar period, Jones—still an unfaltering Baptist—embraced his apostolic status with gusto. As one of the central adherents of Lost Cause mythology, and yet also a Baptist minister, his story illuminates the manner in which sectarian commitments colored the dissemination of the Lost Cause message. His life and work nuance claims that the Lost Cause was a broadly ecumenical movement and attest to the weight and force of denominationalism even among postwar white Southerners aspiring for religious and regional solidarity. In fact, Jones believed that there existed a symbiotic relationship between the Baptist cause and the Lost Cause. To Baptists, he invoked the virtues of Confederate leaders when exhorting his audiences to live holy lives. To ex-Confederates, he lauded spiritual qualities in Confederate leaders that he felt transcended sectarian particularities.

While he was an ardent denominationalist, Jones's Baptistness did not inhibit him from self-identifying as the Confederacy's apostle. He pointed to Lee, Jackson, and Davis as incarnations of Southern virtue—corporeal representations of God's presence for Southerners experiencing divine alienation in the wake of defeat. Of course, there is a certain irony in that Jones—himself a steadfast, even anti-Catholic evangelical—embodied so many non-evangelical concepts: iconography, hagiography, and relic veneration. Even so, he offered to white Southerners the images, saints, and objects through which they could access an inscrutable God.

Jones also accepted the responsibility of supplying and defending an accurate account of Confederate history. He constructed this narrative through copious articles and books, and by editing the *Southern Historical Society Papers*, one of the most potent instruments of Lost Cause diffusion. As the Lost Cause evolved over time—becoming less interested in refighting the Civil War, and more focused on defining the South's role in twentieth-century America—Jones's message shifted as well. Although never relenting his declarations concerning the South's moral and military superiority over the Union, Jones believed that ex-Confederates could freely rejoin the united nation. To his stock narrative that the Confederacy had been more righteous than the Union, Jones added that Southerners had always exemplified the American spirit. For him, far from representing a deficiency in American patriotism, secession confirmed that Southerners had been and remained the truest Americans of all. By grafting the South into a national history that championed freedom and bravery, Jones enabled the next generation of white Southerners to orient themselves within the united nation, but also to safeguard a distinctly Southern identity.

Jones's writings and ministry have a number of broad implications for the study of denominational identity and the development of white Southern memory. First, his role as the Confederacy's apostle spotlights many of the ways in which religion—denominationalism in particular—contributed to the development of the Lost Cause. His career thus supports historian Charles Reagan Wilson's contention that religion played a central role in the development of the mythology. Jones believed the Lost Cause and Protestant Christianity were intimately linked, and through his prolific writings and editorships, white Southerners embraced this linkage as well.

Second, Jones's work modifies prevailing interpretations of ecumenism in nineteenth-century America. Indeed, Lost Causers welcomed the collaboration of various denominations, but also recognized and respected denominational commitments. Studies of religion and the Lost Cause must move away from an ecumenical-denominational dichotomy and must instead acknowledge that postwar ecumenism was situational (tied to wartime stresses), limited (often ignoring Roman Catholics), and pragmatic (cooperative, but not extending into the realm of doctrine). The Lost Cause confirmed that white Southerners could join in a broad literary movement while still holding firmly to denominational identity. The Lost Cause movement benefitted from networking among denominations, but did not necessitate the muting of sectarian particularities.

Third, Jones's example demonstrates that there were limits to the coalescence between nineteenth-century white Southern churches and Southern culture. Helpful here is historian John Lee Eighmy's assertion that white Southern churches largely succumbed to "cultural captivity" with regard to slavery.[4] While the captivity imagery is useful, it can also be misleading. Describing culture as an external and infecting force belies the reality that churches were instrumental in creating the culture in which they were supposedly fettered. Even with this caveat in mind, Jones's labors exhibit that prominent Lost Causers stopped short of sacrificing denominational fidelity for the sake of sustaining regional unity in the postbellum South. From Jones's perspective, there was no conflict between the Baptist denomination and the interdenominational spirit of the Lost Cause. His correspondence and newspaper articles suggest that he would have been profoundly uncomfortable participating in any movement that demanded a cloaking of his Baptistness.

Perhaps the most critical and abiding aspect of Jones's lifework was the attention he gave to Confederate leaders, whom he portrayed as incarnations of God's presence. The value of incarnation for postbellum white Southerners was vital. With the loss of nationhood, Southerners grappled with the idea of a South without a Confederacy. With the loss of the war, Southerners also wrestled with the inscrutability of a God who had allowed the chosen people to be defeated. As one with intimate association with Lee, Jackson, and Davis, the Confederacy's apostle provided for postwar white Southerners palpable representations of the Confederate nation and of divine favor.

✠ ✠ ✠ ✠ ✠

In his eulogy of Jones, W. J. McGlothlin, professor at SBTS, testified that Jones had spoken and written "with the fire and enthusiasm of an actor in the great tragedy."[5] No doubt, Jones saw himself as an actor in the greatest tragedy of American history. He had witnessed the birth of the Southern nation. He had seen the morality of Confederate troops and fought for the righteousness of the Confederate cause. He had recounted the strange and wonderful move of God's spirit in Confederate revivals. He had even fostered deep, personal relationships with heroes who had embodied all that was pure and exceptional about the South. And yet he had also seen God's chosen people defeated and carted into exile. Jones surely thought that the God who had come near in the midst of political chaos and internecine bloodshed would rescue the chosen people once more. As an eyewitness to these triumphs and tragedies, he felt uniquely qualified to serve as the Confederacy's apostle. Not only would he provide white Southerners with tangible exemplars of the faith, but he would vouchsafe to them a narrative by which to order their lives. By holding fast to this gospel, Southerners would persevere long after the age of the apostles was but a distant memory.

Notes

Introduction

1. Mary Anna Jackson, *Life and Letters of General Thomas J. Jackson (Stonewall Jackson) by His Wife* (New York: Harper and Brothers, 1892), 427–28. Unless otherwise noted, I have left the original spelling, structure, and emphasis in all primary source quotations. The epigraph that opens this chapter is from Cassirer's *The Philosophy of Symbolic Forms: Mythical Thought* (New Haven: Yale Univ. Press, 1955), 5.

2. Without attempting to untangle the Gordian knot of terminology related to the Lost Cause specifically, or Southern history in general, a few introductory comments are necessary. First, I am indebted to historian Lloyd Hunter for the term "sacralization" in describing Lost Causers' approach to history. See Hunter, "The Sacred South: Postwar Confederates and the Sacralization of Southern Culture" (PhD diss., Saint Louis Univ., 1978); "The Immortal Confederacy: Another Look at Lost Cause Religion," in Gary W. Gallagher and Alan T. Nolan, *The Myth of the Lost Cause and Civil War History* (Bloomington: Indiana Univ. Press, 2000).

    Definitions of the Lost Cause abound, but a sampling of well-known treatments include the following: Charles Reagan Wilson, *Baptized in Blood: Religion of the Lost Cause, 1865–1920* (Athens: Univ. of Georgia Press, 1980), 1; Gaines Foster, *Ghosts of the Confederacy: Defeat, the Lost Cause and the Emergence of the New South, 1865–1913* (New York: Oxford Univ. Press, 1988), 7–8; W. Scott Poole, *Never Surrender: Confederate Memory and Conservatism in the South Carolina Upcountry* (Athens: Univ. of Georgia Press, 2004), 3, 79; Thomas Lawrence Connelly and Barbara Bellows, *God and General Longstreet: The Lost Cause and the Southern Mind* (Baton Rouge: Louisiana State Univ. Press, 1982), 4–6, 123–24, 137, 146–48; Roland Osterweis, *The Myth of the Lost Cause, 1865–1900* (Hamden, CT: Archon Books, 1973), x; William C. Davis, *The Cause Lost: Myths and Realities of the Confederacy* (Lawrence: Univ. Press of Kansas, 1996), 175–78.

    Following the lead of Wilson and others, I refer to the Lost Cause as a "mythology" and a "civil religion"—both contentious terms among Lost Cause scholars. Some historians reject "mythology" or "civil religion" as appropriate descriptors (Foster, Poole, Hunter), while other historians defend the labels (Osterweis, Davis). For more on myths and the American South, see Paul Gaston, *The New South Creed: A Study in Southern Mythmaking* (Montgomery, AL: New South Books, 2012), 30. I also reference Confederate "nationalism," taking my cue from historians such as Benedict Anderson and Drew Gilpin Faust. See Anderson, *Imagined Communities: Reflections on the Origin and Spread of Nationalism* (New York: Verso Books, 2006), 5–7; Faust, *The Creation of Confederate Nationalism: Ideology and Identity in the Civil War South* (Baton Rouge: Louisiana State Univ. Press, 1990), 16. Other scholars dispute that the Confederacy ever constituted a "nation" (Hunter, Davis); see also Kenneth Stampp, *The Imperiled Union: Essays on the Background of the Civil War* (New York: Oxford Univ. Press, 1980), 255–56; Alan Nolan, *Lee Considered: General Robert E. Lee and Civil War History* (Chapel Hill: Univ. of North Carolina Press, 1991), 28–29.

Wilson anchored his discussion of Southern civil religion in the work of sociologist Robert N. Bellah. See Bellah, "Civil Religion in America," *Daedalus* 96, no. 1 (Jan. 1, 1967): 12. See also Wilson, "The Religion of the Lost Cause: Ritual and Organization of the Southern Civil Religion, 1865–1920," *Journal of Southern History* 46 (May 1980): 219–38. Recently, however, there has been renewed scholarly debate over Lost Cause as civil religion. See Edward R. Crowther, "John the Evangelist Revisited: John William Jones and the Lost Cause," *Journal of Southern Religion* 17 (2015): http:// jsreligion.org/issues /vol17/crowther.html; Keith Harper, "What's Wrong with this Picture? James P. Boyce, John A. Broadus, and Reflections on the Lost Cause," *Journal of Southern Religion* 17 (2015): http:// jsreligion.org/ issues/vol17/harper.html; Arthur Remillard, "From Prizefights to Praying Colonels: Civil Religion, Sports, and a New(ish) Direction for the Lost Cause," *Journal of Southern Religion* 17 (2015): http://jsreligion.org/issues/vol17/remillard.html; Chad Seales, "To Know Good Blood: The Material Morality of Southern Religion," *Journal of Southern Religion* 17 (2015): http://jsreligion.org/ issues/vol17/seales.html; Charles Reagan Wilson, "Assessing the Lost Cause and Southern Civil Religion," *Journal of Southern Religion* 17 (2015): http://jsreligion.org/issues/vol17/wilson.html.

3. Women also played a pivotal role in the spread of the Lost Cause. See Caroline E. Janney, *Burying the Dead but Not the Past: Ladies' Memorial Associations and the Lost Cause* (Chapel Hill: Univ. of North Carolina

Press, 2008); Janney, *Remembering the Civil War: Reunion and the Limits of Reconciliation* (Chapel Hill: Univ. of North Carolina Press, 2013); W. Fitzhugh Brundage, *The Southern Past: A Clash of Race and Memory* (Cambridge, MA: Belknap Press, 2008), 12–54; Cynthia J. Mills and Pamela H. Simpson, eds., *Monuments to the Lost Cause: Women, Art, and the Landscapes of Southern Memory* (Knoxville: Univ. of Tennessee Press, 2003); Karen L. Cox, *Dixie's Daughters: The United Daughters of the Confederacy and the Preservation of Confederate Culture* (Gainesville: Univ. Press of Florida, 2003). For more on women, Southern memory, and race in the late nineteenth century, see David Goldfield, *Still Fighting the Civil War: The American South and Southern History* (Baton Rouge: Louisiana State Univ. Press, 2013), 137–86.

For studies on African Americans and postwar memory, see Brundage, *The Southern Past*; David Blight, "'For Something beyond the Battlefield': Frederick Douglass and the Struggle for the Memory of the Civil War," in David Thelen, *Memory and American History* (Bloomington: Indiana Univ. Press, 1990), 29–49; Blight, *Race and Reunion: The Civil War in American Memory* (Cambridge, MA: Belknap Press, 2002); Edward Blum, *Reforging the White Republic: Race, Religion, and American Nationalism, 1865–1898* (Baton Rouge: Louisiana State Univ. Press, 2007).

Some broad treatments of Civil War or American memory include Alice Fahs and Joan Waugh, eds., *The Memory of the Civil War in American Culture* (Chapel Hill: Univ. of North Carolina Press, 2004); Michael Kammen, *Mystic Chords of Memory: The Transformation of Tradition in American Culture* (New York: Vintage, 1993); Karen E. Fields and Barbara J. Fields, *Racecraft: The Soul of Inequality in American Life* (New York: Verso, 2012), 171–92; Thelen, *Memory and American History*. As do others, Thelen emphasizes that memory is "constructed," not "reproduced." Thus memory is not a passive phenomenon, but a dynamic process shaped in the context of "community, broader politics, and social dynamics" (ix).

4. Wilson portrays Jones as an ecumenist, citing specifically his well-known book, *Christ in the Camp* (1887), in which Jones expressed fond memories of interdenominational cooperation during wartime Confederate revivals. Historian Zachary Dresser has extended this argument by suggesting that Jones's ecumenical account of Confederate revivals was a means of fostering regional unity during a time when denominational factionalism threatened Southern

cohesiveness. In Dresser's view, Jones's work represented in part an attempt to harken back to the interdenominational glory days of wartime revivals in order to resurrect that same ecumenical spirit in the 1870s and 1880s. See Wilson, *Baptized in Blood*, 119–20, 128, 130–32; Dresser, "Onward Christian Soldiers? Confederate Revivalism and Denominationalism in the Nineteenth-Century South" (presented at the Society of Civil War Historians, Baltimore, 2014). In Dresser's estimation, Jones and other Lost Cause writers stood out as anomalies in a culture of intense denominational rivalry. Dresser concludes that such attempts to cultivate denominational union were ultimately unsuccessful, and that denominational sectarianism won the day.

5. In the context of the present study, the term "ecumenism" should not be confused with the modern ecumenical movement, which traces its origins to the Edinburgh Missionary Conference of 1910. The modern ecumenical movement had important antecedents, some of which included the "awakenings" of eighteenth- and nineteenth-century America, and the temperance movement of the early nineteenth century. See C. Douglas Weaver, *In Search of the New Testament Church: The Baptist Story* (Macon, GA: Mercer Univ. Press, 2008), 142; Justo L. Gonzalez, *The Story of Christianity, Vol. 2: The Reformation to the Present Day* (New York: Harper One, 2010), 322; Frank Leslie Cross and Elizabeth A. Livingstone, *The Oxford Dictionary of the Christian Church* (New York: Oxford Univ. Press, 1974), 443.

   Since "ecumenism" has become such a slippery term in the study of Southern history, I have largely avoided its usage in this book. For the sake of clarity—and in order to avoid the risk of inaccurately portraying Jones as one willing to compromise his "Baptistness"—I describe his attitudes and actions toward non-Baptists with descriptors like "cooperative" and "networking." This sentiment is reminiscent of revivalists' attitudes in the First and Second Great Awakenings. Revivalists pooled their efforts for the common goal of evangelism, but did not formally unite denominations; in fact, debates over the revivals often served to split denominations further.

6. According to Wilson, Jones was "the single most important link between Southern religion and the Lost Cause." Wilson also claims that during the years that Jones served as secretary of the *SHSP*, the papers were the "most important publication of the Lost Cause." Historian Gardiner Shattuck agrees, writing that Jones "literally controlled the shape of the Lost Cause through

the publication of documents relating to the Confederacy in volumes of the *Southern Historical Society Papers.*" See Wilson, *Baptized in Blood,* 119–20, 123, 136; Shattuck, *A Shield and Hiding Place: The Religious Life of the Civil War Armies* (Macon: Mercer Univ. Press, 1987), 121. See also Hunter, "The Immortal Confederacy," 186, 194, 211. For the participation of Roman Catholics and Jews in the promotion of the Lost Cause, see Osterweis, *The Myth of the Lost Cause,* 120; Zachary Dresser, "The Theology of Reconstruction: White Southern Religious Leaders in the Aftermath of the Civil War" (PhD diss., Rice Univ., 2013), 150–51.

7. For example, see William Earl Brown, "Pastoral Evangelism: A Model for Effective Evangelism as Demonstrated by the Ministries of John Albert Broadus, Alfred Elijah Dickinson, and John William Jones in the Revival of the Army of Northern Virginia in 1863" (PhD diss., Southeastern Baptist Theological Seminary, 1999); Thomas Lawrence Connelly, *The Marble Man: Robert E. Lee and His Image in American Society* (Baton Rouge: Louisiana State Univ. Press, 1977), 41–42. Wilson pictures Jones as an evangelist of the Lost Cause tradition, while Brown assesses Jones's ministry as a model for Christian evangelism. Connelly, on the other hand, calls Jones a "cunning, ambitious man" who flattered Southern leaders in order to raise funds for the Southern Historical Society.

8. Brown's work provides the fullest treatment of Jones's life and comes closest to placing Jones in a Baptist context. Brown's exploration, however, is largely limited to Jones's relationships with other Baptist ministers. Jones is not the central figure in Brown's work, and his treatment of Jones deals less with Jones's influence on the Lost Cause and more with Jones's ministry as a model for present-day clergy. In a recent dissertation, historian Christopher Martin has provided an astute overview of Jones's historical influence, specifically with regard to Jones's bitter feud with General James Longstreet. Regretfully, the timing of the present publication has precluded me from making full use of Martin's work. See Martin, "The Confederate Crusader: John William Jones and the Lost Cause" (Ph.D. diss. Claremont Graduate University, 2018).

9. Here I borrow the phrasing of historian John Lee Eighmy. See Eighmy and Samuel S. Hill, *Churches in Cultural Captivity: A History of the Social Attitudes of Southern Baptists* (Knoxville: Univ. of Tennessee Press, 1987).

10. Wilson is correct in observing that if Lee was a Christ figure, then Jones was his apostle Paul. Wilson writes that Jones's close relationship with Lee

"symbolically suggested that Jones was an apostle of Lee, who had laid hands on the parson in order that the tradition might be continued." See Wilson, *Baptized in Blood*, 122–23.

11. Jones's life and career also support Wilson's contention that religion played an integral role in the spread of the Lost Cause. For studies that de-emphasize the role of religion in general or clergy in particular in the shaping of the Lost Cause, see Foster, *Ghosts of the Confederacy*, 47; Hunter, "The Immortal Confederacy," 211. For scholars who, like Wilson, highlight religion's influence on the Lost Cause, see Robert J. Miller, *Both Prayed to the Same God: Religion and Faith in the American Civil War* (Lanham, MD: Lexington Books, 2007), 145; Paul Harvey, "'Yankee Faith' and Southern Redemption: White Southern Baptist Ministers, 1850–1890" in Randall M. Miller, Harry S. Stout, and Charles Reagan Wilson, *Religion and the American Civil War* (New York: Oxford Univ. Press, 1998), 167–86; Terrie Dopp Aamodt, *Righteous Armies, Holy Cause: Apocalyptic Imagery and the Civil War* (Macon: Mercer Univ. Press, 2002); Osterweis, *The Myth of the Lost Cause*, 118–29.

CHAPTER ONE *From the Mission Field to the Battlefield: Jones's Early Life and Prewar Years*

1. William Nelson Pendleton, *Personal Recollections of General Lee: An Address Delivered at Washington and Lee University on Gen. Lee's Birth-Day, Jan. 19, 1873* (Baltimore: n.p., 1874), 603–4; Connelly, *The Marble Man*, 38–41. The details of the following account rely heavily on Connelly's work. The epigraph that opens this chapter is in a letter from John Albert Broadus to Cornelia Taliaferro, March 28, 1860, in Archibald Thomas Robertson, *Life and Letters of John Albert Broadus* (Philadelphia: American Baptist Publication Society, 1901), 173–74.

2. Connelly, *The Marble Man*, 40. Connelly hypothesizes that Marshall abandoned the project due to exasperation with the competitiveness among memorial associations.

3. Connelly, 40–42. Washington College added Lee's name almost immediately after his death. See "Our Namesakes: Washington and Lee University," accessed March 16, 2015, http://www.wlu.edu/about-wandl/history-and-traditions /our-namesakes. See also John S. Moore, "John William Jones (1836–1909):

Historian of the Confederacy," *Virginia Baptist Register* 31 (Richmond: Virginia Baptist Historical Society, 1992): 1602.

4. Gardiner H. Shattuck, Jr., "John William Jones," *American National Biography Online*, accessed Dec. 8, 2014, http://www.anb.org; David S. Williams, "J. William Jones (1836–1909)," *New Georgia Encyclopedia*, accessed April 9, 2014, http://www.georgiaencyclopedia.org/articles/history-archaeology /j-william-jones-1836–1909; Moore, "J. William Jones," 1596; Fred Anderson, "Historian of the Confederacy," *Baptist History and Heritage* 32 (July 1997): 47; Wilson, *Baptized in Blood*, 119.

5. Wilson, *Baptized in Blood*, 120; Malcolm Hart Harris, *History of Louisa County, Virginia* (Richmond: Dietz Press, 1936), 189; William H. Whitsitt, "John William Jones, D. D.," *Religious Herald* 82, June 24, 1909, 4–5, 9; *The Seventh Census of the United States: 1850* (Washington, DC: Robert Armstrong, 1853), 285.

   Francis and Ann had eleven children in total: Helen Mary, John William, Francis Pendleton, Philip Edloe, Lucy Marshall, Robert Meade, James Lawrence, Mattie Bernard (listed as Martha in the 1860 census), Willie Page, Clarence, and French. See Moore, "J. William Jones," 1609; Lee Fleming Reese, *The Ashby Book* (San Diego: Western Press, 1976), 1015; "United States Census, 1860," Louisa County, Virginia, database with images, FamilySearch, https://familysearch.org, image 14 of 91; Fold3.com, http://www.fold3.com; citing NARA microfilm publication M653 (Washington, DC: National Archives and Records Administration, n.d.), accessed July 18, 2018.

6. Lyon Gardiner Tyler, *Men of Mark in Virginia: Ideals of American Life; A Collection of Biographies of the Leading Men in the State* 1 (Washington, DC: Men of Mark Publishing Company, 1906), 250–53; Moore, "J. William Jones," 1596; "United States Census, 1850," Louisa County, Virginia, database with images, FamilySearch, https://familysearch.org, image 125 of 163; citing NARA microfilm publication M432 (Washington, DC: National Archives and Records Administration, n.d.), accessed July 18, 2018; *The Seventh Census of the United States*, 272. By 1860, an additional merchant's clerk—William J. Brooks—was residing with the Joneses. See "United States Census, 1860."

7. Historian William Earl Brown suggests that Gray's inclusion among Jones's family members may have indicated that he was a slave. See Brown, "Pastoral Evangelism," 101. See also "United States Census, 1850"; "Unites States Census (Slave Schedule), 1850," Louisa County, Virginia, database with images,

FamilySearch, https://familysearch.org, image 94 of 118; citing NARA micro-film publication M432 (Washington, DC: National Archives and Records Administration, n.d.), accessed July 18, 2018. While the 1850 slave schedule lists Francis W. Jones as "F. W. Jones," context helps confirm this as Francis. The adjacent names are the same (and abbreviated) on both the census and the slave schedule for Louisa County.

8. J. A. C. Chandler et al., eds., *The South in the Building of the Nation: A History of the Southern States Designed to Record the South's Part In the Making of the American Nation; to Portray the Character and Genius, to Chronicle the Achievements and Progress and to Illustrate the Life and Traditions of the Southern People* (Richmond, VA: Southern Historical Publication Society, 1909), 22–23; George Braxton Taylor, *Virginia Baptist Ministers*, 5th Series, 1902–1914 (Lynchburg, VA: J. P. Bell, 1915), 218; Jones, "Varied Experiences In Work Among Young Men," *Religious Herald* 82, April 1, 1909, 4–5 (originally presented before the Richmond Baptist Ministers' Conference on Dec. 7, 1908). Jones and Taylor later became friends and ministered together. See George Braxton Taylor, *Life and Letters of Rev. George Boardman Taylor, D. D.* (Lynchburg, VA: J. P. Bell, 1908), 73, 95, 102–3, 125.

9. Francis William Jones to John William Jones, Oct. 16, 1855, Papers of the Jones Family of Louisa County, VA, Special Collections, Univ. of Virginia Library, Charlottesville (hereafter cited as "Jones Family Papers, UVA"); Chandler, *The South in the Building of the Nation*, 22–23; Jones to Abram Maer Poindexter, Aug. 2, 1859, Missionary File, 1856–1861, Southern Baptist Historical Library and Archives, Nashville, TN (hereafter cited as "Missionary File, SBHLA"); Edward S. Joynes, "In Memoriam—John William Jones, D. D.," *Religious Herald* 82, April 9, 1909, 12; David F. Riggs, *13th Virginia Infantry* (Lynchburg, VA: H. E. Howard, 1988), 122.

10. Taylor, *Virginia Baptist Ministers*, 219; John Lipscomb Johnson, *Autobiographical Notes* (Boulder: Johnson Publishing Company [privately printed], 1958), 108, 122–23. Johnson was also ordained in the same service as Jones, Crawford H. Toy, and James B. Taylor, Jr.

11. Taylor, *Virginia Baptist Ministers*, 219; Jones, "Varied Experiences In Work Among Young Men"; Wilson, *Baptized in Blood*, 120.

12. J. William Jones, Letters, 1857–1861, Special Collections, Univ. of Virginia

Library, Charlottesville (hereafter cited as "Jones Letters, UVA"). By "our denomination," Helen Mary meant Baptists, since she proceeded to request a "letter of dismission" from Broadus's church. These letters transferred membership from one Baptist congregation to another. See Helen Mary Jones to John William Jones, ca. 1854–56, Jones Family Papers, UVA. See also Weaver, *In Search of the New Testament Church* (Ga: Mercer University Press, 2008), 82.

13. Joynes, "In Memoriam"; Brown, "Pastoral Evangelism," 26, 39, 59, 105, 116. Brown writes that while Broadus, Dickinson, and Jones all cooperated with non-Baptists in the context of wartime camp religion, all three remained resolutely Baptist.

14. James Roland Barron, "The Contributions of John A. Broadus to Southern Baptists" (ThD diss., Southern Baptist Theological Seminary, 1972), 25–26.

15. While various sources claim that Jones's and Toy's names on the matriculation list were first and second, respectively, Jones recalled that his name was second. See Jones to A. T. Robertson, May 31, 1899, A. T. Robertson Papers, Special Collections, Southern Baptist Theological Seminary, Louisville, KY (hereafter cited as "Robertson Papers, SBTS"); John R. Sampey, *Southern Baptist Theological Seminary: The First Thirty Years, 1859–1889* (Baltimore: Wharton, Barron and Company, 1890), 126; *General Historical Catalogue of the Southern Baptist Theological Seminary at Greenville, S. C. and Louisville, Ky. 1859–1884*, Special Collections, Southern Baptist Theological Seminary, Louisville, KY. The SBTS curriculum was such that during the course of an eight-month academic year, students could earn diplomas from certain "schools" (departments). Like Jones, many students did not complete the entire three-year curriculum, but left the seminary after one year, having earned selected diplomas. See Gregory A. Wills, *Southern Baptist Theological Seminary, 1859–2009* (New York: Oxford Univ. Press, 2009), 29–30; Charles Hill Ryland, *Recollections of the First Year of the Southern Baptist Theological Seminary: An Address Delivered before the Seminary, at Louisville, Kentucky, Founders Day, January 11th, 1911* (Richmond, VA: 1911), 10–11. Revival and missions had long been important to James Petigru Boyce (1827–1888), the first president of SBTS. While at Brown University, Boyce drew inspiration from the school's president, Francis Wayland (1796–1865), who expressed deep concern for the conversion of students. See John Albert Broadus, *Memoir of James Petigru Boyce, D.D., LL.D.: Late President of the Southern Baptist*

Theological Seminary, Louisville, Ky (New York: A. C. Armstrong and Son, 1893), 43–44, 46; Walter Cochrane Bronson, *The History of Brown University, 1714–1914* (Providence: Brown Univ., 1914), 30–31.

16. "Southern Baptist Theological Seminary Abstract of Principles," accessed April 8, 2015, http://www.sbts.edu/about/truth/abstract/. See also Bill J. Leonard, *God's Last and Only Hope: The Fragmentation of the Southern Baptist Convention* (Grand Rapids, MI: Eerdmans Publishing, 1990), 68–69. Boyce commented that since Baptists were divided on the issue of alien immersion, the abstract intentionally said nothing about the matter. See Wills, *Southern Baptist Theological Seminary*, 106.

17. Robertson, *Life and Letters of John Albert Broadus*, 149; David G. Lyon, "Crawford Howell Toy," *Harvard Theological Review* 13 (Jan. 1920): 3–4; Sampey, *Southern Baptist Theological Seminary*, 32; Brown, "Pastoral Evangelism," 26, 106–7; Broadus to Cornelia Taliaferro, March 28, 1860, in Robertson, *Life and Letters of John Albert Broadus*, 173–74. Broadus would stress again Jones's practical disposition in a wartime letter, calling Jones "surely one of the most useful men in the service." See J. William Jones, *Christ in the Camp or Religion in Lee's Army* (Richmond, VA: B. F. Johnson, 1887), 315.

18. Jones to Broadus, March 30, 1863, in Robertson, *Life and Letters of John Albert Broadus*, 196–98.

19. Lyon, "Crawford Howell Toy," 5–8, 13–15; Billy G. Hurt, "Crawford Howell Toy: Interpreter of the Old Testament" (ThD diss., Southern Baptist Theological Seminary, 1966), 72–74.

20. Jones to Poindexter, Aug. 2, 1859, Missionary File, SBHLA. There is dispute concerning the precise date of Jones and Toy's ordination, with some sources indicating June 9, and others June 10. See Hurt, "Crawford Howell Toy," 31n.

21. Jones to Poindexter, Dec. 15, 1859, Missionary File, SBHLA; Jones to Poindexter, July 16, 1860, Missionary File, SBHLA.

22. Crawford H. Toy to Jones, June 28, 1860, Jones Family Papers, UVA.

23. Jones to Poindexter, Sept. 11, 1860, Missionary File, SBHLA; Jones to Poindexter, Sept. 27, 1860, Missionary File, SBHLA. The companion in question was John Lipscomb Johnson, a fellow UVA student who had been ordained with Jones and Toy. Johnson had received an appointment to Japan, but due to health concerns, the Foreign Mission Board advised him not to go. See

Johnson, *Autobiographical Notes*, 122. Johnson married Toy's sister and eventually served as a Confederate chaplain.

24. Jones to James B. Taylor, Oct. 4, 1860, Missionary File, SBHLA.

25. Jones to Poindexter, Nov. 29, 1860, Missionary File, SBHLA. During the interim, Jones preached in Charlottesville. Here Jones reported preaching to African American members four or five times. See Brown, "Pastoral Evangelism," 108–9.

26. Jones to Broadus, Dec. 17, 1860, in Robertson, *Life and Letters of John Albert Broadus*, 180; Taylor, *Virginia Baptist Ministers*, 220. Jones's sons were Carter Helm, Edloe Pendleton, Frank William, M. Ashby, and Howard Lee. Frank, who did not become a Baptist minister, worked as a lawyer in New York, and also served as an editor for the American Law Book Company. See "Chaplain General J. William Jones," *Confederate Veteran* 17 (May 1909): 239 (hereafter cited as *CV*); Harris, *History of Louisa County, Virginia*, 212–13; Taylor, *Virginia Baptist Ministers*, 228. See also Tyler, *Men of Mark in Virginia*, 250–53; Moore, "J. William Jones," 1607; Jones to Broadus, Feb. 7, 1861, John A. Broadus Papers, Special Collections, Southern Baptist Theological Seminary, Louisville, KY (hereafter cited as "Broadus Papers, SBTS"); "J. William Jones Dies in Georgia," *Times Dispatch* 17, March 18, 1909, 1.

27. Jones to Taylor, Jan. 2, 1861, Missionary File, SBHLA; Jones to Broadus, Dec. 17, 1860, in Robertson, *Life and Letters of John Albert Broadus*, 180.

28. Taylor, *Virginia Baptist Ministers*, 220; Sampey, *Southern Baptist Theological Seminary*, 126; Harris, *History of Louisa County, Virginia*, 199.

29. Jones, "Varied Experiences In Work Among Young Men"; Jones, *Christ in the Camp*, 17; Brown, "Pastoral Evangelism," 55.

30. Jones to Boyce, May 23, 1861, James P. Boyce Papers, Special Collections, Southern Baptist Theological Seminary, Louisville, KY (hereafter cited as "Boyce Papers, SBTS"); "Secession," Library of Virginia, accessed July 25, 2018, http://www.lva.virginia.gov/public/guides/Civil-War/Secession.htm.

31. "Chaplain General J. William Jones," *CV* 17 (May 1909): 239. Hill began as colonel of the 13th but was later promoted to lieutenant general. When Hill was killed at the Battle of Petersburg in April 1865, Jones presided over the funeral. See also Harris, *History of Louisa County, Virginia*, 78–79; Riggs, *13th Virginia Infantry*, 122. Brown, "Pastoral Evangelism," 109–10; Jones, "Gen. A. P. Hill,"

CV 1 (Aug. 1893): 233; Jones, "Reminiscences of the Army of Northern Virginia, or the Boys in Gray, as I Saw Them from 1861 to Appomattox Court-House in 1865," *Southern Historical Society Papers* 9 (Feb. 1881): 90–91 (hereafter cited as *SHSP*); Philip Edloe Jones to Ann Pendleton Jones, June 9, 1861, Jones Family Papers, UVA.

32. Philip Edloe Jones to Francis Pendleton Jones, June 2, 1861, Jones Family Papers, UVA; Philip Edloe Jones to Helen Mary Jones, April 5, 1861, Jones Family Papers, UVA; Philip Edloe Jones to Helen Mary Jones, April 5, 1861; May 12, 1861(?); Philip Edloe Jones to Francis W. Jones, May 12, 1861(?); May 19, 1861(?), Jones Family Papers, UVA. Writing to his father, Ed discussed attending a Roman Catholic service "if I can't do any better."

33. Philip Edloe Jones to Francis W. Jones, Aug. 13, 1861, Jones Family Papers, UVA; Philip Edloe Jones to Ann Pendleton Jones, June 9, 1861, Jones Family Papers, UVA.

34. Jones to Judith Page Helm Jones, June 27, 1861, Jones Family Papers, UVA.

35. Philip Edloe Jones to Ann Pendleton Jones, June 9, 1861, Jones Family Papers, UVA.

36. Riggs, *13th Virginia Infantry*, 29, 74–75, 86. Jones provided conflicting figures about the casualties at Gaines's Mill; on at least two occasions he recorded 13th losses at more than fifty percent. See Jones, *Christ in the Camp*, 251; Jones, "Reminiscences of the Army of Northern Virginia," *SHSP* 9 (Oct.–Dec. 1881): 561; *American Civil War Research Database* (Alexandria, VA: Alexander Street Press, 1997).

37. Francis Pendleton Jones to Francis William Jones, Sept. 23, 1862, Jones Family Papers, UVA; Jones to Judith Page Helm Jones, Jan. 2, 1863, Jones Family Papers, UVA.

38. Jones, *Christ in the Camp*, 19; Drew Gilpin Faust, *This Republic of Suffering: Death and the American Civil War* (New York: Vintage, 2009), 6.

39. Jones, *Christ in the Camp*, 19; Brown, "Pastoral Evangelism," 111. I am indebted to Brown for recognizing the similarities between Jones's account in *Christ in the Camp* and Ed's experience. See also Jones, "Reminiscences of the Army of Northern Virginia," *SHSP* 9 (Oct.–Dec. 1881): 561–62.

40. Riggs, *13th Virginia Infantry*, 122; Jones to Broadus, Sept. 4, 1863, Broadus Papers, SBTS.

41. Jones, *Christ in the Camp*, 433; Brown, "Pastoral Evangelism," 111; Riggs, *13th Virginia Infantry*, 35–36, 41–42.

42. Jones, "Camp Near Petersburg, Jan. 1 '65," *Christian Index* 44, Feb. 2, 1865, 1.

43. Jones to Boyce, May 23, 1861, Boyce Papers, SBTS; Philip Edloe Jones to Ann Pendleton Jones, June 9, 1861, Jones Family Letters, UVA; Jones to Ann Pendleton Jones, Sept. 20, 1861, Jones Family Letters, UVA; Jones, "Varied Experiences In Work Among Young Men"; Brown, "Pastoral Evangelism," 109–10; Riggs, *13th Virginia Infantry*, 122; American Civil War Research Database.

44. Jones, "Camp Near Petersburg, Jan. 12, '65"; Jones, "Camp Near Petersburg, January 23d, 1865," *Christian Index* 44, Feb. 16, 1865, 1; Frank L. Hieronymus, *For Now and Forever: The Chaplains of the Confederate States Army* (Los Angeles: PhD diss., Univ. of California, Los Angeles, 1964), 302, 304. Hieronymus lists the estimates of other denominations as follows: Episcopalians, 86–100; Catholics, 28–30; Cumberland Presbyterians, 23; Lutherans, 10; Disciples, 2; Congregationalists, 1.

45. Hieronymus, *For Now and Forever*, 74–75; Herman Norton, *Rebel Religion: The Story of Confederate Chaplains* (St. Louis, MO: Bethany Press, 1961), 109–10; John Brinsfield, *Faith in the Fight: Civil War Chaplains* (Mechanicsburg, PA: Stackpole Books, 2003), 71. For works that address the way the Civil War challenged and altered Baptist notions of church-state separation, see Bruce Gourley, *Diverging Loyalties: Baptists in Middle Georgia During the Civil War* (Macon: Mercer Univ. Press, 2011); Fredrick J. Dobney, "From Denominationalism to Nationalism in the Civil War: A Case Study," *Texana* 9 (1971): 367–76; Martin Lyndon McMahone, "Liberty More than Separation: The Multiple Streams of Baptist Thought on Church-State Issues, 1830–1900" (PhD diss., Baylor Univ., 2001). See also "Chaplains," *Christian Index* 41, April 15, 1862, 2; J. G. Johnson, "Chaplains," *Christian Index* 42, May 18, 1863, 1.

46. Bertram Wyatt-Brown, "Church, Honor, and Secession," in Randall M. Miller, Harry S. Stout, and Charles Reagan Wilson, *Religion and the American Civil War* (New York: Oxford Univ. Press, 1998), 104; Harry S. Stout, *Upon the Altar of the Nation* (New York: Viking Penguin, 2006), 86; Wilson, *Baptized in Blood*, 6; Drew Gilpin Faust, "Christian Soldiers: The Meaning of Revivalism in the Confederate Army," *Journal of Southern History* 53 (Feb. 1987): 70; Charles F.

Pitts, *Chaplains in Gray: The Confederate Chaplains' Story* (Concord, VA: R. M. J. C. Publications, 1957), 42–43.

47. Pitts, *Chaplains in Gray*, 40–41, 43–44. Hieronymus, *For Now and Forever*, 101–3. Hieronymus contends that by keeping church and state separate, the Confederate government made explicit that the chaplain answered to God alone.

48. Brown, "Pastoral Evangelism," 113, 185.

49. Hieronymus, *For Now and Forever*, 78–80, 87. See also Brinsfield, *Faith in the Fight*, 71–73; Pitts, *Chaplains in Gray*, 43–44. Pitts includes the same categories as does Hieronymus, yet adds "colporteurs," who were lay people or clergy responsible for distributing religious literature in the armies.

50. Taylor, *Virginia Baptist Ministers*, 168; Jones, *Christ in the Camp*, 354; "Annual Report," *Religious Herald* 37, Dec. 29, 1864, 1.

51. The *Confederate Veteran* indicates that Jones became a "missionary chaplain" to Hill's corps when Hill was promoted. This suggests that Jones assumed the position in 1863, the year Stonewall Jackson died and Hill was promoted to lieutenant general. Shattuck and Brinsfield refer to Jones as either a "missionary" or "missionary chaplain," and regimental records seem to confirm this. Taylor and Wilson, however, write that in November 1863 Jones's role changed from chaplain to "evangelist." See "Chaplain General J. William Jones," *CV* 17 (May 1909): 239; Jones, *Christ in the Camp*, 354; Brinsfield, *Faith in the Fight*, 72; Shattuck, "John William Jones"; Wilson, *Baptized in Blood*, 120; Riggs, *13th Virginia Infantry*, 122; Taylor, *Virginia Baptist Ministers*, 68; "To the Churches of the Goshen Association," *Religious Herald* 38, Jan. 5, 1865, 1; "Chaplains' Reunion at Memphis," *Christian Observer* 89, May 8, 1901, 23.

52. Brown, "Pastoral Evangelism," 114.

53. Hieronymus, *For Now and Forever*, 85, 91; Jones, *Christ in the Camp*, 227; Riggs, *13th Virginia Infantry*, 20–21; Jones, "Reminiscences of the Army of Northern Virginia," *SHSP* 9 (Feb. 1881): 93.

54. Broadus, July 6, 1863, and Aug. 17, 1863, in Robertson, *Life and Letters of John Albert Broadus*, 198; Jones, "Army Evangelist," *Religious Herald* 36, Aug. 13, 1863, 1; Brown, "Pastoral Evangelism," 169, 172, 178; Hieronymus, *For Now and Forever*, 135.

55. Jones to Broadus (photocopy), Jan. 4, 1865, J. William Jones Collection, Virginia Baptist Historical Society, Richmond, VA (hereafter cited as "Jones Papers, VBHS"); Jones, *Christ in the Camp*, 522.

56. Phillip Thomas Tucker, *The Confederacy's Fighting Chaplain: Father John B. Bannon* (Tuscaloosa: Univ. of Alabama Press, 1992), 68–69; Hieronymus, *For Now and Forever*, 162–63, 167–69; Jones, *Christ in the Camp*, 312.

57. Jones, *Christ in the Camp*, 321. Jones to Judith Page Helm Jones, Jan. 2, 1863, Jones Family Papers, UVA. "Abstract of Principles."

58. Faust argues that camp religion diluted denominational distinctions on issues such as baptism. See Faust, "Christian Soldiers," 70. See also Wilson, *Baptized in Blood*, 120–21; Taylor, *Virginia Baptist Ministers*, 222–23; "Abstract of Principles"; Jones, *Christ in the Camp*, 255, 383; Jones, "Camp Near Somerville's Ford," *Religious Herald* 36, Oct. 8, 1863; Shattuck, "John William Jones"; Jones, "Varied Experiences In Work Among Young Men." Jones continued ministering outside of the camp, conducting weddings and, on at least one occasion, preaching at an African American church. See "Married," *Richmond Daily Dispatch* 20, Nov. 19, 1861, 2; "Baptist Association," *Richmond Daily Dispatch* 24, June 6, 1863, 1.

59. Riggs, *13th Virginia Infantry*, 29; Taylor, *Virginia Baptist Ministers*, 222; Jones, *Christ in the Camp*, 258.

60. Hieronymus, *For Now and Forever*, 62; Jones, *Christ in the Camp*, 519; Taylor, *Virginia Baptist Ministers*, 221–22; Wilson, *Baptized in Blood*, 120–21, 127–28. Jones had met Stonewall Jackson in the summer of 1861.

61. Jones, "Camp Near Somerville's Ford"; Brown, "Pastoral Evangelism," 184–85; Jones to Broadus, Dec. 29, 1863, Broadus Papers, SBTS.

62. Jones, "Camp Near Petersburg, Jan. 12, '65."

63. Jones, "Camp Near Petersburg, January 23d, 1865."

64. "Baptist Ministers and the Soldiers," *Biblical Recorder* 28, Sept. 30, 1863, 3; "Camp Near Summerville Ford, Rapidan River, Va.," *Biblical Recorder*, Oct. 21, 1863, 2.

65. Crowther, "John the Evangelist Revisited."

CHAPTER TWO *"We Mingled Together in Freest Intercourse":*
Jones the Baptist and Wartime Confederate Religion

1. Jones, *Christ in the Camp*, 271; "To the Friends of the Thirteenth Virginia Regiment," *Daily Dispatch* 20, Dec. 2, 1861, 3; Jones, "Varied Experiences In Work Among Young Men." See also Hieronymus, *For Now and Forever*, 58–59.

Hieronymus writes that there was a shortage of chaplains in 1861–1862, but that numbers improved in late 1862 and 1863. Worth remembering, though, is that chaplains remained in short supply throughout the war's duration.

2. For those dating the revivals immediately after Fredericksburg, see Wilson, *Baptized in Blood*, 120–21; Shattuck, "John William Jones." Jones's obituary in the *Confederate Veteran* also records the revivals as following Fredericksburg. See "Chaplain General J. William Jones," *CV* 17 (May 1909): 239. By contrast, historian Drew Gilpin Faust maintains that the services began soon after Antietam. See Faust, "Christian Soldiers," 71. See also Jones, *Christ in the Camp*, 273, 283; "Varied Experiences In Work Among Young Men."

   Regarding the revivals' spread, Faust writes that the revivals swept from Virginia to the Army of Tennessee and Trans-Mississippi forces. Hieronymus, on the other hand, claims that there was no clear connection between the eastern and western revivals. See Faust, "Christian Soldiers," 65; Hieronymus, *For Now and Forever*, 240.

3. Gorrel Clinton Prim, "Born Again in the Trenches: Revivalism in the Confederate Army" (PhD diss., Florida State Univ., 1982), 39. Prim writes that Confederate revivals came in waves. While there were stirrings of revivals in late 1862, the first major wave of revivals began in early 1863. The second wave of revivals occurred after the Pennsylvania campaign in the summer of 1863; the third wave came in the winter of 1863. While revivals continued from 1864 until the end of the war, they did so to a lesser degree. Hieronymus rightly observes that fewer converts would be expected, since by 1864–1865, there were significantly fewer soldiers than two years prior. See Prim, "Born Again in the Trenches," 139; Hieronymus, *For Now and Forever*, 253–54, 259–60. With regard to the revivals' timing, scholarly discrepancies need not be mutually exclusive. One could speculate that the September 1862 Sharpsburg defeat prompted sporadic revivals, while the December 1862 Fredericksburg victory confirmed for Southerners what would happen if they "returned" to God. With such a divine affirmation, post-Fredericksburg revivals intensified and expanded.

4. Baptist chaplain J. J. D. Renfroe exemplified this line of thinking in an 1863 sermon, proclaiming, "Our cause is just, and God hath greatly blessed us; still we are but men. We have failed to confide in the God of our mercies, we have trusted in our own strength, and he is subjecting us to severe vicissitudes."

See Renfroe, *"The Battle is God's." A sermon preached before Wilcox's brigade, on fast day, the 21st August, 1863, near Orange Court-House, Va. by J. J. D. Renfroe, Chaplain 10th Alabama Regiment* (Richmond, VA: Macfarlane & Fergusson, 1863), 11.

5. Faust, "Christian Soldiers," 66; Jones, *Christ in the Camp*, 242–44.

6. Jones, *Christ in the Camp*, 245–48. Jones's observation that the revivals continued in August 1863 is noteworthy. According to Prim, the second wave of revivals occurred during this period (Prim, "Born Again in the Trenches," 139). Significantly, these revivals came the month after Lee's disastrous defeat at Gettysburg. The timing here adds credence to the contention that revivals followed on the heels of defeat.

7. Jones, *Christ in the Camp*, 246, 248–49; Wilson, *Baptized in Blood*, 119–20, 131.

8. Jones, *Christ in the Camp*, 258, 260–61, 353; Jones, "Camp Near Petersburg, January 23d"; Jones, "Camp Near Petersburg, Jan. 12, '65."

9. Jones, *Christ in the Camp*, 261–62, 468, 471, 481.

10. Jones, "Camp Near Petersburg, Jan. 12, '65." Jones's insistence that victory was attainable at this point of the war supports historian David B. Chesebrough's claim that "[i]t was the ministers who inspired the South to keep on fighting, to continue the shedding of blood, to perpetuate the carnage, when the cause was obviously lost." See Chesebrough, *"God Ordained This War": Sermons on the Sectional crisis, 1830–1865* (Columbia: Univ. of South Carolina Press, 1991), 9. See also James W. Silver, *Confederate Morale and Church Propaganda* (Tuscaloosa: Confederate Publishing Company, 1957).

11. Jones, *Christ in the Camp*, 391–92; Miller, *Both Prayed to the Same God*, 123, 126. Miller also suggests—much to Jones's chagrin, no doubt—that Union armies likely experienced twice as many conversions as did Confederate armies.

12. George C. Rable, *God's Almost Chosen Peoples: A Religious History of the American Civil War* (Chapel Hill: Univ. of North Carolina Press, 2010), 125, 207.

13. Regarding wartime ecumenism, see Faust, "Christian Soldiers," 70. As to postwar ecumenism, historian Zachary Dresser addresses how many white Southerners attempted to emulate the interdenominational nature of Confederate revivals. See Dresser, "The Theology of Reconstruction," 125, 156–58. Dresser notes that postwar Southern ecumenists stressed few doctrinal distinctions aside from the Lord's Supper and baptism, with some advocating for

organic denominational union. Dresser specifically highlights Jones's writings on the Confederate revivals as portraying a "golden age of past unity" to which many postwar Southerners wanted to return. See Dresser, "Onward Christian Soldiers?," 12.

14. Dresser, "The Theology of Reconstruction," 131–32; Weaver, *In Search of the New Testament Church* (Ga: Mercer University Press, 2008)," 87–88, 146; Leonard, *God's Last and Only Hope*, 13, 17–18, 25–31. For a discussion of how denominational divisions paved the way for secession, see Clarence Curtis Goen, "Broken Churches, Broken Nation: Regional Religion and North-South Alienation in Antebellum America," *Church History* 52 (March 1983): 21–35.

15. Pendleton came to be known as the theologian of Landmarkism. Besides Graves and Pendleton, another leader in the movement was Amos Dayton (1813–1865), who spread Landmarker beliefs through his novels. Landmarkers required that those baptized outside of a Landmark church—even if by immersion—be rebaptized before joining a Landmark congregation. Closed communion could also entail giving the Lord's Supper only to members of the particular congregation celebrating communion. See Weaver, *In Search of the New Testament Church*, 153–55; Bill J. Leonard, *Baptist Ways: A History* (Valley Forge, PA: Judson Press, 2003), 183–84.

16. Leonard, *Baptist Ways*, 215; Weaver, *In Search of the New Testament Church*, 158–60; Whitsitt, "John William Jones, D. D." See also Whitsitt, *Genealogy of Jefferson Davis and of Samuel Davies* (New York: Neale Publishing Company, 1910); Hieronymus, *For Now and Forever*, 309. Whitsitt's effusive praise of Jones is even more interesting in light of the role that Jones's son, Carter Helm, played in Whitsitt's resignation. Carter had initially signed a letter of support for Whitsitt, but later met with Whitsitt supporters in order to explain the prudency of resignation. For his part, J. William Jones strongly encouraged Whitsitt to remain at SBTS. See "A Fraternal Statement to Southern Baptists," ca. Sept. 27, 1897, Robertson Papers, SBTS; Wills, *Southern Baptist Theological Seminary, 1859–2009*, 224; J. William Jones, "The Whitsitt Matter," *Religious Herald* 70, Aug. 26, 1897, 1; J. William Jones, "What has Happened Since the Convention at Wilmington," *Religious Herald* 70, Sept. 2, 1897, 2.

17. "Let us Keep our Principles in View," *Biblical Recorder* 28, Dec. 9, 1863, 2.

18. "Preach the Whole Truth," *Biblical Recorder* 29, Jan. 16, 1864, 2.

19. "Army Correspondence," *Confederate Baptist* 1, June 24, 1863, 1. The *Confederate Baptist*, out of Columbia, South Carolina, ran from 1862–1865. The founding editors were prominent Southern Baptists J. L. Reynolds and J. M. C. Breaker. See "The Confederate Baptist," *Religious Herald* 35, Oct. 9, 1862, 1; T. W. Gwin, "An Explanation," *Confederate Baptist* 1, July 22, 1863, 1.

20. Gwin, "An Explanation."

21. "A Pass Through Lines," *Confederate Baptist* 1, July 22, 1863, 2; "A Pass Through the Lines," *Christian Index* 42, Aug. 21, 1863, 2; "Unlawful Baptism," *Biblical Recorder* 28, Aug. 12, 1863, 2. See also historian William Earl Brown's discussion of the Gwin affair: Brown, "Pastoral Evangelism," 61–62.

22. Brown, "Pastoral Evangelism," 8, 61, 65; Prim, "Born Again in the Trenches," 59–60, 63.

23. "Church in the Army," *Christian Index* 42, July 31, 1863, 2. See also "Churches in the Army," *Religious Herald* 36, Aug. 20, 1863, 1.

24. Jones, "Varied Experiences In Work Among Young Men." See also "Church in the Army," *Christian Index* 42, July 31, 1863, 2; Leonard, *Baptist Ways*, 216. One baptismal certificate Jones signed read as follows: "This is to certify that I have this day baptized (name), upon a profession of his faith in Christ. I cordially commend him to the fellowship of any Baptist Church to which this may be presented." See J. William Jones's Baptismal Certificate, Aug. 16, 1863, Jones Papers, VBHS.

25. Jones, *Christ in the Camp*, 223, 305.

26. Jones, 223.

27. Jones, 223–25, 286, 308, 365, 520. One letter to the *Religious Herald* provided an interesting glimpse into the way chaplains welcomed new converts. The letter is signed "Occasional," but the author is likely Jones. Jones often signed his *Herald* letters in this way, and details he provided in *Christ in the Camp* align with the letter's description, timing, and location.

In the letter, Jones commended the way in which chaplains received converts. He observed, "Every day or so 'the doors of the church are opened,' and an opportunity given to all to join the church of their choice, by relating their experiences and being baptized (if they desire it)." At first glance, Jones seemed to imply that converts were not required to be baptized and that he approved of such measures. The rest of Jones's letter, however, made clear that he believed all converts should be baptized. He continued his correspondence by rebuking a minister who felt baptism could wait until soldiers returned to their home churches. Jones countered with biblical examples of converts who were baptized as soon as they made professions of faith.

Not all ministers required baptismal candidates to affiliate with a denomination. Jones mentioned that in a revival led by Episcopalian minister, Hugh Roy Scott, there were seventeen soldiers baptized without identifying with any denomination. See "Letter from Camp," *Religious Herald* 36, April 23, 1863, 1. For corroboration of Jones as the author of the letter, see *Christ in the Camp*, 93–94, 325, 482–83.

28. Prim, "Born Again in the Trenches," 45; Jones, *Christ in the Camp*, 225–26, 230–41, 514–16.

29. Jones, *Christ in the Camp*, 341. Emphasis is Richards's (or Jones's).

30. Jones, *Christ in the Camp or Religion in the Confederate Army* (Atlanta: Martin and Hoyt Company, 1904), 543. This citation comes from the 1904 edition of Jones's work. Beginning with a second edition in 1888, *Christ in the Camp* included an appendix that explored religion in other armies of the Confederacy. By contrast, Jones's 1887 edition had focused on the Army of Northern Virginia. Unless otherwise noted, quotations come from the 1887 edition.

31. Jones, *Christ in the Camp*, 158, 167, 593.

32. W. Harrison Daniel, "The Christian Association: A Religious Society in the Army of Northern Virginia," *Virginia Magazine of History and Biography* 69 (Jan. 1961): 95; Dresser, "Onward Christian Soldiers?," 6; Prim, "Born Again in the Trenches," 64; Brown, "Pastoral Evangelism," 65–67. Describing the nature of nonsectarian associations, Dresser observes that the "purpose was to foster religious life regardless of denominational affiliation, but without destroying such allegiances. Denomination lived on beneath the veneer of Christian union."

33. Jones, *Christ in the Camp*, 244, 334, 354, 385, 484.

34. Jones, *Christ in the Camp*, 17–18, 298, 319, 330; *Christ in the Camp*, 600 (1904 ed.).

35. Jones, *Christ in the Camp*, 20, 29, 39, 207, 234, 265, 271. With vice rampant in the army, there is certainly a tension in Jones's claims that Christ was *in* the Confederate camps at all. Historian Reid Mitchell theorizes that Jones resolved this tension by nuancing how he understood "conversions." Many of these conversions may have involved a heretofore "unchurched" soldier committing to join a congregation. In this way, Jones played both sides of the issue. He could

argue that Southerners were Christians before the war, that these unchurched Christians fell into bad habits while in the army, and that God was present in the Confederate camps as evidenced by how many backsliders recommitted to the faith. See Mitchell, "Christian Soldiers? Perfecting the Confederacy," in *Religion and the American Civil War*, Randall M. Miller, Harry S. Stout, and Charles Reagan Wilson, eds. (New York: Oxford Univ. Press, 1998), 299.

36. Jones, *Christ in the Camp*, 94.

37. Prim, "Born Again in the Trenches," 30.

38. Jones, *Christ in the Camp*, 358, 363–64, 379, 383.

39. Jones, 224.

40. Jones, 168, 216–17, 219, 228.

41. Jones, 148, 177, 184, 214. See also Genesis 28:10–22.

42. Jones, *Christ in the Camp*, 202.

43. Jones, 251, 254, 259, 301, 392. Jones used similar rhetoric in his efforts to recruit more chaplains. "[D]o not delay your coming brethren," he wrote, "for there is many a poor fellow whom you might reach . . . who will fill a soldier's grave in the early spring campaign." See "Now is the Time to Preach in the Army," *Religious Herald* 37, March 10, 1864, 1.

44. Jones, *Christ in the Camp*, 249–50, 253, 272–73, 376. Brown writes that because of Jones's Calvinist theology—which downplayed the role of humans in salvation—Jones did not employ "manipulative techniques" or use "special effects to secure conversions amidst excited group emotions." See Brown, "Pastoral Evangelism," 27. Jones's techniques, however, suggest that he—as did most Confederate chaplains—capitalized on soldiers' fears of death.

45. Jones, *Christ in the Camp*, 276.

46. Jones, 281, 328, 347.

47. Jones, 339.

48. Jones, 235.

49. "Prayer for our Country," *Christian Index* 42, July 31, 1863, 2.

50. Jones, *Christ in the Camp*, 323, 515; Jones, "To the Churches of the Goshen Association," *Religious Herald* 38, Jan. 5, 1865, 1.

51. Jones, *Christ in the Camp*, 235–40.

52. Jones, 232–33, 238–40.

53. Jones, 147, 238–41, 411, 430, 509. See also Faust, "Christian Soldiers," 88.

54. Jones, *Christ in the Camp*, 452, 480, 512.

55. Jones, *Christ in the Camp*, 238–40; Jones, *Christ in the Camp* (1904), 540.

56. Jones, *Christ in the Camp*, 205; Jones, *Christ in the Camp* (1904), 623.

57. "Despondency," *Christian Index* 42, July 31, 1863, 2.

58. Dresser, "Onward Christian Soldiers?," 2, 12.

59. Historian Jay Dolan argues convincingly that nineteenth-century American Catholics were familiar with and open to certain kinds of revivalism, and he lobbies for a broad understanding of the term evangelical. For Dolan, "the term evangelical represents a mood or style of religion which is not peculiar to any one denomination and thus best describes the central thrust of the revival tradition in American history." Of course, such an expansive definition of evangelical would have been quite foreign to Jones, who employed the term more narrowly, usually when referencing Baptists, Methodists, and Presbyterians. See Jay P. Dolan, *Catholic Revivalism: The American Experience, 1830–1900* (Notre Dame: Univ. of Notre Dame Press, 1978), 91.

60. Jones, *Christ in the Camp*, 7, 21, 22, 330, 357, 393–94. At times, Jones used the term evangelical as a general description of ministry focusing on conversion (Jones, 6–7, 32, 167; see also Granberry's introduction, 14). The conversion focus is likely what a writer for the *Petersburg Express* had in mind when describing that the "highly evangelical" nature of colportage would be accepted by "all denominations" (Jones, 162). At other times, Jones used or quoted the term evangelical to refer to "pure" religion or Christian piety (Jones, 20, 68, 338).

61. Jones, *Christ in the Camp*, 223, 225.

62. See Miller, *Both Prayed to the Same God*, 145–46; Osterweis, *The Myth of the Lost Cause, 1865–1900*, 120; Dresser, "The Theology of Reconstruction," 143, 150–51. Osterweis and Dresser also highlight the participation of Jews in the development of the Lost Cause. Yet herein is another example of why the term "ecumenism" has become so unwieldy. Since many historians have used the word to describe the downplaying of doctrinal distinctions, or even the merger of denominational bodies, classifying the inclusion of Roman Catholics and Jews as ecumenical can be misleading. Uniting for the common goal of spreading the Lost Cause was a cooperative venture, but it did not extend into the realm of doctrine.

For more on the role of Jewish chaplains in the war, see E. M. Boswell, "Rebel Religion," *Civil War Times Illustrated* 11 (Oct. 1972): 31. Boswell notes

that while there are no records of the Confederate government commissioning Jewish chaplains, the Confederacy recognized the right of Jewish
chaplains to serve.

63. Jones, *Christ in the Camp*, 204, 408.

64. Jones, 214, 325–26, 350.

65. Wilson, *Baptized in Blood*, 131.

66. Jones, *Christ in the Camp*, 525; Jones, *Christ in the Camp* (1904), 548, 594.

67. Hieronymus estimates that around thirty Roman Catholics served as
Confederate chaplains. Baptists, by comparison, fielded as many as three
hundred. See Hieronymus, *For Now and Forever*, 302, 304. These figures only
reflect those who officially served as chaplains. The numbers do not include
itinerant ministers, Protestant or Roman Catholic, who visited army camps.
See also *American Civil War Research Database* (Alexandria, VA: Alexander
Street Press, 1997); Jones, *Christ in the Camp*, 516, 532. Jones identified
the chaplains of the 47th as S. P. Meredith and S. B. Barber. In his list of
Confederate chaplains, Hieronymus includes a record of a *J. M.* Meredith
but not an *S. P.* Meredith.

68. Patrick J. Hayes, ed., *The Civil War Diary of Father James Sheeran: Confederate
Chaplain and Redemptionist* (Washington, DC: Catholic Univ. of America Press,
2016), 3–4; Jones, *Christ in the Camp* (1904), 530.

69. See William W. Bennett, *A Narrative of the Great Revival Which Prevailed in
the Southern Armies During the Late Civil War Between the States of the Federal
Union* (Philadelphia: Claxton, Remsen and Haffelfinger, 1877). The title of
Jones's 1904 edition of *Christ in the Camp* changed from *Christ in the Camp or
Religion in Lee's Army* to *Christ in the Camp or Religion in the Confederate Army*.
Even though the 1904 edition included the same written material as in Jones's
1888 edition, the title change reflected an effort to broaden the focus of the work
beyond Lee's army (what the 1888 appendix had attempted to do as well).

70. Historians Donald Beagle and Bryan Giemza maintain that Ryan embraced a
"revivalist rhetorical style" during the war. Ryan earned the reputation for his
forceful preaching against sin as well as his ability to motivate listeners to come
to confession. See Beagle and Giemza, *Poet of the Lost Cause: A Life of Father
Ryan* (Knoxville: Univ. of Tennessee Press, 2008), 47–49, 52, 115. If Ryan was
indeed a "Catholic revivalist," it is even more surprising that Jones gave Ryan

no mention. See also Blum, *Reforging the White Republic*, 146; Charles F. Pitts, *Chaplains in Gray: The Confederate Chaplains' Story* (Concord, VA: R. M. J. C. Publications, 1957), 126–28. Even though Pitts refers to Ryan as a Confederate chaplain, historian David O'Connell has argued that Ryan never officially served as army chaplain, though he did minister in Confederate camps. See O'Connell, *Furl That Banner: The Life of Abram J. Ryan, Poet-Priest of the South* (Macon: Mercer Univ. Press, 2006), 54–56. Beagle and Giemza disagree, contending that while Ryan was never officially commissioned as a chaplain, he may have served as a "freelance chaplain" to Louisiana soldiers.

Some of Ryan's most popular postwar poetry included "The Conquered Banner," "The Sword of Robert Lee," "The Lost Cause," and "The March of the Deathless Dead." See Boswell, "Rebel Religion," 31. For work on another popular Roman Catholic minister in the Confederacy, see Phillip Thomas Tucker, *The Confederacy's Fighting Chaplain: Father John B. Bannon* (Tuscaloosa: Univ. of Alabama Press, 1992).

71. For example, see "The Men who Wore the Gray," *SHSP* 10 (June 1882): 279–83; "The Southern Soldier Boy," *SHSP* 10 (April 1882): 186; "The Sword of Lee" and "Robert E. Lee," *SHSP* 11 (Aug./Sept. 1883): 427; "Unveiling of Valentine's Recumbent Figure of Lee at Lexington, Va., June 28, 1883," *SHSP* 11 (Aug./Sept. 1883): 414–15. See also Jones, *Christ in Camp* (1904), 510b.

72. Jones, *Christ in the Camp* (1904), 510.

73. James M. McPherson, *Battle Cry of Freedom: The Civil War Era* (New York: Oxford Univ. Press, 2003), 32–33, 130, 132.

74. McPherson, 131, 135.

75. A good example of this changed attitude is in the letters of Northern chaplain Joseph Hopkins Twichell. See Twichell, *The Civil War Letters of Joseph Hopkins Twichell: A Chaplain's Story* (Athens: Univ. of Georgia Press, 2012), 37, 42, 73. See also Benedict R. Maryniak and John Wesley Brinsfield, Jr., *The Spirit Divided: Memoirs of Civil War Chaplains—The Union* (Macon: Mercer Univ. Press, 2007), 107.

76. "The Bible and the Monk," *Harper's Weekly* 9, Dec. 16, 1865, 785; "The Pope's Bull," *Harper's Weekly* 9, Jan. 28, 1865, 50; Gonzalez, *The Story of Christianity, Vol. 2*, 324–25.

77. "The Unconverted World," *Biblical Recorder* 30, Jan. 25, 1865, 1; "Intellectual Superiority of Protestantism," *Biblical Recorder* 26, Sept. 11, 1861, 1. Here the

Biblical Recorder echoed the views of most Southern Baptists, but Northern
Baptists held similar anti-Catholic sentiments. The eminent Northern Baptist
Francis Wayland associated the Roman Catholic Church with "bigotry, perse-
cution unto death, and the most soul-destroying perversion of the doctrines of
the cross." See Wayland, *Notes on the Principles and Practices of Baptist Churches*
(New York: Sheldon, Blakeman and Company, 1857), 157.

78. "Infallibility of the Pope," *Religious Herald* 5, July 21, 1870, 2; "The Dogma of
Infallibility—Archbishop Spalding's Apology," *Religious Herald* 5, Dec. 22,
1870, 2; "Downfall of the Pope," *Religious Herald* 5, Oct. 20, 1870, 2; "The Proper
Treatment of Roman Catholics," *Religious Herald* 6, Aug. 10, 1871, 2.

79. Jones, *Christ in the Camp*, 350.

80. Shattuck, *A Shield and Hiding Place*, 122.

81. Hieronymus holds that for many Roman Catholics, the language of revivalism
was alien. See Hieronymus, *For Now and Forever*, 239; Prim, "Born Again in
the Trenches," 6. Dolan disagrees, asserting that nineteenth-century revivalism
was not "exclusively a Protestant enterprise." Dolan points to the prevalence of
"parish missions," which had many of the earmarks of what Protestants called
revivals. During the parish mission—which could involve a series of services
lasting more than a week—priests proclaimed the gospel and demanded repentance from congregants. Dolan observes that "revival religion not only found
a home in the Catholic community, it also became the most popular religious
experience of Catholic Americans in the second half of the nineteenth century."
See Dolan, *Catholic Revivalism*, xvi–xvii, 89. For recent study on parish missions
and the history of revivalism among Roman Catholics in America, see Bill J.
Leonard, *A Sense of the Heart: Christian Religious Experience in the United States*
(Nashville, TN: Abingdon Press, 2014), 255–70.

82. Dolan, *Catholic Revivalism*, 24.

83. Faust, "Christian Soldiers," 68; Prim, "Born Again in the Trenches," 43–44;
Hieronymus, *For Now and Forever*, 216, 239–40, 310.

84. Scholars have posited many helpful definitions of evangelicalism, perhaps one of the best known coming from historian David Bebbington.
Bebbington's "quadrilateral"—conversionism, activism, Biblicism, and cruci-
centrism—does not, however, define how contemporaries of a particular time
period used the term evangelical. Historian George Marsden highlights several evangelical foci: Reformation emphasis on scripture, God's saving work,

salvation through personal trust in Christ, evangelism, and life transformation. See Bebbington, *Evangelicalism in Modern Britain: A History from the
1730s to the 1980s* (New York: Routledge, 2003), 2–3; Marsden, "Introduction,"
in *Evangelicalism and Modern America*, ed. George Marsden (Grand
Rapids, MI: Eerdmans Publishing, 1984), ix-x. See also Nathan O. Hatch,
"Evangelicalism as a Democratic Movement," in Marsden, *Evangelicalism
and Modern America*, 73, 75. Hatch states that the "genius of evangelicals long
has been their firm identification with people" and that post-Revolution
American evangelicals "considered the 'common sense' intuition of people
at large more reliable, even in the realm of theology, than the musing of an
educated few."

For recent assessments that challenge or nuance the Bebbington quad-
rilateral, see Darren Dochuk, "Revisiting Bebbington's Classic Rendering of
Modern Evangelicalism at Points of New Departure," *Fides et Historia* 47, no. 1
(Jan. 1, 2015): 63–72; Kelly Cross Elliott, "The Bebbington Quadrilateral Travels
into the Empire," *Fides et Historia* 47, no. 1 (Jan. 1, 2015): 46–53; Thomas S. Kidd,
"The Bebbington Quadrilateral and the Work of the Holy Spirit," *Fides et
Historia* 47, no. 1 (Jan. 1, 2015): 54–57; Mark A. Noll, "Noun or Adjective? The
Ravings of a Fanatical Nominalist," *Fides et Historia*, 47, no. 1 (Winter/Spring
2015): 73–82; Charlie Phillips, "Roundtable: Re-examining David Bebbington's
'Quadrilateral Thesis': Introduction," *Fides et Historia* 47, no. 1 (Jan. 1, 2015):
44–45; Amanda Porterfield, "Bebbington's Approach to Evangelical Christianity
as a Pioneering Effort in Live Religion," *Fides et Historia* 47, no. 1 (Jan. 1, 2015):
58–62; Molly Worthen, "Defining Evangelicalism: Questions that Complement
the Quadrilateral," *Fides et Historia* 47, no. 1 (Jan. 1, 2015): 83–86; Bebbington,
"The Evangelical Quadrilateral: A Response," *Fides et Historia* 47, no. 1 (Jan. 1,
2015): 87–96.

85. Samuel S. Hill, "Northern and Southern Varieties of American Evangelicalism
in the Nineteenth Century," in *Evangelicalism: Comparative Studies of Popular
Protestantism in North America, The British Isles, and Beyond, 1700–1990*, ed.
Mark A. Noll, David Bebbington, and George A. Rawlyk (New York: Oxford
Univ. Press, 1994), 287. Hill also provides a helpful discussion of African
American evangelicals (281–86). See also Paul Harvey, *Redeeming the South:
Religious Cultures and Racial Identities among Southern Baptists, 1865–1925*
(Chapel Hill: Univ. of North Carolina Press, 1997).

86. John Wolffe, "Anti-Catholicism and Evangelical Identity in Britain and the United States, 1830–1860," in *Evangelicalism*, Noll, Bebbington, and Rawlyk, 179–80, 184.

87. Frank Leslie Cross and Elizabeth A. Livingstone, *The Oxford Dictionary of the Christian Church* (New York: Oxford Univ. Press, 2005), 582; Wolffe, "Anti-Catholicism and Evangelical Identity," 190–91.

88. Wolffe, "Anti-Catholicism and Evangelical Identity," 191.

89. Dresser, "The Theology of Reconstruction," 12, 126.

90. Dresser, 12, 126, 138, 147, 150–51; Dresser, "Onward Christian Soldiers?," 2, 8, 12.

91. Jones, *Christ in the Camp*, 225.

92. For example, Faust argues that "[d]enominational differences were all but forgotten in what became an ecumenical movement to bring Christ to the camp. Baptists preached without insisting on baptism as a requirement for the forgiveness of sin. Protestant soldiers flocked to services conducted by Catholic chaplains." See Faust, "Christian Soldiers," 70.

93. Jones, *Christ in the Camp*, 255, 383; Jones, "Camp Near Somerville's Ford," *Religious Herald* 36, Oct. 8, 1863. See also Shattuck, "John William Jones"; Taylor, *Virginia Baptist Ministers*, 223; Wilson, *Baptized in Blood*, 121.

94. Jones, *Christ in the Camp*, 365.

95. Dresser, "The Theology of Reconstruction," 126–27; Dresser, "Onward Christian Soldiers?," 12–13.

96. See Faust, "Christian Soldiers," 70; Miller, *Both Prayed to the Same God*, 145–46. Wilson is closer to the mark in acknowledging the Protestant character of the Lost Cause and admitting that Roman Catholics and Jews participated in Southern civil religion "with some discomfort." See Wilson, "The Religion of the Lost Cause," 233.

97. Dresser, "The Theology of Reconstruction," 125.

CHAPTER THREE *"Our Cause" and the Lost Cause: Jones's Rise to Prominence*

1. "Tidings from Afar," *Religious Herald* 15, June 17, 1880, 2.

2. Jones to John A. Broadus, Oct. 18, 1865, Broadus Papers, SBTS; Jones to James B. Taylor (photocopy), Sept. 21, 1865, Jones Papers, VBHS.

3. "Revival at Goshen Bridge," *Religious Herald* 1, Sept. 6, 1866, 2; Jones to James P. Boyce, June 20, 1866, Boyce Papers, SBTS.

4. Moore, "John William Jones," 1599–604; Brown, "Pastoral Evangelism," 114–17; Whitsitt, "John William Jones, D. D."; Taylor, *Virginia Baptist Ministers*, 225–27. Prior ministers of the Lexington church had been part time, dividing their time (as did Jones) among other churches. With a growing congregation (eighty-five new members between 1865 and 1867), the church desired a full-time minister. See John G. Barrett and John S. Moore, *The History of Manly Memorial Baptist Church* (Lexington, VA: Manly Memorial Baptist Church, 1966) 12–13.

5. Taylor, *Virginia Baptist Ministers*, 225–27; Jones, "Varied Experiences In Work Among Young Men"; Brown, "Pastoral Evangelism," 114–17; Moore, "John William Jones," 1599–604.

6. "News from the Valley," *Religious Herald* 2, Oct. 17, 1867, 2. Members of Lexington allowed the newly formed African American congregation to use the church's lecture room under the conditions that no "stranger" be allowed behind the pulpit and that the group sweep up before leaving. See Barrett and Moore, *The History of Manly Memorial Baptist Church*, 13. For more on the departure of African Americans from Virginia churches, particularly in the eastern part of the state, see Nancy Alenda Hillman, "Drawn Together, Drawn Apart: Black and White Baptists in Tidewater Virginia, 1800–1875" (PhD diss., College of William and Mary, 2013), 295–389. See also Roger Charles Richards, "Actions and Attitudes of Southern Baptists toward Blacks, 1845–1895" (PhD diss., Florida State Univ., 2008), 72–79; Daniel W. Stowell, *Rebuilding Zion: The Religious Reconstruction of the South, 1863–1877* (New York: Oxford Univ. Press, 1998), 66, 73, 79, 87–88, 94, 98.

7. Jones did not make clear whether or not he had an innate aversion to organs in church. If he did, he would have fallen in line with the suspicions of Baptist historian David Benedict that organs might one day exert an "overwhelming influence" in Baptist churches. See Benedict, *Fifty Years Among the Baptists* (New York: Sheldon and Company, 1860), 282–85; "Lexington Baptist Church," *Religious Herald* 3, Oct. 29, 1868, 2.

8. Jones to Broadus, April 15 and Dec. 29, 1869, Broadus Papers, SBTS; Jones to Broadus, Nov. 21, 1870, Broadus Papers, SBTS.

9. Jones to Boyce, Jan. 20, 1872, Boyce Papers, SBTS; Jones to Boyce, Feb. 21, 1871, Boyce Papers, SBTS. Jones's position as seminary agent demonstrated his continued commitment to Baptists despite historian Beth Barton

Schweiger's assertion that Jones "played only a marginal role in the [Baptist] denomination" in the 1870s. Jones's active participation in Baptist life during the 1870s and 1880s at both the local and denominational level as well as through newspaper correspondence problematizes Schweiger's larger argument that denominational publications and "regular pastors" were generally unconcerned with the Lost Cause during this time period. See Schweiger, *The Gospel Working Up: Progress and the Pulpit in Nineteenth-Century Virginia* (New York: Oxford Univ. Press, 2000), 171, 175, 241n.17. Historian Robert Miller persuasively argues that "[w]hite Christian clergy were in many ways the primary 'celebrants' of the religion of the Lost Cause." See Miller, *Both Prayed to the Same God*, 145.

10. "Matters and Things in Georgia," *Religious Herald* 6, Nov. 2, 1871, 3; Jones to Boyce, Jan. 30, Feb. 13, Feb. 17, and March 7, 1872, Boyce Papers, SBTS; Jones to Broadus, March 28, 1872, Broadus Papers, SBTS.

11. "Notes of an Agent's Wanderings," *Religious Herald* 7, April 4, 1872, 3; Jones to Boyce, Aug. 12, 1872, Boyce Papers, SBTS.

12. Jones to Boyce, Aug. 12, 1872, Sept. 9, 1872, Boyce Papers, SBTS; Jones to Broadus, Sept. 16, 1874, Broadus Papers, SBTS; Jones to Boyce, Nov. 2, 1874, Boyce Papers, SBTS.

13. Connelly, *The Marble Man*, 40–42. Even though Jones anticipated contributing to the initial volume—supplying an essay entitled "Incidents and Reminiscences"—he was relatively unknown among most Southerners. An 1870 advertisement for the memorial volume identified Charles Marshall—Lee's aide-de-camp and military secretary—as the author of Lee's biographical sketch. When describing Jones's chapter, however, the flier did not name Jones, and merely referred to him as "a Confederate Chaplain resident at Lexington." See "In Memoriam. General Robert E. Lee," Southern Historical Society (SHS) Files/Correspondence: Miscellaneous, Museum of the Confederacy, Richmond, VA (hereafter cited as "SHS Files, MOC"); Taylor, *Virginia Baptist Ministers*, 225–27.

14. J. L. Rosser, "John William Jones," *Encyclopedia of Southern Baptists* 1 (Nashville, TN: Broadman Press, 1958), 710; Moore, "John William Jones," 1599–604; Sampey, *Southern Baptist Theological Seminary*, 126. See also "Along the Baptist Lines," *Religious Herald* 18, Oct. 23, 1883, 2.

15. "The Herald at the Albemarle Association," *Religious Herald* 5, Sept. 22, 1870, 1. Jones's attitude reflected that of many Southerners toward the ABPS. Jones resisted the ABPS's claim to be the foremost publisher of Baptist literature, and instead lobbied for distinctly Southern publications. See Michael E. Williams, *Isaac Taylor Tichenor: The Creation of the Baptist New South* (Tuscaloosa: Univ. of Alabama Press, 2005), 170–74, 185. Another prominent Southerner who shared Jones's feelings was I. T. Tichenor. Tichenor, a former Confederate chaplain and Southern Baptist minister in Alabama, is perhaps best known for his leadership role in rescuing the Southern Baptist Home Mission Board. He eventually served as the president of what would become Auburn University. See Harvey, *Redeeming the South*, 27–28, 39. See also "The Motion Withdrawn," *Religious Herald* 9, April 23, 1874, 2; "Southern Baptist Convention, Twentieth Annual Session," *Religious Herald* 10, May 13, 1875, 2–3; "Semi-Centennial of the University of Virginia," *Religious Herald* 10, July 15, 1875, 3; Jones to Boyce, May 7, 1877, Boyce Papers, SBTS; Jones to Broadus, Aug. 23, 1880(?), Broadus Papers, SBTS.

16. In a letter to his sister—herself grieving the loss of a child—Jones wrote that he and Judith had also endured the "bitter affliction of having a child snatched from our arms." See Jones to Willie Page Tucker, June 21, 1887, Jones Family Papers, UVA. See also Jones, Jan. 1, 1894, Jones Letters, UVA. Jones and Judith had ten children, five of whom grew to adulthood. See Tyler, *Men of Mark in Virginia*, 250–53. See also "Cloud Turned into Sunshine," *Religious Herald* 12, April 12, 1877, 3; Jones to Boyce, Nov. 5, 1877, Boyce Papers, SBTS; Wilson, *Baptized in Blood*, 123; Moore, "John William Jones," 1599–604.

17. Jones, *Army of Northern Virginia Memorial Volume* (Richmond, VA: J. W. Randolph and English, 1880).

18. "United States Census, 1880," Richmond, Henrico County, Virginia, database with images, FamilySearch, https://familysearch.org, image 76 of 96; citing NARA microfilm publication T9 (Washington, DC: National Archives and Records Administration, n.d.), accessed July 18, 2018.

19. Jones lost the Peabody agency even though he received glowing endorsements from prominent figures such as Joseph E. Johnston, Crawford H. Toy, Edward S. Joynes, James L. Kemper, and John A. Broadus. Interestingly, Broadus was the only reference who provided a somewhat critical review. He admitted that Jones's "elocution has some obvious faults," and that Jones, though

intelligent, was not "eminently a scholar nor a professional educator." See "Testimonial in Favor of J. Wm. Jones for the Position of Agent of the Peabody Educational Fund, 1880," in "John William Jones: John Moore's Research Notes," Virginia Baptist Historical Society, Richmond, VA. Hereafter cited as "John Moore Research Notes, VBHS." In response to Broadus's recommendation, Jones thanked his former mentor for an honest appraisal, yet maintained that "imminent scholarship" was not necessary for the agency in question. See Jones to Broadus, Sept. 15, 1880, Broadus Papers, SBTS; Moore, "John William Jones," 1599–604; Sampey, *Southern Baptist Theological Seminary*, 126.

20. Jones, Letter of Resignation, June 25, 1887, Minutes/Proceedings of the SHS, 1869–1874, Museum of the Confederacy, Richmond, VA. Hereafter cited as "SHS Minutes, MOC." Jones began his position with the HMB in June 1887 and received two thousand dollars per year for his work. See Minutes of the Home Mission Board, John Moore's Research Notes, VBHS.

21. "Good News from the Valley," *Religious Herald* 1, Oct. 4, 1866, 2.

22. "Good News from the Valley."

23. "To the Churches Composing the Goshen Association," *Religious Herald* 1, Nov. 16, 1865, 1.

24. "Baptists in the Valley of Virginia," *Religious Herald* 1, March 15, 1866, 1. The author of this letter wrote from a location where Jones was serving at the time (Goshen Bridge), and the article is signed by a "J. W. J." Jones only occasionally signed correspondence this way, and other *Herald* writers had the same initials. In this instance, Jones confirmed his authorship of the letter in correspondence from early 1867. In Jan. 1867, he wrote another *Herald* letter, also entitled "Baptists in the Valley of Virginia," noting the following: "Under the above caption I wrote a letter for the *Herald* about twelve months ago. Time has only served to strengthen the opinion that I then expressed, that there is a 'future' for the Baptists in Virginia, if we will only use the proper means and look to God for his blessing." See "Baptists in the Valley of Virginia," *Religious Herald* 2, Jan. 31, 1867, 2. The letter to which Jones referred was written in February 1866 (a little more than twelve months prior, as Jones indicated) but printed in March.

25. Jones to Broadus, Feb. 19, 1866, Broadus Papers, SBTS; Jones to Broadus, March 8, 1866, Broadus Papers, SBTS; Jones to Broadus, April 6, 1866, Broadus Papers, SBTS.

26. Jones to Broadus, July 1866, Broadus Papers, SBTS; Jones to Broadus, Dec. 14,

1866, Broadus Papers, SBTS; Jones to Broadus, May 1, 1867, Broadus Papers, SBTS; Jones to Broadus, May 20, 1867, Broadus Papers, SBTS.

27. Jones to Boyce, June 20, 1866, Boyce Papers, SBTS; "Baptists in the Valley of Virginia," *Religious Herald* 2, Jan. 31, 1867, 2.

28. "Southern Baptist Theological Seminary! An Appeal for Help," Nov. 1, 1871, Boyce Papers, SBTS; Jones, Nov. 30, 1871, Broadus Papers, SBTS.

29. Before changing its name to Hollins, the school existed as Valley Union Seminary and as Roanoke Female Seminary. While Bradley was the official founder of the seminary, Charles Lewis Cocke, who took over as principal of the school in 1846, is largely regarded as the founder of the institution. Although Cocke was progressive in his encouragement of female education, the running of the school remained patriarchal, and school officials reinforced women's roles in the domestic sphere. Cocke stressed the nonsectarian nature of the school, yet Jones felt that the institution was amenable to Baptist beliefs and that Baptist parents should send their daughters to attend. Aside from its Baptist heritage, Jones may have been drawn by the school's sectional and patriarchal emphases. See Nancy C. Parrish, *Lee Smith, Annie Dillard, and the Hollins Group: A Genesis of Writers* (Baton Rouge: Louisiana State Univ. Press, 1999), 15, 24. See also Margaret Kidd, "A Benediction for Hollins," accessed June 2, 2015, http://vaheritage.org/2015/05/18/a-benediction-for-hollins/; Hollins Univ., "History and Mission," accessed June 2, 2015, http://www.hollins.edu/who-we-are/history/.

Jones's endorsement of women's education was not an affirmation of women's equality. At the 1885 meeting of the Southern Baptist Convention, he worked on a committee to determine the eligibility of women to serve as convention delegates. Regarding delegate qualifications, the committee unanimously recommended that the convention's constitution be amended to read "brethren" instead of the more inclusive term, "members." The convention passed the amendment with 131 in favor, 42 against. See *Proceedings of the Southern Baptist Convention* (Atlanta: Jas. P. Harrison and Company, 1885), 14, 23.

In an 1890 letter, Jones endorsed a tract written by Broadus entitled "Should Women Speak in Mixed Public Assemblies?" Broadus surveyed New Testament passages on the issue and then systematically argued that women should not be allowed to exercise authority over men. They were allowed, however, to preside over female-only meetings. Interestingly, denominational fidelity figured into Broadus' discussion. He addressed the concerns of some Baptists that groups more open to women—like Methodists—would grow faster than would Baptists. Broadus brushed off the worry, reminding readers that Baptists "let Methodists get all the benefits of infant baptism, of Arminian theology, of centralized organization, because we think these things are contrary to the New Testament." Broadus concluded, "If Baptists are going to abandon New Testament teachings for the sake of falling in with what they regard as a popular movement, the very reason for their existence has ceased." Jones's affirmation of Broadus's letter not only confirmed his own views toward women, but also demonstrated that he, like Broadus, was firmly committed to Baptist particularity. See Broadus, "Should Women Speak in Mixed Public Assemblies?," accessed Nov. 2, 2015, http://www.reformedreader.org/rbb/broadus/women speak.htm. See also Jones to E. L. Compere, Dec. 19, 1890, Ebenezer Lee Compere Papers, Southern Baptist Historical Library and Archives, Nashville, TN. Hereafter cited as "Compere Letters, SBHLA."

30. "A Few more Things about the Valley Association Ministers and Deacons' Meeting—Our Cause in Roanoke—Hollins Institute," *Religious Herald* 5, March 17, 1870, 3; "Leaves from the Scrap Book of a Sunday School Missionary," *Religious Herald* 8, April 17, 1873, 2.

31. Dresser, "The Theology of Reconstruction," 156, 158, 162.

32. "Is it Proper to Baptize a Believer Who Avows his Purposes to Remain Out of the Church," *Religious Herald* 6, Oct. 5, 1871, 2; "Deputation of the Evangelical Alliance," *Religious Herald* 13, May 2, 1878, 2; "Letter from Georgia," *Religious Herald* 6, Oct. 26, 1871, 3.

33. "The Claims of the Presbyterians to Washington and Lee University," *Religious Herald* 8, Aug. 7, 1873, 1.

34. "Leaves from the Scrap-Book of a Sunday School Missionary," *Religious Herald* 8, Jan. 9, 1873, 3. Jones's openness to pulpit exchange is further evidence that he was among the more progressive Virginia Baptists and not a Landmarker. See Weaver, *In Search of the New Testament Church* (Ga: Mercer University Press, 2008), 156. Jones's barb against Methodists is reminiscent of a letter he sent to Broadus in 1863. Writing during his time as chaplain, Jones noted the good supply of chaplains in his brigade, save one Methodist elder who was "rarely ever present except pay day." See Jones to Broadus (photocopy), Jan. 4, 1865, Jones Papers, VBHS.

35. Jones to Broadus, Jan. 28, 1874, Broadus Papers, SBTS.

36. "The Duty of Baptists to Teach their Distinctive Views," *Religious Herald* 16, June 16, 1881, 1.

37. "The Duty of Baptists to Teach their Distinctive Views."

38. "The Duty of Baptists to Teach their Distinctive Views."

39. "Christian Union," *Religious Herald* 1, Jan. 25, 1866, 3.

40. "Religious History Army Northern Va.," *Religious Herald* 2, Jan. 17, 1867, 3.

41. Jones to Boyce, April 20, 1872, Boyce Papers, SBTS.

42. "Character of Preaching in the Confederate Army of Northern Virginia," *Religious Herald* 2, Nov. 7, 1867, 2.

43. "Dr. Hopson's Rebuke to Youth and Inexperience," *Religious Herald* 3, Oct. 8, 1868, 1. For more on Hopson's ministry and military career, see "Winthrop Hartly Hopson," accessed June 3, 2015, http://www.famousamericans.net /winthrophartlyhopson/.

44. "Dr. Hopson's Rebuke to Youth and Inexperience."

45. "Leaves from the Scrap Book of a S. S. Missionary," *Religious Herald* 8, April 10, 1873, 3; Jones to Broadus, April 25, 1878, Broadus Papers, SBTS; "A Visit to Maryland," *Religious Herald* 14, Oct. 16, 1879, 2; "More Georgia Dots," *Religious Herald* 57 (old volume number), May 1, 1884, 2.

46. "The Rappahannock Association," *Religious Herald* 11, Aug. 10, 1876, 2.

47. Jones to Broadus, Sept. 15, 1883, Broadus Papers, SBTS; "Dr. J. Wm. Jones at the University," *Religious Herald* 59, March 4, 1886, 3; "Albemarle County," *Religious Herald* 19, Feb. 14, 1884, 2.

48. Jones to Broadus, Oct. 15, 1874, Broadus Papers, SBTS; Jones to Broadus, April 25, 1878, Broadus Papers, SBTS; Jones to Boyce, March 1, 1888, Boyce Papers, SBTS; Taylor, *Life and Letters of Rev. George Boardman Taylor, D. D.*, 102–3.

49. Jones to Broadus, Aug. 1, 1887, Broadus Papers, SBTS.

50. Jones to Broadus, Aug. 1, 1887.

51. Edward Alfred Pollard, *The Lost Cause: A New Southern History of the War of the Confederates: Comprising a Full and Authentic Account of the Rise and Progress of the Late Southern Confederacy—the Campaigns, Battles, Incidents, and Adventures of the Most Gigantic Struggle of the World's History* (New York: E. B. Treat and Company, Publishers, 1866), 509–10, 606–7.

    As to the phrase, "Lost Cause," scholars generally agree that Pollard popularized the term in two works he wrote soon after the Civil War: *The Lost*

Cause (1866) and *The Lost Cause Regained* (1868). Pollard himself took credit for the popularity of the phrase. See Pollard, *The Lost Cause Regained* (Freeport, NY: Books for Libraries Press, 1970 [1868]), 13. Historians Thomas Connelly and Barbara Bellows have traced usage of the expression back to the works of Sir Walter Scott (1771–1832), whose books were highly influential in the American South. The "Lost Cause" to which Scott referred was Scotland's failed bids for independence. See Connelly and Bellows, *God and General Longstreet*, 2.

52. Pollard, *The Lost Cause*, 91, 456, 482, 581, 659, 727, 729. The "overwhelming odds" argument would become a central theme in later Lost Cause works. Writers like Jones took their inspiration from Lee's farewell address to his beleaguered army after the surrender at Appomattox. In his "General Orders No. 9," Lee indicated that the Army of Northern Virginia had been "compelled to yield to overwhelming numbers and resources." See "Surrender at Appomattox," accessed June 4, 2015, http://www.encyclopediavirginia.org /Surrender_at_Appomattox#start_entry.

53. Pollard, *The Lost Cause*, 43, 47–51, 559–60, 746, 753.

54. "Books about General R. E. Lee," *Christian Index* 50, April 20, 1871, 1; Pollard, *The Lost Cause*, 750–52. See also Wilson, *Baptized in Blood*, 126. Because later Lost Cause writers were less inclined to castigate Davis, some scholars have questioned how influential Pollard was in the development of the Lost Cause. Nevertheless, as historian Rollin Osterweis observes, Pollard "may not have been the architect of the myth, but he was certainly its first prophet." See Osterweis, *The Myth of the Lost Cause, 1865–1900*, 11–12.

55. Pollard, *The Lost Cause Regained*, 13, 15, 18–19, 27–28, 56, 114–15, 117–28.

56. Pollard, 165, 207. Wilson writes that "[r]ace was intimately related to the story of the Lost Cause but was not the basis of it, was not at the center of it." See Wilson, *Baptized in Blood*, 12. Despite Jones's dismissal of Pollard's writings, Jones likewise associated Republican and Reconstruction policies with campaigns for "Negro-equality." See Jones to Broadus, Aug. 1, 1887, Broadus Papers, SBTS.

57. Pendleton, *Personal Recollections of General Lee*, 603–4, 621; Susan Pendleton Lee, *Memoirs of William Nelson Pendleton, D. D.: Rector of Latimer Parish, Lexington, Virginia; Brigadier-General C. S. A.; Chief of Artillery, Army of Northern Virginia* (Philadelphia: J. B. Lippincott Company, 1893), 237, 261, 271–72, 454; Connelly, *The Marble Man*, 38–40.

58. Pendleton, *Personal Recollections of General Lee,* 603–6, 617, 635.

59. Pendleton, 614, 635–36. See also Romans 9:3.

60. Pendleton, *Personal Recollections of General Lee,* 625–27. Initially, Pendleton hesitated to identify Longstreet by name (though there was little doubt to which "lieutenant general" he was referring), but later explicitly pinned the Gettysburg loss on Longstreet. See Lee, *Memoirs of William Nelson Pendleton,* 284–87.

61. Pendleton, *Personal Recollections of General Lee,* 608–10; Lee, *Memoirs of William Nelson Pendleton,* 415.

62. Lee, *Memoirs of William Nelson Pendleton,* 414–15.

63. Gary W. Gallagher, "Jubal A. Early, the Lost Cause, and Civil War History: A Persistent Legacy," in *The Myth of the Lost Cause and Civil War History,* ed. Gallagher and Alan T. Nolan (Bloomington: Indiana Univ. Press, 2010), 39. See also Gallagher, "Shaping Public Memory of the Civil War: Robert E. Lee, Jubal A. Early, and Douglas Southall Freeman," in *The Memory of the Civil War in American Culture,* ed. Alice Fahs and Joan Waugh (Chapel Hill: Univ. of North Carolina Press, 2004), 40–45; Connelly, *The Marble Man,* 73.

64. Jubal A. Early, *The Campaigns of Gen. Robert E. Lee* (Baltimore: J. Murphy and Company, 1872), 28, 45–50.

65. Early, 22, 24, 39, 42.

66. Early, 33–34, 36. See also Jubal A. Early, *Lieutenant General Jubal Anderson Early, C.S.A.: Autobiographical Sketch and Narrative of the War Between the States* (Philadelphia: J. B. Lippincott, 1912), 272, 278.

67. Early, *Lieutenant General Jubal Anderson Early,* ix–x.

CHAPTER FOUR *Southern Hagiography: Jones and the Confederate Trinity*

1. "Dr. J. Wm. Jones with Hon. Jefferson Davis," *Religious Herald* 59, Aug. 19, 1886, 1. The epigraph that opens this chapter is from J. William Jones, *Personal Reminiscences, Anecdotes, and Letters of Gen. Robert E. Lee* (New York: D. Appleton and Company, 1874), 52. Colonel Venable served on Robert E. Lee's staff during the war.

2. "Impending War," *Religious Herald* 59, Sept. 23, 1886, 1.

3. "Rev. J. L. Lodge, D. D., Thanks Dr. J. Wm. Jones," *Religious Herald* 59, Aug. 19, 1886, 1.

4. "General R. E. Lee's Religious Character," *Religious Herald* 5, Oct. 27, 1870, 3.

Cf. Jones, *Christ in the Camp*, 49–60, 65–66, 81. See also "General R. E. Lee's Religious Character," *Christian Index* 49, Nov. 17, 1870, 1.

5. "General R. E. Lee's Religious Character," *Religious Herald* 5, Oct. 27, 1870, 3.

6. Jones, *Personal Reminiscences*, v–vi.

7. Jones, 51, 53, 79.

8. Jones, 129, 133, 135, 147, 491–92. The father of Mary Custis, Lee's wife, was a grandson of Martha Washington from her first marriage. Lost Causers like Jones readily drew attention to connections between Lee and George Washington. For more on these parallels, see Jonathan Horn, *The Man Who Would Not Be Washington: Robert E. Lee's Civil War and His Decision That Changed American History* (New York: Scribner, 2016).

9. Jones, *Personal Reminiscences*, 168–69, 185, 187, 197, 234, 295. See Proverbs 25:21 and Romans 12:20. Despite his insistence that Lee used euphemisms for Union forces, Jones also quoted Lee as calling Northern troops "enemies."

10. Jones, *Personal Reminiscences*, 296, 303, 306, 308.

11. Jones, 416–17, 419, 421–22, 425–26, 440–41, 445.

12. See Shattuck, *A Shield and Hiding Place*, 122–23; Connelly and Bellows, *God and General Longstreet*, 28–29; Osterweis, *The Myth of the Lost Cause*, 9–10; Hunter, "The Sacred South," viii–ix.

13. Jones, *Personal Reminiscences*, 162, 173, 181, 319–20, 326.

14. Jones, 163–65. See Matthew 10:29 and Luke 12:6.

15. Jones, *Personal Reminiscences*, 168, 342–43, 361, 506.

16. Jones, 474–75.

17. In the following discussion, I am indebted to historian Thomas Connelly for highlighting these particular letters as examples of Jones's alterations. See Connelly, *The Marble Man*, 118–19.

18. Jones, *Personal Reminiscences*, 376–77. Robert E. Lee to W. H. F. Lee, May 30, 1858, George Bolling Lee Papers, 1841–1868, Virginia Historical Society, Richmond, VA. Hereafter cited as "George Bolling Lee Papers, VHS."

19. Lee to W. H. F. Lee, Feb. 16, 1862, George Bolling Lee Papers, VHS. For Jones's brief citation, see *Personal Reminiscences*, 387–88. In *Personal Reminiscences*, Jones recorded the letter as being from 1861. In his 1906 book on Lee, Jones corrected the date to 1862. See Jones, *Life and Letters of Robert Edward Lee: Soldier and Man* (New York: Neale Publishing Company, 1906), 160.

20. Lee to W. H. F. Lee, July 9, 1860, George Bolling Lee Papers, VHS.

21. Blum, *Reforging the White Republic*, 89. Blum's work details many of the factors that fueled efforts for reunion between white Northerners and white Southerners. Historian Nell Irvin Painter writes of the 1870s that "as the decade progressed, northern Republicans reinterpreted antiblack and anti-Republican violence in the South less as criminal action and more as proof that traditional political elites needed to return to power." As a result, "[b]y 1877 many northerners were as relieved as southern Democrats to see Reconstruction end and supposedly, if not actually, efficient and honest government return." See Painter, *Standing at Armageddon: The United States, 1877–1919* (New York: W. W. Norton & Company, 1987), 2–3.

22. Jones, *Personal Reminiscences*, 442.

23. Jones, 442–44.

24. For example, see Dresser, "The Theology of Reconstruction," 150. While Dresser uses the term "ecumenism" when referencing the relationship between Jews and evangelical Christians, the term "interfaith" may be a more accurate description.

25. Jones, *Personal Reminiscences*, 110–12.

26. Connelly, *The Marble Man*, 118–19. Lee wrote, "No official intelligence has been used corroborating(?) the rumoured peaceful disposition of the Mormons. Though it is believed that becoming aware of the serious intention of the Govt to punish them, they are much alarmed, and will yield to its demands—How far this will interfere with the movement of the troops for Utah, I do not know. I hope the Mormons will not be permitted to continue where they are but be broken up and expelled [from] the country." Lee to W. H. F. Lee, May 30, 1858, George Bolling Lee Papers, VHS. The context of this letter was Rooney's deployment to suppress the "Mormon rebellion" during the Utah War of 1857–1858.

27. John Esten Cooke, *The Life of Stonewall Jackson: From Official Papers, Contemporary Narratives, and Personal Acquaintance* (New York: C. B. Richardson, 1863); Robert Lewis Dabney, *Life and Campaigns of Lieut.-Gen. Thomas J. Jackson, (Stonewall Jackson)* (Richmond, VA: Blelock and Company, 1866); Mary Anna Jackson, *Life and Letters of General Thomas J. Jackson (Stonewall Jackson) by His Wife*; Mary Anna Jackson, *Memoirs of Stonewall Jackson* (Louisville, KY: Prentice Press, 1895). For more on the mythologizing of Jackson, see Davis, *The Cause Lost*, 162–69.

28. William A. Blair, *Cities of the Dead: Contesting the Memory of the Civil War in the South, 1865–1914* (Chapel Hill: Univ. of North Carolina Press, 2004), 57.

29. For example, see Connelly, *The Marble Man*, 40–42, 81–83.

30. Jones, *Personal Reminiscences*, 158.

31. Jones, Appendix to John Esten Cooke, *Stonewall Jackson: A Military Biography* (New York: D. Appleton and Company, 1876), 534–36.

32. Jones, 468, 470–72, 491.

33. Jones, 475, 490, 497, 560.

34. Jones, 477, 479, 483, 485, 505. For an in-depth treatment of nineteenth-century American conceptions of a "good death," see Faust, *This Republic of Suffering*.

35. See 1 Thessalonians 5:17; Jones, Appendix, 502–4, 506.

36. Jones, Appendix, 492, 499–500.

37. Jones, 501, 559.

38. Jones, 468, 493, 498, 507, 559.

39. Jones, 493.

40. Jones to Jefferson Davis, Dec. 7, 1877, Davis Collection, Museum of the Confederacy, Richmond, VA (hereafter cited as "Davis Collection, MOC").

41. John A. Simpson, "The Cult of the 'Lost Cause,'" *Tennessee Historical Quarterly* 34 (Winter 1975): 352–53.

42. Connelly's assessment of Jones's motives is overly cynical. Connelly suggests that Jones wanted to take advantage of Davis's growing popularity in order to raise money for the society. Connelly concludes that "[t]here was little charity in Jones's efforts." Connelly, *The Marble Man*, 40–42, 78.

43. Jones to Davis, Jan. 6, 1882 and Sept. 22, 1886, Davis Collection, MOC.

44. Jones to Varina Davis, Dec. 18, 1889; Jan. 14, 1890; April 23, 1890, Davis Collection, MOC. See also J. William Jones, *The Davis Memorial Volume, or, Our Dead President, Jefferson Davis and the World's Tribute to His Memory* (Richmond, VA: B. F. Johnson and Company, 1889), v.

45. Jones, *The Davis Memorial Volume*, 452, 456, 460–61.

46. Jones, 462–63. Worth noting here is Jones's emphasis on Davis's specifically *evangelical* religion. Jones claimed that Davis was "in his official position always outspoken and decided on the side of evangelical religion." As he had done in *Christ in the Camp*, Jones stressed evangelical religion in contrast to non-evangelical faiths, such as Roman Catholicism. That said, Wilson goes too

far in proposing that Jones's focus on Davis's "child-like" trust in the doctrines of justification and sanctification was an indication that Jones still envisioned Davis as a Baptist. (Davis grew up Baptist but eventually joined the Episcopal Church.) While Jones may have wanted Davis to be a Baptist, Jones's description of the ex-president was not specifically Baptist. See Wilson, *Baptized in Blood*, 129. Jones actually emphasized the president's broad, interdenominational appeal, noting that Episcopalians, Baptists, Presbyterians, Methodists, Lutherans, and Roman Catholics had all held services of mourning for Davis. Jones even quoted a poem by the prominent Roman Catholic poet, Abram J. Ryan. See Jones, *The Davis Memorial Volume*, 595, 598, 620, 647.

47. Jones, *The Davis Memorial Volume*, vi–ii, 61, 69, 102–3, 114–15, 142.

48. Jones, 241, 243, 254–55, 264–65, 301, 351–52, 389–90, 399–408, 478.

49. Jones, 220–21, 476–77.

50. Jones, 235–36, 252–53.

51. Jones, 283.

52. Jones, 284, 286.

53. Jones, vii, ix, 52, 137, 412, 457.

54. Jones, 514.

55. Jones, 573, 622, 639.

56. "Rev. J. L. Lodge, D. D., Thanks Dr. J. Wm. Jones," *Religious Herald* 59, Aug. 19, 1886, 1; "Jesus in the Camp: Or Religion in Lee's Army," *Religious Herald* 59, July 29, 1886, 1; "Christ in the Camp, or Religion in Lee's Army: Genuineness of the Work of Grace," *Religious Herald* 59, Dec. 23, 1886, 1. The *Religious Herald* serial ran from July to December 1886. Interesting to note is that what would become one of Jones's most popular works was initially directed to Baptists.

57. Details about Bennett's life are scant. Sources for biographical information include the following: "William Woodhull Bennett, D. D, Chaplain, Confederate States of America," accessed Dec. 1, 2012, http://www. arlington cemetery.net; "Rev. Dr. Bennett Dead," *Alexandria Gazette* 88, June 10, 1887, 4; "Dr. W. W. Bennett: Death of a Noted Man of the Methodist Church," *Richmond Dispatch* 11, June 10, 1887, 1; "Dr. Bennett: The Service at Randolph-Macon College Yesterday," *Richmond Dispatch* 11, June 11, 1887, 3. See also "The Virginia Chronicle," accessed July 25, 2015, http://virginiachronicle.com; "Dr. W. W. Bennett," *Richmond Dispatch* 11, June 10, 1887, 1.

58. Bennett, *A Narrative of the Great Revival*, iii; Jones, *Christ in the Camp*, 20.

59. Bennett, *A Narrative of the Great Revival*, iii, 17, 82, 86, 88–89, 91.

60. Granberry, as quoted in Jones, *Christ in the Camp*, 14. See also Jones, *Christ in the Camp*, 21, 461.

61. Bennett, *A Narrative of the Great Revival*, 21, 34, 36, 461; Jones, *Christ in the Camp*, 20.

62. Mitchell, "Christian Soldiers?," 297–99; Wilson, *Baptized in Blood*, 43–44; Shattuck, *A Shield and a Hiding Place*, 120. Jones's book was indeed more successful than Bennett's, despite historian Beth Barton Schweiger's contention that Bennett's work was widely popular while Jones's piece was largely derivative. See Schweiger, *The Gospel Working Up*, 175; 241n.

    Publication dates for *Christ in the Camp* are as follows: 1887 and 1888 (Richmond, VA: B. F. Johnston and Company), 1893 (Philadelphia: World Publishing Company), and 1904 (Atlanta: Martin and Hoyt Company). As perhaps a testament to the vibrancy of Lost Cause ideology, *Christ in the Camp* has been reprinted numerous times in the past few decades (1970, 1976, 1986, 2010). Bennett's work also enjoyed a reprinting surge in the 1970s, 1980s, and 2000s. For more publication dates and details, see "World Cat," accessed Dec. 1, 2012, http://www.worldcat.org.

63. Foster, *Ghosts of the Confederacy*, 6.

64. Mitchell assesses that *Christ in the Camp* was "by far the better fashioned work," whereas Wilson offers that "Bennett's book was the better written and covered a wider geographical area, but Jones's volume exhausted its subject and proved more influential, touching off a series of reminiscences by others." See Mitchell, "Christian Soldiers?," 298; Wilson, *Baptized in Blood*, 43–44. Wilson's note about the "exhaustiveness" of Jones's work warrants qualification. In reality, Bennett's work was highly meticulous, and not only covered a wider geographical area than Jones's, but tracked the Confederate revivals season by season throughout the entire war.

65. As for Bennett, he wrote two other notable works, only one of which came before his *Narrative of the Great Revival* and neither of which was ostensibly related to Lost Cause ideology. See Bennett, *Memorials of Methodism in Virginia: From Its Introduction into the State in the Year 1772 to the Year 1829* (Richmond, VA: William W. Bennett, 1871); Bennett, *A History of Methodism, for Our Young People* (Cincinnati: Hitchcock and Walden, 1878).

66. Jones, *Christ in the Camp*, 5–6.

67. Schweiger, *The Gospel Working Up*, 175.

68. Jones's work (1887 edition) is approximately 530 pages, while Bennett's is roughly 430. Jones cited Jackson more than ninety times; Bennett mentioned Jackson around fifty times. Jones cited Davis more than thirty times; Bennett cited Davis less than twenty. The two works' references to Lee were less disparate.

69. Jones, *Christ in the Camp*, 5, 42–44, 46–48, 60–61, 65, 79, 81–82, 85, 89–90, 92, 97, 99, 102, 104, 106–47. Jones's adulations were not limited to Lee, Jackson, and Davis. Jones tried to counter the image of J. E. B. Stuart as a "gay, rolicksome, laughing soldier," describing him instead as a "humble, earnest Christian, who took Christ as his personal Saviour, lived a stainless life, and died a triumphant death." Along with Stuart, Jones praised the virtues of numerous officers, including John B. Gordon, D. H. Hill, Richard Ewell, Lewis Minor Coleman, and others.

70. Robert Penn Warren, *Segregation: The Inner Conflict in the South* (Athens: Univ. of Georgia Press, 1994 [1956]), 15. In context, Warren's comments referred to both whites and African Americans.

71. Douglas Southall Freeman, *The South to Posterity: An Introduction to the Writing of Confederate History* (Baton Rouge: Louisiana State Univ., 1939), 31.

72. Connelly and Bellows, *God and General Longstreet*, 16–17.

73. This has been the assessment of some scholars. Hunter identifies Jones as an "inveterate name-dropper." Connelly goes further, labeling Jones a "sycophant, a habitual name dropper who relished contact with Confederate notables. He never failed to remind his readers that his words deserved special credence." Connelly continues, "The higher the rank, the more intimate was Jones's supposed acquaintance." See Hunter, "The Sacred South," 110–11; Connelly, *The Marble Man*, 41. In contrast, Wilson calls Jones an "apostle of Lee" and notes that the general "laid hands on the parson in order that the tradition might be continued." See Wilson, *Baptized in Blood*, 123. The year of Jones's death, Baptist historian and one-time president of Southern Baptist Theological Seminary, William H. Whitsitt, also recognized Jones's unique status: "[H]e [Jones] enjoyed the advantage of speaking as an eye-witness. He was a large part of the events that he narrated. He was acquainted with nearly all of the leading actors, and spoke with a degree of authority that must always be respected." See Whitsitt, "John William Jones, D. D."

74. Cf. 1 John 1:1.

75. See Phillip Shaw Paludan, "Religion and the American Civil War," in *Religion and the American Civil War*, ed. Randall M. Miller, Harry S. Stout, and Charles Reagan Wilson (New York: Oxford Univ. Press, 1998), 37. Historians Harry Stout and Christopher Grasso assert that Southerners concluded that "triumphalism was wrong, not the South. God could and did choose losers as well as winners for his chosen people." See Stout and Grasso, "Civil War, Religion, and Communications: The Case of Richmond," in *Religion and the American Civil War*, 348. Appropriately, historian George Rable notes that religion became a "quite malleable instrument for interpreting the great national crisis." See Rable, *God's Almost Chosen Peoples*, 87–88. For more on Southern and Northern understandings of Providence, see Mark A. Noll, *The Civil War as a Theological Crisis* (Chapel Hill: Univ. of North Carolina Press, 2006), 75–94.

76. Jones, *Christ in the Camp*, 101. See also Jones, *Davis Memorial*, ix; Jones, *Personal Reminiscences*, 414; Jones, Appendix, 507.

77. Bennett, *A Narrative of the Great Revival*, 70.

78. Jones, *Christ in the Camp*, 6, 48–49, 82, 102. See also Jones, *Davis Memorial*, 462; Jones, *Personal Reminiscences*, 7; Jones, Appendix, 468, 506.

79. Dresser, "Onward Christian Soldiers?," 2–3; Dresser, "The Theology of Reconstruction," 150.

80. Jones, *Davis Memorial*, 462–63; Jones, *Personal Reminiscences*, 381–86; Jones, Appendix, 502. See also Jones, *Christ in the Camp*, 59; Taylor, *Virginia Baptist Ministers*, 221–22. Despite Jones's praise of Jackson's ranks, historian Bertram Wyatt-Brown writes that Jackson could only supply half of his regiments with chaplains. See Wyatt-Brown, "Church, Honor, and Secession," in *Religion and the American Civil War*, ed. Randall M. Miller, Harry S. Stout, and Charles Reagan Wilson (New York: Oxford Univ. Press, 1998), 104.

81. Jones, *Davis Memorial*, 196, 458; Jones, *Personal Reminiscences*, 130; Jones, Appendix, 473.

82. Jones, *Davis Memorial*, 52–53, 452, 462, 468; Jones, *Personal Reminiscences*, 7, 134, 152–54; Jones, Appendix, 468, 506.

83. Jones, *Davis Memorial*, ix; Jones, *Personal Reminiscences*, 151–52; Jones, Appendix, 493.

84. As Wilson has rightly noted, Jones's work reflected the belief that "old-time Confederate virtue continued to influence Southern souls." See Wilson, *Baptized in Blood*, 10, 44, 138.

85. Jones, *Davis Memorial*, 457, 463–64, 468; Jones, *Personal Reminiscences*, 414.

86. Jones, *Davis Memorial*, ix, 463; Jones, *Personal Reminiscences*, 414; Jones, Appendix, 507.

87. Jones, *Davis Memorial*, ix, 463; Jones, *Personal Reminiscences*, 414; Jones, Appendix, 507.

88. Jones, *Davis Memorial*, ix; Jones, *Personal Reminiscences*, 414; Jones, Appendix, 507; Jones, *Christ in the Camp*, 101. See also William Howard Doane and Elias Henry Johnson, *The Baptist Hymnal: For Use in the Church and Home* (Philadelphia: American Baptist Publication Society, 1883), 214.

89. Jones, *Davis Memorial*, vi–viii, 463–64; Jones, Appendix, 500–1. Cf. Jones, *Personal Reminiscences*, 145 ("fadeless joys").

CHAPTER FIVE *Quest for a Faithful Narrative:*
Jones and the Battle for Southern History

1. "Proceedings of the Fifteenth Annual Meeting and Reunion of the United Confederate Veterans" in Minutes U. C. V. 3 (New Orleans, LA: UCV, 1903–1906), 34–35.

2. Shattuck, *A Shield and Hiding Place*, 121. See also Wilson, *Baptized in Blood*, 123; Connelly and Bellows, *God and General Longstreet*, 33.

3. Hunter, "The Sacred South," 231–32; Connelly, *The Marble Man*, 85–90; "Official Circular, Southern Historical Society."

4. Connelly, *The Marble Man*, 85–90; Richard D. Starnes, "Forever Faithful: The Southern Historical Society and Confederate Historical Memory," *Southern Cultures* 2 (Winter 1996): 178.

5. Gallagher, "Shaping Public Memory of the Civil War," 106–7; Connelly, *The Marble Man*, 40–42, 85–90; Harold Eugene Mahan, "The Final Battle: The Southern Historical Society and Confederate Hopes for History," *Southern Historian* 5 (Spring 1984): 29; Wilson, *Baptized in Blood*, 123.

6. "Official Circular, Southern Historical Society."

7. "Official Circular, Southern Historical Society."

8. Starnes, "Forever Faithful," 178; Mahan, "The Final Battle," 28–30.

9. Wilson, *Baptized in Blood*, 124; Connelly and Bellows, *God and General Longstreet*, 43; Connelly, *The Marble Man*, 85–90; Jones to Jubal Early, March 26,

1878, Jubal Anderson Early Papers, Manuscript Division, Library of Congress (hereafter cited as "Early Papers, LOC").

10. Starnes, "Forever Faithful," 186. See also April 24, 1877, SHS Minutes, MOC; Connelly, *The Marble Man*, 82–83.

11. Oct. 28, 1879, SHS Minutes, MOC.

12. Fitz Lee to Jones, Aug. 10, 1883 and Sept. 4, 1883, J. William Jones Papers, 1861–1892, Accession 21294, Personal papers collection, Library of Virginia, Richmond, VA (hereafter cited as "Jones Papers, LOV"). See also Connelly, *The Marble Man*, 82–83.

13. July–Aug. 1883, SHS Minutes, MOC.

14. July–Aug. 1883, SHS Minutes, MOC.

15. July–Aug. 1883, SHS Minutes, MOC.

16. Feb. 3, 1885, SHS Minutes, MOC; Mahan, "The Final Battle," 31; Susan Speare Durant, "The Gently Furled Banner: The Development of the Myth of the Lost Cause, 1865–1900" (PhD diss., Univ. of North Carolina, 1972), 48–51.

17. R. M. T. Hunter, "Origin of the Late War," *SHSP* 1 (Jan. –June 1876): 4; M. F. Maury, "A Vindication of Virginia and the South," *SHSP* 1 (Feb. 1876): 56–57; "Some Great Constitutional Questions," *SHSP* 12 (Oct. 1884): 485–99.

18. Hunter, "Origin of the Late War," 11.

19. "The Relative Strength of the Armies of Generals Lee and Grant," *SHSP* 2 (July–Dec. 1876): 6. See also "Strength of General Lee's Army in the Seven Days Battles Around Richmond," *SHSP* 1 (June 1876). Sometimes even former Confederates disagreed on troop numbers. Unsurprisingly, Jones and Early favored estimates that downplayed Lee's troop strength, and thus absolved him from any accusation of mismanagement. The troop estimates at Gettysburg would become a point of emphasis for *SHSP* writers. See "General Early's Reply to the Count of Paris," *SHSP* 6 (July 1878): 12–32. See also "Who and What Conquered the South?," *SHSP* 11 (Oct. 1883): 475–77.

20. "Address of Congress to the People of the Confederate States," *SHSP* 1 (Jan.–June 1876): 30–31.

21. Dabney H. Maury, "Grant as a Soldier and Civilian," *SHSP* 5 (May 1878): 231–32, 235, 237. See also "A Northern Opinion of Grant's Generalship," *SHSP* 12 (Jan./Feb. 1884): 20–22. Writers for the *Papers* also wasted no opportunity to

chide or deride William T. Sherman. For example, see "General W. T. Sherman's Visit to the Misses L____ at Canton, Miss., in February, 1864," *SHSP* 8 (March 1880): 120–21; "Sherman's March to the Sea, as seen by a Northern Soldier," *SHSP* 10 (Aug./Sept. 1882): 410–15; "General Sherman's Slanders of Confederate Leaders," *SHSP* 12 (Oct. 1884): 570–72.

22. Daniel Harvey Hill, "Address before the Mecklenburg (N. C.) Historical Society," *SHSP* 1 (May 1876): 389–93.

23. J. B. Hawthorne, "The Courage of the Confederate Soldier," *SHSP* 9 (Jan. 1881): 37.

24. Connelly, *The Marble Man*, 81–83, 93.

25. Jones, "Reminiscences of the Army of Northern Virginia, or the Boys in Gray, as I saw them from Harper's Ferry in 1861 to Appomattox Courthouse," *SHSP* 9 (Oct.–Dec. 1881): 564–65; Robert L. Dabney, "Stonewall Jackson," *SHSP* 11 (Feb./March 1883): 125; "The Truth of History: An open letter from Dr. R. L. Dabney to Dr. J. William Jones," *SHSP* 19 (Jan. 1891): 376–79.

26. "Chancellorsville—Address of General Fitzhugh Lee before the Virginia Division, A. N. V. Association," *SHSP* 7 (Dec. 1879): 23–25, 39.

27. "The Capture of Mr. Jefferson Davis, President of the Confederate States," *SHSP* 4 (Aug. 1877): 91–92; "The Attempt to Fasten the Assassination of President Lincoln on President Davis and other Innocent Parties," *SHSP* 9 (July/Aug. 1881): 313–25; Davis to Jones, Nov. 22, 1883, Davis Collection, MOC.

28. "The Men who Wore the Gray," *SHSP* 10 (June 1882): 279–83; "The Southern Soldier Boy," *SHSP* 10 (April 1882): 186; "The Sword of Lee" and "Robert E. Lee," *SHSP* 11 (Aug./Sept. 1883): 427.

29. Early to Jones, Sept. 4, 1879, SHS Files, MOC; "Unveiling of Valentine's Recumbent Figure of Lee at Lexington, Va., June 28, 1883," *SHSP* 11 (Aug./Sept. 1883): 414–15.

30. "Address of Rabbi J. K. Gutheim," *SHSP* 10 (June 1882): 249–50. In Gutheim's mind, neither the SHS nor the altar symbolized rivalry, but instead a commitment to union.

31. "The Treatment of Prisoners During the War Between the States," *SHSP* 1 (Feb. 1876): 109–10; Starnes, "Forever Faithful," 183.

32. "The Treatment of Prisoners During the War Between the States," *SHSP* 1 (March 1876): 120–28, 162, 168; Durant, "The Gently Furled Banner," 135–36.

33. "The Treatment of Prisoners During the War Between the States," *SHSP* 1 (April 1876): 237, 254, 262, 264.

34. "The Treatment of Prisoners During the War Between the States," 243. See also 235, 237, 239.

35. "The Treatment of Prisoners During the War Between the States," 295, 298–99. The issue of prisoner treatment was not limited to the first year of the *SHSP*. In 1877, Jones remained in a struggle with New York's *The Nation* over the controversy. Durant portrays Jones as daring someone to take his bait and debate the topic. *The Nation* did so, which likely played into Jones's hands. See Durant, "The Gently Furled Banner," 135–36. See also "Editorial Paragraphs," *SHSP* 3 (May/June 1877): 301.

36. Jones to the Comte de Paris, Sept. 1876, SHS Files, MOC; "History of the Civil War in America," *SHSP* 1 (Jan. –June 1876): i; Early, "Comments on the First Volume of the Count of Paris' *Civil War in America*," *SHSP* 3 (March 1877): 151. The Comte published his first volume of the war in 1875 and his second in 1877. His early volumes had been critical of Lee, a sentiment he altered as he cultivated a relationship with (and requested assistance from) the SHS. See Connelly, *The Marble Man*, 85–90.

37. Jones, "Causes of Defeat of Gen. Lee's Army at the Battle of Gettysburg— Opinions of Leading Confederate Soldiers," *SHSP* 4 (Aug. 1877): 1; "Our Gettysburg Series," *SHSP* 5 (Jan./Feb. 1878): 87.

38. Early, "Causes of Defeat of Gen. Lee's Army at the Battle of Gettysburg— Opinions of Leading Confederate Soldiers," *SHSP* 4 (Aug. 1877): 11–16.

39. "Letter from General C. M. Wilcox," "Letter from General A. L. Long, Military Secretary to General R. E. Lee," "Second Paper by Colonel Walter H. Taylor, of General Lee's Staff," *SHSP* 4 (Sept. 1877): 114, 122, 129–30; "Letter from General John B. Hood," "Letter from Major-General Henry Heth," *SHSP* 4 (Oct. 1877): 4, 155; Early to Jones, Oct. 28, 1877, SHS Files, MOC.

40. "Leading Confederates on the Battle of Gettysburg," "Supplement to General Early's Review—Reply to General Longstreet," *SHSP* 4 (Dec. 1877): 1–41, 282–302; "General James Longstreet's Account of the Campaign and Battle," *SHSP* 5 (Jan./Feb. 1878): 54, 68, 71–73, 75; "The Gettysburg Battle: A Second Letter from Gen. Longstreet," *The New York Times*, Feb. 24, 1878;

Jones to Early, March 26, 1878, Early Papers, LOC. See also Mahan, "The Final Battle," 32.

41. "Review of the First Two Days' Operations at Gettysburg and a Reply to General Longstreet by General Fitz Lee," *SHSP* 5 (April 1878): 166–67, 175, 177, 185–93; "General Longstreet's Second Paper on Gettysburg," "Reply to General Longstreet's Second Paper," *SHSP* 5 (June 1878): 6, 8, 13, 287; "Within a Stone's Throw of Independence' at Gettysburg," *SHSP* 12 (March 1884): 111.

42. Connelly, *The Marble Man*, 85–90. Connelly's damning assessment does not stop here. He notes that while Jones was outwardly friendly to the Comte, the editor "secretly attempted to destroy his [the Comte's] credibility as a historian." Connelly also argues that debate over Gettysburg had less to do with historical accuracy and was instead an attempt to save the reputation of Early, who himself had been criticized for his actions at Gettysburg.

Regarding the role of Confederate general J. E. B. Stuart at Gettysburg, Connelly describes a veritable cover-up. Major Henry McClellan, who had served with Stuart, believed that Stuart would have been more effective at Gettysburg if Early's infantry had supported him. Connelly notes a deal between Early and McClellan in which Early would not criticize Stuart's role at Gettysburg (as some had done) if McClellan would not publically criticize Early. By pinning the entire Gettysburg defeat on Longstreet, Early could exonerate both himself and Stuart.

43. William Garrett Piston, *Lee's Tarnished Lieutenant* (Athens: Univ. of Georgia Press, 1990), x; Shattuck, *A Shield and Hiding Place*, 122–23.

44. Hunter, "Origin of the Late War," *SHSP* 1 (Jan.–June 1876): 1.

45. "Address of Congress to the People of the Confederate States," *SHSP* 1 (Jan.–June 1876): 33; Maury, "A Vindication of Virginia and the South," *SHSP* 1 (Feb. 1876): 51–52.

46. Carlton McCarthy, "Detailed Minutiae of Soldier Life in the Army of Northern Virginia," *SHSP* 2 (Sept. 1876): 130–31.

47. James McPherson and James Hogue, *Ordeal By Fire: The Civil War and Reconstruction* (Boston: McGraw-Hill, 2000), 32–33. As historian David Blight puts the matter: "Black people would eventually have a place in the Confederate narrative, but only as time-warped, loyal antebellum slaves. In the Confederate vision of the story, blacks would have to stay in the past, frozen in time, so that ex-Confederates could take their sick souls to a safe place for rehabilitation."

See Blight, "Decoration Days: The Origins of Memorial Day in North and South," in *The Memory of the Civil War in American Culture*, ed. Alice Fahs and Joan Waugh (Chapel Hill: Univ. of North Carolina Press, 2004), 106–7.

48. James R. Chalmers, "Forrest and his Campaigns," *SHSP* 7 (Oct. 1879): 451–52.

49. Chalmers, 452.

50. For more on the conciliatory and subversive nature of biblical interpretation in the postwar South, see Christopher C. Moore, "'Northern Fingers Have Played Our Pianos': Baptists and Reconciliation in Postwar North Carolina, 1865–1877," *Baptist History and Heritage* 48 (Summer 2013): 46–60.

51. "George W. Cable in the Century Magazine," *SHSP* 13 (Jan.–Dec. 1885): 148–49. See George Washing Cable, "The Freedman's Case in Equity," *The Century* 29 (Jan. 1885): 409–19. See also Wilson, *Baptized in Blood*, 124–25.

52. "The Confederate Flag: Editorial in the Southern Illustrated News of March 12th, 1863," *SHSP* 8 (April 1880): 157–58.

53. Carlton McCarthy, "Origin of the Confederate Battle Flag," *SHSP* 8 (Oct.–Dec. 1880): 497, 499.

54. J. B. Hawthorne, "The Courage of the Confederate Soldier," *SHSP* 9 (Jan. 1881): 37.

55. Chalmers, "Forrest and his Campaigns," *SHSP* 7 (Oct. 1879): 452.

56. Gary W. Gallagher, *Causes Won, Lost, and Forgotten: How Hollywood and Popular Art Shape What We Know about the Civil War* (Chapel Hill: Univ. of North Carolina Press, 2013), 2. In his *Race and Reunion*, Blight addresses three visions of postwar memory: reconciliationist, white supremacist, and emancipationist. See Blight, *Race and Reunion*, 2.

57. Blight, *Race and Reunion*, 39. For an insightful treatment of the postwar impulses of Northerners and Southerners to reunite on the basis of shared whiteness, see Blum, *Reforging the White Republic*.

58. As Gallagher has noted, the Reconciliation and Lost Cause strains of memory overlapped to a degree. Gallagher, *Causes Won, Lost, and Forgotten*, 2. Historian Caroline Janney highlights the many Northerners who refused to acquiesce to a Southern-tinted memory of the war. See Janney, *Remembering the Civil War*, 231. For more on how whites, North and South, ignored the role of African American soldiers in the Union Army, see Nell Irvin Painter, *Creating Black Americans: African American History and its Meanings, 1619 to the Present* (New York: Oxford Univ. Press, 2006), 120–24.

59. The future-oriented spirit of the SHS is the focus of Mahan's "The Final Battle." See especially Mahan, 27, 31–32, 34. Mahan writes that the "central theoretical assumption" of the *SHSP* was that future historians would "offer a final vindication" of the Confederacy. Connelly and Bellows write that "[t]he essential factor is that the Inner Lost Cause artists did not expect exculpation in *their* time." By "Inner Lost Cause," Connelly and Bellows mean in part the efforts of ex-Confederates to portray Southerners as superior to Northerners. By comparison, the "National Lost Cause" developed later and involved "pragmatic reunion-oriented" authors who tried to articulate the South's role and identity within the nation. See Connelly and Bellows, *God and General Longstreet*, 4–7, 22, 59, 63.

60. "Official Circular, Southern Historical Society."

61. "Editorial Paragraphs," *SHSP* 1 (Feb. 1876): 109.

62. Jones to Davis, Oct. 2, 1883, Davis Collection, MOC.

63. Jones to Humphreys, Feb. 9, 1875, SHS Files, MOC; "Annual Meeting of the Southern Historical Society," *SHSP* 2 (Nov. 1876): 249; April 12, 1877 and Dec. 6, 1877, SHS Minutes, MOC.

64. "Editorial Paragraphs," *SHSP* 2 (Aug. 1876): 109.

65. "Editorial Paragraphs," *SHSP* 5 (March 1878): 143.

66. "Editorial Paragraphs," *SHSP* 1 (May 1876): 407; "Two Foreign Opinions of the Confederate Cause and People," *SHSP* 10 (Dec. 1882): 560.

67. "'Manufacturing History.' Who Runs the Machine?," *SHSP* 9 (July/Aug. 1881): 378–79.

68. Rossiter Johnson, "Factitious History," *North American Review* (July 1881): 307.

69. Johnson, 308.

70. Johnson, 308–9, 314. Johnson also criticized the South's view of Sherman. Satirically, Johnson wrote that Sherman set Columbia, South Carolina on fire "with his own hands" while Early tried to extinguish the blaze of Chambersburg, Pennsylvania—a fire Early himself had ordered.

71. Johnson, 308–9, 314.

72. Jones rarely published material dealing explicitly with race. Some scholars, however, have argued that Jones expressed his views on race while writing under the pseudonym "Civis." In the spring of 1875, Civis published a series of articles in the *Religious Herald* concerning public education. The author was adamantly against public education, accusing public schools of "atheism," "infidelity," and

breaching church-state separation. The articles provoked significant backlash, and Civis became embroiled in a heated exchange with another *Herald* contributor. See "The Public School—No. 1," *Religious Herald* 10, April 1, 1875, 1. The series of articles, as well as rejoinders, stretched from April to July, ending with "The Public School," *Religious Herald* 10, July 15, 1875, 1.

Civis also published a string of articles in the Richmond journal, *The Southern Planter and Farmer.* These *Southern Planter and Farmer* articles dealt specifically with public education and African Americans. Here Civis claimed that he was a "friend of the negro, but a friend to him in his proper place of subordination." Civis also held that African Americans were instilled with an "instinct of inferiority." At times, Civis's tone bled from paternalism into outright disdain: "No man familiar with the facts involved and competent to form a sound opinion, can believe that the negro is the equal of the Caucasian. The truth is, the negro is incapable of independent civilized existence." Civis continued, "He [the African American] is, by necessity of intellectual weakness, a parasite." In later articles, the author's comments were venomous and replete with scientific racism. He declared that "[t]he whites and the negroes cannot live together as equals" and that "amalgamation" was "too revolting . . . for contemplation." See "The Public School in its Relation to the Negro," *Southern Planter and Farmer* 36, Dec. 1875, 707–11; "The Public School in its Relation to the Negro, No. II," *Southern Planter and Farmer* 37, Jan. 1876, 35–42; "The Public School in its Relation to the Negro, No. III," *Southern Planter and Farmer* 37, Feb. 1876, 108–16; "The Public School in its Relation to the Negro, No. IV," *Southern Planter and Farmer* 37, 325–40.

After months of publishing in the *Religious Herald* and the *Southern Planter and Farmer*, Civis had preserved anonymity. While the editor of the *Southern Planter and Farmer* noted that two authors wrote under the pseudonym, the editor confirmed that the author of the "The Public School in its Relation to the Negro" was the same writer who had published the *Religious Herald* series on public education. Some historians have identified Civis as Jones. See Walter Javan Fraser, "William Henry Ruffner: A Liberal in the Old and New South" (PhD diss., Univ. of Tennessee, 1970), 415; Thomas C. Hunt and Monalisa McCurry-Mullins, *Moral Education in America's Schools: The Continuing Challenge* (Charlotte, NC: Information Age Publishing, Inc., 2005),

63, 129, 139n. Jones, however, was not the author of either the *Religious Herald* or the *Southern Planter and Farmer* series. In August 1876, after he had been outed by a critic, Civis identified himself as Bennett Puryear. See "A Card from Civis," *Southern Planter and Farmer* 37, Aug. 1876, 581. Puryear (1826–1914), a native Virginian, served as a professor at Randolph Macon College, the University of Virginia, and Richmond College. See John G. James, *The Southern Student's Hand-Book of Selections for Reading and Oratory* (New York: A. S. Barnes & Co., 1879), 52–53. For another work that quotes Puryear and Civis interchangeably, see Claude H. Nolen, *The Negro's Image in the South: The Anatomy of White Supremacy* (Lexington: Univ. Press of Kentucky, 2015), 134.

73. Jones, "Work Among Negroes of the South" (Baltimore: Maryland Baptist Mission Rooms, 1891), 2.

74. Jones, 3, 5. Historian Gregory Wills observes that although white Southern Baptist leaders supported slavery as a biblical institution, some were critical of the motivations and practices of slaveholders. Specifically, some Southern Baptists believed that avarice motivated slave traders. Religious leaders also pointed to slaveholder abuses, such as the dismissal of slave marriages or the withholding of religious education from slaves. This last matter was of particular significance for white Southern Baptists, as they readily admitted that Christianization was a benefit—albeit an "unintended consequence"—of slavery. See Wills, *Southern Baptist Theological Seminary*, 57–58.

75. Jones, "Work Among Negroes of the South," 6–7, 10.

76. Jones, 6–7, 10.

77. James M. McPherson, "Long-legged Yankee Lies: The Southern Textbook Crusade" in *The Memory of the Civil War in American Culture*, ed. Alice Fahs and Joan Waugh (Chapel Hill: Univ. of North Carolina Press, 2004), 67. For a work dedicated to the reception of the Lost Cause by children, see Alice Page Elizabeth Hull, "Lessons in Heritage: Southern Children Inherit the Lost Cause" (PhD diss., Univ. of Mississippi, 2006).

78. Jones, *School History of the United States* (Baltimore: R. H. Woodward Company, 1896), 3.

79. Jones, 3–4.

80. Jones, 202, 206, 227, 230–31, 239–41.

81. Jones, 208, 308–10, 317–18.

82. Jones, 215–16, 345–47.

83. Jones, 209–14, 302–4, 306–7, 312, 349–55.

84. Jones, 45, 141, 196, 238, 293.

85. Durant notes that Jones's 1896 edition of the textbook included only a handful of photographs of Union officers. By the 1901 edition, there were forty-nine pictures. Photographs for Confederate officers rose as well, with the 1896 edition including thirty-six and the 1901 edition including ninety-five. See Durant, "The Gently Furled Banner," 293.

86. Jones, *School History of the United States*, 424–25.

CHAPTER SIX *Finishing the Course:*
Jones and the Changing Landscape of the Lost Cause

1. Minutes of the Eleventh Annual Meeting and Reunion of the United Confederate Veterans . . . 1901 (New Orleans, LA: Hopkins' Printing Office, 1902), 108.

2. Connelly and Bellows, *God and General Longstreet*, 4–5, 6, 63, 119–20.

3. Sampey, *Southern Baptist Theological Seminary*, 126; Moore, "John William Jones," 1599–604; "J. William Jones Dies in Georgia," 1, 4.

4. Williams, *Isaac Taylor Tichenor*, 129–30, 134–36. Years after the mission began, Tichenor still had to ward off repeated criticism of the HMB's work in Cuba. For example, see "Dr. Goodwin, Once More," *Religious Herald* 65, April 28, 1892, 1.

5. Jones to John A. Broadus, June 8, 1889, Broadus Papers, SBTS. According to Tichenor, the Southern Baptist Convention (SBC) had requested for the HMB to begin its own publication, as there was not enough space in other Baptist papers to cover the work of the board. See I. T. Tichenor, "Mission Methods— Home Board," *Religious Herald* 65, March 24, 1892, 1; Williams, *Isaac Taylor Tichenor*, 130–32; Jones, "Several Last Words About Home Missions," *Religious Herald* 61, April 19, 1888, 1; Jones, "Virginia Quota for the Havana House," *Religious Herald* 64, Nov. 19, 1891, 2; Jones, "Virginia and the Home Mission Board," *Religious Herald* 65, March 24, 1892, 2; Jones to E. L. Compere, Dec. 12, 1891, Compere Papers, SBHLA.

6. Williams, *Isaac Taylor Tichenor*, 136, 138.

7. Jones to Broadus, Feb. 22 and March 22, 1890, Broadus Papers, SBTS; Jones to Broadus, March 5, 1889, April 20 and Sept. 26, 1890, Broadus Papers, SBTS. According to anecdotes from George Braxton Taylor, Carter had long wanted

to emulate his father. One day, Jones was riding along the Petersburg lines with his son, Carter, on the saddle with him. The young Carter saluted the troops as he passed, until one soldier asked, "How do you do, *General?*" Carter replied, "I am *no General*, Sir. I am a Baptist preacher." On another occasion, Carter informed Robert E. Lee that the boy's ambitions were to attend both the University of Virginia and SBTS, and then to become a Baptist minister. See Taylor, *Virginia Baptist Ministers*, 224.

8. Jones to Broadus, July 14, 1894, Broadus Papers, SBTS; Brown, "Pastoral Evangelism," 119; "John R. Sampey: 1929–1942," Southern Baptist Theological Seminary, accessed July 31, 2018, http://archives.sbts.edu/the-history-of-the-sbts/our-presidents/john-r-sampey-1928–1942/; "Sampey and Lee," Southern Baptist Theological Seminary, accessed July 31, 2018, http://archives.sbts.edu/the-history-of-the-sbts/our-lore/sampey-and-lee/.

9. Jones to Broadus, May 7, 1893, Broadus Papers, SBTS.

10. Jones, "Letter from the University of Virginia," *Religious Herald* 66, Nov. 9, 1893, 1; Jones to Broadus, Dec. 22, 1893, Broadus Papers, SBTS.

11. Jones, "Dr. T. G. Jones at the University," *Religious Herald* 67, June 21, 1894, 2; Jones, "Special Interest at the University," *Religious Herald* 67, Nov. 29, 1894, 3. Historian John S. Moore records that Jones began his chaplaincy at the Miller School in 1895. Letterhead of Jones's correspondence, however, indicates that he was at Miller at least as early as January 1894. This would mean that there was overlap between Jones's chaplaincies at UVA and Miller. While Jones's UVA schedule would have made dual-chaplaincy challenging, the location of both schools in Charlottesville could have made the task feasible. See Moore, "John William Jones," 1605. See also Jones, Jan. 1, 1894, Jones's Letters, UVA.

12. Moore, "John William Jones," 1605–6. See also *Proceedings of the Southern Baptist Convention . . . 1894* (Atlanta: Franklin Printing and Publishing Company, 1894), 22.

13. Moore, "John William Jones," 1606; Jones, "A Word from the New-Comer at Chapel Hill," *Biblical Recorder* 65, June 27, 1900, 2; Brown, "Pastoral Evangelism," 117; Shattuck, "John William Jones," *North Carolina University Magazine* (Chapel Hill: Dialectic and Philanthropic Societies, Univ. of North Carolina, 1901), 94; Jones, "A Word from Chaplain J. W. Jones," *Biblical Recorder* 69, Nov. 5, 1902, 2.

14. Moore, "J. William Jones," 1606–7; *Minutes of the Sixteenth Annual Meeting and Reunion of the United Confederate Veterans . . . 1906* (New Orleans: n.p., n.d.), 18, 61; "J. William Jones Dies in Georgia," 1, 4; "History of Battle Abbey," Virginia Museum of History and Culture, accessed Aug. 9, 2018, https:// www.virginiahistory.org/collections-and-resources/virginia-history-explorer /history-battle-abbey.

15. *CV* 3 (June 1895): 163.

16. Jones, "A Brief Sketch of Gen. R. E. Lee," *CV* 1 (Dec. 1893): 356–57; Jones, "Commands of Lee and Grant in 1864," *CV* 7 (May 1899): 229–30; Jones, "Lee, a Christian Soldier," *Christian Observer* 88, May 9, 1900; Jones, "The Inner Life of Robert Edward Lee," *Chautauquan* 31, May 1900.

17. Jones, "Gen. Lee's Last Office," *CV* 7 (Sept. 1899): 409.

18. Jones, *Life and Letters of Robert Edward Lee*, 11–12.

19. Jones, 82–83, 119–26, 138, 174–75, 309.

20. Jones, 11, 381.

21. Jones, "Dr. Jones's Recollections of Stonewall Jackson," *CV* 1 (Jan. 1893): 19–20; Jones, "Stonewall Jackson: Personal Reminiscences and Anecdotes of His Character," *SHSP* 19 (Jan. 1, 1901): 145; Jones, "Stonewall Jackson," *CV* 12 (April 1904): 174; "Bostonians Like to Hear Confederates," *CV* 15 (May 1907): 229.

22. Jones, "Reminiscences of the Army of Northern Virginia," 564–65; Jones, *Life and Letters of Robert Edward Lee*, 174–75; Jones, "Worked His Way Through," *CV* 9 (Dec. 1901): 535–36.

23. Jones, "Interesting Letter from Dr. J. William Jones," *Biblical Recorder* 67, Feb. 26, 1902, 6. See also Wilson, *Baptized in Blood*, 135.

24. Jones to A. T. Robertson, May 31, 1899, Robertson Papers, SBTS; Jones to Varina Davis, Dec. 7, 1889, Davis Collection, MOC.

25. "The Death of Ex-President Jefferson Davis," *Our Home Field* 2, Jan. 1890, 1.

26. Jones, "The Morale of the Confederate Army," in Clement Anselm Evans, *Confederate Military History: A Library of Confederate States History* (Atlanta: Confederate Publishing Company, 1899), 120–21, 123, 126–27.

27. Jones, "The Private Soldier," *CV* 2 (Sept. 1894): 275; Jones, "Reunion Memorial Services: Address of Chaplain General J. Wm. Jones," *CV* 10 (Aug. 1902): 360; *Minutes of the Eleventh Annual Meeting . . . 1901*, 104.

28. Jones, "The Morale of the Confederate Army," 133, 144–48.

29. Jones, "Opposed to the Name Rebellion," *CV* 2 (July 1894): 199; Jones, "Relative Forces of Lee and Grant," *CV* 7 (Dec. 1899): 555.

30. Jones, "Treatment of Prisoners During the War," *CV* 13 (Sept. 1905): 403; Jones, "The Longstreet-Gettysburg Controversy: Who Commenced It," *SHSP* 23 (Jan.–Dec. 1895): 342. See also Jones, "Longstreet and Gordon," *Biblical Recorder* 69, Feb. 10, 1904, 2.

31. Wilson, *Baptized in Blood*, 125; "Daughters of the Confederacy," *CV* 7 (June 1899): 279; Jones, "A Valuable Confederate History," *CV* 16 (July 1908): 364; *Minutes of the Sixth Annual Meeting and Reunion of the United Confederate Veterans . . . 1896* (Richmond, VA: n.p., n.d.), 7; *Proceedings of the Fourth Annual Meeting and Reunion of the United Confederate Veterans . . . 1894* (Birmingham, AL: n.p., n.d.), 8; Jones, "The Private Soldier," *CV* 2 (Sept. 1894): 275; McPherson, "Long-legged Yankee Lies," 67.

32. H. L. Wayland, "School History of the United States," *The Independent* 49, April 22, 1897, 19; Jones, "The History of Secession and the Prison Mortality of the Late War," *Christian Observer* 85, July 28, 1897, 20.

33. E. C. Dargan, "Jones' School History of the United States," *Christian Index* 76, July 23, 1896, 2.

34. Jones to E. C. Dargan, July 31, 1896, Edwin Charles Dargan Papers, Southern Baptist Historical Library and Archives, Nashville, TN (hereafter cited as "Dargan Papers, SBHLA").

35. Jones to Dargan, July 31, 1896, Dargan Papers, SBHLA. Cf. Galatians 1:6: "I am astonished that you are so quickly deserting the one who called you in the grace of Christ and are turning to a different gospel" (NRSV).

36. Jones, "Interesting Letter from Dr. J. William Jones," *Biblical Recorder* 67, Feb. 26, 1902, 6; Jones, Nov. 14, 1901, Thomas Family Papers, 1828–1924, Virginia Historical Society, Richmond, VA; Jones to Broadus, Aug. 20, 1890, July 14, 1894, and Dec. 27, 1888, Broadus Papers, SBTS; Jones to Dargan, July 31, 1896, Dargan Papers, SBHLA. Interestingly, William H. Whitsitt felt that Jones wrote on Lee not in order to promote the Baptist cause, but out of love for the former general. Whitsitt admitted, however, that Baptists had benefitted from Jones's writings. See Whitsitt, "John William Jones, D. D."

37. Williams, *Isaac Taylor Tichenor*, 131, 134–35.

38. Jones, "A Word about Baptism," *Biblical Recorder* 66, April 3, 1901, 1.

39. James H. Slatton, *W. H. Whitsitt: The Man and the Controversy* (Macon: Mercer

Univ. Press, 2009), 253; Jones, "The Whitsitt Matter," *Religious Herald* 70, Aug. 26, 1897, 1.

40. Jones, "What has Happened Since the Convention at Wilmington," *Religious Herald* 70, Sept. 2, 1897, 2. As was oftentimes the case with Jones, Baptist loyalty and Southern loyalty were two sides of the same coin. According to historian James Slatton, Jones feared that if Whitsitt left SBTS, he would take a recently offered position at the University of Chicago. With Whitsitt in Chicago, Southern students might follow, and thus fall under the influence of "infidel professors." See Slatton, *W. H. Whitsitt*, 310.

Jones was careful to distinguish his defense of Whitsitt's "free thought" from a defense of Whitsitt's "historical opinions." For his part, Jones seldom discussed Landmarkism specifically. At very least, though, Jones's writings revealed that he did not consider the Landmark genealogy of Baptists to be part of the denomination's "cherished principles."

41. Connelly and Bellows, *God and General Longstreet*, 4–5, 6, 63, 119–20.

42. Connelly and Bellows, 7.

43. Jones, "That 'Confederate Yell,'" *Religious Herald* 61, Feb. 2, 1888, 1.

44. Jones, "The Morale of the Confederate Army," 134, 192–93.

45. Jones, 134–35. The colonel's comments concerning foreigners—which likely echoed the nativism of his contemporaries—referred to those he deemed "mercenaries" for the Federal cause. The colonel directed his ire specifically at "stay-at-home patriots" who paid foreigners to serve in their stead. See also *SHSP* 9 (March 1881): 142–43.

46. "Bostonians Like to Hear Confederates," *CV* 15 (May 1907): 229; Jones, *Life and Letters of Robert Edward Lee*, 486.

47. *Minutes of the Eighth Annual Meeting and Reunion of the United Confederate Veterans . . . 1898* (New Orleans: Hopkins' Printing Office, 1899), 14–15. Jones was not alone among Southerners in his plea for the United States. Historian Rufus Spain writes that "[e]vidence of Southern sectionalism among Baptists disappeared during the patriotic upsurge accompanying the Spanish-American War." See Spain, *At Ease in Zion: Social History of Southern Baptists, 1865–1900* (Tuscaloosa: Univ. of Alabama Press, 2003), 31. See also *Minutes of the Eleventh Annual . . . 1901*, 9; *Minutes of the Fifteenth Annual Meeting and Reunion of the United Confederate Veterans . . . 1905* (Louisville, KY: n.p., n.d.), 11; *Minutes of the Sixth Annual Meeting . . . 1896*, 7.

48. Jones, "The National Flag," *CV* 4 (Aug. 1896): 260.

49. Alan Capps, "Coat of Arms," accessed Nov. 20, 2015, http://www.mountvernon .org/ research-collections/digital-encyclopedia/article/coat-of-arms/; Joseph McMillan, "The Arms of George Washington," accessed Nov. 20, 2015, http:// www.americanheraldry.org/pages/index.php?n= President.Washington#toc4; Jones, "The National Flag," *CV* 4 (Aug. 1896): 260.

50. Jones, "The National Flag," *CV* 4 (Aug. 1896): 261.

51. John D. Billings, "Patriotism of the Sections," *CV* 4 (Oct. 1896): 331.

52. Jones, "Dr. Jones's Rejoinder," *CV* 4 (Oct. 1896): 332. Here Jones alluded to Psalm 137 (vv. 5–6), a favorite chapter of postwar white Southerners. Many identified with the sixth-century B. C. E. Babylonian exiles, echoing the lament that opened the chapter: "By the rivers of Babylon, there we sat down, yea, we wept, when we remembered Zion" (v. 1, KJV). In the white Southern appropriation of the narrative, of course, the conquering North was Babylon. Defeated Southerners felt as though they inhabited a "strange land" (v. 4), and they longed for the day when God would rescue the chosen people and punish their oppressors. There is significance, too, in that Psalm 137 concludes with one of the most brutal imprecations in scripture: "O daughter of Babylon, who art to be destroyed; happy shall he be, that rewardeth thee as thou hast served us. Happy shall he be, that taketh and dasheth thy little ones against the stones" (vv. 8–9).

53. Billings, "Patriotism of the Sections," *CV* 4 (Nov. 1896): 369; Jones, "Patriotism and the Sections," *CV* 5 (Jan. 1897): 7–9; Jones, "Nullification and Secession: Record of Massachusetts and New England," *CV* 5 (Feb. 1897): 60.

54. Jones, "Nullification and Secession," 62–63.

55. Clement A. Evans, "Contributions of the South to the Greatness of the American Union," *SHSP* 23 (Jan.–Dec. 1895): 2, 4–6.

56. Evans, 22, 24.

57. *Minutes of the Third Annual Meeting and Reunion of the United Confederate Veterans . . . 1892* (New Orleans: n.p., n.d.), 102; *Proceedings of the Fourth Annual Meeting . . . 1894,* 12–13.

58. Jones, "That Grand Army Invitation," *CV* 2 (May 1894): 154.

59. *Proceedings of the Fourth Annual Meeting . . . 1894,* 33–34. Note Jones's allusion to Lincoln's Second Inaugural Address.

Jones felt that the passage of time only confirmed the rightness of the Confederate cause. One prayer supposedly from Jones while he was chaplain at the University of North Carolina made this point quite clear: "Lord we acknowledge Thee as the all-wise author of every good and perfect gift. We recognize Thy presence and wisdom as much in the terror of lightning as we recognize Thy presence and wisdom in the healing shower. We acknowledge Thou had a divine plan when Thou made the rattle-snake, as well as the song bird, and this was without help from Charles Darwin. But we believe Thou will admit the grave mistake in giving the decision to the wrong side in eighteen hundred and sixty-five."

See Wilson, *Baptized in Blood*, 133. Although Wilson attributes the prayer to Jones, I have found no attesting documentation. That the prayer is Jones's comes from a 1973 quote from Samuel Ervin, former US Senator from North Carolina. See Thad Stem, Jr. and Alan Butler, *Senator Sam Ervin's Best Stories* (Durham, NC: Moore Publishing Company, 1973), 86.

60. Williams, *Isaac Taylor Tichenor*, 181–83; Jones to Compere, Dec. 19, 1890, Compere Papers, SBHLA; Jones to J. M. Frost, May 27, 1897, James Marion Frost Papers, Southern Baptist Historical Library and Archives, Nashville, TN (hereafter cited as "Frost Papers, SBHLA").

61. Jones to Frost, July 30, 1898, April 29, 1901, Sept. 8, 1904, and May 27, 1897, Frost Papers, SBHLA.

62. Williams, *Isaac Taylor Tichenor*, 171, 173–74; Tichenor, "Letter from Dr. Tichenor," *Religious Herald* 63, Jan. 30, 1890, 2. Eventually, the ABPS scaled back the society's employment of African American authors in order to appeal to white Southern readers. See Weaver, *In Search of the New Testament Church* (Ga: Mercer University Press, 2008), 203.

63. "'Kind Words' Circulars," *Religious Herald* 61, Dec. 20, 1888, 2; "Those 'Kind Words' Circulars as They Appear Through the Glasses of a Baltimore Pastor," *Religious Herald* 61, Dec. 20, 1888, 2; "The 'Kind Words' Circulars," *Religious Herald* 61, Dec. 27, 1888, 2; "What Rev. Geo. Cooper, D. D., Thinks of Dr. Jones' Letter," *Religious Herald* 62, Jan. 3, 1889, 3; Tichenor, "Letter from Dr. Tichenor," *Religious Herald* 63, Jan. 30, 1890, 2; Jones, "The 'Kind Words' Circulars," *Religious Herald* 62, Jan. 17, 1889, 2–3.

64. "The 'Circulars,' the Home Board, and the Am. Bap. Pub. Society," *Religious Herald* 62, Jan. 31, 1889, 1; "North Carolina Baptists and the Am. Baptist Publication Society," *Religious Herald* 62, Jan. 10, 1889, 3.

65. *Minutes of the Sixteenth Annual Meeting . . . 1906*, 56.

Conclusion

1. "J. William Jones Dies in Georgia," 1.

2. "Chaplain General J. William Jones," *CV* 12 (May 1909): 239; Joynes, "In Memoriam"; W. J. McGlothlin, *Baptist World* 13, April 1, 1909, 6.

3. H. W. Battle, "Rev. J. William Jones, D. D.," in *Memorial History of the John Bowie Strange Camp, United Confederate Veterans*, ed. Homer Richey (Charlottesville, VA: The Michie Company, 1920), 80.

4. Eighmy and Hill, *Churches in Cultural Captivity*, 20.

5. W. J. McGlothlin, 6.

Bibliography

Primary Sources

MANUSCRIPTS AND ARCHIVES

Albert and Shirley Small Special Collections Library, Univ. of Virginia.
Charlottesville, Virginia.
>J. William Jones Letters, 1857–1861
>Papers of the Jones Family of Louisa County, Virginia
Archives and Special Collections, Southern Baptist Theological Seminary.
Louisville, Kentucky.
>A. T. Robertson Papers
>James P. Boyce Papers
>John A. Broadus Papers
General Historical Catalogue of the Southern Baptist Theological Seminary.
Library of Virginia. Richmond, Virginia.
>J. William Jones Papers, 1861–1892
Manuscript Division, Library of Congress. Washington, DC.
>Jubal Anderson Early Papers
Museum of the Confederacy. Richmond, Virginia.
>Jefferson Davis Collection
>Minutes/Proceedings of the Southern Historical Society, 1869–1874
>Southern Historical Society Files/Correspondence
Southern Baptist Historical Library and Archives. Nashville, Tennessee.
>Ebenezer Lee Compere Papers
>Edwin Charles Dargan Papers
>J. William Jones, Missionary File, 1856–1861
>James Marion Frost Papers
Virginia Baptist Historical Society. Richmond, Virginia.
>J. William Jones Collection
>John Moore's Research Notes
Virginia Historical Society. Richmond, Virginia.
>George Bolling Lee Papers, 1841–1868
>Thomas Family Papers, 1828–1924

NEWSPAPERS AND PERIODICALS

Alexandria Gazette (Alexandria, VA)

Baptist World (Louisville, KY)

Biblical Recorder (Raleigh, NC)

Chautauquan (Jamestown, NY)

Christian Index (Washington, GA; Atlanta, GA)

Christian Observer (Philadelphia, PA)

The Century (New York, NY)

Confederate Baptist (Columbia, SC)

Confederate Veteran (Nashville, TN)

Harper's Weekly (New York, NY)

The Independent (New York, NY)

The New York Times (New York, NY)

North American Review (Boston, MA)

North Carolina University Magazine (Chapel Hill, NC)

Our Home Field (Atlanta, GA)

Religious Herald (Richmond, VA)

Richmond Daily Dispatch (Richmond, VA)

Southern Planter and Farmer (Richmond, VA)

Southern Historical Society Papers (Richmond, VA)

Times Dispatch (Richmond, VA)

ORGANIZATIONAL PUBLICATIONS

Southern Baptist Convention. *Proceedings of the Southern Baptist Convention.*
    Atlanta: Jas. P. Harrison and Company, 1885.
———. *Proceedings of the Southern Baptist Convention.* Atlanta: Franklin and
    Publishing Company, 1894.
United Confederate Veterans. *Minutes of the Third Annual Meeting and Reunion of
    the United Confederate Veterans . . . 1892.* New Orleans: n.p., n.d.
———. *Proceedings of the Fourth Annual Meeting and Reunion of the United
    Confederate Veterans . . . 1894.* Birmingham, AL: n.p., n.d.
———. *Minutes of the Sixth Annual Meeting and Reunion of the United Confederate
    Veterans . . . 1896.* Richmond, VA: n.p., n.d.
———. *Minutes of the Eighth Annual Meeting and Reunion of the United Confederate
    Veterans . . . 1899.* New Orleans: Hopkins' Printing Office, 1899.

———. *Minutes of the Eleventh Annual Meeting and Reunion of the United Confederate Veterans . . . 1901.* New Orleans: Hopkins' Printing Office, 1902.

———. *Minutes of the Fifteenth Annual Meeting and Reunion of the United Confederate Veterans . . . 1905.* Louisville, KY: n.p., n.d.

———. *Minutes of the Sixteenth Annual Meeting and Reunion of the United Confederate Veterans . . . 1906.* New Orleans: n.p., n.d.

BOOKS, ARTICLES, AND RECORDS

Bennett, William W. *Memorials of Methodism in Virginia: From Its Introduction into the State in the Year 1772 to the Year 1829.* Richmond, VA: William W. Bennett, 1871.

———. *A Narrative of the Great Revival Which Prevailed in the Southern Armies During the Late Civil War Between the States of the Federal Union.* Philadelphia: Claxton, Remsen, and Haffelfinger, 1877.

———. *A History of Methodism, for Our Young People.* Cincinnati: Hitchcock and Walden, 1878.

Broadus, John Albert. "Should Women Speak in Mixed Public Assemblies?" Accessed November 2, 2015. http://www.reformedreader.org/rbb/broadus /womenspeak. htm.

———. *Memoir of James Petigru Boyce, D.D., LL.D.: Late President of the Southern Baptist Theological Seminary, Louisville, KY.* New York: A. C. Armstrong and Son, 1893.

Cathcart, William. *The Baptist Encyclopaedia: A Dictionary of the Doctrines, Ordinances, Usages, Confessions of Faith, Sufferings, Labors and Successes, and of the General History of the Baptist Denomination in All Lands; with Numerous Biographical Sketches of Distinguished American and Foreign Baptists, and a Supplement.* Philadelphia: L. H. Everts, 1881.

Cooke, John Esten. *The Life of Stonewall Jackson: From Official Papers, Contemporary Narratives, and Personal Acquaintance.* New York: C. B. Richardson, 1863.

———. *Stonewall Jackson: A Military Biography.* New York: D. Appleton and Company, 1876.

Cooke, John Esten, Moses D. (Moses Drury) Hoge, and J. William (John William) Jones. *Stonewall Jackson: A Military Biography.* New York: D. Appleton and Company, 1876.

Dabney, Robert Lewis. *Life and Campaigns of Lieut.-Gen. Thomas J. Jackson, (Stonewall Jackson).* Richmond, VA: Blelock and Company, 1866.

Early, Jubal A. *The Campaigns of Gen. Robert E. Lee*. Baltimore: J. Murphy and Company, 1872.

———. *Lieutenant General Jubal Anderson Early, C.S.A.: Autobiographical Sketch and Narrative of the War Between the States*. Philadelphia: J. B. Lippincott, 1912.

Furman, Richard. "Exposition of the Views of the Baptists Relative to the Coloured Population In the United States in a Communication to the Governor of South Carolina." Charleston, SC: A. E Miller, 1838.

Graves, James Robinson, and Joshua Soule. "The Great Iron Wheel: Or, Republicanism Backwards and Christianity Reversed: In a Series of Letters Addressed to J. Soule, Senior Bishop of the M. E. Church, South." Nashville, TN: Graves and Marks, 1855.

Jackson, Mary Anna. *Life and Letters of General Thomas J. Jackson (Stonewall Jackson) by His Wife*. New York: Harper and Brothers, 1892.

———. *Memoirs of Stonewall Jackson*. Louisville, KY: Prentice Press, 1895.

Johnson, William B. "William B. Johnson's Address on the Origin of the Southern Baptist Convention." Augusta, GA: 1845.

Jones, John William. *Personal Reminiscences, Anecdotes, and Letters of Gen. Robert E. Lee*. New York: D. Appleton and Company, 1874.

———. *Southern Historical Society Papers*. Richmond, VA: Southern Historical Society, 1876–1887.

———. *Army of Northern Virginia Memorial Volume*. Richmond, VA: J. W. Randolph and English, 1880.

———. *Virginia's Next Governor, Gen. Fitzhugh Lee*. New York: Cheap Publishing Company, 1885.

———. *Christ in the Camp: Or Religion in Lee's Army*. Richmond, VA: B. F. Johnson and Company, 1887. Reprint, Richmond, VA: B. F. Johnson and Company, 1888. Reprint, Atlanta: Martin and Hoyt Company, 1904.

———. *The Davis Memorial Volume, Or, Our Dead President, Jefferson Davis, and the World's Tribute to His Memory*. Richmond, VA: Franklin, 1890.

———. *Work Among Negroes of the South*. Baltimore: Maryland Baptist Mission Rooms, 1891.

———. "The Morale of the Confederate Army." In *Confederate Military History*, ed. Clement Anselm Evans. Atlanta: Confederate Publishing Company, 1899.

———. *School History of the United States*. New York: Univ. Publishing Company, 1901.

———. *Life and Letters of Robert Edward Lee: Soldier and Man*. New York: The Neale Publishing Company, 1906.

———. "Introduction." In *General Turner Ashby: The Centaur of the South*, by Clarence Thomas, ix-xii. Winchester, VA: Eddy Press Corporation, 1907.

Lee, Susan Pendleton. *Memoirs of William Nelson Pendleton, D. D.: Rector of Latimer Parish, Lexington, Virginia Brigadier-General C. S. A. Chief of Artillery, Army of Northern Virginia*. Philadelphia: J. B. Lippincott Company, 1893.

Lipscomb, John. *Autobiographical Notes*. Boulder, CO: Johnson Publishing Company, 1958.

Pendleton, William Nelson. *Personal Recollections of General Lee: An Address Delivered at Washington and Lee University on Gen. Lee's Birth-Day, Jan. 19, 1873*. Baltimore: n.p., 1874.

Pollard, E. A. *The Lost Cause: A New Southern History of the War of the Confederates: Comprising a Full and Authentic Account of the Rise and Progress of the Late Southern Confederacy—the Campaigns, Battles, Incidents, and Adventures of the Most Gigantic Struggle of the World's History*. New York: E. B. Treat and Company Publishers, 1866.

———. *Southern History of the War*. Vols. 1 and 2. New York: Charles B. Richardson, 1866.

———. *The Lost Cause Regained*. New York: G. W. Carleton and Company Publishers, 1868.

Renfroe, J. J. D. *"The Battle is God's." A sermon preached before Wilcox's brigade, on fast day, the 21st August, 1863, near Orange Court-House, Va. by J. J. D. Renfroe, Chaplain 10th Alabama Regiment*. Richmond, VA: MacFarlane & Fergusson, 1863.

Twichell, Joseph Hopkins. *The Civil War Letters of Joseph Hopkins Twichell: A Chaplain's Story*. Athens: Univ. of Georgia Press, 2012.

"United States Census, 1850," Louisa County, Virginia. Accessed July 18, 2018. FamilySearch, https://familysearch.org. Washington, DC: National Archives and Records Administration, n.d.

"United States Census (Slave Schedule), 1850," Louisa County, Virginia. Accessed July 18, 2018. FamilySearch, https://familysearch.org. Washington, DC: National Archives and Records Administration, n.d.

"United States Census, 1860," Louisa County, Virginia. Accessed July 18, 2018. FamilySearch, https://familysearch.org. Washington, DC: National Archives and Records Administration, n.d.

"United States Census, 1870," Lexington, Rockbridge County, Virginia. Accessed
July 18, 2018. FamilySearch, https://familysearch.org. Washington, DC:
National Archives and Records Administration, n.d.

"United States Census, 1880," Richmond, Henrico County, Virginia. Accessed
July 18, 2018. FamilySearch, https://familysearch.org. Washington, DC:
National Archives and Records Administration, n.d.

"Virginia Marriages, 1785–1940." Accessed July 18, 2018. FamilySearch, https://
familysearch. org.

Warren, E. W. "Scriptural Vindication of Slavery." Macon, GA: n.p., 1861.

Wayland, Francis. *Notes on the Principles and Practices of Baptist Churches*. New York:
Sheldon, Blakeman and Company, 1857.

SECONDARY SOURCES

Aamodt, Terrie Dopp. *Righteous Armies, Holy Cause: Apocalyptic Imagery and the
Civil War*. Macon, GA: Mercer Univ. Press, 2002.

Ahlstrom, Sydney E. *A Religious History of the American People*. 2nd ed. New Haven:
Yale Univ. Press, 2004.

American Civil War Research Database. Alexandria, VA: Alexander Street Press, 1997.

Anderson, Benedict. *Imagined Communities: Reflections on the Origin and Spread of
Nationalism*. New York: Verso Books, 2006.

Anderson, Fred. "Historian of the Confederacy." *Baptist History and Heritage* 32,
no. 3–4 (July 1, 1997): 47.

Arlington Cemetery. "William Woodhull Bennett, D. D., Chaplain, Confederate
States of America." Accessed December 1, 2012. http://www. arlington
cemetery.net.

Armitage, Thomas. *A History of the Baptists—Vol. 1*. Paris, AR: The Baptist Standard
Bearer, 2001.

Barrett, John Gilchrist, and John S. Moore. *The History of Manly Memorial Baptist
Church, Lexington, Virginia*. Lexington, VA: Manly Memorial Baptist
Church, 1966.

Barron, James Roland. "The Contributions of John A. Broadus to Southern
Baptists." PhD diss., Southern Baptist Theological Seminary, 1972.

Beagle, Donald, and Byan Giemza. *Poet of the Lost Cause: A Life of Father Ryan*.
Knoxville: Univ. of Tennessee Press, 2008.

Bebbington, David W. *Evangelicalism in Modern Britain: A History from the 1730s to the 1980s*. New York: Routledge, 2003.

Bellah, Robert N. "Civil Religion in America." *Daedalus* 96, no. 1 (January 1, 1967): 1–21.

Benedict, David. *Fifty Years Among the Baptists*. New York: Sheldon and Company, 1860.

Blair, William A. *Cities of the Dead: Contesting the Memory of the Civil War in the South, 1865–1914*. Chapel Hill: Univ. of North Carolina Press, 2004.

Blevins, Carolyn DeArmond. "Baptist State Papers: Shapers or Reflectors of Southern Baptist Thought?" *Baptist History and Heritage* 28, no. 3 (July 1993): 4–13.

Blight, David W. *Race and Reunion: The Civil War in American Memory*. Cambridge, MA: Belknap Press, 2002.

Blum, Edward J. *Reforging the White Republic: Race, Religion, and American Nationalism, 1865–1898*. Baton Rouge: Louisiana State Univ. Press, 2007.

Blum, Edward J, and W. Scott Poole. *Vale of Tears: New Essays on Religion and Reconstruction*. Macon: Mercer Univ. Press, 2005.

Boles, John B. *The Great Revival, 1787–1805: The Origins of the Southern Evangelical Mind*. Lexington: Univ. Press of Kentucky, 1982.

Boswell, E. M. "Rebel Religion." *Civil War Times Illustrated* 11 (October 1972): 26–33.

Brackney, William Henry. *Baptists in North America: An Historical Perspective*. Malden, MA: Blackwell Publishing, 2006.

Brinsfield, John Wesley. *Faith in the Fight: Civil War Chaplains*. Mechanicsburg, PA: Stackpole Books, 2003.

Bronson, Walter Cochrane. *The History of Brown University, 1714–1914*. Providence: Brown Univ., 1914.

Brown, William Earl. "Pastoral Evangelism: A Model for Effective Evangelism as Demonstrated by the Ministries of John Albert Broadus, Alfred Elijah Dickinson, and John William Jones in the Revival of the Army of Northern Virginia in 1863." PhD diss., Southeastern Baptist Theological Seminary, 1999.

Brundage, W. Fitzhugh. *The Southern Past: A Clash of Race and Memory*. Cambridge, MA: Belknap Press, 2008.

Capps, Alan. "Coat of Arms." Accessed November 20, 2015. http://www.mount vernon.org/research-collections/digital-encyclopedia/article/coat-of-arms/.

Carmichael, Peter S. *The Last Generation: Young Virginians in Peace, War, and Reunion*. Chapel Hill: Univ. of North Carolina Press, 2009.

Cassirer, Ernst. *The Philosophy of Symbolic Forms: Mythical Thought*. New Haven: Yale Univ. Press, 1955.

Chandler, J. A. C., et al., eds. *The South in the Building of the Nation: A History of the Southern States Designed to Record the South's Part In the Making of the American Nation; to Portray the Character and Genius, to Chronicle the Achievements and Progress and to Illustrate the Life and Traditions of the Southern People*. Richmond, VA: Southern Historical Publication Society, 1909.

Cheseborough, David B. *"God Ordained This War": Sermons on the Sectional crisis, 1830–1865*. Columbia: Univ. of South Carolina Press, 1991.

"Civil War Diaries and Letters Digital Collection—The University of Iowa Libraries." Accessed March 18, 2013. http://digital.lib.uiowa.edu/cwd/.

"Civil War Journals Online—Confederate." *Squidoo*. Accessed September 20, 2013. http://vallain.squidoo.com/civil-war-journals-online-confederate.

Coker, Joe L. *Liquor in the Land of the Lost Cause: Southern White Evangelicals and the Prohibition Movement*. Lexington: Univ. Press of Kentucky, 2007.

Connelly, Thomas Lawrence. *The Marble Man, Robert E. Lee and His Image in American Society*. Baton Rouge: Louisiana State Univ. Press, 1977.

Connelly, Thomas Lawrence, and Barbara Bellows. *God and General Longstreet: The Lost Cause and the Southern Mind*. Baton Rouge: Louisiana State Univ. Press, 1982.

Cox, Karen L. *Dixie's Daughters: The United Daughters of the Confederacy and the Preservation of Confederate Culture*. Gainesville: Univ. Press of Florida, 1982.

Crowther, Edward R. *Southern Evangelicals and the Coming of the Civil War*. Lewiston, NY: E. Mellen Press, 2000.

———. "John the Evangelist Revisited: John William Jones and the Lost Cause." *Journal of Southern Religion* 17 (2015): http://jsreligion.org/issues/ vol17 /crowther.html.

Cross, Frank Leslie, and Elizabeth A. Livingstone. *The Oxford Dictionary of the Christian Church*. New York: Oxford Univ. Press, 1974. Reprint, New York: Oxford Univ. Press, 2005.

Culbreth, David Marvel Reynolds. *The University of Virginia: Memories of Her Student-life and Professors*. New York: Neale Publishing Company, 1908.

Daniel, W. Harrison. "The Christian Association: A Religious Society in the Army of Northern Virginia." *Virginia Magazine of History and Bibliography* 69 (January 1961): 93–100.

———. "Virginia Baptists and the Negro in the Antebellum Era." *Journal of Negro History* 56, no. 1 (January 1971): 1–16.

Davis, Andrew P. "Temporal Defeat, Divine Victory: The Origins of the Religion of the Lost Cause, 1860–1870." MA thesis, College of Charleston, 2012.

Davis, William C. *The Cause Lost: Myths and Realities of the Confederacy.* Lawrence: Univ. Press of Kansas, 1996.

"Diaries and Journals of the American Civil War." Accessed September 20, 2013. http://www.rarebooks.nd.edu/digital/civil_war/diaries_journals/index.shtml.

Dill, Jacob Smiser, and Southern Baptist Convention Sunday School Board. *Isaac Taylor Tichenor, the Home Mission Statesman.* Nashville, TN: Sunday School Board, Southern Baptist Convention, 1908.

"Discovery Commons, Virginia Tech." Accessed October 31, 2013. https://dcr.emd .vt. edu/vital/access/manager/Index.

Doan, William Howard, and Elias Henry Johnson. *The Baptist Hymnal: For Use in the Church and Home.* Philadelphia: American Baptist Publication Society, 1883.

Dobney, Fredrick J. "From Denominationalism to Nationalism in the Civil War: A Case Study." *Texana* 9, no. 4 (1971): 367–76.

"Documenting the American South." Accessed September 29, 2013. http:// docsouth.unc.edu/index.html.

Dolan, Jay P. *Catholic Revivalism: The American Experience, 1830–1900.* Notre Dame: Univ. of Notre Dame Press, 1978.

Dollar, Kent T. *Soldiers of the Cross: Confederate Soldier-Christians and the Impact of War on Their Faith.* Macon: Mercer Univ. Press, 2005.

Dresser, Zachary Woods. "The Theology of Reconstruction: White Southern Religious Leaders in the Aftermath of the Civil War." PhD diss., Rice Univ., 2013.

———. "Onward Christian Soldiers? Confederate Revivalism and Denominationalism in the Nineteenth-Century South." Paper delivered at the Society of Civil War Historians, Baltimore, June 12–14, 2014.

Durant, Susan Speare. "The Gently Furled Banner: The Development of the Myth of the Lost Cause, 1865–1900." PhD diss., Univ. of North Carolina at Chapel Hill, 1972.

Eighmy, John Lee, and Samuel S. Hill. *Churches in Cultural Captivity: A History of the Social Attitudes of Southern Baptists.* Knoxville: Univ. of Tennessee Press, 1987.

Elder, Robert. "Southern Saints and Sacred Honor: Evangelicalism, Honor, Community, and the Self in South Carolina and Georgia, 1784–1860." PhD diss., Emory Univ., 2011.

Fahs, Alice, and Joan Waugh, eds. *The Memory of the Civil War in American Culture.* Chapel Hill: Univ. of North Carolina Press, 2004.

Faulkner, William. *Intruder in the Dust.* New York: Vintage Books, 1991.

Faust, Drew Gilpin. "Christian Soldiers: The Meaning of Revivalism in the Confederate Army." *Journal of Southern History* 53 (February 1987): 63–90.

———. *The Creation of Confederate Nationalism Ideology and Identity in the Civil War South.* Baton Rouge: Louisiana State Univ. Press, 1990.

———. *This Republic of Suffering: Death and the American Civil War.* New York: Vintage, 2009.

Fields, Karen E., and Barbara J. Fields. *Racecraft: The Soul of Inequality in American Life.* New York: Verso, 2012.

Fleche, Andre. *The Revolution of 1861: The American Civil War in the Age of Nationalist Conflict.* Chapel Hill: Univ. of North Carolina Press, 2012.

Flynt, Wayne. *Alabama Baptists: Southern Baptists in the Heart of Dixie.* Tuscaloosa: Univ. of Alabama Press, 1998.

Foner, Eric. *Reconstruction: America's Unfinished Revolution, 1863–1877.* New York: Perennial Classics, 2002.

———. *Forever Free: The Story of Emancipation and Reconstruction.* New York: Vintage Books, 2006.

Foster, Gaines M. *Ghosts of the Confederacy: Defeat, the Lost Cause and the Emergence of the New South, 1865–1913.* New York: Oxford Univ. Press, 1988.

Fountain, Daniel L. *Slavery, Civil War, and Salvation: African American Slaves and Christianity, 1830–1870.* Baton Rouge: Louisiana State Univ. Press, 2010.

Fraser, Walter Javan. "William Henry Ruffner: A Liberal in the Old and New South." PhD diss., Univ. of Tennessee, 1970.

Freeman, Douglas Southall. *The South to Posterity: An Introduction to the Writing of Confederate History.* Baton Rouge: Louisiana State Univ., 1939.

Freeman, Douglas Southall, Richard Harwell, and James M. McPherson. *Lee.* New York: Scribner, 1997.

Fuller, A. James. *Chaplain to the Confederacy: Basil Manly and Baptist Life in the Old South*. Baton Rouge: Louisiana State Univ. Press, 2000.

Gallagher, Gary W. *The Confederate War*. Cambridge: Harvard Univ. Press, 1999.

———. *Lee and His Generals in War and Memory*. Baton Rouge: Louisiana State Univ. Press, 2004.

———. *Causes Won, Lost, and Forgotten: How Hollywood and Popular Art Shape What We Know about the Civil War*. Chapel Hill: Univ. of North Carolina Press, 2013.

Gallagher, Gary W., and Alan T. Nolan, eds. *The Myth of the Lost Cause and Civil War History*. Bloomington: Indiana Univ. Press, 2010.

Gaston, Paul. *The New South Creed: A Study in Southern Mythmaking*. Montgomery, AL: New South Books, 2012.

Gaustad, Edwin S., ed. *A Documentary History of Religion in America to 1877*. 3rd ed. William B. Eerdmans Publishing Company, 2003.

Genovese, Eugene D. *A Consuming Fire: The Fall of the Confederacy in the Mind of the White Christian South*. Athens: Univ. of Georgia Press, 1998.

Goen, Clarence Curtis. "Broken Churches, Broken Nation: Regional Religion and North-South Alienation in Antebellum America." *Church History* 52, no. 1 (March 1, 1983): 21–35.

Goldfield, David. *Still Fighting the Civil War: The American South and Southern History*. Baton Rouge: Louisiana State Univ. Press, 2013.

Gonzalez, Justo L. *The Story of Christianity, Vol. 2: The Reformation to the Present Day*. New York: Harper One, 2010.

Gourley, Bruce T. *Diverging Loyalties: Baptists in Middle Georgia During the Civil War*. Macon: Mercer Univ. Press, 2011.

Guelzo, Allen C. *Fateful Lightning: A New History of the Civil War and Reconstruction*. New York: Oxford Univ. Press, 2012.

Harper, Keith. "What's Wrong with this Picture? James P. Boyce, John A. Broadus, and Reflections on the Lost Cause." *Journal of Southern Religion* 17 (2015): http://jsreligion.org/issues/vol17/harper.html.

Harris, Malcolm Hart. *History of Louisa County, Virginia*. Richmond, VA: Dietz Press, 1936.

Harvey, Paul. *Redeeming the South: Religious Cultures and Racial Identities Among Southern Baptists, 1865–1925*. Chapel Hill: Univ. of North Carolina Press, 1997.

Hatch, Nathan O. *The Democratization of American Christianity*. New Haven: Yale Univ. Press, 1991.

Hayes, Patrick J., ed. *The Civil War Diary of Father James Sheeran: Confederate Chaplain and Redemptionist*. Washington, DC: Catholic Univ. of America Press, 2016.

Hieronymus, Frank L. "For Now and Forever: The Chaplains of the Confederate States Army." PhD diss., Univ. of California, Los Angeles, 1964.

Hill, Samuel S. *Southern Churches in Crisis Revisited*. Tuscaloosa: Univ. of Alabama Press, 1999.

Hill, Samuel S., Charles H. Lippy, and Charles Reagan Wilson. *Encyclopedia of Religion in the South*. Macon: Mercer Univ. Press, 2005.

Hillman, Nancy Alenda. "Drawn Together, Drawn Apart: Black and White Baptists in Tidewater Virginia, 1800–1875." PhD diss., College of William and Mary, 2013.

Hollins University. "History and Mission." Accessed June 2, 2015. http://www. hollins. edu/who-we-are/history/.

Horn, Jonathan. *The Man Who Would Not Be Washington: Robert E. Lee's Civil War and His Decision That Changed American History*. New York: Scribner, 2016.

Horwitz, Tony. *Confederates in the Attic: Dispatches from the Unfinished Civil War*. New York: Vintage Books, 1999.

Hull, Alice Page Elizabeth. "Lessons in Heritage: Southern Children Inherit the Lost Cause." PhD diss., Univ. of Mississippi, 2006.

Hunt, Thomas C., and Monalisa McCurry-Mullins. *Moral Education in America's Schools: The Continuing Challenge*. Charlotte, NC: Information Age Publishing, Inc., 2005.

Hunter, Lloyd Arthur. "The Sacred South: Postwar Confederates and the Sacralization of Southern Culture." PhD diss., Saint Louis Univ., 1978.

Hurt, Billy G. "Crawford Howell Toy: Interpreter of the Old Testament." ThD diss., Southern Baptist Theological Seminary, 1966.

James, John G. *The Southern Student's Hand-Book of Selections for Reading and Oratory*. New York: A. S. Barnes & Co., 1879.

Janney, Caroline E. *Burying the Dead but Not the Past: Ladies' Memorial Associations and the Lost Cause*. Chapel Hill: Univ. of North Carolina Press, 2008.

———. *Remembering the Civil War: Reunion and the Limits of Reconciliation*. Chapel Hill: Univ. of North Carolina Press, 2013.

Kammen, Michael. *Mystic Chords of Memory: The Transformation of Tradition in American Culture*. New York: Vintage Books, 1993.

Kidd, Margaret. "A Benediction for Hollins." Accessed June 2, 2015. http://vaheritage.org/2015/05/18/a-benediction-for-hollins/.

Killingsworth, Vernon Blake. "'Tis God That Afflicts You: The Roots of the Religion of the Lost Cause among Charleston Baptists, 1847–1861." PhD diss., Texas Christian Univ., 2011.

Leonard, Bill J. *God's Last and Only Hope: The Fragmentation of the Southern Baptist Convention*. Grand Rapids, MI: Eerdmans Publishing, 1990.

———. *Baptist Ways: A History*. Valley Forge, PA: Judson Press, 2003.

———. *A Sense of the Heart: Christian Religious Experience in the United States*. Nashville, TN: Abingdon Press, 2014.

Lyon, David G. "Crawford Howell Toy." *Harvard Theological Review* 13 (January 1920): 1–22.

Mahan, Harold Eugene. "The Final Battle: The Southern Historical Society and Confederate Hopes for History." *Southern Historian* 5 (Spring 1984): 27–37.

Marsden, George, ed. *Evangelicalism and Modern America*. Grand Rapids, MI: Eerdmans Publishing, 1984.

Marty, Martin E. *Religion and Republic: The American Circumstance*. Boston: Beacon Press, 1989.

Maryniak, Benedict R., and John Wesley Brinsfield, Jr. *The Spirit Divided: Memoirs of Civil War Chaplains—The Union*. Macon: Mercer Univ. Press, 2007.

Mathews, Donald G. *Religion in the Old South*. Chicago: Univ. of Chicago Press, 1979.

———. "The Southern Rite of Human Sacrifice." *The Journal of Southern Religion* 3 (2000). Accessed September 4, 2014. http://jsr.as.wvu.edu.

McBeth, Leon. *The Baptist Heritage*. Nashville, TN: Broadman Press, 1987.

McMahone, Martin Lyndon. "Liberty More than Separation: The Multiple Streams of Baptist Thought on Church-State Issues, 1830–1900." PhD diss., Baylor Univ., 2001.

McMillan, Joseph. "The Arms of George Washington." Accessed November 20, 2015. http://www.americanheraldry.org/pages/index.php?n=President.Washington#toc4.

McPherson, James M. *Battle Cry of Freedom: The Civil War Era*. New York: Oxford Univ. Press, 2003.

McPherson, James, and James Hogue. *Ordeal By Fire: The Civil War and Reconstruction*. Boston: McGraw-Hill, 2000.

Miller, Randall M., Harry S. Stout, and Charles Reagan Wilson. *Religion and the American Civil War*. New York: Oxford Univ. Press, 1998.

Miller, Robert J. *Both Prayed to the Same God: Religion and Faith in the American Civil War*. Lanham, MD: Lexington Books, 2007.

Mills, Cynthia J., and Pamela H. Simpson, eds. *Monuments to the Lost Cause: Women, Art, and the Landscapes of Southern Memory*. Knoxville: Univ. of Tennessee Press, 2003.

Moore, Christopher C., "'Northern Fingers Have Played Our Pianos': Baptists and Reconciliation in Postwar North Carolina, 1865–1877. *Baptist History and Heritage* 48 (Summer 2013): 46–60.

Moore, John S. "John William Jones (1836–1909): Historian of the Confederacy." In *Virginia Baptist Register* 31. Richmond, VA: Virginia Baptist Historical Society, 1992.

Neff, John R. *Honoring the Civil War Dead: Commemoration and the Problem of Reconciliation*. Lawrence: Univ. Press of Kansas, 2005.

Nolan, Alan T. *Lee Considered: General Robert E. Lee and Civil War History*. Chapel Hill: Univ. of North Carolina Press, 1991.

Nolen, Claude H. *The Negro's Image in the South: The Anatomy of White Supremacy*. Lexington: Univ. Press of Kentucky, 2015.

Noll, Mark A. *America's God: From Jonathan Edwards to Abraham Lincoln*. New York: Oxford Univ. Press, 2002.

———. *The Civil War as a Theological Crisis*. Chapel Hill: Univ. of North Carolina Press, 2006.

Noll, Mark A., David Bebbington, and George A. Rawlyk, eds. *Evangelicalism: Comparative Studies of Popular Protestantism in North America, The British Isles, and Beyond, 1770–1990*. New York: Oxford Univ. Press, 1994.

Norton, Herman. *Rebel Religion: The Story of Confederate Chaplains*. St. Louis: Bethany Press, 1961.

O'Connell, David. *Furl That Banner: The Life of Abram J. Ryan, Poet-Priest of the South*. Macon: Mercer Univ. Press, 2006.

O'Connell, Edward T. "Public Commemoration of the Civil War and Monuments to Memory: The Triumph of Robert E. Lee and the Lost Cause." PhD diss., State Univ. of New York at Stony Brook, 2008.

Osterweis, Rollin Gustav. *The Myth of the Lost Cause, 1865–1900*. Hamden, CT: Archon Books, 1973.

Painter, Nell Irvin. *Standing at Armageddon: The United States, 1877–1919*. New York: W. W. Norton & Company, 1987.

———. *Creating Black Americans: African American History and its Meanings, 1619 to the Present*. New York: Oxford Univ. Press, 2006.

Parrish, Nancy C. *Lee Smith, Annie Dillard, and the Hollins Group: A Genesis of Writers*. Baton Rouge: Louisiana State Univ. Press, 1999.

Piston, William Garrett. *Lee's Tarnished Lieutenant*. Athens: Univ. of Georgia Press, 1990.

Pitts, Charles F. *Chaplains in Gray: The Confederate Chaplains' Story*. Concord, VA: R. M. J. C. Publications, 1957.

Poole, W. Scott. *Never Surrender: Confederate Memory and Conservatism in the South Carolina Upcountry*. Athens: Univ. of Georgia Press, 2004.

Prim, Gorrell Clinton. "Born Again in the Trenches: Revivalism in the Confederate Army." PhD diss., Florida State Univ., 1982.

Rable, George C. *God's Almost Chosen Peoples: A Religious History of the American Civil War*. Chapel Hill: Univ. of North Carolina Press, 2010.

Raboteau, Albert J. *Slave Religion: The "Invisible Institution" in the Antebellum South*. New York: Oxford Univ. Press, 2004.

Reese, Lee Fleming. *The Ashby Book*. San Diego: Western Press, 1976.

Remillard, Arthur. "From Prizefights to Praying Colonels: Civil Religion, Sports, and a New(ish) Direction for the Lost Cause." *Journal of Southern Religion* 17 (2015): http://jsreligion.org/issues/vol17/remillard.html.

Richards, Roger Charles. "Actions and Attitudes of Southern Baptists toward Blacks, 1845–1895." PhD diss., Florida State Univ., 2008.

Richey, Homer, ed. *Memorial History of the John Bowie Strange Camp, United Confederate Veterans*. Charlottesville, VA: The Michie Company, 1920.

Richey, Russell E. *American Civil Religion*. San Francisco: Edwin Mellen Press, 1990.

Riggs, David F. *13th Virginia Infantry*. Lynchburg, VA: H. E. Howard, 1988.

Robertson, Archibald Thomas. *Life and Letters of John Albert Broadus*. Philadelphia: American Baptist Publication Society, 1901.

Rosser, J. L. "John William Jones." In *Encyclopedia of Southern Baptists*, vol. 1. Nashville, TN: Broadman Press, 1958.

Ryland, Charles Hill. *Recollections of the First Year of the Southern Baptist Theological Seminary: An Address Delivered before the Seminary, at Louisville, Kentucky, Founders Day, January 11th, 1911*. Richmond, VA: n.p., 1911.

Sampey, John R. *Southern Baptist Theological Seminary: The First Thirty Years, 1859–1889*. Baltimore: Wharton, Barron, and Company, 1890.

Schweiger, Beth Barton. *The Gospel Working Up: Progress and the Pulpit in Nineteenth-Century Virginia*. New York: Oxford Univ. Press, 200.

Seales, Chad. "To Know Good Blood: The Material Morality of Southern Religion." *Journal of Southern Religion* 17 (2015): http://jsreligion.org/issues /vol17/seales.html.

"Secession." Library of Virginia. Accessed July 25, 2018, http://www.lva.virginia.gov /public/guides/Civil-War/Secession.htm.

Shattuck, Gardiner H., Jr. *A Shield and Hiding Place: The Religious Life of the Civil War Armies*. Macon: Mercer Univ. Press, 1987.

———. "John William Jones." *American National Biography Online*. Accessed August 20, 2014. http://www.anb.org.

Silver, James W. *Confederate Morale and Church Propaganda*. New York: W. W. Norton and Company, Incorporated, 1967.

Simpson, John A. "The Cult of the 'Lost Cause.'" *Tennessee Historical Quarterly* 34 (Winter 1975): 350–61.

Slatton, James H. *W. H. Whitsitt: The Man and the Controversy*. Macon: Mercer Univ. Press, 2009.

Southern Baptist Theological Seminary. "Abstract of Principles." Accessed April 8, 2015. http://www.sbts.edu/about/truth/abstract/.

———. "John R. Sampey: 1929–1942." Accessed July 31, 2018. http://archives.sbts .edu/the-history-of-the-sbts/our-presidents/john-r-sampey-1928-1942/.

———. "Sampey and Lee." Accessed July 31, 2018. http://archives.sbts.edu /the-history-of-the-sbts/our-lore/sampey-and-lee/.

Spain, Rufus. *At Ease in Zion: Social History of Southern Baptists, 1865–1900*. Nashville: Vanderbilt Univ. Press, 1967.

Stampp, Kenneth. *The Imperiled Union: Essays on the Background of the Civil War*. New York: Oxford Univ. Press, 1980.

Starnes, Richard D. "Forever Faithful: The Southern Historical Society and Confederate Historical Memory." *Southern Cultures* 2 (Winter 1996): 177–94.

Stem, Thad, Jr., and Alan Butler. *Senator Sam Ervin's Best Stories*. Durham, NC: Moore Publishing Company, 1973.

Stout, Harry S. *Upon the Altar of the Nation*. New York: Viking Penguin, 2006.

Stowell, Daniel W. *Rebuilding Zion: The Religious Reconstruction of the South, 1863–1877*. New York: Oxford Univ. Press, 1998.

Strickland, Arthur Barsazou. *Roger Williams: Prophet and Pioneer of Soul-Liberty*. Boston: Judson Press, 1919.

"Surrender at Appomattox." *Encyclopedia Virginia*. Accessed June 4, 2015. http://www.encyclopediavirginia.org/Surrender_at_Appomattox#start_entry.

Taylor, George Braxton. *Life and Letters of Rev. George Boardman Taylor, D. D.* Lynchburg, VA: J. P. Bell Company, 1908.

———. *Virginia Baptist Ministers*, 5th Series, 1902–1914. Lynchburg, VA: J. P. Bell Company, 1913.

Thelen, David. *Memory and American History*. Bloomington: Indiana Univ. Press, 1990.

Towns, W. Stuart. *Enduring Legacy: Rhetoric and Ritual of the Lost Cause*. Tuscaloosa: Univ. of Alabama Press, 2012.

Tucker, Phillip Thomas. *The Confederacy's Fighting Chaplain: Father John B. Bannon*. Tuscaloosa: Univ. of Alabama Press, 1992.

Tyler, Lyon Gardiner. *Men of Mark in Virginia: Ideals of American Life; A Collection of Biographies of the Leading Men in the State*, vol. 1. Washington, DC: Men of Mark Publishing Company, 1906.

"The Virginia Chronicle." Accessed July 25, 2015. http://virginiachronicle.com.

Virginia Museum of History and Culture. "History of Battle Abbey." Accessed August 9, 2018. https://www.virginiahistory.org/collections-and-resources/virginia-history-explorer/history-battle-abbey.

Virtual American Biographies. "Winthrop Hartly Hopson." Accessed June 3, 2015. http://www.famousamericans.net/winthrophartlyhopson/.

Warren, Robert Penn. *Segregation: The Inner Conflict in the South*. Athens: Univ. of Georgia Press, 1994 (1956).

Washington and Lee Univ. "Our Namesakes." Accessed March 16, 2015. http://www.wlu.edu/about-wandl/history-and-traditions/our-namesakes.

Weaver, C. Douglas. *In Search of the New Testament Church: The Baptist Story*. Macon: Mercer Univ. Press, 2008.

Whitsitt, William H. *Genealogy of Jefferson Davis and of Samuel Davies*. New York: Neale Publishing Company, 1910.

Wiley, Bell Irvin. *The Life of Billy Yank: The Common Soldier of the Union*. Baton Rouge: Louisiana State Univ. Press, 2008.

Williams, David S. "J. William Jones (1836–1909)." *New Georgia Encyclopedia*. Accessed September 4, 2014. http://www.georgiaencyclopedia.org.

Williams, Michael E. *Isaac Taylor Tichenor: The Creation of the Baptist New South*. Tuscaloosa: Univ. of Alabama Press, 2005.

Wills, Gregory A. *Southern Baptist Theological Seminary, 1859–2009*. New York: Oxford Univ. Press, 2009.

Wilson, Charles Reagan. "The Religion of the Lost Cause: Ritual and Organization of the Southern Civil Religion, 1865–1920." *Journal of Southern History* 46 (May 1980): 219–38.

———. *Baptized in Blood the Religion of the Lost Cause, 1865–1920*. Athens: Univ. of Georgia Press, 2009.

———. "Assessing the Lost Cause and Southern Civil Religion." *Journal of Southern Religion* 17 (2015): http://jsreligion.org/issues/vol17/wilson.html.

Woodward, C. Vann. *Origins of the New South, 1877–1913*. Baton Rouge: Louisiana State Univ. Press, 1971.

———. *The Strange Career of Jim Crow*. New York: Oxford Univ. Press, 2001.

———. *The Burden of Southern History*. Baton Rouge: Louisiana State Univ. Press, 2008.

Woodworth, Steven E. *While God Is Marching On: The Religious World of Civil War Soldiers*. Lawrence: Univ. Press of Kansas, 2003.

"World Cat." Accessed December 1, 2012. http://www.worldcat.org.

Wyatt-Brown, Bertram. *Southern Honor: Ethics and Behavior in the Old South*. New York: Oxford Univ. Press, 2007.

Index

Page numbers in **boldface** refer to illustrations.

"Abstract of Principles" (SBTS), 13, 29, 218n16

African Americans, 111, 120, 152, 157, 235n85, 250n70, 259–60n72; and the American Baptist Publication Society, 200, 267n62; and Baptists, 140, 165–67, 171, 188, 236n6; and J. William Jones, 11, 71–72, 76, 219n25, 223n58; and the Lost Cause, 93, 95, 97; and memory, 211n3, 258n58; and reconciliation, 160–61

American Baptist Publication Society (ABPS), 75, 90, 199–201, 238n15, 267n62

American flag, 171, 193–94, 196–97

American Revolution, 126, 147, 169, 193, 234n84

Anderson, Josephus W., 9

Andersonville prison, 151

Antietam, 20, 34, 96, 224n2

Appomattox, 36, 111, 113, 133, 169, 243n52

army churches, 41–42, 44–45

army evangelists, 25–27, 29, 31, 77, 222n51

army missionaries, 24–27, 31, 43, 56, 222n51

Army of Northern Virginia, 70, 75, 86–87, 96–97, 195, 243n52;

battle flag, 159; and Chaplains' Association, 30, 44; in *Christ in the Camp*, 58–59, 228n30; revivals, 36–38; in the *Southern Historical Society Papers*, 144, 163

associations, 44–45, 130, 228n32

Atlanta, burning of, 169

Bagley, G. W., 31

baptism, 10, 66, 71, 83, 201, 226n13, 241n29; and camp converts, 29–30, 36, 49, 227n24, 227–28n27; denominational competition, 47, 55, 78, 80–81, 188; denominational cooperation, 43–44, 77, 223n58, 235n92; and Landmarkism, 39–40, 189, 226n15; wartime controversy, 41–43

Barber, S. B., 58, 231n67

Battle Abbey, 179

Beauregard, P. G. T., 141, 159

Bennett, William W., 38, 59, 128, 249n57, 250n65; work compared with Jones's, 128–31, 133, 249n62, 249–50n64, 250n68

Billings, John D., 194–95

Blaine, James G., 151

Boyce, James P., 18, 23, 73–74, 85, 89, 218nn15–16

Bradley, Joshua, 81, 240n29

Bragg, Braxton, 141

287

Braxton, Carter, 16

Broaddus, Andrew, 51

Broadus, John Albert, 79–80,
88–90, **104**, 116, 217nn12–13;
and anti-Catholicism, 83–84;
correspondence with Jones, 16–17,
22, 30, 73, 187, 242n34; friendship
with Jones, 176, 178, 239n19;
opinion of Jones, 7, 13–14, 218n17;
preaching in Confederate camp,
25–26, 28, 36; and women in
ministry, 241n29

Brown, John, 169, 196

Buchanan, James, 169

Cable, George Washington, 158

Calhoun, John C., 124

Calvinism, 20

Carroll, B. H., 40

Cassirer, Ernst, 1

Chalmers, James R., 157–58, 160

Chancellorsville, 21, 35, 49, **102**, 117–18,
121, 148–49

chaplains, 86–87, 117, 128–29, 131,
225n4, 238n15; and Baptists,
30–31, 41–42, 47, 66; and the
Confederate government, 24–25,
34, 222n47; Crawford H. Toy, 14;
denominational cooperation, 38,
43–45, 48–55, 116; denominational
identity, 32, 55, 67; and
evangelicals, 24, 30, 56–57; and
evangelism, 48–51, 229n44;
and Jews, 231n62; and John A.
Broadus, 12; and John Lipscomb

Johnson, 11, 219n23; and Jones
(postwar), 177–79, 193, 201,
203, 262n11, 267n59; and Jones
(wartime), 1, 8, 23–24, 70–71,
77, 85, 90, 222n51, 242n34; and
revivals, 38, 227n27; and Robert E.
Lee, 111; roles, 28–29; and Roman
Catholics, 58–60, 66–67, 231n67,
232n70, 232n75, 235n92; shortage,
45–48, 224n1, 229n43; and
Stonewall Jackson, 120, 252n80;
terminology, 26–27, 222n51; and
war, 36

Chaplains' Association, 28, 30–31, 44,
46, 52, 57–58

Charlottesville Baptist Church, 12–13

China, 15, 17–18

chosenness, 24, 113, 117, 122, 138; and
defeat, 1, 95, 206–7, 251n75, 266n52;
and divine retribution, 51–52; and
evangelicals, 188; and Jones, 8; and
revivals, 33, 204

Christ in the Camp, 33, 56–60, 87–90,
148, 227–28n27; and camp worship,
35; compared with the work of
William W. Bennett, 128–34;
and Confederate leaders, 58, 133,
149; editions, 228n30, 231n69,
249n62; evangelical emphasis,
56–57, 84, 248n46; and hospitals,
49; as newspaper serial, 2,
108–9; and non-Baptists, 45, 65,
211n4; popularity, 130, 249n64;
publication, 76–78, 174; references
to Jones's brothers, 21–22, 221n39

Christian Index, 23, 31, 41–42, 52, 54, 108, 186
Christian soldiers, 53–54
Church of Jesus Christ of Latter-day Saints, 113, 117, 246–47n26
church-state separation, 4, 24–25, 221n45, 259n72
civil religion, 53, 209–10n2, 235n96
Civil War, 2, 14, 18, 69, 164, 243n51; and American history, 192, 197, 205; and church-state separation, 221n45; and Jubal Early, 96, 153, 155; and memory, 8, 160; and Robert E. Lee, 94; and Roman Catholics, 61–62; in *School History of the United States*, 165, 168, 178, 186; and slavery, 91, 98, 115, 126; in the *Southern Historical Society Papers*, 75; studies of, 3–4, 211n3; textbooks, 139
Cocke, Charles Lewis, 240n29
Cohen, A. D., 48
Coleman, Lewis Minor, 250n69
colportage, 44, 48–49, 111, 132, 134, 222n49, 230n60
Confederacy, 89, 91, 97, 139, 168, 194, 202, 204; and American history, 191; apostleship of Jones, 3–5, 8, 87, 108, 134, 197, 204, 209; and chaplains, 25; chosenness, 24; in *Christ in the Camp*, 59, 228n30; and denominational cooperation, 55; and disembodiment, 132; flags, 159, 196, 198; and Jefferson Davis, 123–24, 132, 177; and Jews, 231n62;

leadership, 86, 98, 108, 127–28, 184, 206; motto, 137; narrative, 2, 68, 77, 85, 88, 136, 138, 183; nationhood, 210n2; and religion, 4, 33, 90, 205; and Robert E. Lee, 179; and Roman Catholics, 232n70; in *School History of the United States*, 169; and slavery, 98–99, 115, 125; and the *Southern Historical Society Papers*, 140–41, 151, 155, 163, 213n6, 258n59; and Stonewall Jackson, 122; and war, 34, 163
Confederate flags, 54, 120, 159, 168, 196, 198
Confederate Memorial Association, 179
Confederate Veteran, 173, 184, 203, 222n51, 224n2
Constitution (CSA), 169
Constitution (US), 108, 135, 146, 157, 170–71, 184, 195
Cooke, John Esten, 117–18, 149
Corcoran, William W., 143
Corron, J. P., 72
Cridlin, R. W., 54
Cuba, 175–76, 188, 261n4
Custis, George Washington Parke, 114

Dabney, Robert L., 117, 148, 158, 170, 182
Daniel, John W., 125–26
Dargan, E. C., 186–87
Darwin, Charles, 14, 267n59
Davis, Jefferson, 75, **102**, 118, 180, 203; canonization, 2, 68, 90, 108, 122,

eschatology, 13

Evangelical Alliance, 64, 81

Evangelical Tract Society, 44

evangelicals: and African Americans, 235n85; in *Christ in the Camp*, 56–58, 62, 65–66, 78, 84–85, 131, 230n60, 248n46; definition, 234n84; denominational competition, 55, 78–82, 98, 188; denominational cooperation, 30, 39, 47–48, 77; and Jefferson Davis, 124, 248n46; and Jews, 246n24; and John A. Broadus, 12, 84–85; and Jones, 17, 66–68, 77, 136, 166–67, 177, 205; and the Lost Cause, 68, 70, 99; and revivals, 35, 63; and Robert E. Lee, 94, 116; and Roman Catholics, 62–64, 67–68, 98, 150, 188, 204, 230n59, 248n46; in *School History of the United States*, 169

Evans, Clement A., 184, 195–97

evolution, 112, 267n59

Ewell, Richard, 19, 250n69

fifteenth amendment, 111

First Bull Run, 34

First Great Awakening, 221n5

First Manassas. *See* First Bull Run

Foreign Mission Board (FMB), 14–15, 70, 219n23

Fort Sumter, 169

fourteenth amendment, 111

Fredericksburg (battle), 19, 21, 34, 224n2, 224–25n3

Freeman, Douglas Southall, 132

Frost, J. M., 199–200

Fugitive Slave Act, 195

Gaines's Mill (battle), 21, 220n36

Georgia, 31, 47, 73, 81, 203

Gettysburg, 22–23, 254n19, 256n42; and James Longstreet, 23, 94, 97, 153–55, 170, 185, 244n60, 256n42; and Robert E. Lee, 76, 118, 225n6;

Gordon, John B., 75, 110, 250n69

Goshen Bridge Baptist Church, 70–71, 77–78, 82, 239n24

Granberry, J. C., 33, 45, 129

Grand Army of the Republic (GAR), 198

Grant, Ulysses S., 36, 125, 147–48, 152, 160, 164, 169; compared with Robert E. Lee, 91, 97, 110–11, 180, 185

Graves, James R., 39, 226n15

Gray, Alphonso, 9–10, 216n7

Gutheim, J. K., 150, 255n30

Gwin, T. W., 41, 227n21

hagiography, 1, 4, 88, 107, 205; and incarnation, 128, 133–34, 138

Hampton, Wade, 110

Hardwick, J. B., 49

Harvard University, 14

Havana House, 175

Hawthorne, J. B., 147–48, 160

Hayne, Paul H., 112

Helm (Jones), Judith Page. *See* Jones, Judith

Herrenvolk democracy, 157

Heth, Henry, 154

Hiden, John C., 11, 187

Hill, Ambrose Powell (A. P.), 18, 26–27, 220n21, 222n51

Hill, Daniel Harvey (D. H.), 142–43, 147, 190, 250n69

Hoge, Moses D., 119–121

Hoge, William J., 43

Holcombe, James P., 112

Hollins Institute, 81, 240n29

Hollywood Cemetery, 203

Home Mission Board (HMB), 188, 238n15, 261nn4–5; and Jones, 2, 76, 165, 174–77, 199–201, 239n20

Home Mission Society (HMS), 199

Hood, John B., 154

Hopson, Winthrop Hartly, 86–87, 242n43

hospitals, 28, 48–49, 151

Humphreys, Andrew A., 162

Hunter, R. M. T., 146–56

immigration, 60

invincibility, 34, 54, 121, 143

Jackson, Mary Anna, 1, 117

Jackson, Thomas J. "Stonewall," 18–19, 86–87, **102**, 153, 251–52n80; and African Americans, 120, 166–67; and Baptists, 88–90, 166–67; canonization, 2, 180; in *Christ in the Camp*, 131–33, 250nn68–69; death, 119, 121–22, 222n51; and denominational cooperation, 46, 121; as incarnation, 127, 183, 206;

interaction with Jones, 85, 223n60; invincibility, 54, 118; and Jones, 68, 98–99, 173, 192, 194, 203–4; and Mary Anna Jackson, 1, 117; and religion, 117–20, 181–82; rivalry with Robert E. Lee, 118–19, 148–49, 163, 170, 182; in the *Southern Historical Society Papers*, 148–49, 163; vindication, 136–37; virtues, 4–5, 108–9, 127, 134–36, 205; and William Pendleton, 93–94

Jefferson, Thomas, 194

jeremiads, 52

Jews, 116, 177, 246n24; and the Lost Cause, 65, 150, 213n6, 230–31n62, 235n96

Johnson, Andrew, 170

Johnson, John Lipscomb, 11, 217n10, 219n23

Johnson, Rossiter, 163–65, 258–59n70

Johnston, Albert Sydney, 157

Johnston, Joseph E., 239n19

Jones, Ann Pendleton (Ashby), 9, 19–22, 215n5

Jones, Carter Helm, 176, 178, 219n26, 226n16, 262n7

Jones, Edith, 76

Jones, Edloe Pendleton, 176, 178, 219n26

Jones, Francis Pendleton ("Pen"), 9, 19, 21–23, 215n5

Jones, Francis William, 9–10, 215n5, 216n7

Jones, Frank William, 177, 219n26

Jones, Helen Mary, 9, 12, 215n5, 217n12

Jones, Howard Lee, 176, 219n26

Jones, Ida, 76

Jones, J. William, **101**; and African
  Americans, 11, 71–72, 76, 165–67,
  259–60n72; and American Baptist
  Publication Society, 199–200,
  238n15; as apostle, 3–5, 8, 77, 85, 108,
  171, 205, 213–14n10; and baptism,
  43–44, 66, 227n24, 227–28n27;
  Baptist identity, 2, 66–67, 75,
  78–84, 150; battles, 20–21, 220n36;
  as chaplain, 23–25; conversion, 10;
  death, 203–4; death of brothers,
  21–23, 220–21n39; denominational
  cooperation, 3, 9, 30, 43–45,
  77, 134, 212n5; early life, 9–17;
  and ecumenism, 2–3, 211–12n4;
  enlistment, 18–20; as evangelist,
  25–27, 222n51; friendship
  with Jefferson Davis, 85, 107,
  123–24, 183, 206; friendship with
  Robert E. Lee, 30, 69, 85, 123; and
  incarnation, 128, 132–34, 138, 206–7;
  influence among Baptists, 69–70,
  88, 99, 109, 237n9; and James
  Longstreet, 23, 94, 153–56; and
  Jefferson Davis, 122–27, 134–37, 170,
  182–83, 248n46; late career, 174–79,
  183–201; lectures, 74, 85–86, 88–90;
  marriage, 15–16, 20; as missionary,
  14–17; *Personal Reminiscences*,
  8, 74, 108–9; postwar ministry,
  70–75; and Robert E. Lee, 108–17,
  134–37, 170, 180–81; and revivals,
  33–38, 45, 225n6; and Roman
  Catholics, 55–68, 84, 134, 149–50,

187–88, 248n46; and secession, 16;
  and slavery, 9–10, 76, 99, 140; and
  Southern Historical Society, 75,
  96, 141–46; and *Southern Historical
  Society Papers*, 140–41, 143, 145–65,
  171, 185, 205, 212n6; and Stonewall
  Jackson, 117–22, 134–37, 170, 181–82;
  and temperance, 71; textbook, 169–
  71, 185–87, 261n85; theology, 13, 29,
  52–55; as transitional figure, 173–74,
  190–97; wartime ministry, 28–30,
  48–50; and "Whitsitt controversy,"
  189–90, 226n16, 265n40; and
  women's education, 81, 240–41n29

Jones, John M., 22

Jones, Judith, 16–17, 20–21, 182–83, 187,
  238n16

Jones, Lucy, 9, 215n5

Jones, M. Ashby, 73, 176–78, 199, 203,
  219n26

Jones, Philip Edloe ("Ed"), 9, 19, 20–22,
  24, 215n5, 220n32, 221n39

Jones, Robert, 9, 215n5

Joynes, Edward S., 10–11, 203

Kemper, James L., 239n19

Key, Francis Scott, 193

Know-Nothings, 60–61

Ku Klux Klan, 73

Lacy, B. T., 30, 44, 46, 51–54, 109

Landmarkism, 13, 39–40, 189, 226n15,
  242n34, 265n40

Lee, Fitz, 144, 148, 155

Lee, Mary Custis, 110, 245n8

Lee, Robert E., 22, 36, 70, **101**, 125, 176–77, 262n7; and Baptists, 88–89, 265n36; canonization, 2, 5, 90, 127, 179–81, 183, 204; in *Christ in the Camp*, 58–59, 231n69, 250nn68–69; commissioning Jones, 1, 5, 8, 68, 76, 131, 213–14n10, 251n73; and common soldiers, 184; and Confederate flags, 159; death, 7, 73–74, 237n13; and denominational cooperation, 115–17; and E. A. Pollard, 91; friendship with Jones, 30, 69, 85, 123; and George Washington, 245n8; as incarnation, 155, 183, 205–6; invincibility, 34, 110, 143; and James Longstreet, 23, 94, 97, 153–56, 170; and Jubal Early, 96–98; in *Life and Letters of Robert Edward Lee*, 246n19; and the Lost Cause, 75–76, 185; and Mormons, 113, 117, 246–47n26; overwhelmed, 96, 243n52, 254n19; in *Personal Reminiscences*, 8, 74, 108; as president of Washington College, 71, 74, 79, 82, 110, 214n3; and reconciliation, 192, 194, 203; and religion, 87, 99, 109–13, 122, 131–38, 173; and revivals, 225n6; and Roman Catholics, 150; rivalry with Stonewall Jackson, 118–19, 148–49, 163, 170, 182; in *School History of the United States*, 169–70, 186; and slavery, 113–15, 134, 157; and Southern Historical Society, 144; in *Southern Historical Society Papers*, 151, 161, 163–64, 255n36; surrender, 70, 91, 96, 111–12, 118, 169, 243n52; and Union troops, 245n9; vindication, 136–37; virtues, 4, 205; and William Pendleton, 93–95

Lee, S. D., 127

Lee, William Henry Fitzhugh (Rooney), 113–14, 117, 247n26

Lee Memorial Association, 7, 89, 93

Lexington Baptist Church, 70–73, 236n4, 236n6

Life and Letters of Robert Edward Lee: Soldier and Man, 179–80

Lincoln, Abraham, 18, 149, 157, 169–70, 267n59

Long, A. L., 154

Longstreet, James, **103**, 213n8; and Gettysburg, 23, 94, 97, 154–55, 170, 185, 244n60; and Jubal Early, 97, 154–55, 256n42; and the *Southern Historical Society Papers*, 153–56, 163

Lord's Supper, 13, 39, 83, 226n13, 226n15

Lost Cause: and Baptist cooperation, 32, 55, 67, 187, 190; and Baptist identity, 70, 85, 87–89, 167, 183; and children, 260–61n77; and *Christ in the Camp*, 128–33, 249n62, 250n65; definition, 1, 174, 190–91, 209–10n2, 243n51, 258n59; and denominationalism, 2, 4–5, 55, 65, 80, 175, 204, 206, 212n4; and E. A. Pollard, 90–93, 96, 98, 177, 243n51, 243n54; and George Washington,

mythology (*continued*)

denominationalism, 77, 204;
and E. A. Pollard, 96; and
evangelicals, 68; "Inner" and
"National" Lost Cause, 190, 197,
202; and Jefferson Davis, 108;
and religion, 3, 205; and revivals,
38; and Robert E. Lee, 108;
and Stonewall Jackson, 108, 117,
247n27; and troop numbers, 185;
and Virginia

nationalism, 210n2
nativism, 60, 265n45
Northern Baptists, 198–99, 201, 233n77

Our Home Field, 175, 183

Palmer, Benjamin Morgan, 142
Paris, Comte de, 153–54, 255n36, 256n42
paternalism, 140, 166–67, 175, 259n72
patriotism, 54, 173, 196, 205
Pendleton, James Madison, 39, 226n15
Pendleton, William Nelson, 90, **103**,
117, 244n60; and Robert E. Lee, 7,
74, 93–96, 98
*Personal Reminiscences, Anecdotes and
Letters of Gen. Robert E. Lee*, 8, 74,
108–9, 113–15
Petersburg (battle), 21, 23, 30–31, 36–37,
180, 220n31, 262n7
Pickett, George, 153–54
Pius IX, 61
Poindexter, Abram Maer, 14–15
Pollard, Edward Alfred (E. A.), 90–93,

96, 98, 243n51, 243n54, 244n56;
criticism of Jefferson Davis, 91–92,
122, 177
Powers, W. C., 30
Presbyterians, 12, 41, 53, 116–17, 119, 142,
248n46; and Baptist competition,
47, 72, 78, 79–80, 82, 177; and
Baptist cooperation, 30, 43–45,
56, 58; as chaplains, 24, 221n44; as
"evangelicals," 230n59
Preston, John S., 112
prisoners, 161; exchange, 125, 147;
mistreatment by Union troops,
147, 152, 184–86; in *Southern
Historical Society Papers*, 151–53, 163,
255n35
Protestants, 4, 57, 66, 231n67, 235n92;
and anti-Catholicism, 60–62,
83–84; and the Lost Cause, 3, 205,
235n96; and revivals, 58, 62–63, 67,
233n81
Providence, 9, 32, 54, 119, 181, 251n75
Puryear, Bennett, 260n72
Pusey, E. B., 64

race, 10, 120, 126, 196, 211n3; and Jones,
98, 115, 140, 165–66, 170, 259n72;
and the Lost Cause, 91–93, 95, 97;
and the *Southern Historical Society
Papers*, 156–58, 160–61
reconciliation, 171, 196, 257n50; in *Christ
in the Camp*, 128–29; Jones, 75, 191,
194, 197–99; and memory, 203,
257n56, 258n58; and Robert E.
Lee, 115; in *School History of the*

Sheeran, James, 58, 59

Sherman, William T., 31, 169, 254n21, 258n70

slavery, 35, 37, 61, 64, 71, 196, 206; defense of, 4, 92–93, 126; and Jefferson Davis, 125–26; and Jones, 98–99, 166–67, 170–71, 195; and the Jones's family, 9–10, 76, 216n7; and the Lost Cause, 18, 76, 91–93, 95, 97–98, 153, 257n47; and Robert E. Lee, 95, 113–15, 135, 181; and Southern Baptists, 260n74; and the *Southern Historical Society Papers*, 140, 146, 156–61; and Stonewall Jackson, 120; and William W. Bennett, 129

Soldiers' Tract Association, 128

South Carolina, 12, 16, 41, 110, 195, 227n19, 258–59n70

Southern Baptist Convention (SBC), 2, 14, 78, 199–200, 240–41n29; and the Home Mission Board, 76, 165, 174, 261n5; and William H. Whitsitt, 39–40, 189

Southern Baptist Theological Seminary (SBTS), 18, 203, 207, 217–18n15, 237n9, 262n7; and Crawford H. Toy, 14; and Jones, 12–13, 71–74, 79–81, 85–86, 89, 176–77, 186–87; theology, 29; and William H. Whitsitt, 40, 189, 226n16, 265n40, 251n73

Southern Baptists, 3; and African Americans, 165; identity, 39; and Jones, 85, 88, 108–9, 175, 199–200,

227n19, 238n15; and Northern Baptists, 75, 191, 198; and Roman Catholics, 62, 233n77; and slavery, 260n74

Southern Historical Society (SHS), **105**, 147, 151, 153, 161–65, 171, 258n59; debt, 144–46, 213n7; founding, 140–43; and Jews, 150, 255n30; Jones, 75–76, 88–89, 122–23, 130, 168, 174–75; and Roman Catholics, 149–50; and Virginia, 96

Southern Historical Society Papers (*SHSP*); and the Army of Northern Virginia, 144; and Jones, 22, 68, 75, 165, 171, 205, 212n6; and the Lost Cause, 2, 140–41, 172, 212n6; and Roman Catholics, 59; and secession, 146, 192; and the Southern Historical Society, 96, 143, 145; themes, 99, 146–62, 169, 185, 190, 255n35, 258n59

Spanish-American War, 193, 266n47

Spotsylvania Court House, 20

"Star-Spangled Banner," 193

Stearns, Shubal, 9

Stephens, Alexander, 151

Stuart, James Ewell Brown (J. E. B.), 117, 154, 203, 250n69, 256n42

successionism, 39

Sunday School and Bible Board of the General Association of Virginia, 74

Sunday School Board (of the SBC), 70, 199–200

Syllabus of Errors, 61

Taylor, George Boardman, 10, 79, 89

Taylor, George Braxton, 262n7

Taylor, James Barnett, Jr., 217n10

Taylor, James Barnett, Sr., 15, 17, 49, 57, 70

Taylor, Richard, 141

Taylor, Walter H., 154

temperance, 71, 212n5

Tennessee, 58, 72, 122, 193

textbooks, 139–40, 165, 168–71, 178, 185, 261n85

13th Virginia Infantry, 18–24, 27–28, 59, 220n31, 220n36

Tichenor, Isaac T., 175–77, 188, 200, 238n15, 261nn4–5

Toy, Crawford H., 12–17, 217n10, 217n15, 218n20, 219n23, 239n19

Tractarian Movement, 64

Twichell, Joseph Hopkins, 232n75

Uncle Tom's Cabin, 153

Unitarians, 14

United Brethren, 30

United Confederate Veterans (UCV), 179–80, 193, 198, 201

United Daughters of the Confederacy (UDC), 185

University of North Carolina, 61, 178, 189, 267n59

University of Virginia (UVA), 10–13, 203, 219n23, 262n7; and Jones's chaplaincy, 177–78, 262n11; and Jones's lectures, 88, 180

Utah, 113, 246–47n26

Van den Berghe, Pierre L., 157

Venable, Charles S., 75, 107, 245n1

Virginia, 14, 44, 69, 81, 112, 128, 260n72; in American history, 193–95; and Baptists, 72–73, 75, 78–80, 236n6, 239–40n24, 242n34; and the Civil War, 20, 22, 95; and Jones, 9, 17, 70, 74, 178; revivals, 34, 224n2; and Robert E. Lee, 74, 94, 181, 192; and Roman Catholicism, 61; and secession, 16, 18; and slavery, 125–26, 156, 170; and the Southern Historical Society, 96, 142–44

Virginia Baptist Colportage and Sunday-School Board, 26

Virginia Military Institute (VMI), 71

War of 1812, 194

Warren, Robert Penn, 132, 250n70

Washington, George, 82, 110, 147, 193–94, 245n8

Washington, Martha, 245n8

Washington and Lee University, 79, 82, 116; name change, 214n3; and Robert E. Lee, 7–8, 69, 71, 73–74, 116, 150, 180

Washington College. *See* Washington and Lee University

Wayland, Francis, 218n15, 233n77

Wayland, H. L., 185–86

Wellhausen, Julius, 14

Whitsitt, William H., 39–40, 71, 189–90, 226n16, 251n73, 265n36, 265n40

Wilcox, C. M., 154
Wilderness (battle), 22
Witherspoon, T. D., 47–48
women: abuses by Union troops, 147,
    152, 184; education, 81, 240–41n29;

and the Lost Cause, 210–11n3; in
ministry, 240–41n29

Young Men's Christian Association
    (YMCA), 11, 71, 178

www.ingramcontent.com/pod-product-compliance
Lightning Source LLC
Chambersburg PA
CBHW031937090426

42811CB00002B/207